The International Aspects
of China's Tax Law

中国
涉外税法

李 娜 ◎ 著

厦门大学出版社 国家一级出版社
XIAMEN UNIVERSITY PRESS 全国百佳图书出版单位

图书在版编目（CIP）数据

中国涉外税法：英文 / 李娜著. -- 厦门：厦门大
学出版社，2023.3
    ISBN 978-7-5615-7149-1

Ⅰ．①中… Ⅱ．①李… Ⅲ．①涉外税收－税法－中国
－教材－英文 Ⅳ．①D922.229

中国版本图书馆CIP数据核字(2018)第235227号

出 版 人	郑文礼
责任编辑	李　宁　郑晓曦
封面设计	张雨秋
技术编辑	许克华

出版发行 厦门大学出版社

社　　址	厦门市软件园二期望海路39号
邮政编码	361008
总　　机	0592-2181111　0592-2181406(传真)
营销中心	0592-2184458　0592-2181365
网　　址	http://www.xmupress.com
邮　　箱	xmup@xmupress.com
印　　刷	厦门市竞成印刷有限公司

开本	720 mm×1 020 mm　1/16
印张	26
插页	1
字数	606 千字
版次	2023 年 3 月第 1 版
印次	2023 年 3 月第 1 次印刷
定价	86.00 元

本书如有印装质量问题请直接寄承印厂调换

厦门大学出版社
微信二维码

厦门大学出版社
微博二维码

Preface

This book is written primarily to be used as a textbook for people learning the international aspects of China's tax law. Therefore, the book does not cover all aspects of China's tax regime and all governing laws, rather it focuses on a few Chinese taxes and treaties which are applicable to cross-border transactions involving China.

How many taxes are there in China? Which taxes are applicable when doing business in China? What are the governing tax laws? How to pay taxes in China? How to relieve double taxation for incomes derived from China? All these are the typical questions I have heard from students, professors as well as business people when I taught the course "The International Aspects of China's Tax Law" in Australia, several European countries, and Russia in the past decade. However, it's difficult to answer these questions with simple words because there is no general tax code governing all taxes in China. The eighteen (18) Chinese taxes currently are provided in 18 separate laws and regulations, and these taxes are imposed on different taxpayers as well as on different incomes and activities. Hence some professors and students suggested I write a book addressing these questions in plain language and considering the syllabus, materials (especially the case studies), and English translation of the relevant Chinese tax laws which I have used in my lectures.

I was inspired by these suggestions and started to write this book in 2018. Very soon I realized that I was facing significant difficulties. A few Chinese domestic tax laws were under the process of amendments, and some important tax reforms have been going on for years. For example, the reform on tax administration took place in 2018, the new Chinese individual income tax regime came into force in 2019, and the value added tax (VAT) law is currently under enactment at the National People's Congress. At the same time, the Chinese tax treaty network continues to expand, and China becomes more and more active in global tax governance projects. Hence this book in a form of the first edition is written according to the tax laws and regulations in force as of 31 March, 2023. And I plan to publish the second edition in the coming years for the purpose of adopting the most updated developments of tax laws and regulations in China.

Thanks to the editors for their hard work. Thanks to all my colleagues, friends, peers, and students for their comments and suggestions. Thanks to the East China University of Political Science and Law (ECUPL) for sponsoring the publication. The first edition of this book comes to publish as scheduled in 2023, and I am now collecting materials for writing the second edition which I promise will be a better one.

Na Li
Shanghai, March 2023

Abbreviations

APA	advance pricing agreement
BEPS	base erosion and profit shifting
CFC	controlled foreign corporation
DTA	double tax agreement double tax arrangement
EIT	enterprise income tax
EOI	exchange of information
FDI	foreign direct investment
TIEA	tax information exchange agreement
GACC	General Administration of Customs of China
GAAR	general anti-tax avoidance rule
G20	Group of Twenty
GST	goods and services tax
IIT	individual income tax
LOB	limitation on benefit
LSA	location specific advantage
MAP	mutual agreement procedure
MOF	Ministry of Finance
NPC	National People's Congress

续表

OECD	Organization for Economic Cooperation and Development
PE	permanent establishment
PPT	principal purpose test
PRC	People's Republic of China
RMB	renminbi
MLI	Multilateral Convention to Implement Tax Treaty Related Measures to Prevent Base Erosion and Profit Shifting
SAAR	specific anti-tax avoidance rule
SAT	State Administration of Taxation
UN	United Nations
VAT	value added tax

Contents

CHAPTER 1 INTRODUCTION   / 001 /

  1.1 Overview   / 001 /

  1.2 Framework of China's Tax Regime   / 002 /

  1.3 Taxes   / 002 /

  1.4 Tax Mix   / 006 /

  1.5 Main Players in China's Tax Regime   / 009 /

  1.6 History of China's Tax Regime   / 010 /

  Appendix: Exercises   / 012 /

CHAPTER 2 SOURCE OF LAW   / 013 /

  2.1 Introduction   / 013 /

  2.2 Domestic Tax Laws   / 013 /

  2.3 Tax Treaties   / 019 /

  Appendix Ⅰ: Chinese Tax Treaties(As of March 2021)   / 020 /

  Appendix Ⅱ: Exercises   / 027 /

CHAPTER 3 VALUE ADDED TAX   / 028 /

  3.1 Introduction   / 028 /

  3.2 Structure of the VAT Legislations   / 029 /

  3.3 Taxpayers   / 030 /

  3.4 Taxable Events   / 031 /

  3.5 Tax Rates   / 034 /

  3.6 Exemption   / 036 /

  3.7 Tax Timing   / 042 /

  3.8 Calculation of VAT   / 042 /

  3.9 Tax Administration   / 044 /

Appendix Ⅰ: VAT Provisional Regulation (2017 Revision)   / 046 /

Appendix Ⅱ: Circular Caishui 〔2016〕 No. 36   / 056 /

Appendix Ⅲ: Practice Questions   / 155 /

CHAPTER 4   EXCISE TAX   / 157 /

4.1   Introduction   / 157 /

4.2   Structure of the Consumption Tax Provisional Regulation   / 157 /

4.3   Taxpayers   / 158 /

4.4   Taxable Goods and Tax Rates   / 158 /

4.5   Tax Timing   / 161 /

Appendix: Consumption Tax Provisional Regulation

(2008 Amendment)   / 161 /

CHAPTER 5   INDIVIDUAL INCOME TAX   / 168 /

5.1   Introduction   / 168 /

5.2   Structure of the IIT Legislations   / 169 /

5.3   Taxpayers   / 170 /

5.4   Taxable Income   / 172 /

5.5   Tax Payable   / 177 /

5.6   Special Adjustments   / 185 /

5.7   Tax Administration   / 185 /

Appendix Ⅰ: IIT Law (2018 Amendment)   / 188 /

Appendix Ⅱ: Exercises   / 199 /

CHAPTER 6   ENTERPRISE INCOME TAX   / 203 /

6.1   Introduction   / 203 /

6.2   Structure of the EIT Legislations   / 204 /

6.3   Taxpayers   / 204 /

6.4   Source Rules   / 207 /

6.5   Calculation of EIT   / 208 /

6.6   Taxable Income   / 209 /

6.7   Deductions   / 216 /

6.8   Losses of Previous Years   / 225 /

6.9   Tax Exemption and Deduction   / 226 /

6.10   Foreign Tax Credit   / 226 /

6.11   Tax Administration   / 227 /

6.12   Special Rules for Non-Chinese Tax Residents   / 229 /

Appendix Ⅰ: EIT Law (2018 Amendment)   / 230 /

Appendix Ⅱ: Exercises   / 245 /

CHAPTER 7   RELIEF OF DOUBLE TAXATION   / 247 /

7.1   Introduction   / 247 /

7.2   Unilateral Approach: The Credit Method in Domestic Law   / 249 /

7.3   Bilateral Approach: Tax Treaties   / 250 /

Appendix Ⅰ: An Example of Relief of Double Taxation in China   / 290 /

Appendix Ⅱ: Exercises   / 300 /

CHAPTER 8   TAX ADMINISTRATION   / 302 /

8.1   Introduction   / 302 /

8.2   The Governing Law   / 303 /

8.3   Collection of Taxes   / 304 /

8.4   Collection of Social Contributions   / 305 /

8.5   Tax Audit   / 305 /

8.6   Taxpayers' Rights   / 306 /

8.7   Exchange of Information   / 307 /

Appendix Ⅰ: Tax Administration Law(2015 Amendment)   / 309 /

Appendix Ⅱ: Exercises   / 340 /

CHAPTER 9   ANTI-TAX AVOIDANCE MEASURES   / 342 /

9.1   Introduction   / 342 /

9.2   Domestic Measures   / 343 /

9.3   Anti-treaty Abuse Measures   / 355 /

9.4   Implementation of the BEPS Project   / 358 /

Appendix: Exercises   / 371 /

CHAPTER 10   TAX DISPUTE RESOLUTION   / 373 /

10.1　Introduction   / 373 /

10.2　Tax Cases   / 375 /

10.3　Judicial Cases   / 376 /

10.4　Administrative Investigations   / 397 /

Appendix：Exercises   / 404 /

CHAPTER 1   **INTRODUCTION**

1.1   Overview

The People's Republic of China (hereafter "China" or "PRC") is a unitary state having a vast land of 9.6 million square kilometres. It consists of four autonomous municipalities (i. e. Beijing, Shanghai, Tianjin and Chongqing), five autonomous regions (i.e. Inner Mongolia, Guangxi, Xizang, Ningxia and Xinjiang), two special administrative regions (i.e. Hong Kong and Macao) and twenty-three provinces (including Taiwan). Since Hong Kong, Macao and Taiwan apply different tax systems from the mainland part of China[①], this book addresses only the international aspects of the tax laws of the mainland part of China.

China is not an Organisation for Economic Cooperation and Development (OECD) member state but is a member of the G20 and the United Nations (UN). Since 2011, China has become the second largest economy in the world, but its per capita GDP in 2018 accounts for about only 86 percent of the world average and was ranked the 72nd globally.[②]Therefore, China is still a developing country. For most of the last three decades, China was one

---

① State Council of China, "Administrative division of the People's Republic of China", http://www. gov. cn/guoqing/2005-09/13/content _ 5043917. htm (accessed on 30 March, 2021).

② World Bank's database: https://data. worldbank. org/indicator/NY. GDP. PCAP. CD? end=2018&locations=CN&most_recent_value_desc=false&start=1960&type=points&view=chart (accessed on 30 March, 2021).

of the largest capital importers in the world. But since 2014 it has become a net exporter of capital (i.e. capital exported is greater than capital imported), and accordingly China is changing its international tax policy from that of a pure source state to a mixed position of being both a residence state and a source state.

1.2　Framework of China's Tax Regime

The framework of China's current tax regime consists of two parts:

(1) the domestic taxes, including 18 taxes; and

(2) the tax treaty network, including more than 100 bilateral tax treaties and a few multilateral tax treaties.

In terms of the notion of "the international aspects of China's tax law", it is necessary to make it clear in this introduction section that there is no tax in China officially named as the "international tax" and there is no Chinese tax treaty formally named as the "international tax treaty". All Chinese taxes should be included into the scope of "international taxation in China", as long as they are confined to taxable subjects and object of or relating to cross-border transactions. Also, this notion should include those bilateral treaties and multilateral treaties which have been concluded by Chinese government for or relating to tax matters.

This book although will address only a number of taxes (i.e. income taxes, value added tax and excise tax) and tax treaties which are closely relevant to cross-border transactions involving China, one should not neglect the importance of the remaining taxes and treaties of China.

1.3　Taxes

As of March 2021, the framework of China's domestic tax consists of 18 specific types of taxes, which in general can be divided into three categories:

(1) goods and services taxes: value added tax (VAT), excise tax, vehicle purchase tax, and customs duty;

(2) income taxes: enterprise income tax (EIT) and individual income tax (IIT);

(3) property and behaviour taxes: land value-added tax, real estate tax, urban and town land use tax, farmland occupation tax, deed tax, resource tax, environmental protection tax, vehicle and vessel tax, stamp duty, urban maintenance and construction tax, tobacco tax, and vessel tonnage tax.

These 18 taxes are imposed on different taxpayers and on different incomes and activities.

1.3.1 Goods and Services Taxes

The goods and services taxes include four types, which are imposed to different taxpayers (but sometimes could overlap) on different tax base and at different tax rates. The following table (Table 1-1) summarizes the main features of these four taxes; and Chapters 3 and 4 of this book will address on the VAT and excise tax respectively.

Table 1-1　Goods and services taxes

Taxes	Taxpayers	Tax Subject	Tax Rates
Value Added Tax (VAT)	entities and individuals	Import, production or sale of goods, provision of services, transfer of properties in China	Varying in a range from 0 to 16%
Excise Tax	entities and individuals	Producing or consigned processing taxable goods; importing taxable goods into China. At present, 15 types of goods are taxable goods, for example, tobacco, alcohol, cosmetics, refined oil products, expensive watches, etc	Ad valorem tax, per unit tax, or a combination

Continued

Taxes	Taxpayers	Tax Subject	Tax Rates
Vehicle Purchase Tax	Entities and individuals	Purchasing taxable vehicles, including cars, motorcycles, trams, trailers and agricultural-used vehicles in China	10%
Customs Duty	Consignee of imports, consignor of exports, and owners of imported goods	Importing goods into China, or exporting a few number of goods from China	Ad valorem tax, per unit tax, or a combination

1.3.2 Income Taxes

China has two separate income tax regimes: the individual income tax which is applicable to individuals; and the enterprise income tax which is applicable to entities, organization and other units. These income taxes are governed by two separate tax laws, namely the Individual Income Tax Law (IIT Law) and the Enterprise Income Tax Law of China (EIT Law). The following table (Table 1-2) summarizes the main features of these two income taxes; and the details will be addressed respectively in Chapter 5 and Chapter 6 of this book.

Table 1-2　Income taxes

Taxes	Taxpayers	Tax Subject	Tax Rates
Individual Income Tax (IIT)	Individuals	Worldwide income of Chinese tax residents, and income sourced from China for non-tax residents	Varying in a range from 3% to 45%
Enterprise Income Tax (EIT)	Enterprises, institution and other organizations, except for partnership	Worldwide income of Chinese tax residents, and income sourced from China for non-tax residents	Tax residents:25% Non-tax residents: 20%

1.3.3 Property and Behavior Taxes

Although this book will not address any particular type of property and behavior taxes, it is still important to know that these taxes may apply to some cross-border transactions as well. The following table (Table 1-3) illustrates the main features of these taxes.

Table 1-3   Property and behavior taxes

Taxes	Taxpayers	Tax Subject	Tax Rates
Land Value-added Tax	Entities and individuals	Releasing gains on transfer of right to use state-owned land, buildings and associated structures thereon in China	Varying in a range from 30% to 60%
Real Estate Tax	Owners or mortgagees of real estate	owning houses or mortgaging houses which are located in cities, county towns, administrative towns and industrial and mining districts in China	1. 2% for self-used houses and 12% or 4% for leased-out houses
Urban and Town Land Use Tax	Entities and individuals	Occupying land in cities, county towns, administrative towns and industrial and mining districts in China	Different rates for different locations
Farmland Occupation Tax	entities and individuals	Occupying arable land in China to build houses or for other non-agricultural construction purpose	Different rates for different locations
Deed Tax	Assignees or transferees	Assigning or transferring ownership title of the land use rights and/or the buildings in China	Varying in a range from 1% to 5%
Resource Tax	Entities and individuals	Exploiting taxable mineral resources (such as crude oil, natural gas, coal, etc.) or producing salt in China	Ad valorem or per unit
Environmental Protection Tax	Entities	Discharging pollutants (such as air pollutants, water pollutants and noise pollution) within China	Different rates for different pollutants

Continued

Taxes	Taxpayers	Tax Subject	Tax Rates
Vehicle and Vessel Tax	Owners	Owning vehicles or vessels in China	Different rates for different swept volumes
Stamp Duty	Entities and individuals	Concluding or receiving taxable documents (such as various types of contracts, documents of the transfer of property title, business books and accounts, etc.) in China	Different rates for different documents
Urban Maintenance and Construction Tax	Entities and individuals	When taxpayers paying VAT or excise tax, this is a supplementary tax	Different rates for different locations
Tobacco Tax	Entities and individuals	Purchasing tobacco leaves in China	20%
Vessel Tonnage Tax	In-charge person of the vessels	Vessels entering Chinese ports from overseas ports	Different rates for different tonnages

1.4　Tax Mix

China's tax revenue has been rising steadily in the past three decades. As it is shown in the following figure (Figure 1-1), the Chinese tax revenue in 2019 was almost 40 times of that in 1993. And when calculating on the comparable basis, tax revenue in 2019 was increased by 215.5 billion RMB on a year-on-year basis, registering growth of 1.3 percent.[①] In 2018, the share of tax revenue in GDP was 17.4 percent.

Furthermore, with regard to the total tax revenue collected in 2019, the tax revenue of goods and services tax (GST), income taxes, property and

---

[①]　See website of the State Taxation of Administration of China: http://www.china-tax.gov.cn/eng/c101270/c101273/c5157941/content.html (accessed on 30 March, 2021).

billion RMB   ▦ Tax Revenue   ▦ Growth Rate

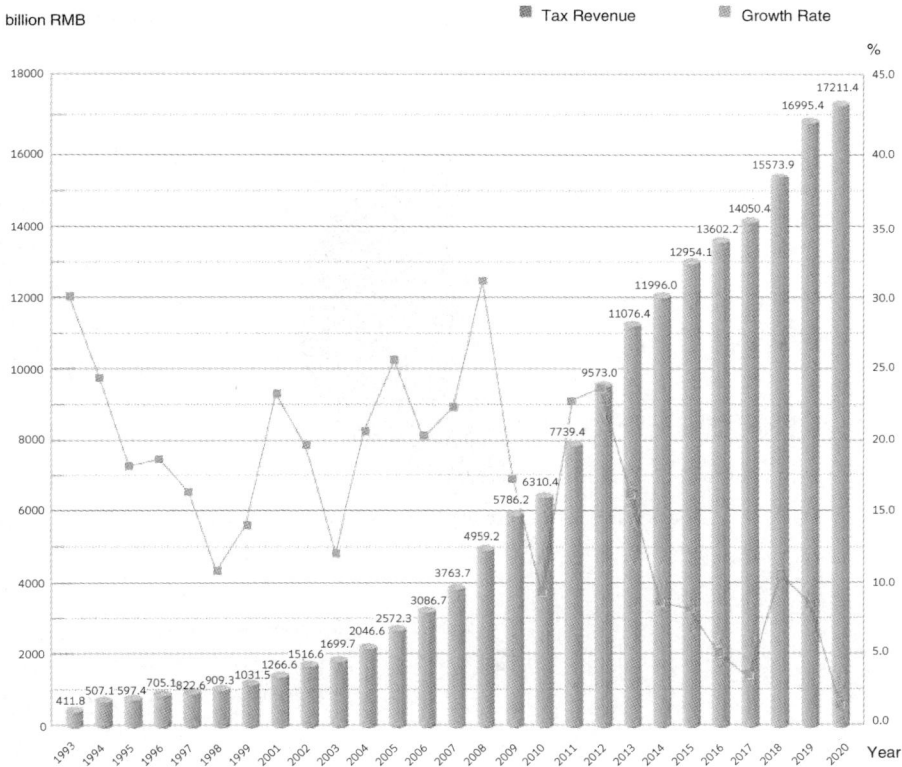

Figure 1-1   Tax Revenue Growth(1993-2019)

behavior taxes was 9454.9 billion RMB, 4790.4 billion RMB and 2966.1 billion RMB, accounting for 54.9%, 27.8% and 17.3% respectively. Clearly,
as shown in the following figure (Figure 1-2), the revenue of GST remained
to be the major portion of China's total tax revenue in 2019.

 While looking into the specific taxes, the revenues of VAT, enterprise
income tax, excise tax, and individual income tax in 2019 were 7756.8 billion
RMB, 3751.6 billion RMB, 1348.2 billion RMB, 1038.9 billion RMB, accounting for 45.1%, 21.8%, 7.8%, and 6.0% of the total tax revenue re-
spectively(Figure 1-3).

 The above figures of the tax revenue in 2019 were consistent with the
tax mixes of the previous years, where the goods and services taxes (especially the VAT) have been the most important revenue source in China for

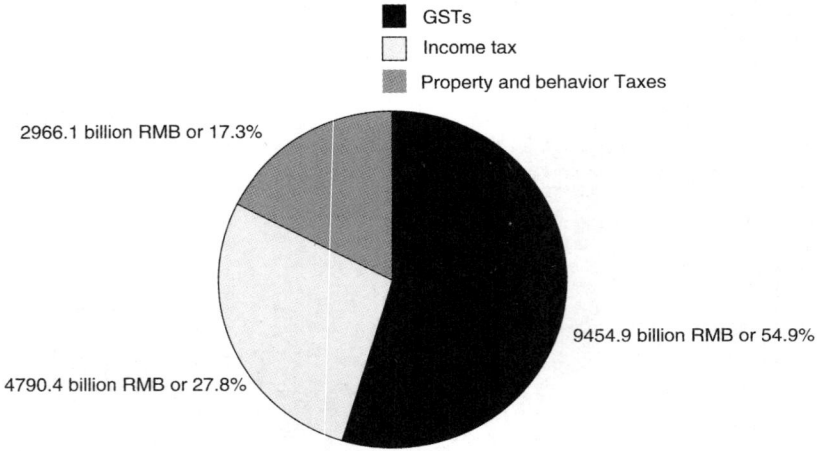

Figure 1-2   Tax revenue by tax category in 2019

GSTs
Income tax
Property and behavior Taxes

2966.1 billion RMB or 17.3%

9454.9 billion RMB or 54.9%

4790.4 billion RMB or 27.8%

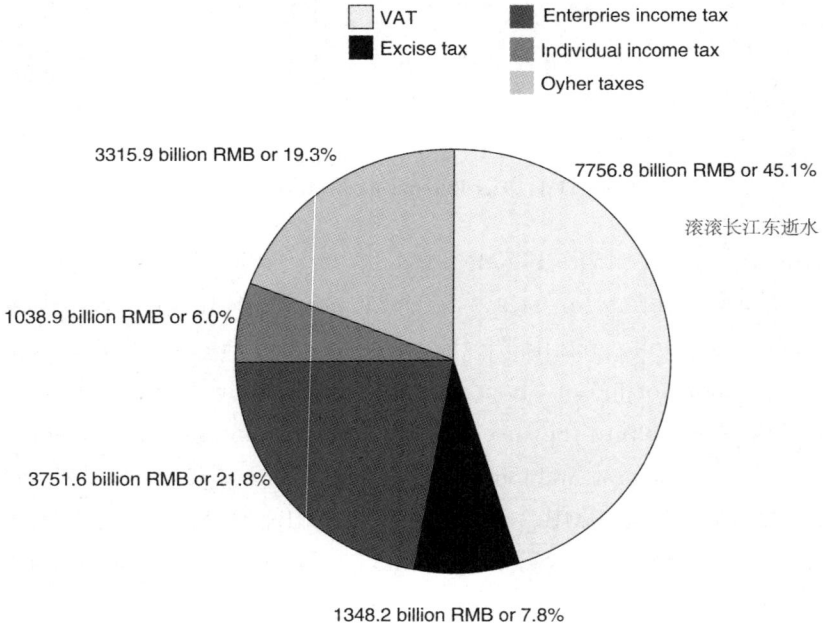

Figure 1-3   Tax revenue by tax type in 2019

VAT   Enterpries income tax
Excise tax   Individual income tax
                   Oyher taxes

3315.9 billion RMB or 19.3%

7756.8 billion RMB or 45.1%

滚滚长江东逝水

1038.9 billion RMB or 6.0%

3751.6 billion RMB or 21.8%

1348.2 billion RMB or 7.8%

two decades. Such a tax mix may reflect the facts of China's economic developments which focused on manufacturing and trading industries in the past decades. It also implies why the Chinese tax authorities have been putting significant efforts into collection of goods and services taxes, especially the VAT which is under a quite strict invoice system for both administration and tax collections.

1.5   Main Players in China's Tax Regime

The main players in China's tax regimes could be divided into the following three groups (see Figure 1-4):

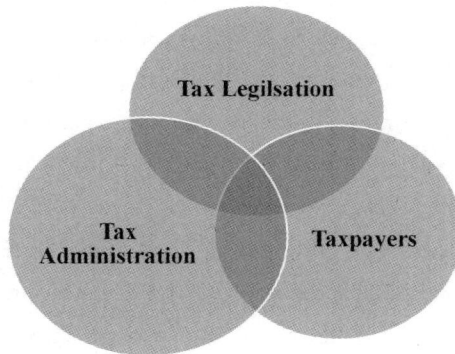

Figure 1-4   Main players in China's tax regime

(1) The first group is the ones who enact the tax legislations, including tax laws, regulations, circulars as well as tax treaties. Chapter 2 of this book will provide the names and roles of these players in Chinese tax legislations.

(2) The second group is the ones who implement the tax legislations and treaties. Chapter 8 of the this book will address the details on these players.

(3) The third group is the taxpayers, who are the ones paying the taxes to the players in the second group in accordance with the tax legislations enacted by the players of the first group. The players in the third group may be individuals, enterprises, organizations and other forms of units, depending

on the specific types of the taxes and tax treaties. These players could be Chinese individuals and enterprises or foreign individuals or enterprises. Therefore, it is necessary to pay particular attention to the question when reading the Chapters 3.7: who are the taxpayers for that specific tax?

1.6　History of China's Tax Regime

The current tax regime of China is a result of several rounds of tax reforms over the past 40 years. Following China's reform and opening up in the late 1970s, there arose the demands for a stable tax regime which could be compatible with the new strategy of the nation's market economy.[①]Thus two approaches were carried out in parallel to build up China's tax regime.

One approach was to establish a domestic tax framework. Efforts were made in the 1980s to introduce the income taxes and several indirect taxes, which were applied to domestic and foreign taxpayers separately and differently.[②] Then in the 1990s, China conducted a milestone fiscal reform (the "1994 Reform"), which targeted both tax structure and tax administration. A single legislation for value added tax, excise tax, business tax and other indirect taxes was enacted respectively by the State Council, and these indirect taxes started to apply to domestic and foreign taxpayers with the same tax rates and method.[③]The unification of domestic and foreign enterprise income tax systems was however delayed until the Enterprise Income Tax Law came into force on 1 January, 2008. In addition, the 1994 Reform established a tax-revenue-sharing system between the central and provincial governments of China, and the tax administration was accordingly separated in-

---

① Jin Li and Richard Krever, Globalization and Modernization as Drivers for Tax Reform in the Socialist Market Economy, *Theoretical Inquiries in Law*, 2010, Vol.11, No.2.

② Jinyan Li, China's Tax System: An Evaluation, *Denver Journal of International Law and Policy*, 1989, Vol.3.

③ Mario Blejer and Gyorgy Szapara, The Evolving Role of Tax Policy in China, *Journal of Comparative Economics*, 1990, Vol.14, p.452, 462.

to central and local.[1] The present tax regime of China is still based on the a-bove fundamental structure of the 1994 Reform.[2]

Another approach was to build up a tax treaty network. China concluded its first tax treaty with Japan in 1983, and then it continued to negotiate and conclude tax treaties (arrangements) with 110 jurisdictions as of March 2021 for the purpose of preventing double taxation and eliminating tax evasion in terms of incomes.[3]

A clear trend of development in Chinese tax regime, both in terms of domestic taxes and tax treaties, is from the position of a source state to a residence state. One example is the tax incentives in Chinese income tax laws. When China opened its door to foreign investment in the late 1970s, its economy and infrastructures at that time were of little attraction to inves-tors. In order to compensate its disadvantages, China commenced using tax factors, in particular tax incentives, at the beginning of 1980s to attract FDIs (foreign direct investments). Hence, the first income tax laws respec-tively for foreign equity joint venture and foreign enterprise came into force in 1980 and 1981[4], which provided generous tax incentives with a clear aim of attracting both foreign capital and technology. The tax incentives in forms of tax holidays, lower income tax rates, accelerated depreciation, and re-funds of tax paid on reinvestment were obviously designed to attract foreign capital, while the tax incentives in forms of exempting with holding tax on

---

① Yasheng Huang, Central-Local Relations in China During the Reform Era: The Economic and Institutional Dimensions, *WORLD DEV*. 1996, Vol.24, p.655, 660.

② Liu Zuo, *Thirty Years of Tax Reforms in China*, Beijing: China Finance and E-conomics Press, 2008.

③ China International Taxation Research Institute, *Forty Years of China's Interna-tional Taxation*, Beijing: China Taxation Press, 2018.

④ The Income Tax Law of the People's Republic of China Concerning Joint Ventures Using Chinese and Foreign Investment passed by the National People's Congress (NPC) on 10 September, 1980 applied to equity joint ventures formed by a foreign investor and a Chi-nese partner. The Income Tax Law of the People's Republic of China Concerning Foreign Enterprises was promulgated by the NPC on 13 December, 1981. It applied to foreign in-vestment including contractual joint ventures, joint explorations, and wholly foreign-owned enterprises.

royalties, lower income tax rates, and tax holidays for hi-tech foreign investment were designed to attract foreign technology. These FDI-specific incentives continued (even though China promulgated a new income tax law for foreign investment in 1991)[①] for almost three decades, until China's Enterprise Income Tax Law came into force on 1 January, 2008.[②] Under this 2008 Enterprise Income Tax Law, those foreign-oriented tax incentives were abolished and the same tax incentive measures apply to both domestic and foreign investment in environmental protection, high-advanced technology, as well as those in less developed regions of China.

Appendix: Exercises

(1) How many taxes are there in China? Which taxes are relevant to cross-border transactions involving?

(2) Who are the taxpayers for the goods and services taxes?

(3) Who are actually undertaking the tax burdens for the goods and services taxes?

(4) Who are the taxpayers for the income taxes?

(5) Who are actually undertaking the tax burdens for the income taxes?

(6) In terms of China's tax mix, which tax is the most important revenue source for Chinese government? Why?

(7) Comparing China's tax regime with the tax regime of your own jurisdiction, what are the similarities? What are the differences?

---

① Enterprise Income Tax Law for Foreign Invested Enterprises and Foreign Enterprises the People's Republic of China promulgated by the NPC on 9 April, 1991, which came into effect on 1 July, 1991. This new income law abolished the former two income tax laws promulgated in 1980 and 1981 respectively applicable to foreign investments.

② Enterprise Income Tax Law of People's Republic of China, promulgated by the NPC on 16 March, 2007 and came into force on 1 January, 2008.

CHAPTER 2　SOURCE OF LAW

2.1　Introduction

There is not a single tax law or a general tax code governing all taxes in China, and there is no case law in China either. Rather separate laws and regulations are imposing different taxes on different taxpayers and on different incomes and activities. Meanwhile, more than 100 tax treaties are also important parts of the source of law in China in terms of taxation and tax administration. In case of any conflict between domestic law and tax treaties, the provisions of tax treaties will prevail[①]. Hence this chapter will address the source of Chinese tax laws from two perspectives: the domestic tax laws and the tax treaties.

2.2　Domestic Tax Laws

The framework of Chinese domestic tax laws stand like a pyramid with

---

① 　Article 91 of the Law on the Levying and Collection of Taxes promulgated at the 27th Meeting of the Standing Committee of the 7th NPC on September 4, 1992, amended by the Standing Committee of the 9th NPC on April 28, 2001, and effective on May 1, 2001; and Article 58 of the Enterprise Income Tax Law promulgated by the NPC on 6 March, 2007 and effective on January 1, 2008.

three tiers[①](see Figure 2-1):

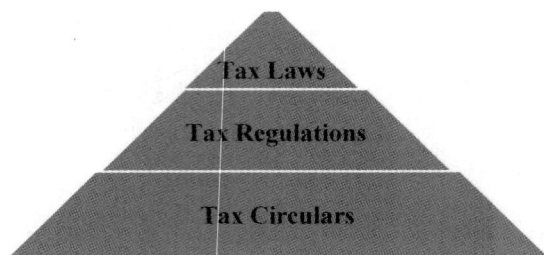

Figure 2-1   Framework of China's domestic tax laws

(1) On the top are a number of tax laws promulgated by the National People's Congress ("NPC") and its Standing Committee, which are legislative organs in China.

(2) On the second tier are the tax regulations enacted by the State Council which is the highest executive organ in China but has been delegated with certain legislative power from the NPC to ① enact the detailed rules for implementing the tax laws promulgated by the NPC; and ② enact provisional regulations governing a number of taxes before the NPC promulgates a governing law. While in recent years, the NPC has been working on enacting laws to replace these provisional regulations. Thus we may expect to see in the coming years that more and more Chinese taxes will be governed by the "laws" promulgated by the NPC rather than by the "provisional regulations" enacted by the State Council.

(3) The bottom are the ministerial rules and circulars in an amount of more than 5000 enacted by the Ministry of Finance (MOF), the State Administration of Taxation (SAT) and the General Administration of Customs of China (GACC) under the legislative power re-delegated from the State Council to them. These ministerial rules and circulars provide detailed rules to interpret and apply tax treaties in China.

---

① Dongmei Qiu, *Legal Interpretation of Tax Law: China*, in *Legal Interpretation of Tax Law*, Robert F. van Brederode and Richard Krever eds., published by Kluwer Law International BV, The Netherlands in 2014.

2.2.1 Tax Laws

The NPC is the highest organ of state power in China. The NPC consists of approximately 3000 delegates elected by the administrative regions and the military forces. Its permanent body is the Standing Committee of the NPC located in Beijing. The NPC and its Standing Committee exercise the legislative power of tax law in China. In general, the laws promulgated by the NPC only set out the general principles and rules in forms of a quite limited number of articles, thus it leaves to the State Council and the relevant government departments to enact the detailed rules and regulations on how to implement these laws.

As of March 30, 2021, the NPC and its Standing Committee have promulgated the following tax laws (Table 2-1):

Table 2-1   Tax laws as of March 30, 2021

No.	Name of the Law	Time of Promulgation
Laws on specific taxes		
1	Individual Income Tax Law	September 10, 1980
2	Enterprise Income Tax Law	March 16, 2007
3	Vehicle and Vessel Tax Law	February 25, 2011
4	Environmental Protection Tax Law	December 25, 2016
5	Vessel Tonnage Tax Law	December 27, 2017
6	Tobacco Leaf Tax Law	December 27, 2017
7	Vehicle Acquisition Tax Law	December 29, 2018
8	Farmland Occupation Tax Law	December 29, 2018
9	Resource Tax Law	August 26, 2019
10	Urban Maintenance and Construction Tax Law	August 11, 2020
11	Deed Tax Law	August 11, 2020
Laws on tax administration and collection		
12	Law of the People's Republic of China on the Administration of Tax Collection	September 4, 1992

At a provincial level, local People's Congresses and their Standing Committees are empowered to make local rules and regulations, provided that they do not contravene the Constitution Law, the laws promulgated by the NPC or the administrative regulations made by State Council.

2.2.2 Tax Regulations

The State Council, headed by the Premier Minister, is the highest executive body of state power in China. Administrative regulations enacted by the State Council are normally named as "regulations", "provisions" or "measures", and these administrative regulations are ranking immediately below the laws promulgated by the NPC.

In terms of tax legislations, the State Council is empowered with a legislative power partially from the Legislation Law[①] and partially from the delegated legislative power from the NPC[②]. The tax legislations enacted by the State Council normally consist of two parts:

---

① Legislation Law of the People's Republic of China, promulgated at the Third Session of the Ninth National People's Congress on 15 March, 2000, and amended at the Third Session of the Twelfth National People's Congress on 15 March, 2015. Article 9 of the Legislation Law empowers the State Council to enact administrative regulations, rules and measures to implement the tax laws promulgated by the NPC and its Standing Committee. For example, the Implementing Regulations of the Law on Enterprise Income Tax, promulgated on 6 December, 2007; Implementing Regulations of the Individual Income Tax Law, promulgated on 28 January, 1994 and amended on 19 July, 2011; the Implementing Regulations of the Vehicle and Vessel Tax Law, promulgated on 23 November, 2011 and effective on 1 January, 2012.

② Decision of the NPC Standing Committee to Authorize the State Council to Reform the System of Industrial and Commercial Taxes and Issue Relevant Draft Tax Regulations for Trial Application, issued by the NPC on 18 September, 1984 and repealed on 27 June, 2009; Decision of the NPC on Authorizing the State Council to Formulate Interim Provisions or Regulations Concerning Economic Structural Reform and Open Policy, issued by the NPC on 10 April, 1985. The delegated legislative power from the NPC to the State Council was for the latter to enact provisional regulations before the NPC formally enacted them, for example, Provisional Regulations on the value-added tax, promulgated by the State Council on 13 December, 1993; Provisional Regulations on Business Tax, promulgated by the State Council on 13 December, 1993; and Provisional Regulations on Consumption Tax promulgated by the State Council on 13 December, 1993.

(1)The implementation rules which the State Council enacted to provide detailed rules for implementing the tax laws promulgated by the NPC.

It is necessary to enact these implementing rules, because the tax laws promulgated by the NPC usually set out the general principles of the respective taxes in a limited number of articles. Thus it depends on the implementing rules enacted by the State Council to provide detailed provisions concerning the scope of the tax, applicable persons, calculation of tax charge, timing of payment, etc. For example, the NPC promulgated the Enterprise Income Tax Law on 16 March, 2007, and then the State Council enacted the Implementation Regulations on the Enterprise Income Tax Law on 6 December, 2007.

(2) The second part refers to those provisional regulations governing specific taxes, for which the NPC has not promulgated the tax laws yet. Such provisional regulations are less in terms of numbers, as the NPC is making tax laws to replace these provisional regulations. For example, the NPC is promulgating a VAT law to replace the currently applicable Provision Regulation on value-added tax which was enacted by the State Council on 13 December, 1993.

The following table lists out the provisional regulations which have not be replaced by a tax law yet by March 2021(Table 2-2).

Table 2-2

No.	Name of the Law	Enacting Time	Status as of March 2021
1	Provisional Regulation on Real Estate Tax	15 September, 1986	Valid
2	Provisional Regulation on Stamp Duty	6 August, 1988	Valid
3	Provisional Regulation on Urban and Town Land Use Tax	27 September, 1988	Valid
4	Provisional Regulation on Business Tax	13 December, 1993	Abolished on 19 November, 2017
5	Provisional Regulation on value-added tax	13 December, 1993	Valid

Continued

No.	Name of the Law	Enacting Time	Status as of March 2021
6	Provisional Regulation on Consumption Tax	13 December, 1993	Valid
7	Provisional Regulation on Land Value-Added Tax	13 December , 1993	Valid
8	Regulations on Import and Export Duties	23 November, 2003	Valid

2.2.3 Tax Circulars

The MOF, the SAT and the GACC are authorized by the State Council to issue circulars, jointly or separately, for the purpose of clarifying the issues arising from implementation of tax laws and regulations. These circulars are addressed mainly to the branches and offices of the MOF, the GACC and the SAT, therefore it has been a long-time debate on their binding effects: Should they be binding only on these authorities? Or should they also have a binding effect on taxpayers? In practice, these tax circulars have significant impact on both tax administration and tax compliance.

Furthermore, a concern on the conflict of interest issue has been on the SAT as well. The SAT is also the highest level tax authority in China, which supervises all Chinese tax authorities to implement tax laws and regulations in terms of their tax administration functions; meanwhile, the SAT has enacted thousands of tax circulars interpreting how the tax laws, regulations and treaties should be implemented. Such dual functions of the SAT unavoidably brought concerns in taxpayers on the fairness and integrity of the SAT in performing its roles.[1]

---

[1]　Wei Cui, What Is the "Law" in Chinese Tax Administration?, *Asia Pacific Law Review*, 2016.

2.3   Tax Treaties

China has built up a quite broad tax treaty network, which includes more than 100 bilateral tax treaties and a number of multilateral tax treaties. These tax treaties also constitute a part of the source law of China's tax law.

2.3.1 DTAs

As of March 2021, China has concluded bilateral tax agreements with 107 countries and the bilateral arrangements which Chinese Mainland signed with Hong Kong, Macao and Taiwan respectively for the purpose of relieving double taxation and prevention of fiscal evasion with respect to taxes on income. Collectively, these bilateral tax agreements and arrangements are called "double tax agreements" (DTAs). Details on how to implement these DTAs will be addressed in Chapter 7 of this book.

2.3.2 Tax Information Exchange Agreements (TIEAs)

China has concluded bilateral agreements with ten low-tax or no-tax jurisdictions during the period from 2009 to 2014 for the purpose of exchanging information relating to taxes. These agreements are collectively called "tax information exchange agreements" (TIEAs). These TIEAs have no provision regarding relief of double taxation, but only provide a regime for exchange of tax information upon request between China and the contracting states. These ten contracting States are Bahamas, British Virgin Islands, Isle of Man, Guernsey, Jersey, Bermuda, Argentina, Cayman Islands, San Marino, and Liechtenstein.

2.3.3 Multilateral Tax Conventions

As of March 2021, China has signed three multilateral tax treaties:

(1)Multilateral Convention on Mutual Administrative Assistance in Tax Matters as mended by the 2010 protocol, which imposes an obligation of mutual administrative assistance on China and the other Contracting States in terms of exchange of information, recovery of tax claims and service of documents. China singed this multilateral convention on 27 August, 2013 and the convention became effective on 1 January, 2017.

(2) Multilateral Competent Authority Agreement on Automatic Exchange of Financial Account Information, which imposes an obligation on China and the other Contracting States to exchange their tax-related financial account information automatically on a multilateral basis. China singed this multilateral convention on 16 December, 2015 and the convention became effective in China in May 2017.

(3)Multilateral Convention to Implement Tax Treaty Related Measures to Prevent Base Erosion and Profit Shifting, which will be applied to amend a number of Chinese DTAs by incorporating certain anti-tax evasion and avoidance measures.

Appendix I : Chinese Tax Treaties (As of March 2021)

(1)DTAs (Table 2-3)

Table 2-3   DTAs

No.	Jurisdiction	Signing Date	Effective Date	Implementation Date
1	Japan	1983-09-06	1984-06-26	1985-01-01
2	U.S.A.	1984-04-30	1986-11-21	1987-01-01
3	France	1984-05-30	1985-02-21	1986-01-01
		2013-11-26	2014-12-28	2015-01-01

Continued

No.	Jurisdiction	Signing Date	Effective Date	Implementation Date
4	U.K.	1984-07-26	1984-12-23	1985-01-01
		2011-06-27	2013-12-13	China: 2014-01-01 UK: (1)Income tax and capital gains: 2014-04-06; (2)Corporation tax: 2014-04-01
5	Belgium	1985-04-18	1987-09-11	1988-01-01
		2009-10-07	2013-12-29	2014-01-01
6	Germany	1985-06-10	1986-05-14	1985-01-01/07-01
		2014-03-28	2016-04-06	2017-01-01
7	Malaysia	1985-11-23	1986-09-14	1987-01-01
8	Norway	1986-02-25	1986-12-21	1987-01-01
9	Denmark	1986-03-26	1986-10-22	1987-01-01
		2012-06-16	2012-12-27	2013-01-01
10	Singapore	1986-04-18	1986-12-11	1987-01-01
		2007-07-11	2007-09-18	2008-01-01
11	Canada	1986-05-12	1986-12-29	1987-01-01
12	Finland	1986-05-12	1987-12-18	1988-01-01
		2010-05-25	2010-11-25	2011-01-01
13	Sweden	1986-05-16	1987-01-03	1987-01-01
14	New Zealand	1986-09-16	1986-12-17	1987-01-01
		2019-04-01	2019-12-027	2020-01-01
15	Thailand	1986-10-27	1986-12-29	1987-01-01
16	Italy	1986-10-31	1989-11-14	1990-01-01
		2019-03-23	Not yet	
17	The Netherlands	1987-05-13	1988-03-05	1989-01-01
		2013-05-31	2014-08-31	2015-01-01
18	Czechoslovakia	1987-06-11	1987-12-23	1988-01-01
19	Poland	1988-06-07	1989-01-07	1990-01-01
20	Australia	1988-11-17	1990-12-28	1991-01-01

Continued

No.	Jurisdiction	Signing Date	Effective Date	Implementation Date
21	Yugoslavia (Bosnia and Herzegovina)	1988-12-02	1989-12-16	1990-01-01
22	Bulgaria	1989-11-6	1990-05-25	1991-01-01
23	Pakistan	1989-11-15	1989-12-27	1989-01-01
24	Kuwait	1989-12-25	1990-07-20	1989-01-01
25	Switzerland	1990-07-06	1991-09-027	1990-01-01
		2013-09-25	2014-11-15	2015-01-01
26	Cyprus	1990-10-25	1991-10-05	1992-01-01
27	Spain	1990-11-22	1992-05-20	1993-01-01
		2018-11-28	Not yet	Not yet
28	Romania	1991-01-16	1992-03-05	1993-01-01
		2016-07-04	2017-06-17	2018-01-01
29	Austria	1991-04-10	1992-11-01	1993-01-01
30	Brazil	1991-08-05	1993-01-06	1994-01-01
31	Mongolia	1991-08-26	1992-06-23	1993-01-01
32	Hungary	1992-06-17	1994-12-31	1995-01-01
33	Malta	1993-02-02	1994-03-20	1995-01-01
		2010-10-18	2011-08-25	2012-01-01
34	United Arab Emirates	1993-07-01	1994-07-14	1995-01-01
35	Luxembourg	1994-03-012	1995-07-28	1996-01-01
36	Korea	1994-03-28	1994-09-27	1995-01-01
37	Russia	1994-05-27	1997-04-10	1998-01-01
		2014-10-13	2016-04-09	2017-01-01
38	Papua New Guinea	1994-07-14	1995-08-16	1996-01-01
39	India	1994-07-18	1994-11-19	1995-01-01
40	Mauritius	1994-08-01	1995-05-04	1996-01-01
41	Croatia	1995-01-09	2001-05-18	2002-01-01
42	Belarus	1995-01-17	1996-10-03	1997-01-01

Continued

No.	Jurisdiction	Signing Date	Effective Date	Implementation Date
43	Slovenia	1995-02-13	1995-12-27	1996-01-01
44	Israel	1995-04-08	1995-12-22	1996-01-01
45	Vietnam	1995-05-17	1996-10-18	1997-01-01
46	Turkey	1995-05-23	1997-01-20	1998-01-01
47	Ukraine	1995-12-04	1996-10-18	China: 1997-01-01 Ukraine: (1)Dividend, interest, royalties and individual income tax: 1996-12-17; (2)corporate income tax: 1997-01-01
48	Armenia	1996-05-05	1996-11-28	1997-01-01
49	Jamaica	1996-06-03	1997-03-15	1998-01-01
50	Iceland	1996-06-03	1997-02-05	1998-01-01
51	Lithuania	1996-06-03	1996-10-18	1997-01-01
52	Latvia	1996-06-07	1997-01-27	1998-01-01
53	Uzbekistan	1996-07-03	1996-07-03	1997-01-01
54	Bangladesh	1996-09-12	1997-04-10	China: 1998-01-01 Bangladesh: 1998-07-01
55	Yugoslavia (Serbia And Montenegro)	1997-03-21	1998-01-01	1998-01-01
56	Sudan	1997-05-30	1999-02-09	2000-01-01
57	Macedonia	1997-06-09	1997-11-29	1998-01-01
58	Egypt	1997-08-13	1999-03-24	2000-01-01
59	Portugal	1998-04-21	2000-06-07	2001-01-01
60	Estonia	1998-05-12	1999-01-08	2000-01-01
61	Laos	1999-01-25	1999-06-22	2000-01-01
62	Seychelles	1999-08-26	1999-12-17	2000-01-01
63	The Philippines	1999-11-18	2001-03-23	2002-01-01
64	Ireland	2000-04-19	2000-12-29	China: 2001-01-01 Ireland: 2001-04-06
65	South Africa	2000-04-25	2001-01-07	2002-01-01

Continued

No.	Jurisdiction	Signing Date	Effective Date	Implementation Date
66	Barbados	2000-05-15	2000-10-27	2001-01-01
67	Moldova	2000-06-07	2001-05-26	2002-01-01
68	Katar	2001-04-02	2008-10-21	2009-01-01
69	Cuba	2001-04-13	2003-10-17	2004-01-01
70	Venezuela	2001-04-17	2004-12-23	2005-01-01
71	Nepal	2001-05-14	2010-12-31	2011-01-01
72	Kazakhstan	2001-09-12	2003-07-27	2004-01-01
73	Indonesia	2001-11-07	2003-08-25	2004-01-01
74	Oman	2002-03-25	2002-07-20	2003-01-01
75	Nigeria	2002-04-15	2009-03-21	2010-01-01
76	Tunis	2002-04-16	2003-09-23	2004-01-01
77	Iran	2002-04-20	2003-08-14	2004-01-01
78	Bahrain	2002-05-16	2002-08-08	2003-01-01
79	Greece	2002-06-03	2005-11-01	2006-01-01
80	Kyrgyzstan	2002-06-24	2003-03-29	2004-01-01
81	Morocco	2002-08-27	2006-08-16	2007-01-01
82	Srilanka	2003-08-11	2005-05-22	2006-01-01
83	Trinidad and Tobago	2003-09-18	2005-05-22	2005-06-01 and 2006-01-01 respectively for different incomes
84	Albania	2004-09-13	2005-07-28	2006-01-01
85	Brunei	2004-09-21	2006-12-29	2007-01-01
86	Azerbaijan	2005-03-17	2005-08-17	2006-01-01
87	Georgia	2005-06-22	2005-11-10	2006-01-01
88	Mexico	2005-09-12	2006-03-01	2007-01-01
89	Saudi Arabia	2006-01-23	2006-09-01	2007-01-01
90	Algeria	2006-11-06	2007-07-27	2008-01-01
91	Tajikistan	2008-08-27	2009-03-28	2010-01-01

Continued

No.	Jurisdiction	Signing Date	Effective Date	Implementation Date
92	Ethiopia	2009-05-14	2012-12-25	2013-01-01
93	Turkmenistan	2009-12-13	2010-05-30	2011-01-01
94	Czech	2009-08-28	2011-05-04	2012-01-01
95	Zambia	2010-07-26	2011-06-30	2012-01-01
96	Syria	2010-10-31	2011-09-01	2012-01-01
97	Uganda	2012-01-11	Not yet	
98	Botswana	2012-04-11	2018-09-19	China: 2019-01-01 Botswana: withholding taxes 2018-10-19; other taxes 2019-07-01
99	Ecuador	2013-01-21	2014-03-06	2015-01-01
100	Chile	2015-05-25	2016-08-08	2017-01-01
101	Zimbabwe	2015-12-01	2016-09-29	2017-01-01
102	Cambodia	2016-10-13	2018-01-26	2019-01-01
103	Kenya	2017-09-21	Not yet	Not yet
104	Gabon	2018-09-01	Not yet	Not yet
105	The Republic of Congo	2018-09-05	Not yet	Not yet
106	Angola	2018-10-09	Not yet	Not yet
107	Argentina	2018-12-02	Not yet	Not yet

(2)Tax Arrangements(Table 2-4)

Table 2-4   Tax Arrangements

No.	Region	Signing Date	Effective Date	Implementation Date
1	Hong Kong	2006-08-21	2006-12-08	Chinese mainland: 2007-01-01 HK:2007-04-01
2	Macao	2003-12-27	2003-12-30	2004-01-01
3	Taiwan	2015-08-25	Not yet	Not yet

(3)TIEAs(Table 2-5)

Table 2-5   TIEAs

No.	Jurisdiction	Signing Date	Effective Date	Implementation Date
1	Bahamas	2009-12-01	2010-08-28	2011-01-01
2	The British Virgin Islands	2009-12-07	2010-12-30	2011-01-01
3	the Isle of Man	2010-10-26	2011-08-14	2012-01-01
4	Guernsey	2010-10-27	2011-08-17	2012-01-01
5	Jersey	2010-10-29	2011-11-10	2012-01-01
6	Bermuda	2010-12-02	2011-12-31	2012-01-01
7	Argentina	2010-12-13	2011-09-16	2012-01-01
8	Cayman	2011-09-26	2012-11-15	2013-01-01
9	San Marino	2012-07-09	2013-04-30	2014-01-01
10	Liechtenstein	2014-01-27	2014-08-02	2015-01-01

(4)Multilateral Conventions(Table 2-6)

Table 2-6   Multilateral Conventions

No.	Name	Signing Date	Effective Date	Implementation Date
1	Multilateral Convention on Mutual Administrative Assistance in Tax Matters amended by the 2010 Protocol	2013-08-27	2016-02-01	2017-01-01
2	Multilateral Competent Authority Agreement on Automatic Exchange of Financial Account Information	2015-12-16	2017-05	2017-07
3	Multilateral Convention to Implement Tax Treaty Related Measures to Prevent Base Erosion and Profit Shifting	2017-06-07	Not yet	Not yet

Appendix Ⅱ : Exercises

1. What are the legal sources of Chinese tax law?

2. Who are making tax laws in China?

3. Who enacts provisional tax regulations in China?

4. Who issues tax circulars in China?

5. What roles do the SAT play in China's tax regime?

6. How many tax treaties have China concluded?

7. In what aspects (income activities or other tax matters) the Chinese tax treaties are for?

8. What's the relationship between China's domestic law and tax treaties?

CHAPTER 3   VALUE ADDED TAX[①]

3.1   Introduction

The value added tax (VAT) and the business tax co-existed in China during the period from 1993 to 2016. The VAT was imposed at all stages of manufacturing, distribution and sales, as well as on import of goods by taxpayers; whereas the business tax was imposed on services except for processing, replacement and repair services which were subject to VAT. This bifurcated turnover tax system was considered inefficient, as the business tax was a tax without input tax credit and the overlapping of VAT and business tax created an unfair tax burden on taxpayers. Hence the Chinese government launched a VAT reform pilot program in Shanghai on 1 January, 2012 with the aim to transitioning all taxable items under the business tax into the scope of VAT. Since 1 May, 2016, the reform has been rolled out nationwide to all industries, which previously were subject to the business tax. Therefore, the business tax was no longer imposed after 1 May, 2016, and since then the VAT has been imposed on all imports of goods, provision of services, supply of goods and transfer of properties in China.

[①]   The content of this chapter is based on the publications of Dr. Li on journals, books and international conferences. For example, her papers "24 Years Later: China Finally Centralizes Its Tax Administration", co-authored with Richard Krever(Tax Notes International, 2018, Vol.4, No.8); and "Taxing Digital Businesses in China"(Asia-Pacific Tax Bulletin, 2020, Vol.26, No.2).

Therefore, the legislations governing VAT in China consist of the following regulations and circulars:

(1) The Provincial Regulation on value-added tax of the People's Republic of China (the "VAT Provisional Regulation"), enacted by the State Council in 1993 and latest amended in 2017; and the Implementation Rules of the VAT Provisional Regulation, enacted by the MOF and the SAT in 2008 and latest amended in 2011.

The VAT Provisional Regulation effective from 1 January, 2014 provides a VAT regime applicable to manufacturing, distribution and sales of goods in China, import of goods into China and provision of processing, replacement and repair services in China.

(2) The tax circulars issued by the MOF and the SAT with regard to implementation of the VAT Provision Regulation and with regard to the reform of transition from the Business Tax to VAT in the 2010s, especially the Circular Caishui 〔2016〕 No. 36.

According to the Circular Caishui 〔2016〕 No. 36, since 1 May, 2016 all services and transfers of properties have been transit to be subject to the VAT, instead of the business tax, in China. The Circular Caishui 〔2016〕 No. 36 provides detailed rules for imposing the VAT on services and transfer of properties.

3.2   Structure of the VAT Legislations

The VAT Provisional Regulation and the tax circulars (especially the Circular Caishui 〔2016〕 No. 36) are applicable in parallel governing the VAT compliance and administrations in China. The NPC is in a process of promulgation of a law governing the VAT regime (Table 3-1).

Table 3-1 Structure of the VAT Regulations

Covered Issues	VAT Provisional Regulation	Circular Caishui 〔2016〕 No. 36
Ⅰ.Taxpayer, Taxable Events and Withholding Agent	Art. 1 and Art. 18	Arts. 1-14
Ⅱ.Tax Rates	Art. 2	Arts. 15-16
Ⅲ.Taxable Income	Art. 3	Arts. 37-44
Ⅳ.Tax Payable by general taxpayer	Arts. 4-10	Arts. 17-18 and Arts. 21-33
Ⅴ. Tax Payable by Small-Scale Taxpayer	Arts. 11-13	Art. 19 and Arts. 34-36
Ⅵ.Tax Payable for Imports	Art. 14	
Ⅶ.Tax Payable by Withholdings		Art. 20
Ⅷ.Exemption	Arts. 15-17	Arts. 48-50
Ⅸ.Tax Administration	Arts. 19-26	Arts. 45-47 and Arts. 51-55
Ⅹ.Supplementary Provisions	Arts. 27-28	

3.3 Taxpayers

The VAT taxpayers are entities and individuals, who are engaged in supply of goods, provision of services or transfer of properties in China, or import of goods into China. The term "entities" herein refers to all enterprises, administrative institutions, public institutions, military institutions, social organizations, and other types of entities. While the term "individual" means both the natural persons and the household entrepreneurs.

These VAT taxpayer sare divided into two categories: the "general taxpayers" and the "small-scale taxpayers". The general taxpayers are subject to the normal rates of VAT, are entitled to input tax credit on purchases, and must issue special VAT invoices; whereas the small-scale taxpayers are taxed at a low rate, but have neither the right to claim input VAT nor the right to issue special VAT invoices. The thresholds for registration as a general taxpayer have been changed a number of times, as a result of both the VAT reforms and enhancement of tax administration capacity. Thresholds applicable in 2020 were as follows:

(1)As for a taxpayer engaging in provision of services, its annual business revenue should be no less than RMB 5 million;

(2)As for a taxpayer engaging in wholesale or retail sales of goods, its annual business revenue should be no less than RMB 800,000;

(3)As for a taxpayer engaging in manufacture and productions, its annual business revenue should be no less than RMB 500,000.

However, where a small-scale taxpayer may have adequate accounting records with accurate tax information, it may apply for being recognized as a "general taxpayer". Once being approved, such taxpayer shall be subject to VAT according to the approach applicable to the general taxpayers.

3.4   Taxable Events

The taxable events of VAT are quite broad in China, including supply of goods, provision of services and transfer of property in China, as well as import of goods into China, except for activities expressly exempted by laws and regulations. The taxable events in general should be provided for consideration, which is the price paid for goods or services as well as any additional charges which are not included in the price. A consideration denominated in foreign currencies must be converted into RMB at the average exchange rate on the date of the transaction or the first day of the month in which the transaction takes place.

3.4.1 Supply of Goods

Supply of goods refers to transfer of ownership of goods for considerations in cash, or in forms of property or other economic benefits. The following activities shall be deemed as supply of goods and be subject to VAT in China:

(1) delivery of goods to other entities or individuals for sale on a consignment basis;

(2) sales of consigned goods;

(3) delivery of goods from one site of a taxpayer to its other sites for sales, when such taxpayer has more than one site and pays taxes for those sites on a consolidation basis, unless sites involved in delivery of goods are situated in the same county or in the same city in China;

(4) use of taxable goods in manufacturing non-taxable goods or services;

(5) use of taxable goods for welfare or personal consumption;

(6) transfer of taxable goods as investments into entities or individual entrepreneurs;

(7) transfer of taxable goods as dividend distribution to shareholders or investors;

(8) gift of taxable goods to other entities or individuals.

The notion "goods" herein includes tangible movable property, industrial products and certain products used in the agricultural sector, including electricity, heating, power, gas, forage and chemical fertilizers.

3.4.2 Import of Goods

Import of goods into China, including the self-use articles carried or mailed into China, shall be subject to VAT. Such VAT should be paid to the Chinese Customs authorities, along with the customs duty and excise tax if applicable. Therefore, some laws and regulations issued by the Chinese Customs for or relating to VAT shall also be applicable for import of goods into China.

3.4.3 Export of Goods

Export of goods in principle should subject to VAT, but the applicable VAT rate is usually 0 unless otherwise specified by the State Council. The general taxpayers engaging in export of goods are entitled to a refund of the input VAT paid for purchasing the goods or relevant materials for producing the exported goods.

3.4.4 Provision of Services

Provision of services shall be subject to VAT in China when the service provider or the service receiver is inside of China, unless exemption treatments are provided according to applicable laws and regulations. But if the service has been wholly performed outside China by entities or individuals outside China to entities or individuals within the territory of China, then such service shall not become a taxable event in China for the VAT purpose. As for those services being provided free of charge, they shall be deemed as taxable unless such services were provided for public welfare purpose.

3.4.5 Export of Services

In principle, exported services should be subject to VAT in China since the service provider is inside of China. However, the Circular Caishui [2016] No. 36 provides exemption treatment to certain exported services when the actual recipients of services are outside China and such services are irrelevant to cargo or immovable property within China. The details of these exempted services are provided in Section 6 herein.

3.4.6 Transfer of Property

Transfer of property in China shall be subject to VAT, unless such transfer is entitled with an exemption treatment according to the governing laws and regulations. The property herein includes immovable property located in China, movable property and intangible property. The notion "transfer" refers to both transfer of ownership of the property (for example, sales of the property' title) and the transfer of the use right of the property (for example, lease of the property).

However, the following two types of transfer shall not be subject to

VAT:

(1)Sales of intangible property that is used wholly outside of China and is provided by entities or individuals outside China to entities or individuals within the territory of China.

(2) Sales of tangible movable property that is used wholly outside of China and is provided by entities or individuals outside China to entities or individuals within the territory of China.

3.5 Tax Rates

3.5.1 Rates Applicable to General Taxpayers

3.5.1.1 Standard VAT Rates

The following table(Table 3-2) lists the standard VAT rates provided in the VAT Provisional Regulation and the Circular Caishui 〔2016〕 No. 36 applicable to the general taxpayers. It is notable that these VAT rates may be changed from time to time by the SAT and MOF in forms of tax circulars.

Table 3-2   VAT Rates

Taxable Events	Tax Rates
Import of goods	17%
Export of goods	0
Supply of goods	17%
Operating leases or financial leases of equipments	17%
Transportation, postal, telecom, construction, sales or leases of real property	11%
All remaining services and transfer of property	6%

3.5.1.2 Reduced VAT Rates

A reduced VAT rate of 11% shall apply to the general VAT payers when importing or selling the following goods:

(1)grain and other agricultural products, edible vegetable oil, and edible salt;

(2)tap water, heating, cooling, hot water, coal gas, liquefied petroleum gas, natural gas, diethyl ether, methane, and coal products for residential use;

(3)books, newspapers, magazines, audio-visual recordings, and electronic publications;

(4)feed, fertilizer, pesticide, agricultural machinery, and agricultural films;

(5)other goods specified by the State Council.

3.5.2 Rates Applicable to Small-Scale Taxpayers

A rate of 3% is the single VAT rate applicable to small-scale taxpayers for the taxable events, unless it is provided otherwise by the MOF and the SAT in forms of tax circulars. This 3% rate is called the VAT collection rate.

3.5.3 Zero Rate (0)

The following exported services provided by entities or individuals inside of China could be subject to a VAT rate of zero percent (0). But the service providers are allowed to waive the zero rate, but opt to an exemption treatment or opt to pay the VAT, as long as the service providers shall comply with opted treatment for a period of at least 36 months:

(1)International transportation services provided in forms of ① transporting passengers or cargo from China to abroad; ② transporting into China passengers or cargo from abroad; or ③ transporting passengers or cargo outside China;

(2)air transport services;

(3)services provided for foreign entities that are fully consumed outside China, including ① R&D services; ② energy management contracting services; ③ design services; ④ production and distribution services of radio, film, and television programs (or works); ⑤ software services; ⑥ circuit design and testing services; ⑦ information system services; ⑧ business process management services; ⑨ offshore service outsourcing business, such as information technology outsourcing (ITO), technical business process outsourcing (BPO), and technical knowledge process outsourcing (KPO) service; and ⑩ transfer of technologies;

(4)Other services as prescribed by the MOF and the SAT.

3.6　Exemption

3.6.1 Exempted Services

The Circular Caishui〔2016〕No. 36 provides with a long list of the services which shall be exempted from VAT in China, even when both the service providers and the recipients are inside of China:

(1)nursing and teaching services provided by nurseries and kindergartens;

(2)elderly care services provided by elderly care institutions;

(3)nursing services provided by charity agencies for the disabled;

(4)matrimonial agency services;

(5)funeral and interment services;

(6)services provided by disabled persons to the society;

(7)medical services provided by medical institutions;

(8)educational services provided by schools that provide education for academic credentials;

(9)services provided by students participating in work-study programs;

(10)agricultural mechanical ploughing, irrigation and drainage, prevention and treatment of plant diseases and insect pests, plant protection, agriculture and animal husbandry insurance, and related technical training, and breeding as well as the prevention and treatment of diseases of poultry, livestock and aquatic animals;

(11)income obtained from selling tickets at the first entrance admission in the provision of cultural and sports services by memorial halls, museums, cultural centers, governing bodies of protected historic and cultural sites, art galleries, exhibition halls, academies of painting and calligraphy, and libraries in their own places;

(12)income obtained from selling tickets for cultural and religious activities held in Buddha temples, Taoist temples, mosques and churches;

(13)government funds and administrative charges collected by entities other than administrative entities in compliance with the conditions prescribed in Article 10 of the Measures for the Implementation of the Pilot Program;

(14)individuals' transfer of copyright;

(15)individuals' sale of housing units built and used by themselves;

(16)public rental housing units leased by business management entities of public rental housing units before December 31, 2018;

(17) transport income obtained in the mainland by Taiwan shipping companies and airline companies from the direct shipping and direct air transport services across the Taiwan Strait;

(18)direct or indirect international cargo transport agency services provided by taxpayers;

(19)a number of interest income, including ① interest for small loans of financial institutions for farmer households before December 31, 2016; ② national student loans; ③ national debts, and debts of local governments; ④ loans granted by the People's Bank of China to financial institutions; ⑤ individual housing loans granted by housing provident fund management centers with housing provident funds at designated authorized banks; ⑥ foreign exchange loans granted by financial institutions as authorized by foreign exchange administrative departments in the business operation of state foreign exchange reserves; ⑦ interest charged by an enterprise group or any core enterprise of the enterprise group from the enterprise group or entities subordinated to the group at a rate not higher than the interest rate of loans paid to financial institutions or the nominal interest rate of paid bonds in the uniform lending and repayment business;

(20) revoked financial institutions pay debts with goods, immovable property, intangible assets, negotiable securities, negotiable instruments and other property;

(21) premium income derived from personal insurance products with a term of one year or more launched by an insurance company;

(22) income from the transfer of the following financial commodities: ① trading of securities by domestic companies upon the entrustment of qualified foreign institutional investors (QFIIs) in China; ② trading of A shares by investors on the Hong Kong market (including entities and individuals) listed on the Shanghai Stock Exchange through the Shanghai-Hong Kong Stock Connect; ③ trading of fund shares in the mainland with investors on the Hong Kong market (including entities and individuals) through mutual fund recognition; ④ trading of stocks and bonds by management institutions of securities investment funds (closed-end securities investment funds and open-end securities investment funds) using funds; ⑤ individuals' transfer of financial commodities;

(23) interest income from the inter-bank business of financial institutions;

(24) incomes obtained by a guarantee institution concurrently meeting the following conditions from the credit guarantee or re-guarantee business for small-sized and medium-sized enterprises (excluding the income from credit ratings, consulting, and training, etc.) shall be exempted from VAT for a period of three years;

(25) interest subsidy income and price margin subsidy income obtained from the Central Treasury or local public finance departments by national commodity reserves management entities and their directly subordinated enterprises undertaking commodity reserves;

(26) technology transfer and technical development and related technical consulting and technical services provided by taxpayers;

(27) energy management contracting (EMC) services concurrently meeting certain conditions;

(28) ticket proceeds of popular science publicity entities and the ticket

proceeds arising from popular science activities carried out by the Party and government departments and associations for science and technology at or above the county level before December 31, 2017;

(29) income gained from giving classes of advanced study or training classes by colleges and universities, secondary schools and elementary schools (excluding their subordinated entities) funded by governments which is fully attributable to the school;

(30) income obtained from the provision of "modern services" (excluding financial leasing services, advertising services and other modern services) and "life services" (excluding cultural and sports activities, other life services, sauna, and oxygen bars), which are formed by vocational schools launched by the government mainly for the purpose of providing place of practice for in-school students, funded, run and managed by such schools, and the business income of which is owned by the schools;

(31) income obtained from the provision of home care services by home care service staff members subject to the staffing system of home care service enterprises;

(32) income from the issuance of welfare lotteries and sports lotteries;

(33) income from the rental of surplus real property of the army;

(34) income from the sale of housing units by enterprises and administrative institutions at the cost price or at the standard price in support of the housing system reform of the state;

(35) transfer of the right to use land to agricultural producers for agricultural production;

(36) individuals' free transfer of real estate and the right to use land involved in the division of housing property;

(37) land owner sells the right to use land and the land user returns the right to use land to the land owner;

(38) assignment, transfer or recovery of the right to use natural resources (excluding the right to use land) by local people's governments at or above the county level or natural resources administrative departments;

(39) employment of family members living with military service members;

(40)employment of demobilized military officers.

Furthermore, the Circular Caishui 〔2016〕 No. 36 provides with a preferential policy of "immediate refund after payment of the VAT" to the following services:

(1)For pipeline transportation services provided by a general taxpayer, the VAT policy of refund immediately after payment shall apply to the portion of actual VAT burden on the taxpayer in excess of 3%.

(2)For financial leasing of tangible personal property and sale and leaseback financing of tangible personal property provided by a general taxpayer among pilot taxpayers engaged in financial leasing as approved by the People's Bank of China (PBC), the China Banking and Insurance Regulatory Commission (CBRC), or the Ministry of Commerce, the VAT policy of refund immediately after payment shall apply to the portion of actual tax burden on the pilot taxpayer in excess of 3%. If the paid-in capital of a general taxpayer among pilot taxpayers engaged in financial leasing and sale and leaseback financing as approved by a provincial commerce department or a state economic and technological development zone authorized by the Ministry of Commerce reaches 170 million yuan after May 1, 2016, the aforesaid provisions shall apply from the month when the paid-in capital reaches the threshold, or if the paid-in capital fails to reach 170 million yuan but the registered capital reaches 170 million yuan after May 1, 2016, the aforesaid provisions may also apply from the first day of the next month before July 31, 2016. The financial leasing of tangible personal property and sale and leaseback financing of tangible personal property conducted after August 1, 2016 shall no longer be governed by the aforesaid provisions.

The notion of the "actual VAT burden" herein means the portion of VAT actually paid by a taxpayer on taxable services provided for the current period to the total price and additional fees obtained by the taxpayer from providing taxable services during the current period.

3.6.2 Exported Services

According to the Circular Caishui 〔2016〕 No. 36, the following exported services provided by entities or individuals inside of China shall be exempted from VAT, when the actual recipients of services are outside China and such services are irrelevant to cargo or immovable property within China.

(1) The services listed as follows:

①construction services of engineering projects located outside China;

②engineering supervision services for engineering projects located outside China;

③engineering prospecting and exploration services for projects and mineral resources located outside China;

④conference and exhibition services for conferences and exhibitions located outside China;

⑤warehousing services for warehouses located outside China;

⑥tangible personal property rental services with the subject matter used outside China;

⑦broadcasting services provided outside China for radio, film, and television programs (or works);

⑧culture and sports services, education and medical services, and tourism services provided outside China.

(2) Postal services, receipt and delivery services, and insurance services provided for export cargo, including insurance for export cargo and insurance for export credit.

(3) The following services provided for foreign entities that are fully consumed outside China:

①telecommunications services;

②intellectual property services;

③logistics support services (excluding warehousing services and receipt and delivery services);

④authentication and consultation services;

⑤professional technical services;

⑥business support services;

⑦advertising services with advertisements released outside China.

(4) International transportation services provided in the mode of carriage without means of transport.

(5) Direct paid financial services provided for monetary financing and other financial services among foreign entities, and such services are irrelevant to the cargo, intangible assets, and real estate within China.

(6) Other services as prescribed by the MOF and the SAT.

3.7   Tax Timing

The VAT shall be imposed at the time the consideration of the transaction is paid or becomes payable under a contract or the date of receiving the VAT invoices.

For import of goods, the date of the customs declaration is determinant. For supply of goods, the time of taxation is the time when ① the payment is received; ② goods are delivered; ③ a sales agreement is signed; or ④ invoices are issued.

For provision of services, the time of taxation is any one of the following: ① the date on which the service is provided or the payment received; ② the date of payment agreed in a contract; ③ the date on which the invoice is issued in advance; ④ the date on which the advance payment is received in respect of a lease of tangibles or construction business operating with the advance payment system; ⑤ the date on which the ownership of financial products is transferred; and ⑥ in the case of a deemed service supply, the date on which the deemed supply of services takes place.

3.8   Calculation of VAT

3.8.1 General Taxpayers

The general taxpayers are entitled to input tax credit for VAT paid on purchasing of business inputs. The input tax credit is the VAT paid or payable on purchases of goods and services in China and on goods imported into China to the extent to which the goods are used in producing taxable goods or services. The VAT paid on property and services for use partly in taxable supplies may be recovered on a proportional basis.

The creditable input VAT is the amount of tax which the general taxpayers are entitled to offset against their VAT liabilities. In principle, the taxpayer may only use input tax credit to offset against output tax. Excess input tax is, except for exports, not refundable, but may be carried forward indefinitely. The unused input tax credit is lost in the case of liquidation. Although agricultural products are exempt from VAT, for the purpose of input tax credits, the purchaser is deemed to have paid VAT at the rate of 10% on the purchase price.

The input tax may not be credited in respect of the purchases of: ① goods and services that are used for non-taxable supplies; ② goods and services used for exempt supplies; ③ real estate and real estate under construction, supplied by a small-scale taxpayer; ④ goods and services for personal consumption such as food and beverage; ⑤ goods and services for personal consumption or welfare of employees; and ⑥ goods and services that are lost as a result of natural disasters, theft, mildew or deterioration due to poor management.

There is no input tax credit available for interest expenses, as well as for fees and charges directly imposed on loans of a general taxpayer. However, input tax paid by financial institutions on fixed, immovable and intangible assets is creditable for VAT purposes even if such institutions are only partially taxable.

To offset the input VAT, the amount of creditable input VAT must be supported by special VAT invoices. Enterprises must complete a VAT application form on a monthly or quarterly basis and submit various other documents and invoices to the competent state tax authorities which must process the application in 15 days.

Under certain circumstances, the tax authorities may deny an input tax credit, e.g. if invoices or other compulsory documents do not meet the requirements as prescribed by relevant laws and regulations, or the accounting records are incomplete.

3.8.2 Small-Scale Taxpayers

A small-scale taxpayer must apply the simplified method when calculating its VAT. With this method, the output VAT is paid at a reduced rate of 3% and the small-scale taxpayer is unable to claim input VAT credits in relation to that transaction.

3.9　Tax Administration

3.9.1 Registration and Payments

Enterprises and individuals must register with the local tax authorities before the commencement of business activity. At the time of registration, the tax authorities determine whether the taxpayer is a "general taxpayer" or a "small-scale taxpayer".

Depending on the business sector and amount of the VAT payable, the tax period varies from 1 day to 1 quarter as determined by the competent tax authorities. In most sectors, the tax period is a month, and tax returns must be filed, and the tax must be remitted within 15 days following the tax period. The tax period for banks and financial companies is a quarter and they are required to file VAT returns and to remit the tax within 15 days following the quarter.

Given that VAT registration usually takes place at the branch level, a legal entity having multiple branches may have multiple VAT registrations. As a result, supplies between branches shall be subject to VAT in China. Therefore, a head office and each of its branches are required to remit applicable VAT to local tax authorities in the place where each is located.

However, with the approval of the SAT, a head office may make payments on a consolidated basis for all its branches.

3.9.2 Invoices

The general taxpayers are only allowed to issue special VAT invoices which are purchased from the tax authorities. The invoices are processed and registered by using a special machine and the system is called the "Golden Tax System".

The amount of allowable input VAT must be supported by special VAT invoices which must be verified by the tax authorities on a monthly basis. Each VAT invoice is in triplicate (one for the customer, one for input tax investigation and one for accounting purposes) and numbered, and taxpayers may not claim an input tax credit until they have obtained the relevant invoices issued or signed by the vendor.

Small-scale taxpayers engaged in certification, consulting services and other designated sectors may, as part of a pilot project, issue special VAT invoices by using the VAT invoice issuing system themselves and no longer need to apply to the tax authorities for the invoices.[1] Ordinary invoices must be issued for goods and services that are exempt from VAT or sold to consumers or exempt suppliers.

3.9.3 Withholding Obligation

Non-resident who have no establishment in China may not register for VAT purposes in China. Therefore, they are required to pay VAT through their agents in China; otherwise, if there is not any agent to withhold the VAT, the purchaser or importer shall have an obligation to pay the tax. There is no turnover threshold for non-resident taxpayers. However, a non-resident taxpayer may qualify as a small-scale taxpayer based on turnover and be taxed at a lower VAT rate. The recipient of the supply must withhold

---

①　SAT Public Notice 〔2017〕 No. 4.

the VAT from the price and the parties must take this VAT withholding into account in their contract on services and in their accounting systems.

Non-resident taxpayers having an establishment in China are required to file a VAT return on a quarterly basis if having frequent taxable transactions. If the taxpayer does not have frequent taxable transactions, a VAT return must be filed per transaction. The return must be filed and the VAT due must be remitted within 15 days following the end of the tax quarter or the date of transaction.

Non-resident taxpayers having no establishment in China must remit VAT through an agent or recipients of goods or services, who is required to file a separate return for non-resident supplies.

Appendix Ⅰ: VAT Provisional Regulation (2017 Revision)①

English Translation	Chinese Version
Provisional Regulation of the People's Republic of China on value-added tax	中华人民共和国增值税暂行条例
(Promulgated by Order No. 134 of the State Council of the People's Republic of China on December 13, 1993; revised at the 34th Executive Meeting of the State Council on November 5, 2008; and revised in accordance with the Decision of the State Council on Amending Some Administrative Regulation on February 6, 2016; and revised for the second time in accordance with the Decision of the State Council to Repeal the Provisional Regulation of the People's Republic of China on Business Tax and Amend the Provisional Regulation of the People's Republic of China on Value Added Tax on November 19, 2017)	(1993 年 12 月 13 日中华人民共和国国务院令第 134 号公布 2008 年 11 月 5 日国务院第 34 次常务会议修订通过 根据 2016 年 2 月 6 日《国务院关于修改部分行政法规的决定》第一次修订 根据 2017 年 11 月 19 日《国务院关于废止〈中华人民共和国营业税暂行条例〉和修改〈中华人民共和国增值税暂行条例〉的决定》第二次修订)

---

① The English version was translated with a reference of the translations on the website of www.pkulaw.com.

Continued

English Translation	Chinese Version
Article 1 Entities and individuals that sell goods or labor services of processing, repair or replacement (hereinafter referred to as "labor services"), sell services, intangible assets, or immovables, or import goods within the territory of the People's Republic of China are taxpayers of value added tax ("VAT"), and shall pay VAT in accordance with this Regulation.	**第一条**　在中华人民共和国境内销售货物或者加工、修理修配劳务(以下简称劳务),销售服务、无形资产、不动产以及进口货物的单位和个人,为增值税的纳税人,应当依照本条例缴纳增值税。
Article 2 The VAT rate is:	**第二条**　增值税税率:
(1)17%, for taxpayers selling goods, labor services, or tangible movable property leasing services or importing goods, except as otherwise specified in items (2), (4) and (5) hereof;	(一)纳税人销售货物、劳务、有形动产租赁服务或者进口货物,除本条第二项、第四项、第五项另有规定外,税率为17%。
(2)11%, for taxpayers selling transportation, postal, basic telecommunications, construction, or immovable leasing services, selling immovables, transferring the rights to use land, or selling or importing the following goods:	(二)纳税人销售交通运输、邮政、基础电信、建筑、不动产租赁服务,销售不动产,转让土地使用权,销售或者进口下列货物,税率为11%:
(a)grain and other agricultural products, edible vegetable oil, and edible salt;	1.粮食等农产品、食用植物油、食用盐;
(b)tap water, heating, cooling, hot water, coal gas, liquefied petroleum gas, natural gas, dimethyl ether, methane, and coal products for residential use;	2.自来水、暖气、冷气、热水、煤气、石油液化气、天然气、二甲醚、沼气、居民用煤炭制品;
(c) books, newspapers, magazines, audio-visual recordings, and electronic publications;	3.图书、报纸、杂志、音像制品、电子出版物;
(d)feed, fertilizer, pesticide, agricultural machinery, and agricultural films; and	4.饲料、化肥、农药、农机、农膜;
(e)other goods specified by the State Council.	5.国务院规定的其他货物。
(3)6%, for taxpayers selling services or intangible assets, except as otherwise specified in items (1), (2) and (5) hereof;	(三)纳税人销售服务、无形资产,除本条第一项、第二项、第五项另有规定外,税率为6%。
(4)zero, for taxpayers exporting goods, except as otherwise specified by the State Council; or	(四)纳税人出口货物,税率为零;但是,国务院另有规定的除外。
(5)zero, for domestic entities and individuals selling services or intangible assets within the scope prescribed by the State Council across national borders.	(五)境内单位和个人跨境销售国务院规定范围内的服务、无形资产,税率为零。

Continued

English Translation	Chinese Version
Any adjustments to the tax rates shall be decided by the State Council.	税率的调整，由国务院决定。
Article 3 For a taxpayer concurrently engaged in goods or taxable services at different tax rates, the sales amounts for goods or taxable services at different tax rates shall be calculated separately, otherwise, the higher tax rate shall apply.	**第三条** 纳税人兼营不同税率的项目，应当分别核算不同税率项目的销售额；未分别核算销售额的，从高适用税率。
Article 4 Except for the provisions in Article 11 of this Regulation, for a taxpayer engaged in selling goods or supplying taxable services, the payable tax amount shall be the balance after offsetting or deducting the input tax amount for the current period against or from the output tax amount for the current period. The formula for computing the payable tax amount is:	**第四条** 除本条例第十一条规定外，纳税人销售货物、劳务、服务、无形资产、不动产（以下统称应税销售行为），应纳税额为当期销项税额抵扣当期进项税额后的余额。应纳税额计算公式：
The payable tax amount = The output tax amount for the current period — the input tax amount for the current period	应纳税额＝当期销项税额－当期进项税额
If the output tax amount for the current period is less than and insufficient to offset against or deduct the input tax amount for the current period, the deficiency can be carried forward to the following period for offset or deduction.	当期销项税额小于当期进项税额不足抵扣时，其不足部分可以结转下期继续抵扣。
Article 5 The VAT tax amount that a taxpayer occurrence of any taxable sale calculates on the basis of the sales amount and at the tax rate as prescribed in Article 2 of this Regulation and collects from the buyer is the output tax amount. The formula for the calculation of the output tax amount:	**第五条** 纳税人发生应税销售行为，按照销售额和本条例第二条规定的税率计算收取的增值税额，为销项税额。销项税额计算公式：
The output tax amount = The sales amount × The tax rate	销项税额＝销售额×税率
Article 6 The sales amount shall be the full price and ex-price fees that a taxpayer charges the buyer for the occurrence of any taxable sale, but exclude the output tax amount collected.	**第六条** 销售额为纳税人发生应税销售行为收取的全部价款和价外费用，但是不包括收取的销项税额。
The sales amount shall be calculated in RMB. Where a taxpayer settles the sales amount in a currency other than RMB, it (he) shall convert it into RMB.	销售额以人民币计算。纳税人以人民币以外的货币结算销售额的，应当折合成人民币计算。

Continued

English Translation	Chinese Version
Article 7 If the price of the goods occurrence of any taxable sale by a taxpayer is obviously low without a justifiable reason, the competent taxation organ shall verify and determine the sales amount.	**第七条**　纳税人发生应税销售行为的价格明显偏低并无正当理由的,由主管税务机关核定其销售额。
Article 8 The VAT amount that a taxpayer pays or bears for purchasing goods, labor services, services, intangible assets, or immovables is the input tax amount.	**第八条**　纳税人购进货物、劳务、服务、无形资产、不动产支付或者负担的增值税额,为进项税额。
The following input tax amounts are allowed to be off-set against or be deducted from the input tax amounts:	下列进项税额准予从销项税额中抵扣:
(1) the VAT amount as indicated in the special VAT invoice obtained from the seller;	(一)从销售方取得的增值税专用发票上注明的增值税额。
(2) the VAT amount as indicated in the special bill of payment of import VAT obtained from the customs house;	(二)从海关取得的海关进口增值税专用缴款书上注明的增值税额。
(3) for the purchase of agricultural products, besides obtaining the special VAT invoice or customs special bill of payment of import VAT, the amount of input tax as calculated according to the purchase price of the agricultural product indicated on the agricultural product purchase invoice or sales invoice and a deduction rate of 11%, except as otherwise specified by the State Council. The formula for the calculation of the input tax amount is:	(三)购进农产品,除取得增值税专用发票或者海关进口增值税专用缴款书外,按照农产品收购发票或者销售发票上注明的农产品买价和 11% 的扣除率计算的进项税额,国务院另有规定的除外。进项税额计算公式:
The input tax amounts = The purchase price × The deduction rate	进项税额=买价×扣除率
(4) The VAT amount indicated on the tax payment certificate for withheld taxes obtained from the tax authority or withholding agent for the purchase of labor services, services, intangible assets, or domestic immovables from entities or individuals outside China.	(四)自境外单位或者个人购进劳务、服务、无形资产或者境内的不动产,从税务机关或者扣缴义务人取得的代扣代缴税款的完税凭证上注明的增值税额。
Any adjustments to the allowed deduction items and rates shall be decided by the State Council.	准予抵扣的项目和扣除率的调整,由国务院决定。
Article 9 For a taxpayer purchasing goods, labor services, services, intangible assets, or immovable, if the VAT deduction voucher it (he) obtains does not conform to law, administrative regulation, or relevant provisions of the taxation administrative department of the State Council, the input tax amount shall not be offset against or deducted from the output tax amount.	**第九条**　纳税人购进货物、劳务、服务、无形资产、不动产,取得的增值税扣税凭证不符合法律、行政法规或者国务院税务主管部门有关规定的,其进项税额不得从销项税额中抵扣。

Continued

English Translation	Chinese Version
Article 10 The amount of input tax on any of the following items shall not be deducted from the amount of output tax：	**第十条** 下列项目的进项税额不得从销项税额中抵扣：
(1) Goods，labor services，services，intangible assets，or immovables purchased for taxable items to which the simple tax computation method applies，VAT-exempt items，or collective welfare or individual consumption.	（一）用于简易计税方法计税项目、免征增值税项目、集体福利或者个人消费的购进货物、劳务、服务、无形资产和不动产；
(2) The purchased goods suffering from abnormal losses and relevant labor services and transportation services.	（二）非正常损失的购进货物，以及相关的劳务和交通运输服务；
(3) The purchased goods (excluding fixed assets)，labor services，and transportation services consumed by work-in-process or finished products suffering from abnormal losses.	（三）非正常损失的在产品、产成品所耗用的购进货物（不包括固定资产）、劳务和交通运输服务；
(4) Other items as specified by the State Council.	（四）国务院规定的其他项目。
Article 11 For occurrence of any taxable sale of a small-scale taxpayer, a simple approach shall be employed to calculate the payable tax amount on the basis of the sales amount and at the tax rate and the input tax amount shall not be offset or deducted. The formula for the calculation of the payable amount：	**第十一条** 小规模纳税人发生应税销售行为，实行按照销售额和征收率计算应纳税额的简易办法，并不得抵扣进项税额。应纳税额计算公式：
The payable tax amount＝The sales amount×The tax rate	应纳税额＝销售额×征收率
the criterions for small-scale taxpayers shall be formulated by the finance and taxation administrative departments of the State Council.	小规模纳税人的标准由国务院财政、税务主管部门规定。
Article 12 The levy rate of VAT on small-scale taxpayers shall be 3%，except as otherwise specified by the State Council.	**第十二条** 小规模纳税人增值税征收率为3%，国务院另有规定的除外。
Article 13 A taxpayer other than a small-scale taxpayer shall undergo registration with the appropriate tax authority. The specific registration measures shall be developed by the taxation department of the State Council.	**第十三条** 小规模纳税人以外的纳税人应当向主管税务机关办理登记。具体登记办法由国务院税务主管部门制定。
Where a small-scale taxpayer with adequate accounting is able to provide accurate tax data, it may undergo registration with the appropriate tax authority not as a small-scale taxpayer, and calculate the taxes payable according to the relevant provisions of this Regulation.	小规模纳税人会计核算健全，能够提供准确税务资料的，可以向主管税务机关办理登记，不作为小规模纳税人，依照本条例有关规定计算应纳税额。

Continued

English Translation	Chinese Version
Article 14 For goods imported by a taxpayer, the payable tax amount shall be calculated on the basis of the composite assessable value and the tax rates as given in Article 2 of this Regulation. The formulas for the calculation of the composite assessable value and the payable tax amount are:	**第十四条**　纳税人进口货物,按照组成计税价格和本条例第二条规定的税率计算应纳税额。组成计税价格和应纳税额计算公式:
The composite assessable value = The customs duty-paid value + The customs duty + The consumption tax	组成计税价格=关税完税价格+关税+消费税
The payable tax amount = The composite assessable value × The tax rate	应纳税额=组成计税价格×税率
Article 15 The following items shall be exempted from the VAT:	**第十五条**　下列项目免征增值税:
(1) self-produced agricultural products sold by agricultural producers;	(一)农业生产者销售的自产农产品;
(2) contraceptive medicines and devices;	(二)避孕药品和用具;
(3) antique books;	(三)古旧图书;
(4) apparatus and equipment imported and directly used for scientific research, experiment and teaching;	(四)直接用于科学研究、科学试验和教学的进口仪器、设备;
(5) imported materials and equipment from foreign governments and international organizations as gratuitous aid;	(五)外国政府、国际组织无偿援助的进口物资和设备;
(6) articles exclusively for persons with disabilities that are directly imported by organizations of persons with disabilities; and	(六)由残疾人的组织直接进口供残疾人专用的物品;
(7) self-used articles sold by the seller.	(七)销售的自己使用过的物品。
Except for the provisions of the preceding paragraph, the VAT exemption and reduction items shall be prescribed by the State Council. No other region or department shall prescribe any tax exemption or reduction item.	除前款规定外,增值税的免税、减税项目由国务院规定。任何地区、部门均不得规定免税、减税项目。
Article 16 For a taxpayer concurrently engaged in VAT-free or VAT reduction items, it (he) shall calculate the sales amounts of the VAT-free or VAT reduction items separately, otherwise, it (he) shall not enjoy the tax exemptions or reductions.	**第十六条**　纳税人兼营免税、减税项目的,应当分别核算免税、减税项目的销售额;未分别核算销售额的,不得免税、减税。

Continued

English Translation	Chinese Version
Article 17 If the sales amount of a taxpayer does not reach the VAT threshold as prescribed by the finance and taxation administrative departments of the State Council, it shall be exempted from the VAT. If it reaches the aforesaid threshold, the VAT shall be calculated and paid in full amount on the basis of this Regulation.	第十七条 纳税人销售额未达到国务院财政、税务主管部门规定的增值税起征点的,免征增值税;达到起征点的,依照本条例规定全额计算缴纳增值税。
Article 18 Where an entity or individual outside the territory of the People's Republic of China supplies taxable services inside the territory of the People's Republic of China, and it (he) has not established a business institution within China, its (his) agent within China shall be the withholding obligor. If it (he) has no agent within China, the purchaser shall be the withholding obligor.	第十八条 中华人民共和国境外的单位或者个人在境内销售劳务,在境内未设有经营机构的,以其境内代理人为扣缴义务人;在境内没有代理人的,以购买方为扣缴义务人。
Article 19 The time when an obligation to pay the VAT arises shall be as follows:	第十九条 增值税纳税义务发生时间:
(1) For the occurrence of any taxable sale, it is the date on which the sales price payment is received or the sales voucher as requested is obtained. If an invoice is issued in advance, it shall be the same day when the invoice is issued.	(一)发生应税销售行为,为收讫销售款项或者取得索取销售款项凭据的当天;先开具发票的,为开具发票的当天。
(2) For imported goods, it is the date of customs declaration for import.	(二)进口货物,为报关进口的当天。
The time when an obligation to withhold the VAT arises shall be the same day when an obligation to pay the VAT arises.	增值税扣缴义务发生时间为纳税人增值税纳税义务发生的当天。
Article 20 The VAT shall be collected by taxation organs and the VAT on imported goods shall be withheld by the customs houses.	第二十条 增值税由税务机关征收,进口货物的增值税由海关代征。
The VAT on self-use articles carried or mailed into China by individuals shall be levied together with the customs duties. The specific measures shall be formulated by the Tariff Policy Committee of the State Council in conjunction with relevant departments.	个人携带或者邮寄进境自用物品的增值税,连同关税一并计征。具体办法由国务院关税税则委员会会同有关部门制定。

Continued

English Translation	Chinese Version
Article 21 The taxpayer of occurrence of any taxable sale shall issue a special VAT invoice to the buyer requesting a special VAT invoice and give clear indications of the sales amount and output tax amount on it.	**第二十一条**　纳税人发生应税销售行为,应当向索取增值税专用发票的购买方开具增值税专用发票,并在增值税专用发票上分别注明销售额和销项税额。
Under any of the following circumstances，no special VAT invoice shall be issued：	属于下列情形之一的,不得开具增值税专用发票：
(1) The purchaser in the taxable sale is an individual consumer；and	(一)应税销售行为的购买方为消费者个人的;
(2) the tax-free provisions apply to the occurrence of any taxable sale.	(二)发生应税销售行为适用免税规定的。
Article 22 The VAT payment places：	**第二十二条**　增值税纳税地点：
1. Business with a fixed establishment shall file tax returns with the competent taxation organ at the locality where the establishment is located. If the head office and its branch are not situated in the same county (or city)，they shall file tax returns separately to their respective local competent taxation organ. The head office may，upon the approval of the finance or taxation administrative department of the State Council or its authorized finance or taxation organ，file tax returns with the competent taxation organ at the locality where the establishment is located on a consolidated basis.	(一)固定业户应当向其机构所在地的主管税务机关申报纳税。总机构和分支机构不在同一县(市)的,应当分别向各自所在地的主管税务机关申报纳税;经国务院财政、税务主管部门或者其授权的财政、税务机关批准,可以由总机构汇总向总机构所在地的主管税务机关申报纳税。
2. Business with fixed premises that sells goods or labor services in another county (or city) shall report its business conducted in such other county (or city) to the tax authority at the place where the institution is located，and file a tax return with the tax authority at the place where the institution is located；if it fails to report the same，it shall file a tax return with the tax authority at the place where goods are sold or labor services occur；or if it fails to file a tax return with the tax authority at the place where goods are sold or labor services occur，the tax authority at the place where the institution is located shall collect the taxes in arrears.	(二)固定业户到外县(市)销售货物或者劳务,应当向其机构所在地的主管税务机关报告外出经营事项,并向其机构所在地的主管税务机关申报纳税;未报告的,应当向销售地或者劳务发生地的主管税务机关申报纳税;未向销售地或者劳务发生地的主管税务机关申报纳税的,由其机构所在地的主管税务机关补征税款。

Continued

English Translation	Chinese Version
(3) Business without a fixed establishment selling goods or labor services shall file tax returns with the competent taxation organ at the locality where the sales activities take place or where the taxable services occur. If it fails to do so, the competent taxation organ at the locality where it is located or resides shall levy the overdue taxes.	（三）非固定业户销售货物或者劳务,应当向销售地或者劳务发生地的主管税务机关申报纳税;未向销售地或者劳务发生地的主管税务机关申报纳税的,由其机构所在地或者居住地的主管税务机关补征税款。
(4) For imported goods, tax returns shall be filed with the customs house at the locality where the customs declaration is made.	（四）进口货物,应当向报关地海关申报纳税。
A withholding obligor shall file tax returns and pay the tax amounts, which it withholds, to the competent taxation organ at the place where its institution or domicile is located.	扣缴义务人应当向其机构所在地或者居住地的主管税务机关申报缴纳其扣缴的税款。
Article 23 The VAT taxable period shall be one day, three days, five days, 10 days, 15 days, one month or one quarter. The specific taxable period of a taxpayer shall be determined respectively by the competent taxation organ on the basis of the payable tax amount of the taxpayer. If the tax cannot be paid on a regular period basis, it can be assessed on a transaction-by-transaction basis.	第二十三条　增值税的纳税期限分别为1日、3日、5日、10日、15日、1个月或者1个季度。纳税人的具体纳税期限,由主管税务机关根据纳税人应纳税额的大小分别核定;不能按固定期限纳税的,可以按次纳税。
A taxpayer who adopts one month or one quarter as a taxable period shall file tax returns within 15 days after the expiration of such a period. If it (he) adopts one day, three days, five days, 10 days or 15 days as a taxable period, it (he) shall prepay the tax within five days after the expiration of such a period and within 15 days of the following month, file a tax return and settle the payable tax amount of the immediately previous month.	纳税人以1个月或者1个季度为1个纳税期的,自期满之日起15日内申报纳税;以1日、3日、5日、10日或者15日为1个纳税期的,自期满之日起5日内预缴税款,于次月1日起15日内申报纳税并结清上月应纳税款。
The time limit for a withholding obligor to deliver tax payment shall be governed by the preceding two paragraphs.	扣缴义务人解缴税款的期限,依照前两款规定执行。
Article 24 A taxpayer of imported goods shall pay the tax within 15 days from the date on which the customs house fills out the special bill of payment of import VAT issued by the customs offices.	第二十四条　纳税人进口货物,应当自海关填发海关进口增值税专用缴款书之日起15日内缴纳税款。

Continued

English Translation	Chinese Version
Article 25 A taxpayer exporting tax-rebate (exemption) goods shall go through the export formalities in the customs house and within the prescribed time limit for applying for tax rebate (exemption) and on a monthly basis, apply to the competent taxation organ for handling the tax rebate (exemption) for the exported goods on the strength of export declaration forms, or where the tax refund (exemption) provisions are applicable to the sale of any service or intangible asset across national borders by an entity or individual within in the territory of China, declarations for tax refund (exemption) shall be filed with the tax authority on schedule. The concrete measures shall be formulated by the finance or taxation administrative department of the State Council.	第二十五条　纳税人出口货物适用退(免)税规定的,应当向海关办理出口手续,凭出口报关单等有关凭证,在规定的出口退(免)税申报期内按月向主管税务机关申报办理该项出口货物的退(免)税;境内单位和个人跨境销售服务和无形资产适用退(免)税规定的,应当按期向主管税务机关申报办理退(免)税。具体办法由国务院财政、税务主管部门制定。
Where any exported goods are returned or a customs declaration is withdrawn after the completion of the tax rebate on the exported goods, the taxpayer shall pay back the said tax rebate according to law.	出口货物办理退税后发生退货或者退关的,纳税人应当依法补缴已退的税款。
Article 26 The administration of collection of the VAT shall be governed by the Law of the People's Republic of China on the Administration of Tax Collection and the relevant provisions in this Regulation.	第二十六条　增值税的征收管理,依照《中华人民共和国税收征收管理法》及本条例有关规定执行。
Article 27 Where any matters concerning taxpayers' payment of VAT are otherwise specified in any provisions issued by the State Council or by the finance or taxation administrative department of the State Council with the consent of the State Council, such provisions shall prevail.	第二十七条　纳税人缴纳增值税的有关事项,国务院或者国务院财政、税务主管部门经国务院同意另有规定的,依照其规定。
Article 28 This Regulation shall come into force as of January 1, 2009.	第二十八条　本条例自 2009 年 1 月 1 日起施行。

Appendix Ⅱ：Circular Caishui 〔2016〕 No. 36①

English Translation	Chinese Version
Notice of the Ministry of Finance and the State Administration of Taxation on Implementing the Pilot Program of Replacing Business Tax with value-added tax in an All-round Manner	财政部、国家税务总局关于全面推开营业税改征增值税试点的通知
(Caishui〔2016〕No. 36)	（财税〔2016〕36 号）
The public finance departments（bureaus）, state taxation bureaus, and local taxation bureaus of all provinces, autonomous regions, municipalities directly under the Central Government, and cities under separate state planning; and the Financial Bureau of Xinjiang Production and Construction Corps:	各省、自治区、直辖市、计划单列市财政厅（局）、国家税务局、地方税务局,新疆生产建设兵团财务局:
With the approval of the State Council, as of May 1, 2016, the pilot program of replacing business tax with value-added tax（VAT）shall be implemented across the country, all business tax taxpayers in the construction industry, the real estate industry, the financial industry, and the living service industry shall be included in the scope of the pilot program, and the payment of business tax shall be replaced by the payment of VAT. Measures for Implementing the Pilot Program of Replacing Business Tax with value-added tax, Provisions on Relevant Matters Concerning the Pilot Program of Replacing Business Tax with value-added tax, Provisions on the Transitional Policies for the Pilot Program of Replacing Business Tax with value-added tax, and Provisions on the Application of Zero VAT Rate and VAT Exemption Policy to Cross-Border Taxable Activities are hereby issued to you for your compliance and implementation.	经国务院批准,自 2016 年 5 月 1 日起,在全国范围内全面推开营业税改征增值税(以下称营改增)试点,建筑业、房地产业、金融业、生活服务业等全部营业税纳税人,纳入试点范围,由缴纳营业税改为缴纳增值税。现将《营业税改征增值税试点实施办法》、《营业税改征增值税试点有关事项的规定》、《营业税改征增值税试点过渡政策的规定》和《跨境应税行为适用增值税零税率和免税政策的规定》印发你们,请遵照执行。

---

① The English version was translated with a reference of the translations on the website of www.pkulaw.com.

Continued

English Translation	Chinese Version
The Annexes to this Notice shall come into force as of May 1, 2016, unless a different time is set for implementation. Notice of the Ministry of Finance and the State Administration of Taxation on Including the Railway Transportation and Postal Services Industries in the Pilot Program of Replacing Business Tax with value-added tax (No. 106 〔2013〕, Ministry of Finance), Supplementary Notice of the Ministry of Finance and the State Administration of Taxation on the Relevant Policies on the Pilot Program of Levying value-added tax in Lieu of Business Tax on Railway Transportation and Postal Services Sectors (No. 121 〔2013〕, Ministry of Finance), Notice of the Ministry of Finance and the State Administration of Taxation on Including the Telecommunications Industry in the Pilot Program of Levying value-added tax in Lieu of Business Tax (No. 43 〔2014〕, Ministry of Finance), Supplementary Notice of the Ministry of Finance and the State Administration of Taxation on the Zero value-added tax Rate Policy for International Water Transportation (No. 50 〔2014〕, Ministry of Finance); and the Notice of the Ministry of Finance and the State Administration of Taxation on the Application of the Zero value-added tax Rate Policy to Film and Television and Other Export Services (No. 118 〔2015〕, Ministry of Finance) shall be repealed accordingly, with the exception of those provisions that have been otherwise differently provided for.	本通知附件规定的内容,除另有规定执行时间外,自 2016 年 5 月 1 日起执行。《财政部 国家税务总局关于将铁路运输和邮政业纳入营业税改征增值税试点的通知》(财税〔2013〕106 号)、《财政部 国家税务总局关于铁路运输和邮政业营业税改征增值税试点有关政策的补充通知》(财税〔2013〕121 号)、《财政部 国家税务总局关于将电信业纳入营业税改征增值税试点的通知》(财税〔2014〕43 号)、《财政部 国家税务总局关于国际水路运输增值税零税率政策的补充通知》(财税〔2014〕50 号)和《财政部 国家税务总局关于影视等出口服务适用增值税零税率政策的通知》(财税〔2015〕118 号),除另有规定的条款外,相应废止。
All competent local authorities shall attach great importance to the pilot program of replacing business tax with VAT, effectively strengthen the organization and leadership of the pilot program, make elaborate arrangements, specify the responsibilities, take various effective measures, make good preparations for the implementation of the pilot program, effectively conduct monitoring analysis, publicity, interpretation, and other work in the implementation of the pilot program, and ensure the stable, orderly, and smooth progress of reform. Any problems encountered during the implementation process shall be reported to the Ministry of Finance and the State Administration of Taxation in a timely manner.	各地要高度重视营改增试点工作,切实加强试点工作的组织领导,周密安排,明确责任,采取各种有效措施,做好试点前的各项准备以及试点过程中的监测分析和宣传解释等工作,确保改革的平稳、有序、顺利进行。遇到问题请及时向财政部和国家税务总局反映。

Continued

English Translation	Chinese Version
Annexes:	附件:
1. Measures for Implementing the Pilot Program of Replacing Business Tax with value-added tax	1.营业税改征增值税试点实施办法
2. Provisions on Relevant Matters Concerning the Pilot Program of Replacing Business Tax with value-added tax	2.营业税改征增值税试点有关事项的规定
3. Provisions on the Transitional Policies for the Pilot Program of Replacing Business Tax with value-added tax	3.营业税改征增值税试点过渡政策的规定
4. Provisions on the Application of Zero VAT Rate and VAT Exemption Policy to Cross-Border Taxable Activities	4.跨境应税行为适用增值税零税率和免税政策的规定
Ministry of Finance	财政部
State Administration of Taxation	国家税务总局
March 23，2016	2016 年 3 月 23 日
Annex 1	附件 1
Measures for the Implementation of the Pilot Program of Replacing Business Tax with value-added tax	营业税改征增值税试点实施办法
Chapter Ⅰ Taxpayers and Withholding Agents	**第一章　纳税人和扣缴义务人**
Article 1 The entities and individuals that sell services, intangible assets or immovable properties（hereinafter referred to as "taxable acts"）within the territory of the People's Republic of China are value-added tax（VAT）payers, and shall pay VAT instead of business tax in accordance with these Measures.	**第一条**　在中华人民共和国境内(以下称境内)销售服务、无形资产或者不动产(以下称应税行为)的单位和个人,为增值税纳税人,应当按照本办法缴纳增值税,不缴纳营业税。
"Entities" means enterprises, administrative entities, public institutions, military institutions, social organizations, and other entities.	单位,是指企业、行政单位、事业单位、军事单位、社会团体及其他单位。
"Individuals" means individual industrial and commercial households and other individuals.	个人,是指个体工商户和其他个人。

Continued

English Translation	Chinese Version
Article 2 Where an entity conducts business operations through contracting, leasing, or affiliation, if the contractor, lessee, or party affiliated to another party (hereinafter collectively referred to as the "contractor") conducts business operations in the name of the employer, lessor, or party to which it is affiliated (hereinafter collectively referred to as the "employer"), and the employer assumes the relevant legal liabilities, the employer shall be the taxpayer; otherwise, the contractor shall be the taxpayer.	**第二条**　单位以承包、承租、挂靠方式经营的,承包人、承租人、挂靠人(以下统称承包人)以发包人、出租人、被挂靠人(以下统称发包人)名义对外经营并由发包人承担相关法律责任的,以该发包人为纳税人。否则,以承包人为纳税人。
Article 3 Taxpayers are divided into general taxpayers and small-scale taxpayers.	**第三条**　纳税人分为一般纳税人和小规模纳税人。
The taxpayers whose annual sales amount of their taxable acts subject to VAT (hereinafter referred to as the "taxable sales amount") exceeds the thresholds as prescribed by the Ministry of Finance and the State Administration of Taxation are general taxpayers, and the taxpayers whose taxable annual sales amount do not exceed the prescribed standard are small-scale taxpayers.	应税行为的年应征增值税销售额(以下称应税销售额)超过财政部和国家税务总局规定标准的纳税人为一般纳税人,未超过规定标准的纳税人为小规模纳税人。
Other individuals whose annual taxable sales amount exceed the prescribed standard are not general taxpayers. The entities and individual industrial and commercial households whose annual taxable sales amount exceed the prescribed standard but which do not regularly conduct taxable acts may choose to pay taxes as small-scale taxpayers.	年应税销售额超过规定标准的其他个人不属于一般纳税人。年应税销售额超过规定标准但不经常发生应税行为的单位和个体工商户可选择按照小规模纳税人纳税。
Article 4 Where a taxpayer whose annual taxable sales amount does not exceed the prescribed threshold has a sound accounting system, and is able to provide accurate tax-related materials, the taxpayer may apply to the competent tax authority for registration as a general taxpayer and pay VAT as a general taxpayer.	**第四条**　年应税销售额未超过规定标准的纳税人,会计核算健全,能够提供准确税务资料的,可以向主管税务机关办理一般纳税人资格登记,成为一般纳税人。
"Have a sound accounting system" means that a taxpayer is able to set up account books under the uniform accounting system of the state and conduct accounting based on lawful and valid vouchers.	会计核算健全,是指能够按照国家统一的会计制度规定设置账簿,根据合法、有效凭证核算。

Continued

English Translation	Chinese Version
Article 5 A taxpayer eligible as a general taxpayer shall apply to the competent tax authority for registration as a general taxpayer. The specific measures for registration shall be developed separately by the State Administration of Taxation.	第五条　符合一般纳税人条件的纳税人应当向主管税务机关办理一般纳税人资格登记。具体登记办法由国家税务总局制定。
Unless otherwise prescribed by the State Administration of Taxation, no general taxpayer may be converted into a small-scale taxpayer once it is registered as a general taxpayer.	除国家税务总局另有规定外，一经登记为一般纳税人后，不得转为小规模纳税人。
Article 6 Where an entity or individual outside of the territory of the People's Republic of China (hereinafter referred to as "outside China") conducts any taxable act within the territory of China, but has no business institution within the territory of China, the purchaser shall be the withholding agent of VAT, except as otherwise provided for by the Ministry of Finance and the State Administration of Taxation.	第六条　中华人民共和国境外（以下称境外）单位或者个人在境内发生应税行为，在境内未设有经营机构的，以购买方为增值税扣缴义务人。财政部和国家税务总局另有规定的除外。
Article 7 With the approval of the Ministry of Finance and the State Administration of Taxation, two or more taxpayers may be deemed one taxpayer to pay taxes on a consolidated basis. The specific measures shall be developed separately by the Ministry of Finance and the State Administration of Taxation.	第七条　两个或者两个以上的纳税人，经财政部和国家税务总局批准可以视为一个纳税人合并纳税。具体办法由财政部和国家税务总局另行制定。
Article 8 Taxpayers shall conduct VAT accounting according to the uniform accounting rules of the state.	第八条　纳税人应当按照国家统一的会计制度进行增值税会计核算。
Chapter II Taxation Coverage	第二章　征税范围
Article 9 The specific scope of taxable acts shall be governed by Explanatory Notes on the Sales of Services, Intangible Assets or Immovable Properties.	第九条　应税行为的具体范围，按照本办法所附的《销售服务、无形资产、不动产注释》执行。
Article 10 "Sales of services, intangible assets or immovable properties" means the paid provision of services, and the paid transfer of intangible assets or immovable properties, except for the following non-business activities:	第十条　销售服务、无形资产或者不动产，是指有偿提供服务、有偿转让无形资产或者不动产，但属于下列非经营活动的情形除外：
(1)the charge of governmental funds or administrative levies by administrative entities that concurrently meet the following conditions.	（一）行政单位收取的同时满足以下条件的政府性基金或者行政事业性收费。

Continued

English Translation	Chinese Version
(a) The governmental funds are established with the approval of the State Council or the Ministry of Finance, or the administrative levies are established with the approval of the State Council or a provincial people's government or the competent public finance or price department thereof.	1.由国务院或者财政部批准设立的政府性基金,由国务院或者省级人民政府及其财政、价格主管部门批准设立的行政事业性收费;
(b) Financial receipts printed by or the printing of which is supervised by the public finance department at or above the provincial level are issued at the time of collection.	2.收取时开具省级以上(含省级)财政部门监(印)制的财政票据;
(c) All payments collected are turned over to the treasury in full amount.	3.所收款项全额上缴财政。
(2) The provision of services by employees of the entities or individual industrial and commercial households to the entities or employers in exchange of wages or salaries.	(二)单位或者个体工商户聘用的员工为本单位或者雇主提供取得工资的服务。
(3) The provision of services by entities or individual industrial and commercial households to their employees.	(三)单位或者个体工商户为聘用的员工提供服务。
(4) Other circumstances as prescribed by the Ministry of Finance and the State Administration of Taxation.	(四)财政部和国家税务总局规定的其他情形。
Article 11 "Paid" means obtainment of money, goods or other economic benefits from the provision of services.	**第十一条** 有偿,是指取得货币、货物或者其他经济利益。
Article 12 "Sales of services, intangible assets or immovable properties within the territory of China" means that:	**第十二条** 在境内销售服务、无形资产或者不动产,是指:
(1) the sellers or purchasers of the services (excluding the lease of immovable properties) or intangible assets (excluding the rights to use natural resources) are within the territory of China;	(一)服务(租赁不动产除外)或者无形资产(自然资源使用权除外)的销售方或者购买方在境内;
(2) the immovable properties sold or leased are within the territory of China;	(二)所销售或者租赁的不动产在境内;
(3) the natural resources whose use rights are sold are within the territory of China; or	(三)所销售自然资源使用权的自然资源在境内;
(4) other circumstances as prescribed by the Ministry of Finance and the State Administration of Taxation.	(四)财政部和国家税务总局规定的其他情形。

Continued

English Translation	Chinese Version
Article 13 The following circumstances do not fall within the scope of sales of services or intangible assets within the territory of China：	第十三条　下列情形不属于在境内销售服务或者无形资产：
(1)Sales of the services that occur completely outside China by entities or individuals outside China to entities or individuals within the territory of China.	（一）境外单位或者个人向境内单位或者个人销售完全在境外发生的服务。
(2)Sales of the intangible assets that are used completely outside China by entities or individuals outside China to entities or individuals within the territory of China.	（二）境外单位或者个人向境内单位或者个人销售完全在境外使用的无形资产。
(3)Sales of the tangible movable properties that are used completely outside China by entities or individuals outside China to entities or individuals within the territory of China.	（三）境外单位或者个人向境内单位或者个人出租完全在境外使用的有形动产。
(4)Other circumstances as prescribed by the Ministry of Finance and the State Administration of Taxation.	（四）财政部和国家税务总局规定的其他情形。
Article 14 The following circumstances shall be deemed as sales of services， intangible assets or immovable properties：	第十四条　下列情形视同销售服务、无形资产或者不动产：
(1)The provision of free services by entities or individual industrial and commercial households for other entities or individuals，except when such services are used for the public welfare undertakings or for the public.	（一）单位或者个体工商户向其他单位或者个人无偿提供服务，但用于公益事业或者以社会公众为对象的除外。
(2) The transfer of intangible assets or immovable properties free of charge by entities or individuals to other entities or individuals，except when such intangible assets or immovable properties are used for the public welfare undertakings or for the public.	（二）单位或者个人向其他单位或者个人无偿转让无形资产或者不动产，但用于公益事业或者以社会公众为对象的除外。
(3)Other circumstances as prescribed by the Ministry of Finance and the State Administration of Taxation.	（三）财政部和国家税务总局规定的其他情形。
Chapter Ⅲ Tax Rates and Levy Rates	第三章　税率和征收率
Article 15 VAT rates：	第十五条　增值税税率：
(1)Where a taxpayer conducts any taxable act，the tax rate shall be 6%，except when the taxpayer falls within the scope of the circumstance as prescribed in Item (2)，(3) or (4).	（一）纳税人发生应税行为，除本条第（二）项、第（三）项、第（四）项规定外，税率为6%。

Continued

English Translation	Chinese Version
(2) Where a taxpayer provides transportation，postal services，basic telecommunications，construction or immovable property leasing services，sells any immovable property，or transfers the right to use land，the tax rate shall be 11%.	(二) 提供交通运输、邮政、基础电信、建筑、不动产租赁服务,销售不动产,转让土地使用权,税率为 11%。
(3) Where a taxpayer provides tangible movable property leasing services，the tax rate shall be 17%.	(三) 提供有形动产租赁服务,税率为 17%。
(4) For a cross-border taxable act conducted by an entity or individual within the territory of China，the tax rate shall be zero. The specific scope shall be provided for separately by the Ministry of Finance and the State Administration of Taxation.	(四) 境内单位和个人发生的跨境应税行为,税率为零。具体范围由财政部和国家税务总局另行规定。
Article 16 The levy rate of VAT shall be 3%，unless it is otherwise differently provided for by the Ministry of Finance and the State Administration of Taxation.	第十六条　增值税征收率为 3%,财政部和国家税务总局另有规定的除外。
Chapter IV Calculation of Tax Amount Payable	第四章　应纳税额的计算
Section 1 General Provisions	第一节　一般性规定
Article 17 The method for calculating VAT shall include the general tax computation method and the simple tax computation method.	第十七条　增值税的计税方法,包括一般计税方法和简易计税方法。
Article 18 The general tax computation method shall apply to the taxable acts conducted by general taxpayers.	第十八条　一般纳税人发生应税行为适用一般计税方法计税。
General taxpayers may choose to calculate the tax on their special taxable acts as prescribed by the Ministry of Finance and the State Administration of Taxation with the simple tax computation method，and such method，once chosen，shall not be changed for 36 months.	一般纳税人发生财政部和国家税务总局规定的特定应税行为,可以选择适用简易计税方法计税,但一经选择,36 个月内不得变更。
Article 19 The simple tax computation method shall apply to the taxable acts conducted by small-scale taxpayers.	第十九条　小规模纳税人发生应税行为适用简易计税方法计税。
Article 20 Where an overseas entity or individual conducts any taxable act within the territory of China，and has established no business institution within the territory of China，the withholding agent shall calculate the deductible tax under the following formula：	第二十条　境外单位或者个人在境内发生应税行为,在境内未设有经营机构的,扣缴义务人按照下列公式计算应扣缴税额：

Continued

English Translation	Chinese Version
Deductible tax = Payment made by the purchaser ÷ (1 + Tax rate) × Tax rate	应扣缴税额＝购买方支付的价款÷（1+税率）×税率
Section 2 General Tax Computation Method	**第二节　一般计税方法**
Article 21 The tax amount payable calculated under the general tax computation method means the balance after deducting the input tax for the current period from the output tax for the current period. The formula for calculating the tax amount payable is as follows：	**第二十一条**　一般计税方法的应纳税额，是指当期销项税额抵扣当期进项税额后的余额。应纳税额计算公式：
Tax amount payable = Output tax for the current period − Input tax for the current period	应纳税额＝当期销项税额−当期进项税额
If the output tax for the current period is less than the input tax for the current period，and is insufficient to offset，the deficiency can be carried forward for deduction in the following period.	当期销项税额小于当期进项税额不足抵扣时，其不足部分可以结转下期继续抵扣。
Article 22 "Output tax" means the VAT amount on the taxable act conducted by a taxpayer calculated on the basis of the sales amount and the VAT tax rate. The formula for calculating the output tax is as follows：	**第二十二条**　销项税额，是指纳税人发生应税行为按照销售额和增值税税率计算并收取的增值税额。销项税额计算公式：
Output tax = Sales amount × Tax rate	销项税额＝销售额×税率
Article 23 The sales amount calculated with the general tax computation method shall exclude the output tax. Where a taxpayer adopts the pricing method of combining the sales amount with the output tax, the sales amount shall be calculated according to the following formula：	**第二十三条**　一般计税方法的销售额不包括销项税额，纳税人采用销售额和销项税额合并定价方法的，按照下列公式计算销售额：
Sales amount = Sales amount including tax ÷ (1 + Tax rate)	销售额＝含税销售额÷（1+税率）
Article 24 "Input tax" means the VAT amount paid or borne by a taxpayer for purchasing goods，and processing or repairing labor services，intangible assets or immovable properties.	**第二十四条**　进项税额，是指纳税人购进货物、加工修理修配劳务、服务、无形资产或者不动产，支付或者负担的增值税额。
Article 25 The following amounts of input tax may be deducted from the output tax：	**第二十五条**　下列进项税额准予从销项税额中抵扣：
(1)VAT amount indicated on the special VAT invoice obtained from the seller (including the uniform invoice for the sale of motor vehicles issued with a tax control machine，hereinafter the same).	（一）从销售方取得的增值税专用发票（含税控机动车销售统一发票，下同）上注明的增值税额。

Continued

English Translation	Chinese Version
(2) VAT amount indicated on the customs special bill of payment for VAT on imported goods obtained from the customs office.	（二）从海关取得的海关进口增值税专用缴款书上注明的增值税额。
(3) Input tax calculated on the basis of the purchase price indicated on the invoice for the purchase or sale of agricultural products and at the deduction rate of 13% in addition to obtaining the special VAT invoice or the customs special bill of payment for VAT on imported goods for the purchase of agricultural products. The formula for calculating the input tax is as follows:	（三）购进农产品，除取得增值税专用发票或者海关进口增值税专用缴款书外，按照农产品收购发票或者销售发票上注明的农产品买价和13%的扣除率计算的进项税额。计算公式为：
Input tax = Purchase price × Deduction rate	进项税额＝买价×扣除率
"Purchase price" means the price indicated on the invoice for the purchase or sale of agricultural products when the taxpayer purchases such products, and the tobacco tax which is paid according to the relevant provisions.	买价，是指纳税人购进农产品在农产品收购发票或者销售发票上注明的价款和按照规定缴纳的烟叶税。
The "agricultural products purchased" shall not include those on which the input tax is deducted in accordance with Measures for the Implementation of the Pilot Program of Assessment and Deduction of Input value-added tax on Agricultural Products.	购进农产品，按照《农产品增值税进项税额核定扣除试点实施办法》抵扣进项税额的除外。
(4) VAT amount indicated on the tax payment certificate for payment of withheld taxes obtained from the tax authority or withholding agent for the purchase of services, intangible assets or immovable properties from entities or individuals outside China.	（四）从境外单位或者个人购进服务、无形资产或者不动产，自税务机关或者扣缴义务人取得的解缴税款的完税凭证上注明的增值税额。
Article 26 Where the VAT deduction voucher obtained by a taxpayer does not comply with any law, administrative regulation or relevant provision of the State Administration of Taxation, the input tax shall not be deducted from the output tax.	**第二十六条**　纳税人取得的增值税扣税凭证不符合法律、行政法规或者国家税务总局有关规定的，其进项税额不得从销项税额中抵扣。
"VAT deduction voucher" means a special VAT invoice, a customs special bill of payment for VAT on imported goods, an invoice for the purchase of agricultural products, an invoice for the sale of agricultural products, or a tax payment certificate.	增值税扣税凭证，是指增值税专用发票、海关进口增值税专用缴款书、农产品收购发票、农产品销售发票和完税凭证。

Continued

English Translation	Chinese Version
Where the taxpayer deducts the input tax based on the taxpayment certificate, it shall have a written contract, a payment certificate and a statement or invoice issued by the entity outside China. If the materials are not complete, the input tax shall not be deducted from the output tax.	纳税人凭完税凭证抵扣进项税额的,应当具备书面合同、付款证明和境外单位的对账单或者发票。资料不全的,其进项税额不得从销项税额中抵扣。
Article 27 The input tax of the following items shall not be deducted from the output tax:	第二十七条 下列项目的进项税额不得从销项税额中抵扣:
(1) Goods purchased, or processing or repair labor or services, intangible assets or immovable properties for the taxable items to which the simple tax computation method applies, non-VAT taxable items, collective welfare or individual consumption. The "fixed assets, intangible assets or immovable properties" there of involved only means the fixed assets, intangible assets (excluding other equity intangible assets) and immovable properties which are specially used for the aforesaid items.	(一)用于简易计税方法计税项目、免征增值税项目、集体福利或者个人消费的购进货物、加工修理修配劳务、服务、无形资产和不动产。其中涉及的固定资产、无形资产、不动产,仅指专用于上述项目的固定资产、无形资产(不包括其他权益性无形资产)、不动产。
Social entertainment expenses of taxpayers fall within the scope of individual consumption.	纳税人的交际应酬消费属于个人消费。
(2) Goods purchased under abnormal losses, or relevant processing or repair labor and services or transportation services.	(二)非正常损失的购进货物,以及相关的加工修理修配劳务和交通运输服务。
(3) Goods purchased (excluding fixed assets), processing or repair labor and services or transportation services under abnormal losses that are consumed by products or finished products.	(三)非正常损失的在产品、产成品所耗用的购进货物(不包括固定资产)、加工修理修配劳务和交通运输服务。
(4) Immovable properties under abnormal losses, and the goods purchased, design services and construction services consumed by such immovable properties.	(四)非正常损失的不动产,以及该不动产所耗用的购进货物、设计服务和建筑服务。
(5) Goods purchased, design services and construction services consumed by immovable property projects under construction under abnormal losses.	(五)非正常损失的不动产在建工程所耗用的购进货物、设计服务和建筑服务。
Taxpayers' new building, rebuilding, expansion, renovation and decoration of immovable properties all fall within the scope of immovable property projects under construction.	纳税人新建、改建、扩建、修缮、装饰不动产,均属于不动产在建工程。

Continued

English Translation	Chinese Version
(6) Passenger transportation services, loan services, catering services, residents' daily services entertainment services purchased.	(六)购进的旅客运输服务、贷款服务、餐饮服务、居民日常服务和娱乐服务。
(7) Other circumstances as prescribed by the Ministry of Finance and the State Administration of Taxation.	(七)财政部和国家税务总局规定的其他情形。
The term "goods" as mentioned in Articles (4) and (5) of this Article means the materials and equipment constituting the physical immovable properties, including building and decoration materials, water supply and drainage, heating, sanitation, ventilation, lighting, communications, gas, fire control, central air conditioning, elevator, electrical and intelligent building equipment and supporting facilities.	本条第(四)项、第(五)项所称货物,是指构成不动产实体的材料和设备,包括建筑装饰材料和给排水、采暖、卫生、通风、照明、通讯、煤气、消防、中央空调、电梯、电气、智能化楼宇设备及配套设施。
Article 28 The specific scope of immovable properties and intangible assets shall be governed by Explanatory Notes on the Sales of Services, Intangible Assets and Immovable Properties.	第二十八条　不动产、无形资产的具体范围,按照本办法所附的《销售服务、无形资产或者不动产注释》执行。
"Fixed assets" means the machines, machinery, means of transportation, and other tangible movable property such as equipment, tools, and appliances related to production and distribution with a service life of more than 12 months.	固定资产,是指使用期限超过 12 个月的机器、机械、运输工具以及其他与生产经营有关的设备、工具、器具等有形动产。
"Abnormal loss" means the loss resulting from pilferage, loss, mildew, rot or deterioration caused by mismanagement, or the confiscation, destruction or demolition of goods or immovable properties caused by violations of laws or regulations.	非正常损失,是指因管理不善造成货物被盗、丢失、霉烂变质,以及因违反法律法规造成货物或者不动产被依法没收、销毁、拆除的情形。
Article 29 Where a taxpayer to which the general tax computation method applies concurrently operates any taxable item to which the simple tax computation method applies or VAT-exempt item, and it is unable to identify the non-deductible input tax, the non-deductible input tax shall be calculated according to the following formula:	第二十九条　适用一般计税方法的纳税人,兼营简易计税方法计税项目、免征增值税项目而无法划分不得抵扣的进项税额,按照下列公式计算不得抵扣的进项税额:
Non-deductible input tax = Total input tax unidentifiable for the current period×(Sales amount of the taxable item to which the simple tax computation method applies for the current period + Sales amount of the VAT-exempt item)÷Total sales amounts for the current period	不得抵扣的进项税额=当期无法划分的全部进项税额×(当期简易计税方法计税项目销售额+免征增值税项目销售额)÷当期全部销售额

Continued

English Translation	Chinese Version
The competent tax authority may liquidate the non-deductible input tax according to the annual data under the aforesaid formula.	主管税务机关可以按照上述公式依据年度数据对不得抵扣的进项税额进行清算。
Article 30 Where the purchased goods (excluding fixed assets), labor and services, taxable services whose input tax has been deducted fall within any of the circumstances as prescribed in Article 27 of these Measures (excluding taxable items to which the simple tax computation method applies and the VAT-exempt items), the input tax for such purchased goods or services shall be deducted from the input tax of the current period; and if such input tax cannot be determined, the deductible input tax shall be calculated according to the actual costs in the current period.	**第三十条** 已抵扣进项税额的购进货物(不含固定资产)、劳务、服务,发生本办法第二十七条规定情形(简易计税方法计税项目、免征增值税项目除外)的,应当将该进项税额从当期进项税额中扣减;无法确定该进项税额的,按照当期实际成本计算应扣减的进项税额。
Article 31 If any fixed asset, intangible asset or immovable property for which the input tax amount has been deducted falls within any of the circumstances as prescribed in Article 27 of these Measures, the input tax amount which shall not be deducted shall be calculated according to the following formula:	**第三十一条** 已抵扣进项税额的固定资产、无形资产或者不动产,发生本办法第二十七条规定情形的,按照下列公式计算不得抵扣的进项税额:
Nondeductible input tax amount = Net value of the fixed asset, intangible asset or immovable property × Applicable tax rate	不得抵扣的进项税额＝固定资产、无形资产或者不动产净值×适用税率
The "net value of the fixed asset, intangible asset or immovable property" means the balance after the taxpayer makes provisions for depreciation or amortization according to the financial and accounting rules.	固定资产、无形资产或者不动产净值,是指纳税人根据财务会计制度计提折旧或摊销后的余额。
Article 32 The VAT amount refunded by a taxpayer that adopts the general tax computation method to a purchaser due to sales allowance, suspension or refund shall be deducted from the output tax of the current period; and the VAT amount recovered due to sales allowance, suspension return shall be deducted from the input tax of the current period.	**第三十二条** 纳税人适用一般计税方法计税的,因销售折让、中止或者退回而退还给买方的增值税额,应当从当期的销项税额中扣减;因销售折让、中止或者退回而收回的增值税额,应当从当期的进项税额中扣减。
Article 33 Under any of the following circumstances, the tax payable shall be calculated on the basis of the sales amount and the VAT rate, but no input tax shall be deducted from output tax, and no special VAT invoice shall be used:	**第三十三条** 有下列情形之一者,应当按照销售额和增值税税率计算应纳税额,不得抵扣进项税额,也不得使用增值税专用发票:

Continued

English Translation	Chinese Version
(1) A general taxpayer does not have a sound accounting system or is unable to provide accurate tax information.	（一）一般纳税人会计核算不健全，或者不能够提供准确税务资料的。
(2) A taxpayer should have undergone the formalities for the registration of the qualification as a general taxpayer but fails to do so.	（二）应当办理一般纳税人资格登记而未办理的。
Section 3 Simple Tax Computation Method	第三节　简易计税方法
Article 34 "Tax amount payable calculated with the simple tax computation method" means the VAT amount calculated on the basis of the sales amount and the VAT levy rate, without deducting the input tax. The formula for calculating the tax amount payable is as follows：	第三十四条　简易计税方法的应纳税额，是指按照销售额和增值税征收率计算的增值税额，不得抵扣进项税额。应纳税额计算公式：
Tax amount payable＝Sales amount×Levy rate	应纳税额＝销售额×征收率
Article 35 The sales amount calculated with the simple tax computation method shall not include the tax payable, and if the taxpayer adopts the pricing method of combining the sales amount with tax payable, the sales amount shall be calculated according to the following formula：	第三十五条　简易计税方法的销售额不包括其应纳税额，纳税人采用销售额和应纳税额合并定价方法的，按照下列公式计算销售额：
Sales amount＝Sales amount including tax÷(1＋Levy rate)	销售额＝含税销售额÷（1＋征收率）
Article 36 The sales amount refunded by a taxpayer that adopts the simple tax computation method to a purchaser due to sales allowance, suspension or refund shall be deducted from the sales amount of the current period. If overpayment of tax is caused by any balance after deduction from the sales amount of the current period, such tax may be deducted from the tax payable in the following period.	第三十六条　纳税人适用简易计税方法计税的，因销售折让、中止或者退回而退还给购买方的销售额，应当从当期销售额中扣减。扣减当期销售额后仍有余额造成多缴的税款，可以从以后的应纳税额中扣减。
Section 4 Determination of Sales Amount	第四节　销售额的确定
Article 37 "Sales amount" means the full prices and ex-price charges obtained by taxpayers from conducting taxable acts, except as otherwise provided for by the Ministry of Finance and the State Administration of Taxation.	第三十七条　销售额，是指纳税人发生应税行为取得的全部价款和价外费用，财政部和国家税务总局另有规定的除外。

Continued

English Translation	Chinese Version
"Ex-price charges" means charges of various natures in addition to prices，excluding the following items：	价外费用，是指价外收取的各种性质的收费，但不包括以下项目：
(1)Governmental funds or administrative charges collected on behalf of others，which comply with the provisions of Article 10 of these Measures.	(一)代为收取并符合本办法第十条规定的政府性基金或者行政事业性收费。
(2)Funds collected on behalf of the clients by issuing invoices on behalf of the clients.	(二)以委托方名义开具发票代委托方收取的款项。
Article 38 Sales amount shall be calculated in RMB.	第三十八条　销售额以人民币计算。
Where a taxpayer settles the sales amount in a currency other than RMB，the taxpayer shall convert the currency into RMB，and the conversion rate may be the central parity rate for RMB quoted either on the day when the sales amount occurs or on the first day of that month. The taxpayer shall determine in advance the applicable conversion rate，which，once being determined，shall not be changed within 12 months.	纳税人按照人民币以外的货币结算销售额的，应当折合成人民币计算，折合率可以选择销售额发生的当天或者当月 1 日的人民币汇率中间价。纳税人应当在事先确定采用何种折合率，确定后 12 个月内不得变更。
Article 39 A taxpayer concurrently engaged in the sale of goods，labor，services，intangible assets or immovable properties，to which different tax rates or levy rates apply，shall separately account the sales amounts to which different tax rates or levy rates apply；otherwise，the higher tax rate shall apply.	第三十九条　纳税人兼营销售货物、劳务、服务、无形资产或者不动产，适用不同税率或者征收率的，应当分别核算适用不同税率或者征收率的销售额；未分别核算的，从高适用税率。
Article 40 A sale act involving both services and goods shall be regarded as a mixed sale. The mixed sales by entities or individual industrial and commercial households engaged in the production，wholesale or retail of goods shall be subject to VAT as sale of goods，and the mixed sales by other entities or individual industrial and commercial households shall be subject to VAT as sale of services.	第四十条　一项销售行为如果既涉及服务又涉及货物，为混合销售。从事货物的生产、批发或者零售的单位和个体工商户的混合销售行为，按照销售货物缴纳增值税；其他单位和个体工商户的混合销售行为，按照销售服务缴纳增值税。
For the purpose of this Article，"entities or individual industrial and commercial households engaged in the production，wholesale or retail of goods" includes entities or individual industrial and commercial households mainly engaged in the production，wholesale or retail of goods and concurrently engaged in the sale of services.	本条所称从事货物的生产、批发或者零售的单位和个体工商户，包括以从事货物的生产、批发或者零售为主，并兼营销售服务的单位和个体工商户在内。

Continued

English Translation	Chinese Version
Article 41 A taxpayer concurrently engaged in tax exemption or reduction items shall calculate separately the sales amount of the tax exemption or tax reduction items; otherwise, no tax exemption or reduction shall be allowed.	**第四十一条** 纳税人兼营免税、减税项目的,应当分别核算免税、减税项目的销售额;未分别核算的,不得免税、减税。
Article 42 Where, after a taxpayer issues a special VAT invoice for conducting any taxable act, the invoice is found wrongly issued, or the sales allowance, suspension or refund occurs or is under any other circumstance, the taxpayer shall issue a special VAT invoice in red characters according to the provisions of the State Administration of Taxation; if it fails to issue the said invoice as required, the deduction of input tax from output tax or the deduction of sales amount as prescribed in Article 32 or 36 of these Measures shall not be allowed.	**第四十二条** 纳税人发生应税行为,开具增值税专用发票后,发生开票有误或者销售折让、中止、退回等情形的,应当按照国家税务总局的规定开具红字增值税专用发票;未按照规定开具红字增值税专用发票的,不得按照本办法第三十二条和第三十六条的规定扣减销项税额或者销售额。
Article 43 Where a taxpayer conducting any taxable act indicates separately the price and the amount of discount on the same invoice, the sales amount shall be the price after discount; and if the price and the amount of discount are not indicated on the same invoice, the sales amount shall be the price and the amount of discount shall not be allowed.	**第四十三条** 纳税人发生应税行为,将价款和折扣额在同一张发票上分别注明的,以折扣后的价款为销售额;未在同一张发票上分别注明的,以价款为销售额,不得扣减折扣额。
Article 44 Where a taxpayer conducts any taxable act at an evidently low or high price for no justifiable commercial purpose, or conducts any taxable act as listed in Article 14 of these Measures but has no sales amount, the competent tax authority shall have the power to determine the sales amount in the following sequence:	**第四十四条** 纳税人发生应税行为价格明显偏低或者偏高且不具有合理商业目的的,或者发生本办法第十四条所列行为而无销售额的,主管税务机关有权按照下列顺序确定销售额:
(1)The sales amount shall be determined at the average price for the taxpayer's sale of services, intangible assets or immovable properties of the same kind in the latest period.	(一)按照纳税人最近时期销售同类服务、无形资产或者不动产的平均价格确定。
(2)The sales amount shall be determined at the average price for other taxpayers' sales of services, intangible assets or immovable properties of the same kind in the latest period.	(二)按照其他纳税人最近时期销售同类服务、无形资产或者不动产的平均价格确定。

Continued

English Translation	Chinese Version
(3)The sales amount shall be determined on the basis of the composite taxable value. The formula for calculating the composite taxable value is as follows:	(三)按照组成计税价格确定。组成计税价格的公式为:
Composite taxable value＝Costs ×（1＋Cost-profit ratio)	组成计税价格＝成本×（1＋成本利润率)
The cost-profit ratio shall be determined by the State Administration of Taxation.	成本利润率由国家税务总局确定。
The expression "for no justifiable commercial purpose" means that the taxpayer, for the primary purpose of seeking tax profits, reduces, exempts or delays the payment of VAT amount, or increases the refund of VAT amount through intentional arrangements.	不具有合理商业目的,是指以谋取税收利益为主要目的,通过人为安排,减少、免除、推迟缴纳增值税税款,或者增加退还增值税税款。
Chapter Ⅴ Time of Occurrence of Tax Payment Obligations and Withholding Obligations and Place of Tax Payment	**第五章　纳税义务、扣缴义务发生时间和纳税地点**
Article 45 The time of occurrence of tax payment obligations and withholding obligations is as follows:	**第四十五条**　增值税纳税义务、扣缴义务发生时间为:
(1)The day when a taxpayer conducts a taxable act and receives the sales payment or obtains a voucher for demanding payment; or the day when an invoice is issued if the invoice is issued in advance.	(一)纳税人发生应税行为并收讫销售款项或者取得索取销售款项凭据的当天;先开具发票的,为开具发票的当天。
"Receives the sales payment" means that a taxpayer receives payment during or after the sale of service, intangible asset or immovable property.	收讫销售款项,是指纳税人销售服务、无形资产、不动产过程中或者完成后收到款项。
The "day when a taxpayer obtains a voucher for demanding payment" means the payment date determined in a written contract; or the day when the transfer of the service, intangible asset or immovable property is completed or the day when the ownership of the immovable property changes if there is no such written contract or the payment date is not determined in the written contract.	取得索取销售款项凭据的当天,是指书面合同确定的付款日期;未签订书面合同或者书面合同未确定付款日期的,为服务、无形资产转让完成的当天或者不动产权属变更的当天。
(2)Where a taxpayer provides construction services or leasing services by means of prepayment, the time of occurrence of its payment obligations shall be the day when the advance payment is received.	(二)纳税人提供建筑服务、租赁服务采取预收款方式的,其纳税义务发生时间为收到预收款的当天。

Continued

English Translation	Chinese Version
(3) The day when the ownership of financial commodities is transferred if the taxpayer is engaged in the transfer of financial commodities.	(三)纳税人从事金融商品转让的,为金融商品所有权转移的当天。
(4) Where a taxpayer falls within any of the circumstances as prescribed in Article 14 of these Measures, the time of occurrence of its payment obligations shall be the day when the transfer of services or intangible assets is completed or the day when the ownership of immovable property changes.	(四)纳税人发生本办法第十四条规定情形的,其纳税义务发生时间为服务、无形资产转让完成的当天或者不动产权属变更的当天。
(5) The time of the occurrence of VAT withholding obligations shall be the day when a taxpayer's VAT payment obligations occur.	(五)增值税扣缴义务发生时间为纳税人增值税纳税义务发生的当天。
Article 46 The place of VAT payment is as follows:	**第四十六条**　增值税纳税地点为:
(1) A business operator with a fixed premise shall file a tax return with the competent tax authority at the place where the institution is located or the individual resides. If the head office and branch offices of the business operator are not in a same county (or city), they shall file separate tax returns with the local competent tax authorities respectively. With the approval of the Ministry of Finance and the State Administration of Taxation or the public finance and tax authorities authorized by the Ministry of Finance or the State Administration of Taxation, the head office may file a tax return on a consolidated basis with the competent tax authority at the place where the head office is located.	(一)固定业户应当向其机构所在地或者居住地主管税务机关申报纳税。总机构和分支机构不在同一县(市)的,应当分别向各自所在地的主管税务机关申报纳税;经财政部和国家税务总局或者其授权的财政和税务机关批准,可以由总机构汇总向总机构所在地的主管税务机关申报纳税。
(2) A business operator without a fixed premise shall file a return with the competent tax authority at the place where the taxable act occurs; and if no tax return is so filed, the competent tax authority at the place where the institution is located or the individual resides shall collect the overdue taxes.	(二)非固定业户应当向应税行为发生地主管税务机关申报纳税;未申报纳税的,由其机构所在地或者居住地主管税务机关补征税款。
(3) Other individuals that provide construction services, sell or lease immovable properties, or transfer the rights to use natural resources shall file tax returns with the competent tax authorities at the places where the construction services occur, the immovable properties are located or the natural resources are located.	(三)其他个人提供建筑服务,销售或者租赁不动产,转让自然资源使用权,应向建筑服务发生地、不动产所在地、自然资源所在地主管税务机关申报纳税。

Continued

English Translation	Chinese Version
(4)A withholding agent shall file a return of withheld taxes with the competent tax authority at the place where the institution is located or the individual resides.	(四)扣缴义务人应当向其机构所在地或者居住地主管税务机关申报缴纳扣缴的税款。
Article 47 The VAT payment period shall be one day, three days, five days, 10 days, 15 days, one month or one quarter, where applicable. The specific payment period for a taxpayer shall be verified and determined by the competent tax authority on the basis of the tax amount payable of the taxpayer. The provisions on the payment period of one quarter shall apply to small-scale taxpayers, banks, finance companies, trust investment companies, credit unions and other taxpayers as prescribed by the Ministry of Finance and the State Administration of Taxation. Where tax cannot be paid on a regular period basis, it may be paid on a transaction-by-transaction basis.	第四十七条 增值税的纳税期限分别为1日、3日、5日、10日、15日、1个月或者1个季度。纳税人的具体纳税期限,由主管税务机关根据纳税人应纳税额的大小分别核定。以1个季度为纳税期限的规定适用于小规模纳税人、银行、财务公司、信托投资公司、信用社,以及财政部和国家税务总局规定的其他纳税人。不能按照固定期限纳税的,可以按次纳税。
A taxpayer that may pay tax during a period of one month or one quarter shall file a tax return within 15 days after the expiry of such period. If the payment period is one day, three days, five days, 10 days or 15 days, the taxpayer shall prepay the tax within five days after the expiry of such period, file a tax return within 15 days as of the first day of the following month, and settle the tax payable of the preceding month.	纳税人以1个月或者1个季度为1个纳税期的,自期满之日起15日内申报纳税;以1日、3日、5日、10日或者15日为1个纳税期的,自期满之日起5日内预缴税款,于次月1日起15日内申报纳税并结清上月应纳税款。
The time limit for a withholding agent to pay the withheld taxes shall be governed by the preceding two paragraphs.	扣缴义务人解缴税款的期限,按照前两款规定执行。
Chapter VI Handling of Tax Reduction or Exemption	**第六章 税收减免的处理**
Article 48 Where the provisions on VAT exemption or reduction apply to any taxable act conducted by a taxpayer, the taxpayer may waive the tax exemption or reduction, and pay VAT in accordance with the provisions of these Measures. The taxpayer may not reapply for tax exemption or reduction within 36 months after waiving the tax exemption or reduction.	第四十八条 纳税人发生应税行为适用免税、减税规定的,可以放弃免税、减税,依照本办法的规定缴纳增值税。放弃免税、减税后,36个月内不得再申请免税、减税。
Where any tax exemption and zero rate provisions concurrently a apply to a taxpayer that conducts a taxable act, the taxpayer may choose the application of tax exemption or zero tax rate.	纳税人发生应税行为同时适用免税和零税率规定的,纳税人可以选择适用免税或者零税率。

Continued

English Translation	Chinese Version
Article 49 Where the sales amount of any taxable act conducted by an individual does not reach the threshold for levy of VAT, the individual shall be exempted from VAT; otherwise, VAT shall be calculated and paid in full amount.	第四十九条　个人发生应税行为的销售额未达到增值税起征点的,免征增值税;达到起征点的,全额计算缴纳增值税。
The thresholds for VAT shall not apply to the individual industrial and commercial households.	增值税起征点不适用于登记为一般纳税人的个体工商户。
Article 50 The ranges of the thresholds for levy of VAT are as follows:	第五十条　增值税起征点幅度如下:
(1)5,000-20,000 yuan in monthly sales (including the figures mentioned), if VAT is paid on a regular basis.	(一)按期纳税的,为月销售额5000～20000 元(含本数)。
(2)300-500 yuan in sales amount per transaction (or per day) (including the figures mentioned), if VAT is paid on a transaction-by-transaction basis.	(二)按次纳税的,为每次(日)销售额 300～500 元(含本数)。
Any adjustments to the thresholds for levy of VAT shall be prescribed by the Ministry of Finance and the State Administration of Taxation. The public finance departments (bureaus) and state taxation bureaus of provinces, autonomous regions, and municipalities directly under the Central Government shall, according to their actual circumstances, determine the applicable local thresholds for levy of VAT within the prescribed ranges, and report such local thresholds to the Ministry of Finance and the State Administration of Taxation for recordation.	起征点的调整由财政部和国家税务总局规定。省、自治区、直辖市财政厅(局)和国家税务局应当在规定的幅度内,根据实际情况确定本地区适用的起征点,并报财政部和国家税务总局备案。
The enterprises or non-enterprise entities with a monthly sales amount of less than 20,000 yuan among small-scale VAT taxpayers shall be exempt from VAT. Prior to December 31, 2017, the small-scale VAT taxpayers with the monthly sales amount of 20,000 yuan (including the figures mentioned) to 30,000 yuan shall be exempt from VAT.	对增值税小规模纳税人中月销售额未达到 2 万元的企业或非企业性单位,免征增值税。2017年 12 月 31 日前,对月销售额 2 万元(含本数)至 3 万元的增值税小规模纳税人,免征增值税。
Chapter Ⅶ Collection Administration	**第七章　征收管理**
Article 51 The State Administration of Taxation shall be responsible for collecting VAT levied in lieu of business tax. The VAT on the immovable properties sold by taxpayers and the immovable properties leased by other individuals shall be temporarily collected by local taxation bureaus upon the authorization of the State Administration of Taxation.	第五十一条　营业税改征的增值税,由国家税务局负责征收。纳税人销售取得的不动产和其他个人出租不动产的增值税,国家税务局暂委托地方税务局代为征收。

Continued

English Translation	Chinese Version
Article 52 A taxpayer that conducts any taxable act to which zero tax rate applies shall apply for tax refund (or exemption) to the competent tax authority on a regular basis, and the specific measures shall be developed by the Ministry of Finance and the State Administration of Taxation.	第五十二条　纳税人发生适用零税率的应税行为,应当按期向主管税务机关申报办理退(免)税,具体办法由财政部和国家税务总局制定。
Article 53 A taxpayer that conducts any taxable act shall issue a special VAT invoice to the purchaser that requests a special VAT invoice and give clear indications of the sales amount and output tax amount on it.	第五十三条　纳税人发生应税行为,应当向索取增值税专用发票的购买方开具增值税专用发票,并在增值税专用发票上分别注明销售额和销项税额。
Under any of the following circumstances, no special VAT invoice shall be issued:	属于下列情形之一的,不得开具增值税专用发票:
(1)The services, intangible assets or immovable properties are sold to individual consumers.	(一)向消费者个人销售服务、无形资产或者不动产。
(2) The provisions on VAT-exemption apply to the taxable act.	(二)适用免征增值税规定的应税行为。
Article 54 A small-scale taxpayer that conducts any taxable act may apply to the competent tax authority for issuance of a special VAT invoice on behalf of the taxpayer to a purchaser which requests a special VAT invoice.	第五十四条　小规模纳税人发生应税行为,购买方索取增值税专用发票的,可以向主管税务机关申请代开。
Article 55 The administration of collection of VAT from taxpayers shall be governed by these Measures, the Law of the People's Republic of China on the Administration of Tax Collection, and the current provisions on the administration of VAT collection.	第五十五条　纳税人增值税的征收管理,按照本办法和《中华人民共和国税收征收管理法》及现行增值税征收管理有关规定执行。
Annex: Explanatory Notes on the Sales of Services, Intangible Assets and Immovable Properties	附:销售服务、无形资产、不动产注释
Annex:	附:
Explanatory Notes on the Sales of Services, Intangible Assets and Immovable Properties	销售服务、无形资产、不动产注释
I. Sales of Services	一、销售服务
"Sales of services" means the provision of transportation services, postal services, telecommunications services, construction services, financial services, modern services, and life services.	销售服务,是指提供交通运输服务、邮政服务、电信服务、建筑服务、金融服务、现代服务、生活服务。

Continued

English Translation	Chinese Version
(1)Transportation Services	(一)交通运输服务
"Transportation services" means the business activities of conveying cargo or passengers to a destination by means of transportation, resulting in the shifting of the spatial location of cargo or passengers, including land, water, air and pipeline transportation services.	交通运输服务,是指利用运输工具将货物或者旅客送达目的地,使其空间位置得到转移的业务活动。包括陆路运输服务、水路运输服务、航空运输服务和管道运输服务。
(a)Land Transportation Services	1.陆路运输服务
"Land transportation services" means the transportation business activities of conveying cargo or passengers by land (aboveground or underground), including railway transportation services as well as other land transportation services.	陆路运输服务,是指通过陆路(地上或者地下)运送货物或者旅客的运输业务活动,包括铁路运输服务和其他陆路运输服务。
(ⅰ) "Railway transportation services" means the transportation business activities of conveying cargo or passengers by railway.	(1)铁路运输服务,是指通过铁路运送货物或者旅客的运输业务活动。
(ⅱ) "Other land transportation services" means the land transportation business activities other than railway transportation services, including road, cable car, ropeway, subway, and urban light rail transportation, etc.	(2)其他陆路运输服务,是指铁路运输以外的陆路运输业务活动。包括公路运输、缆车运输、索道运输、地铁运输、城市轻轨运输等。
The VAT on the management fees collected by a taxi company from taxi drivers using taxis owned by the taxi company shall be paid according to the rate for land transportation services.	出租车公司向使用本公司自有出租车的出租车司机收取的管理费用,按照陆路运输服务缴纳增值税。
(b)Water Transportation Services	2.水路运输服务
"Water transportation services" means the transportation business activities of conveying cargo or passengers by river, lake, stream, and other natural or artificial waterways or sea lanes.	水路运输服务,是指通过江、河、湖、川等天然、人工水道或者海洋航道运送货物或者旅客的运输业务活动。
The voyage charter business and time charter business in water transportation fall within the scope of water transportation services.	水路运输的程租、期租业务,属于水路运输服务。
"Voyage charter business" means business whereby a transportation enterprise completes the transportation task on a certain voyage for the charterer and collects a charter fee.	程租业务,是指运输企业为租船人完成某一特定航次的运输任务并收取租赁费的业务。

Continued

English Translation	Chinese Version
"Time charter business" means the business whereby a transportation enterprise charters a vessel equipped with operators to another party for use during a specified period, the vessel is at the command of the charterer during the specified period, and the transportation enterprise collects a charter fee on a daily basis from the charterer whether the vessel is in operation or not, with the ship-owner assuming all the fixed costs incurred therefrom.	期租业务,是指运输企业将配备有操作人员的船舶承租给他人使用一定期限,承租期内听候承租方调遣,不论是否经营,均按天向承租方收取租赁费,发生的固定费用均由船东负担的业务。
(c) Air Transportation Services	3.航空运输服务
"Air transportation services" means the transportation business activities of conveying cargo or passengers by air routes.	航空运输服务,是指通过空中航线运送货物或者旅客的运输业务活动。
The wet-lease business in air transportation falls within the scope of air transportation services.	航空运输的湿租业务,属于航空运输服务。
"Wet-lease business" means the business whereby an air transportation enterprise leases an unstaffed airplane to another party for use during a specified period, the airplane is at the command of the lessee during the specified period, and the air transportation enterprise collects rentals according to a certain rate from the lessee whether the airplane is in operation or not, with the lessee assuming all the fixed costs incurred therefrom.	湿租业务,是指航空运输企业将配备有机组人员的飞机承租给他人使用一定期限,承租期内听候承租方调遣,不论是否经营,均按一定标准向承租方收取租赁费,发生的固定费用均由承租方承担的业务。
The VAT on space transportation services shall be paid according to the rate for air transportation services.	航天运输服务,按照航空运输服务缴纳增值税。
"Space transportation services" means the business activities of launching satellites, space probes, and other space crafts to an orbit in the outer space by using rockets and other carriers.	航天运输服务,是指利用火箭等载体将卫星、空间探测器等空间飞行器发射到空间轨道的业务活动。
(d) Pipeline Transportation Services	4.管道运输服务
"Pipeline transportation services" means the transportation business activities of conveying gas, liquid, and solid materials through pipeline facilities.	管道运输服务,是指通过管道设施输送气体、液体、固体物质的运输业务活动。
The VAT on the carriage business without a means of transport shall be paid according to the rate for transportation services.	无运输工具承运业务,按照交通运输服务缴纳增值税。

Continued

English Translation	Chinese Version
"Carriage business without a means of transport" means the business activity of an operator which concludes a transportation service contract with the consignor as a carrier, collects freight and assumes the liabilities of the carrier, and then authorizes the actual carrier to complete the transportation services.	无运输工具承运业务,是指经营者以承运人身份与托运人签订运输服务合同,收取运费并承担承运人责任,然后委托实际承运人完成运输服务的经营活动。
(2)Postal Services	(二)邮政服务
"Postal services" means the business activities of providing mail delivery, postal remittance, confidential correspondence and other basic postal services by China Post Group and its affiliated postal enterprises, including universal postal services, special postal services, and other postal services.	邮政服务,是指中国邮政集团公司及其所属邮政企业提供邮件寄递、邮政汇兑和机要通信等邮政基本服务的业务活动。包括邮政普遍服务、邮政特殊服务和其他邮政服务。
(a)Universal Postal Services	1.邮政普遍服务
"Universal postal services" means the business activities of delivering correspondence, parcels and other mail, issuing post stamps, distributing newspapers and magazines, and providing postal remittance, etc.	邮政普遍服务,是指函件、包裹等邮件寄递,以及邮票发行、报刊发行和邮政汇兑等业务活动。
"Correspondence" means letters, printed matters, postage-paid envelops and cards, unaddressed letters, and small postal packages, etc.	函件,是指信函、印刷品、邮资封片卡、无名址函件和邮政小包等。
"Parcels" means articles independently packed and delivered to a specific individual or entity according to the name and address on the package, the weight of which does not exceed 50 kilograms, the size of each side of which does not exceed 150 cm, and the total of the length, width, and height of which does not exceed 300 cm.	包裹,是指按照封装上的名址递送给特定个人或者单位的独立封装的物品,其重量不超过五十千克,任何一边的尺寸不超过一百五十厘米,长、宽、高合计不超过三百厘米。
(b)Special Postal Services	2.邮政特殊服务
"Special postal services" means the business activities of delivering ordinary mail of compulsory servicemen, confidential correspondence, Braille books, and legacies of revolutionary martyrs, etc.	邮政特殊服务,是指义务兵平常信函、机要通信、盲人读物和革命烈士遗物的寄递等业务活动。
(c)Other Postal Services	3.其他邮政服务
"Other postal services" means the business activities of selling stamp albums and other postal products and providing postal agency, etc.	其他邮政服务,是指邮册等邮品销售、邮政代理等业务活动。

Continued

English Translation	Chinese Version
(3) Telecommunications Services	（三）电信服务
"Telecommunications services" means the business activities of providing voice call services，and transmitting，sending，receiving or applying images，text messages and other electric data and information through wired or wireless electromagnetic or optoelectronic systems or by using other various communications network resources，including basic telecommunications services and value-added telecommunications services.	电信服务，是指利用有线、无线的电磁系统或者光电系统等各种通信网络资源，提供语音通话服务，传送、发射、接收或者应用图像、短信等电子数据和信息的业务活动。包括基础电信服务和增值电信服务。
(a) Basic Telecommunications Services	1.基础电信服务
"Basic telecommunications services" means the business activities of providing voice call services and renting or selling such network elements as bandwidth and wavelength via fixed network，mobile network，satellites and Internet.	基础电信服务，是指利用固网、移动网、卫星、互联网，提供语音通话服务的业务活动，以及出租或者出售带宽、波长等网络元素的业务活动。
(b) Value-Added Telecommunications Services	2.增值电信服务
"Value-added telecommunications services" means the business activities of providing text message and multimedia message services，electric data as well as information transmission and application services，and Internet access services，etc.，via fixed network，mobile network，satellites，Internet and cable television networks.	增值电信服务，是指利用固网、移动网、卫星、互联网、有线电视网络，提供短信和彩信服务、电子数据和信息的传输及应用服务、互联网接入服务等业务活动。
The VAT on ground transfer services for satellite television signals shall be paid according to the rate for value-added telecommunications services.	卫星电视信号落地转接服务，按照增值电信服务缴纳增值税。
(4) Construction Services	（四）建筑服务
"Construction services" means the business activities of the building，repair and decoration of various buildings，structures and ancillary facilities，and the installation of lines，pipes，equipment and facilities，etc.，and other engineering operations，including engineering services，installation services，repair services，decoration services and other construction services.	建筑服务，是指各类建筑物、构筑物及其附属设施的建造、修缮、装饰，线路、管道、设备、设施等的安装以及其他工程作业的业务活动。包括工程服务、安装服务、修缮服务、装饰服务和其他建筑服务。
(a) Engineering Services	1.工程服务

Continued

English Translation	Chinese Version
"Engineering services" means the engineering operations of new building and rebuilding of various buildings and structures, including the engineering operations of installation or decoration of various equipment or pillars and operating platforms connected to the buildings, as well as the engineering operations of various kilns and metal structures.	工程服务,是指新建、改建各种建筑物、构筑物的工程作业,包括与建筑物相连的各种设备或者支柱、操作平台的安装或者装设工程作业,以及各种窑炉和金属结构工程作业。
(b)Installation Services	2.安装服务
"Installation services" means the engineering operations of the assembly and arrangement of production equipment, power equipment, hoisting equipment, transportation equipment, transmission equipment, medical laboratory equipment, as well as a variety of other equipment and facilities, including the engineering operation of installation of operating platforms, laddersand balustrades connected to the installed equipment, and the engineering operations of insulation, anti-corrosion, heat preservation and painting for the installed equipment, among others.	安装服务,是指生产设备、动力设备、起重设备、运输设备、传动设备、医疗实验设备以及其他各种设备、设施的装配、安置工程作业,包括与被安装设备相连的工作台、梯子、栏杆的装设工程作业,以及被安装设备的绝缘、防腐、保温、油漆等工程作业。
The VAT on installation fees, initial installation fees, account-opening fees, capacity expansion fees and similar charges charged by operators of fixed-line telephones, cable television, broadband water, electricity, gas and heating installation, etc. from users shall be paid according to the rate for installation services.	固定电话、有线电视、宽带、水、电、燃气、暖气等经营者向用户收取的安装费、初装费、开户费、扩容费以及类似收费,按照安装服务缴纳增值税。
(c)Repair Services	3.修缮服务
"Repair services" means the engineering operations of repairing, reinforcing, maintaining and improving the buildings and structures, so as to restore them to their original use value or extend their service life.	修缮服务,是指对建筑物、构筑物进行修补、加固、养护、改善,使之恢复原来的使用价值或者延长其使用期限的工程作业。
(d)Decoration Services	4.装饰服务
"Decoration services" means the engineering operation of decorating the buildings and structures, so that they will look more beautiful or have a particular purpose.	装饰服务,是指对建筑物、构筑物进行修饰装修,使之美观或者具有特定用途的工程作业。
(e)Other Construction Services	5.其他建筑服务

Continued

English Translation	Chinese Version
"Other construction services" means various engineering operations other than the aforesaid engineering operations, such as the engineering operations of drilling wells (sinking wells), demolishing buildings or structures, levelling land, landscaping, dredging (excluding waterway dredging), shifting of buildings, putting up scaffolding, blasting, mining perforation, surface attachments (including rock, soil and sand beds, etc.) stripping and cleaning, etc.	其他建筑服务，是指上列工程作业之外的各种工程作业服务，如钻井（打井）、拆除建筑物或者构筑物、平整土地、园林绿化、疏浚（不包括航道疏浚）、建筑物平移、搭脚手架、爆破、矿山穿孔、表面附着物（包括岩层、土层、沙层等）剥离和清理等工程作业。
(5) Financial Services	（五）金融服务
"Financial services" means the business activities of operating financial insurance, including loan services, direct paid financial services, insurance services and transfer of financial commodities.	金融服务，是指经营金融保险的业务活动。包括贷款服务、直接收费金融服务、保险服务和金融商品转让。
(a) Loan Services	1.贷款服务
"Loan" means the business activity of lending money to others for use so as to obtain interest income.	贷款，是指将资金贷与他人使用而取得利息收入的业务活动。
The VAT on the income obtained from various funds occupied and lent, including the income of interest (capital-guarantee earnings, remunerations, fund possession fees, and compensatory payment, among others) of financial commodities gained during the period when they are held, interest income from the overdraft of credit cards, interest income from the reverse repurchase of financial commodities, interest income from margin trading and short selling, and interest and interest income obtained from financing sale and leaseback, documentary credit, default interest, discount of bills, relending and other business, shall be paid according to the rate for loan services.	各种占用、拆借资金取得的收入，包括金融商品持有期间（含到期）利息（保本收益、报酬、资金占用费、补偿金等）收入、信用卡透支利息收入、买入返售金融商品利息收入、融资融券收取的利息收入，以及融资性售后回租、押汇、罚息、票据贴现、转贷等业务取得的利息及利息性质的收入，按照贷款服务缴纳增值税。
"Financing sale and leaseback" means the business activity whereby an enterprise engaged in the financing sale and leaseback business leases back to the lessee an asset which has been sold by the lessee to the enterprise engaged in the financing sale and leaseback business for the purpose of financing.	融资性售后回租，是指承租方以融资为目的，将资产出售给从事融资性售后回租业务的企业后，从事融资性售后回租业务的企业将该资产出租给承租方的业务活动。
The VAT on the fixed profits or minimum profits collected on the basis of monetary fund investment shall be paid according to the rate for loan services.	以货币资金投资收取的固定利润或者保底利润，按照贷款服务缴纳增值税。

Continued

English Translation	Chinese Version
(b)Direct Paid Financial Services	2.直接收费金融服务
"Direct paid financial services" means the business activities of providing relevant services and receives compensation for monetary fund accommodation and other financial business, including provision of money exchange, account management, electronic banking, credit cards, letters of credit, financial guarantees, asset management, trust management, fund management, financial trading venue (platform) management, financial settlement, fund liquidation, financial payment and other services.	直接收费金融服务,是指为货币资金融通及其他金融业务提供相关服务并且收取费用的业务活动。包括提供货币兑换、账户管理、电子银行、信用卡、信用证、财务担保、资产管理、信托管理、基金管理、金融交易场所(平台)管理、资金结算、资金清算、金融支付等服务。
(c)Insurance Services	3.保险服务
"Insurance services" means the commercial insurance acts whereby an insurance applicant pays an insurance premium to an insurer under an insurance contract and the insurer undertakes to pay the insurance money to compensate for the property loss caused by the occurrence of a potential incident specified in the insurance contract or pay the insurance money when the insurant dies, becomes disabled or sick or reaches a specified age, time limit or any other condition specified in the contract, including personal insurance services and property insurance services.	保险服务,是指投保人根据合同约定,向保险人支付保险费,保险人对于合同约定的可能发生的事故因其发生所造成的财产损失承担赔偿保险金责任,或者当被保险人死亡、伤残、疾病或者达到合同约定的年龄、期限等条件时承担给付保险金责任的商业保险行为。包括人身保险服务和财产保险服务。
"Personal insurance services" means a type of insurance business activity which takes the life and body of human beings as the subject matter insured.	人身保险服务,是指以人的寿命和身体为保险标的的保险业务活动。
"Property insurance services" means a type of insurance business activity which takes property and relevant interests as the subject matter insured.	财产保险服务,是指以财产及其有关利益为保险标的的保险业务活动。
(d)Transfer of Financial Commodities	4.金融商品转让
"Transfer of financial commodities" means the business activity of transferring the ownership of foreign exchange, negotiable securities, non-goods futures, and other financial commodities.	金融商品转让,是指转让外汇、有价证券、非货物期货和其他金融商品所有权的业务活动。
The "transfer of other financial commodities" includes the transfer of funds, trust and wealth management commodities and a variety of other asset management products and financial derivatives.	其他金融商品转让包括基金、信托、理财产品等各类资产管理产品和各种金融衍生品的转让。

Continued

English Translation	Chinese Version
(6) Modern Services	(六) 现代服务
"Modern services" means the business activities of providing technical and knowledge-based services for the manufacturing industry, cultural industry, modern logistics industry and other industries, including research, development and technical services, information technology services, cultural and creative services, logistics support services, leasing services, attestation and consultation services, radio, film and television services, business support services and other modern services.	现代服务,是指围绕制造业、文化产业、现代物流产业等提供技术性、知识性服务的业务活动。包括研发和技术服务、信息技术服务、文化创意服务、物流辅助服务、租赁服务、鉴证咨询服务、广播影视服务、商务辅助服务和其他现代服务。
(a) Research, Development and Technical Services	1. 研发和技术服务
"Research, development and technical services" includes research and development services, energy performance contracting services, engineering prospecting and exploration services, and professional technical services.	研发和技术服务,包括研发服务、合同能源管理服务、工程勘察勘探服务、专业技术服务。
(ⅰ) "Research and development services," also known as technological development services, means the business activities of research, experiment, and development of new technologies, new products, new processes, or new materials, and their systems.	(1) 研发服务,也称技术开发服务,是指就新技术、新产品、新工艺或者新材料及其系统进行研究与试验开发的业务活动。
(ⅱ) "Energy performance contracting services" means the business activities whereby an energy service company agrees on energy conservation objectives with an energy consumption entity in a contract, the energy services company provides necessary services, and the energy consumption entity pays from its savings resulting from energy conservation to the energy service company for the latter's investment and reasonable remuneration.	(2) 合同能源管理服务,是指节能服务公司与用能单位以契约形式约定节能目标,节能服务公司提供必要的服务,用能单位以节能效果支付节能服务公司投入及其合理报酬的业务活动。
(ⅲ) "Engineering prospecting and exploration services" means the business activities of conducting on-site investigation of topography, geological structure, and reserves of underground resources before and after mining or engineering construction.	(3) 工程勘察勘探服务,是指在采矿、工程施工前后,对地形、地质构造、地下资源蕴藏情况进行实地调查的业务活动。
(ⅳ) "Professional technological services" means meteorological services, seismic services, marine services, surveying services, urban planning, environment and ecological monitoring services and other special technical services.	(4) 专业技术服务,是指气象服务、地震服务、海洋服务、测绘服务、城市规划、环境与生态监测服务等专项技术服务。

Continued

English Translation	Chinese Version
(b)Information Technology Services	2.信息技术服务
"Information technology services" means the business activities of producing, collecting, disposing, processing, storing, transporting, searching and utilizing information through computers, communication networks or other technologies and providing information services, including software services, circuit designing and testing services, information system services, business process management services and value-added information system services.	信息技术服务,是指利用计算机、通信网络等技术对信息进行生产、收集、处理、加工、存储、运输、检索和利用,并提供信息服务的业务活动。包括软件服务、电路设计及测试服务、信息系统服务、业务流程管理服务和信息系统增值服务。
(ⅰ)"Software services" means the business activities of providing software development services, software maintenance services, and software testing services, among others.	(1)软件服务,是指提供软件开发服务、软件维护服务、软件测试服务的业务活动。
(ⅱ)"Circuit designing and testing services" means the business activities of providing integrated circuit and electronic circuit designing and testing and the relevant technical support services.	(2)电路设计及测试服务,是指提供集成电路和电子电路产品设计、测试及相关技术支持服务的业务活动。
(ⅲ)"Information system services" means the business activities of providing information system integration, network management, website content maintenance, desktop management and maintenance, information system application, integration of basic information technology management platforms, management of information technology infrastructures, data centers, hosting centers, information security services, online antivirus, and web hosting, etc., including network operation services offered by websites to a non-self-owned online games.	(3)信息系统服务,是指提供信息系统集成、网络管理、网站内容维护、桌面管理与维护、信息系统应用、基础信息技术管理平台整合、信息技术基础设施管理、数据中心、托管中心、信息安全服务、在线杀毒、虚拟主机等业务活动。包括网站对非自有的网络游戏提供的网络运营服务。
(ⅳ)"Business process management services" means the business activities of providing human resource management, financial and economic management, audit management, tax management, logistics information management, business information management, call centers and other services by relying on information technologies.	(4)业务流程管理服务,是指依托信息技术提供的人力资源管理、财务经济管理、审计管理、税务管理、物流信息管理、经营信息管理和呼叫中心等服务的活动。
(ⅴ)"Value-added information system services" means the additional information technology services provided to users by utilizing information system resources, including data processing, analysis and integration, database management, data backup, data storage, disaster recovery services, and e-commerce platform, etc.	(5)信息系统增值服务,是指利用信息系统资源为用户附加提供的信息技术服务。包括数据处理、分析和整合、数据库管理、数据备份、数据存储、容灾服务、电子商务平台等。

Continued

English Translation	Chinese Version
(c)Cultural and Creative Services	3.文化创意服务
"Cultural and creative services" includes design services, intellectual property services, advertising services as well as conference and exhibition services.	文化创意服务,包括设计服务、知识产权服务、广告服务和会议展览服务。
(ⅰ)"Design services" means the business activities of expressing plans, programs and conceptions through words, language, pictures, sound, vision and other forms, including industrial design, internal management design, business operation design, supply chain design, model design, costume design, environment design, graphic design, packaging design, animation design, online game design, exhibition design, website design, mechanical design, engineering design, advertisement design, creative design, and copying and blue print, etc.	(1)设计服务,是指把计划、规划、设想通过文字、语言、图画、声音、视觉等形式传递出来的业务活动。包括工业设计、内部管理设计、业务运作设计、供应链设计、造型设计、服装设计、环境设计、平面设计、包装设计、动漫设计、网游设计、展示设计、网站设计、机械设计、工程设计、广告设计、创意策划、文印晒图等。
(ⅱ)"Intellectual property services" means the business activities of handling intellectual property right affairs, including the registration, identification, appraisal, authentication, and retrieval services for patents, trademarks, copyrights, software, and integrated circuit layout designs.	(2)知识产权服务,是指处理知识产权事务的业务活动。包括对专利、商标、著作权、软件、集成电路布图设计的登记、鉴定、评估、认证、检索服务。
(ⅲ)"Advertising services" means the business activities of publicizing clients' commodities, operating service items, cultural and sports programs, announcements, statements, and other entrusted matters and providing relevant services in various forms, such as books, newspapers, magazines, broadcasting, television, movie, slide show, billboard, poster, showcase, neon light, lamp box, and Internet, etc., including advertising agency and the release, broadcasting, publicity, and exhibition, etc., of advertisements.	(3)广告服务,是指利用图书、报纸、杂志、广播、电视、电影、幻灯、路牌、招贴、橱窗、霓虹灯、灯箱、互联网等各种形式为客户的商品、经营服务项目、文体节目或者通告、声明等委托事项进行宣传和提供相关服务的业务活动。包括广告代理和广告的发布、播映、宣传、展示等。
(ⅳ)"Conference and exhibition services" means the business activities of holding or organizing and arranging various kinds of exhibitions and conferences for commodity circulation, sales promotion, exhibition, economic and trade talks, non-governmental exchanges, enterprise communication and international exchanges, etc.	(4)会议展览服务,是指为商品流通、促销、展示、经贸洽谈、民间交流、企业沟通、国际往来等举办或者组织安排的各类展览和会议的业务活动。
(d)Logistics Support Services	4.物流辅助服务

Continued

English Translation	Chinese Version
"Logistics support services" includes aviation services, port terminal services, cargo and passenger terminal services, salvage and rescue services, loading/unloading and handling services, warehousing services and collection and delivery services.	物流辅助服务,包括航空服务、港口码头服务、货运客运场站服务、打捞救助服务、装卸搬运服务、仓储服务和收派服务。
(ⅰ)"Aviation services" includes aviation ground services and general aviation services.	(1)航空服务,包括航空地面服务和通用航空服务。
"Aviation ground services" means the business activities of providing navigation and labor-related ground services by air liners, airports, civil aviation administrations and terminals, etc. to Chinese and foreign airplanes or other aircrafts which navigate within the territory of China or land in airports within the territory of China, including passenger security check services, parking apron management services, airport departure hall management services, airplane cleaning and disinfection services, flight management services, airplane movement services, airplane communication services, ground signal services, airplane safety services, airplane runway management services and air transportation management services, etc.	航空地面服务,是指航空公司、飞机场、民航管理局、航站等向在境内航行或者在境内机场停留的境内外飞机或者其他飞行器提供的导航等劳务性地面服务的业务活动。包括旅客安全检查服务、停机坪管理服务、机场候机厅管理服务、飞机清洗消毒服务、空中飞行管理服务、飞机起降服务、飞行通讯服务、地面信号服务、飞机安全服务、飞机跑道管理服务、空中交通管理服务等。
"General aviation services" means the business activities of providing flight services for professional work, including aerial photography, aviation training, aerial surveying, aerial prospecting, aerial forest fire fighting, aerial seeding and pesticide spraying, aerial artificial rain, aeronautical meteorological sounding, aviation marine monitoring, and aeronautical science experiments, etc.	通用航空服务,是指为专业工作提供飞行服务的业务活动,包括航空摄影、航空培训、航空测量、航空勘探、航空护林、航空吊挂播洒、航空降雨、航空气象探测、航空海洋监测、航空科学实验等。
(ⅱ)"Port terminal services" means the business activities of vessel dispatching services at ports, vessel communication services, waterway management services, waterway dredging services, lighthouse management services, navigation mark management services, shipping pilot services, tallying services, mooring and unmooring services, berthing and berth shifting services, cleaning of vessel oil spilt on the sea, water transportation management services, professional vessel cleaning, disinfection and testing services, vessel oil spill prevention services, and other services for vessels.	(2)港口码头服务,是指港务船舶调度服务、船舶通讯服务、航道管理服务、航道疏浚服务、灯塔管理服务、航标管理服务、船舶引航服务、理货服务、系解缆服务、停泊和移泊服务、海上船舶溢油清除服务、水上交通管理服务、船只专业清洗消毒检测服务和防止船只漏油服务等为船只提供服务的业务活动。

Continued

English Translation	Chinese Version
The VAT on port facility security fees charged by port facility operators shall be paid according to the rate for port terminal services.	港口设施经营人收取的港口设施保安费按照港口码头服务缴纳增值税。
(ⅲ)"Cargo and passenger terminal services" means the business activities of providing cargo stowage services, transportation organization services, transit and transfer services, vehicle dispatching services, ticket services, cargo packing and reconditioning services, railway line use services, passenger carriage addition services, special railway luggage and parcel delivery services, railway arrival and transfer services, railcar connection and disconnection services, vehicle addition services, railway overhead contact system services, railway locomotive traction services, and other services by cargo and passenger terminals.	(3)货运客运场站服务,是指货运客运场站提供货物配载服务、运输组织服务、中转换乘服务、车辆调度服务、票务服务、货物打包整理、铁路线路使用服务、加挂铁路客车服务、铁路行包专列发送服务、铁路到达和中转服务、铁路车辆编解服务、车辆挂运服务、铁路接触网服务、铁路机车牵引服务等业务活动。
(ⅳ)"Salvage and rescue services" means the business activities of providing vessel personnel rescue, vessel property salvage, marine salvage, and sunken ship and article salvage services.	(4)打捞救助服务,是指提供船舶人员救助、船舶财产救助、水上救助和沉船沉物打捞服务的业务活动。
(ⅴ)"Loading/unloading and handling services" means the business activities of loading/unloading and handling of cargo between means of transportation, between loading and unloading sites, or between means of transportation and loading and unloading sites by using loading/unloading and handling tools, manpower, or animal power.	(5)装卸搬运服务,是指使用装卸搬运工具或者人力、畜力将货物在运输工具之间、装卸现场之间或者运输工具与装卸现场之间进行装卸和搬运的业务活动。
(ⅵ)"Warehousing services" means the business activities of storage and safekeeping of goods in warehouses, goods yards, or other places for customers.	(6)仓储服务,是指利用仓库、货场或者其他场所代客贮放、保管货物的业务活动。
(ⅶ)"Collection and delivery services" means the business activities of completing the services of collection, sorting, and delivery of correspondence and parcels during a promised period as consigned by the sender.	(7)收派服务,是指接受寄件人委托,在承诺的时限内完成函件和包裹的收件、分拣、派送服务的业务活动。
"Collection services" means the business activities of collecting correspondence and parcels from the sender and conveying the same to the distribution center of the service provider in the same city.	收件服务,是指从寄件人收取函件和包裹,并运送到服务提供方同城的集散中心的业务活动。
"Sorting services" means the business activities of classification and distribution of correspondence and parcels by the service provider at its distribution center.	分拣服务,是指服务提供方在其集散中心对函件和包裹进行归类、分发的业务活动。

Continued

English Translation	Chinese Version
"Delivery services" means the business activities whereby a service provider delivers correspondence and parcels to the recipient in the same city from its distribution center.	派送服务,是指服务提供方从其集散中心将函件和包裹送达同城的收件人的业务活动。
(e)Leasing Services	5.租赁服务
"Leasing services" includes financial leasing services and operating leasing services.	租赁服务,包括融资租赁服务和经营租赁服务。
(ⅰ)"Financial leasing services" means the leasing activities characterized by financing and transfer of ownership, that is, the lessor purchases any tangible movable property or immovable property and leases it to the lessee according to the specifications, model, performance and other conditions as required by the lessee; the lessor owns, and the lessee only has the right to use, the tangible movable property or immovable property during the term of the contract; and, after paying off the rentals upon the expiry of the contract, the lessee is entitled to purchasing the tangible movable property or immovable property at its residual value to own the property. It is financial leasing whether the lessor sells the tangible movable property or immovable property to the lessee or not.	(1)融资租赁服务,是指具有融资性质和所有权转移特点的租赁活动。即出租人根据承租人所要求的规格、型号、性能等条件购入有形动产或者不动产租赁给承租人,合同期内租赁物所有权属于出租人,承租人只拥有使用权,合同期满付清租金后,承租人有权按照残值购入租赁物,以拥有其所有权。不论出租人是否将租赁物销售给承租人,均属于融资租赁。
According to different subject matters, financial leasing services may be divided into the services of financial leasing of tangible movable property and the services of financial leasing of immovable property.	按照标的物的不同,融资租赁服务可分为有形动产融资租赁服务和不动产融资租赁服务。
The VAT on financing sale and leaseback shall not be paid under this tax item.	融资性售后回租不按照本税目缴纳增值税。
(ⅱ)"Operating leasing services" means the business activities of transferring tangible movable property or immovable property to others for use during an agreed period without changing the ownership of the leased property.	(2)经营租赁服务,是指在约定时间内将有形动产或者不动产转让他人使用且租赁物所有权不变更的业务活动。
According to different subject matters, financial leasing services may be divided into the services of operating leasing of tangible movable property and the services of operating leasing of immovable property.	按照标的物的不同,经营租赁服务可分为有形动产经营租赁服务和不动产经营租赁服务。

Continued

English Translation	Chinese Version
The VAT on the leasing of the advertising space for such immovable properties as buildings and structures or such tangible movable properties as airplanes and vehicles to other entities or individuals for publishing advertisements shall be paid according to the rate for operating leasing services.	将建筑物、构筑物等不动产或者飞机、车辆等有形动产的广告位出租给其他单位或者个人用于发布广告,按照经营租赁服务缴纳增值税。
The VAT on vehicle parking services, road traffic services (including tolls, bridge tolls, and lockage fees, etc.) shall be paid according to the rate for the services for the operating leasing of immovable properties.	车辆停放服务、道路通行服务(包括过路费、过桥费、过闸费等)等按照不动产经营租赁服务缴纳增值税。
The bareboat charter business in waterway transportation and dry-lease business in air transportation fall within the scope of operating leasing.	水路运输的光租业务、航空运输的干租业务,属于经营租赁。
"Bareboat charter business" means the business activity whereby a transportation enterprise leases a vessel equipped with no operators to another party for use during an agreed period, and only collects fixed rentals, without assuming various expenses incurred during the transportation.	光租业务,是指运输企业将船舶在约定的时间内出租给他人使用,不配备操作人员,不承担运输过程中发生的各项费用,只收取固定租赁费的业务活动。
"Dry-lease business" means the business activity whereby an air transportation enterprise leases an unstaffed airplane to another party for use during an agreed period, and only collects fixed rentals, without assuming the expenses incurred during the transportation.	干租业务,是指航空运输企业将飞机在约定的时间内出租给他人使用,不配备机组人员,不承担运输过程中发生的各项费用,只收取固定租赁费的业务活动。
(f) Attestation and Consultation Services	6.鉴证咨询服务
"Attestation and consultation services" includes certification services, attestation services, and consultation services.	鉴证咨询服务,包括认证服务、鉴证服务和咨询服务。
(i) "Certification services" means the business activities whereby entities with professional qualifications certify the compliance of products, services and management systems with the relevant technical specifications and the compulsory requirements or standards thereof by inspection, testing, measurement and other technologies.	(1)认证服务,是指具有专业资质的单位利用检测、检验、计量等技术,证明产品、服务、管理体系符合相关技术规范、相关技术规范的强制性要求或者标准的业务活动。

Continued

English Translation	Chinese Version
(ii)"Attestation services" means the business activities whereby entities with professional qualifications are entrusted with the attestation of relevant matters to issue opinions with a probative force, including accounting attestation, taxation attestation, legal attestation, occupational technical ability appraisal, project cost attestation, project supervision, assets appraisal, environmental assessment, real estate land evaluation, construction drawing review, and medical malpractice identification, etc.	(2)鉴证服务,是指具有专业资质的单位受托对相关事项进行鉴证,发表具有证明力的意见的业务活动。包括会计鉴证、税务鉴证、法律鉴证、职业技能鉴定、工程造价鉴证、工程监理、资产评估、环境评估、房地产土地评估、建筑图纸审核、医疗事故鉴定等。
(iii)"Consultation services" means the business activities of providing information, suggestions, plans, consultation and other services, including the consultation in such aspects as finance, software, technology, financial affairs, taxation, law, internal management, business operation, process management, and health, etc.	(3)咨询服务,是指提供信息、建议、策划、顾问等服务的活动。包括金融、软件、技术、财务、税收、法律、内部管理、业务运作、流程管理、健康等方面的咨询。
The VAT on translation services and market research services shall be paid according to the rate for consultation services.	翻译服务和市场调查服务按照咨询服务缴纳增值税。
(g)Radio, Film and Television Services	7.广播影视服务
"Radio, film and television services" includes services for the production, distribution and broadcasting of radio, film, and television programs (or works).	广播影视服务,包括广播影视节目(作品)的制作服务、发行服务和播映(含放映,下同)服务。
(i)"Services for the production of radio, film, and television programs (or works)" means the services for the production of special topics (or special programs), special columns, variety shows, sports, cartoons, radio plays, teleplays, movies, and other radio, film, and television programs and works, including the planning, collecting and editing, filming, recording, production of audio/video text and picture materials, scene layout, post-cutting, translation (or translation and editing), subtitling, production of titles, credits, and trailers, special effect production, film fix, cataloging, and confirmation of rights, etc. related to radio, film, and television programs and works.	(1)广播影视节目(作品)制作服务,是指进行专题(特别节目)、专栏、综艺、体育、动画片、广播剧、电视剧、电影等广播影视节目和作品制作的服务。具体包括与广播影视节目和作品相关的策划、采编、拍摄、录音、音视频文字图片素材制作、场景布置、后期的剪辑、翻译(编译)、字幕制作,片头、片尾、片花制作,特效制作,影片修复,编目和确权等业务活动。

Continued

English Translation	Chinese Version
(ⅱ)"Services for the distribution of radio, film, and television programs (or works)" means the business activities of distributing radio, film, and television programs (or works) and transferring the rights to report and broadcast sporting events and other activities to cinemas, radio stations, television stations, websites, and other entities and individuals in such a manner as box office split, buy-out, or commission.	(2)广播影视节目(作品)发行服务,是指以分账、买断、委托等方式,向影院、电台、电视台、网站等单位和个人发行广播影视节目(作品)以及转让体育赛事等活动的报道及播映权的业务活动。
(ⅲ)"Services for the broadcasting of radio, film, and television programs (or works)" means the business activities of broadcasting radio, film, and television programs (or works) in cinemas, theatres, video halls, and other venues or through radio stations, television stations, satellite communications, Internet, cable television, and other wireless or wired devices.	(3)广播影视节目(作品)播映服务,是指在影院、剧院、录像厅及其他场所播映广播影视节目(作品),以及通过电台、电视台、卫星通信、互联网、有线电视等无线或者有线装置播映广播影视节目(作品)的业务活动。
(h)Business Support Services	8.商务辅助服务
"Business support services" includes enterprise management services, brokerage and agency services, human resource services, and security protection services.	商务辅助服务,包括企业管理服务、经纪代理服务、人力资源服务、安全保护服务。
(ⅰ)"Enterprise management services" means the business activities of providing headquarters management, investment and asset management, market management, property management, comprehensive daily management and other services.	(1)企业管理服务,是指提供总部管理、投资与资产管理、市场管理、物业管理、日常综合管理等服务的业务活动。
(ⅱ)"Brokerage and agency services" means all types of brokerage, intermediary and agency services, including financial agency, intellectual property agency, freight forwarding, customs declaration agency, legal representation, real estate intermediary agency, employment intermediary agency, marriage intermediary agency, agent bookkeeping, and auction, etc.	(2)经纪代理服务,是指各类经纪、中介、代理服务。包括金融代理、知识产权代理、货物运输代理、代理报关、法律代理、房地产中介、职业中介、婚姻中介、代理记账、拍卖等。
"Freight forwarding services" means the business activities of handling relevant formalities for the freightage, loading and unloading, storage, port entry and departure of a vessel, pilotage and berthing, etc., as an agent of the consignee or the consignor of goods, or the owner, charterer, or operator of the vessel, for theconsignor and in the name of the consignor.	货物运输代理服务,是指接受货物收货人、发货人、船舶所有人、船舶承租人或者船舶经营人的委托,以委托人的名义,为委托人办理货物运输、装卸、仓储和船舶进出港口、引航、靠泊等相关手续的业务活动。

Continued

English Translation	Chinese Version
"Customs declaration agency services" means the business activities of agency handling of customs declaration formalities as entrusted by the consignee or consignor of imported or exported goods.	代理报关服务,是指接受进出口货物的收、发货人委托,代为办理报关手续的业务活动。
(ⅲ)"Human resources services" means the business activities of public employment, labor dispatch, commissioned talent recruitment, labor outsourcing and other services.	(3)人力资源服务,是指提供公共就业、劳务派遣、人才委托招聘、劳动力外包等服务的业务活动。
(ⅳ)"Security protection services" means the business activities of providing services for protecting personal safety and property security, and maintaining social order, among others, including place and residence security protection, special security, security system monitoring, and other security protection services.	(4)安全保护服务,是指提供保护人身安全和财产安全,维护社会治安等的业务活动。包括场所住宅保安、特种保安、安全系统监控以及其他安保服务。
(I) Other Modern Services	9.其他现代服务
"Other modern services" means the modern services other than research and development and technical services, information technology services, cultural and creative services, logistics support services, leasing services, attestation and consultation services, radio, film and television services, and business support services.	其他现代服务,是指除研发和技术服务、信息技术服务、文化创意服务、物流辅助服务、租赁服务、鉴证咨询服务、广播影视服务和商务辅助服务以外的现代服务。
(7)Living Services	(七)生活服务
"Living services" means various services provided for the purpose of meeting the needs of urban and rural residents' daily life, including cultural and sports services, education and medical services, tourism and entertainment services, catering and accommodation services, residents' daily services and other living services.	生活服务,是指为满足城乡居民日常生活需求提供的各类服务活动。包括文化体育服务、教育医疗服务、旅游娱乐服务、餐饮住宿服务、居民日常服务和其他生活服务。
(a)Cultural and Sports Services	1.文化体育服务
"Cultural and sports services" includes cultural services and sports services.	文化体育服务,包括文化服务和体育服务。

Continued

English Translation	Chinese Version
（ⅰ）"Cultural services" means the various services provided for the purpose of meeting the needs of the cultural life of the general public，including literary and artistic creations，artistic performances，cultural competitions，borrowing of books and reference materials from libraries，administration of the archives in archival repositories，protection of cultural relics and intangible heritages，organization and holding of religious activities，scientific and technological activities，cultural activities，and the provision of tourist sites.	（1）文化服务，是指为满足社会公众文化生活需求提供的各种服务。包括：文艺创作、文艺表演、文化比赛，图书馆的图书和资料借阅，档案馆的档案管理，文物及非物质遗产保护，组织举办宗教活动、科技活动、文化活动，提供游览场所。
（ⅱ）"Sports services" means the business activities of organizing and holding sports competitions，sports performances，and sports activities，and providing sports trainings，sports guidance and sports management.	（2）体育服务，是指组织举办体育比赛、体育表演、体育活动，以及提供体育训练、体育指导、体育管理的业务活动。
（b）Educational and Medical Services	2.教育医疗服务
"Educational and medical services" includes educational services and medical services.	教育医疗服务，包括教育服务和医疗服务。
（ⅰ）"Educational services" means the business activities of providing academic education services，non-academic education services，and educational support services.	（1）教育服务，是指提供学历教育服务、非学历教育服务、教育辅助服务的业务活动。
"Academic education services" means the business activities of the organization of teaching according to the enrollment and teaching programs determined or recognized by the administrative departments of education and the issuance of corresponding academic certificates，including elementary education，junior secondary education，senior secondary education，and higher education，etc.	学历教育服务，是指根据教育行政管理部门确定或者认可的招生和教学计划组织教学，并颁发相应学历证书的业务活动。包括初等教育、初级中等教育、高级中等教育、高等教育等。
"Non-academic education services" includes preprimary education and various trainings，speeches，lectures and seminars，etc.	非学历教育服务，包括学前教育、各类培训、演讲、讲座、报告会等。
"Educational support services" includes education appraisal，examination，enrollment and other services.	教育辅助服务，包括教育测评、考试、招生等服务。

Continued

English Translation	Chinese Version
(ⅱ)"Medical services" means the services in such aspects as medical examination, diagnosis, treatment, rehabilitation, prevention, health care, child delivery, family planning, and epidemic services, and the business of providing drugs, medical materials and appliances, ambulance, patient accommodation and catering services related to these services.	(2)医疗服务,是指提供医学检查、诊断、治疗、康复、预防、保健、接生、计划生育、防疫服务等方面的服务,以及与这些服务有关的提供药品、医用材料器具、救护车、病房住宿和伙食的业务。
(c)Tourism and Entertainment services	3.旅游娱乐服务
"Tourism and entertainment services" include tourism services and entertainment services.	旅游娱乐服务,包括旅游服务和娱乐服务。
(ⅰ)"Tourism services" means the business activities of organizing and arranging traffic, sightseeing, accommodation, catering, shopping, cultural recreation, business and other services.	(1)旅游服务,是指根据旅游者的要求,组织安排交通、游览、住宿、餐饮、购物、文娱、商务等服务的业务活动。
(ⅱ)"Entertainment services" means the business activity of concurrently providing sites and services for recreational activities.	(2)娱乐服务,是指为娱乐活动同时提供场所和服务的业务。
Specifically including: cabarets, ballrooms, nightclubs, bars, billiards, golf, bowling, and recreation (including shooting, hunting, horse racing, game machines, bungee jumping, karts, fire balloons, powered parachute, archery and darts).	具体包括:歌厅、舞厅、夜总会、酒吧、台球、高尔夫球、保龄球、游艺(包括射击、狩猎、跑马、游戏机、蹦极、卡丁车、热气球、动力伞、射箭、飞镖)。
(d)Catering and Accommodation Services	4.餐饮住宿服务
"Catering and accommodation services" include catering services and accommodation services.	餐饮住宿服务,包括餐饮服务和住宿服务。
(ⅰ)"Catering services" means the business activities of providing customers with catering consumption services through concurrently offering food and places for eating.	(1)餐饮服务,是指通过同时提供饮食和饮食场所的方式为消费者提供饮食消费服务的业务活动。
(ⅱ)"Accommodation services" means the activities of providing accommodations and supporting services, etc., including hotels, guest houses, hostels, resorts and other commercial accommodations.	(2)住宿服务,是指提供住宿场所及配套服务等的活动。包括宾馆、旅馆、旅社、度假村和其他经营性住宿场所提供的住宿服务。
(e)Residents' Daily Services	5.居民日常服务

Continued

English Translation	Chinese Version
"Residents' daily services" means the services provided mainly for meeting the daily living needs of individual residents and their families, including city appearance and municipal administration, housekeeping, wedding celebration, pension, funeral and interment, care and nursing, relief assistance, hairdressing and beauty, massage, sauna, oxygen bar, foot massage, bath, washing and dying, photographic enlargements and other services.	居民日常服务,是指主要为满足居民个人及其家庭日常生活需求提供的服务,包括市容市政管理、家政、婚庆、养老、殡葬、照料和护理、救助救济、美容美发、按摩、桑拿、氧吧、足疗、沐浴、洗染、摄影扩印等服务。
(f)Other Living Services	6.其他生活服务
"Other living services" means the living services other than cultural and sports services, educational and medical services, tourism and entertainment services, catering and accommodation services and residents' daily services.	其他生活服务,是指除文化体育服务、教育医疗服务、旅游娱乐服务、餐饮住宿服务和居民日常服务之外的生活服务。
II. Sales of Intangible Assets	二、销售无形资产
"Sales of intangible assets" means the business activities of transferring the ownership of or the right to use intangible assets. "Intangible assets" means the assets that are not in physical form but can bring about economic benefits, including the rights to use technologies, trademarks, copyrights, business reputation, natural resources and other equity intangible assets.	销售无形资产,是指转让无形资产所有权或者使用权的业务活动。无形资产,是指不具实物形态,但能带来经济利益的资产,包括技术、商标、著作权、商誉、自然资源使用权和其他权益性无形资产。
"Technologies" includes patent technologies and non-patent technologies.	技术,包括专利技术和非专利技术。
"Rights to use natural resources" includes the rights to use land, the rights to use sea areas, exploration rights, mining rights, water-drawing rights, and the rights to use other natural resources.	自然资源使用权,包括土地使用权、海域使用权、探矿权、采矿权、取水权和其他自然资源使用权。
"Other equity intangible assets" includes the rights to operate infrastructure assets, public utility concessions, quotas, management rights (including franchised management rights, chain management rights and other management rights), dealership, distribution rights, power of agency, membership rights, seat right, virtual props of online games, domain names, name rights, portrait rights, naming rights, and transfer fees, etc.	其他权益性无形资产,包括基础设施资产经营权、公共事业特许权、配额、经营权(包括特许经营权、连锁经营权、其他经营权)、经销权、分销权、代理权、会员权、席位权、网络游戏虚拟道具、域名、名称权、肖像权、冠名权、转会费等。
III. Sales of Immovable Properties	三、销售不动产

Continued

English Translation	Chinese Version
"Sales of immovable property" means the business activities of transferring the ownership of immovable property. "Immovable property" means the property which are immovable or the natures or shapes of which will change after being moved, including buildings and structures, etc.	销售不动产,是指转让不动产所有权的业务活动。不动产,是指不能移动或者移动后会引起性质、形状改变的财产,包括建筑物、构筑物等。
"Buildings" includes residences, commercial business buildings, office buildings and other buildings available for living, work or other activities.	建筑物,包括住宅、商业营业用房、办公楼等可供居住、工作或者进行其他活动的建造物。
"Structures" includes roads, bridges, tunnels, dams and other constructions.	构筑物,包括道路、桥梁、隧道、水坝等建造物。
The VAT on the transfer of the limited property rights or permanent rights to use buildings, the transfer of the ownership of the buildings or structures under construction, or the concurrent transfer of the rights to use the land occupied by any buildings or structures when such buildings or structures are transferred shall be paid according to the rate for the sale of immovable properties.	转让建筑物有限产权或者永久使用权的,转让在建的建筑物或者构筑物所有权的,以及在转让建筑物或者构筑物时一并转让其所占土地的使用权的,按照销售不动产缴纳增值税。
Annex 2	附件 2
Provisions on Matters Concerning the Pilot Program of Replacing Business Tax with value-added tax	营业税改征增值税试点有关事项的规定
I. During the implementation of the pilot program of replacing business tax with value-added tax (VAT) (hereinafter referred to as the "pilot program"), relevant policies on pilot taxpayers [meaning taxpayers which pay value-added tax ("VAT") in accordance with the Measures for Implementing the Pilot Program of Replacing Business Tax with value-added tax, hereinafter referred to as the "Measures for Implementing the Pilot Program")	一、营改增试点期间,试点纳税人[指按照《营业税改征增值税试点实施办法》(以下称《试点实施办法》)缴纳增值税的纳税人]有关政策
1. Concurrent Operations	(一)兼营
A pilot taxpayer that sells goods or provides processing, repair, or maintenance labor and services, intangible assets or immovable properties to which different tax rates or levy rates apply shall calculate respectively the sales amounts to which different tax rates or levy rates apply; otherwise, the applicable tax rates or levy rates shall be as follows:	试点纳税人销售货物、加工修配劳务、服务、无形资产或者不动产适用不同税率或者征收率的,应当分别核算适用不同税率或者征收率的销售额,未分别核算销售额的,按照以下方法适用税率或者征收率:

Continued

English Translation	Chinese Version
(1)In the case of selling goods or providing processing, repair, or maintenance labor or services, intangible assets or immovable properties to which different tax rates apply, the highest of the tax rates shall apply.	1.兼有不同税率的销售货物、加工修理修配劳务、服务、无形资产或者不动产,从高适用税率。
(2)In the case of selling goods or providing processing, repair, or maintenance labor or services, intangible assets or immovable properties to which different levy rates apply, the highest of the levy rates shall apply.	2.兼有不同征收率的销售货物、加工修理修配劳务、服务、无形资产或者不动产,从高适用征收率。
(3)In the case of selling goods or providing goods or providing processing, repair, or maintenance labor or services, intangible assets or immovable properties to which different tax rates and levy rates apply, the highest of the tax rates shall apply.	3.兼有不同税率和征收率的销售货物、加工修理修配劳务、服务、无形资产或者不动产,从高适用税率。
2. Items Not Subject to VAT	(二)不征收增值税项目
(1)Railway transportation services and air transportation services provided free of charge under instructions from the state, which fall within the scope of the services for the public good as set out in Article 14 of the Measures for Implementing the Pilot Program.	1.根据国家指令无偿提供的铁路运输服务、航空运输服务,属于《试点实施办法》第十四条规定的用于公益事业的服务。
(2)Interest on deposits.	2.存款利息。
(3)Insurance compensation obtained by the insured.	3.被保险人获得的保险赔付。
(4)Special maintenance funds for residential properties collected by real estate administrative departments or the institutions, housing provident fund management centers, developers or property management entities designated by them on behalf of taxpayers.	4.房地产主管部门或者其指定机构、公积金管理中心、开发企业以及物业管理单位代收的住宅专项维修资金。
(5) The transfer of immovable properties or land use right involved in the process of asset restructuring, where all or part of the physical assets of a taxpayer and the creditor's rights, liabilities and labor force associated therewith are transferred multiple times by means such as merger, split, sale, and swap.	5.在资产重组过程中,通过合并、分立、出售、置换等方式,将全部或者部分实物资产以及与其相关联的债权、负债和劳动力一并转让给其他单位和个人,其中涉及的不动产、土地使用权转让行为。
3. Sales Amount	(三)销售额
(1)The sales amount of loan services shall be the total interest and income of an interest nature obtained from the provision of loans services.	1.贷款服务,以提供贷款服务取得的全部利息及利息性质的收入为销售额。

Continued

English Translation	Chinese Version
(2) The sales amount of financial services with direct charges shall be the various expenses collected for the provision of financial services with direct charges, i.e., handling charges, commissions, fees, management fees, service fees, processing fees, fees for opening accounts, transfer fees, settlement fees and custodian fees, etc.	2.直接收费金融服务,以提供直接收费金融服务收取的手续费、佣金、酬金、管理费、服务费、经手费、开户费、过户费、结算费、转托管费等各类费用为销售额。
(3) In the transfer of financial products, the sales amount of such products shall be the balance of the selling price thereof minus the purchase price thereof.	3.金融商品转让,按照卖出价扣除买入价后的余额为销售额。
For the positive and negative balances in the transfer of financial products, the sales amount of such products is the balance after offsetting losses against profits. Where there is still a negative balance after offsetting, it may be carried forward to the next tax payment period for offsetting against the sales amount of the financial products to be transferred in the next period; however, where there is still a negative balance at the end of the year, it may not be carried forward to the next fiscal year.	转让金融商品出现的正负差,按盈亏相抵后的余额为销售额。若相抵后出现负差,可结转下一纳税期与下期转让金融商品销售额相抵,但年末时仍出现负差的,不得转入下一个会计年度。
The purchase price of financial products may choose to be calculated by the weighted average method or the moving weighted average method, and once the method is chosen, the method shall not be changed within 36 months.	金融商品的买入价,可以选择按照加权平均法或者移动加权平均法进行核算,选择后 36 个月内不得变更。
No special VAT invoice shall be issued for the transfer of financial products.	金融商品转让,不得开具增值税专用发票。
(4) The sales amount of brokerage services shall be the balance of the full prices and ex-price charges obtained minus the contributions to a governmental fund or administrative charges collected from and paid on behalf of a client. No special VAT invoice shall be issued for the contributions to a governmental fund or administrative charges collected from a client.	4.经纪代理服务,以取得的全部价款和价外费用,扣除向委托方收取并代为支付的政府性基金或者行政事业性收费后的余额为销售额。向委托方收取的政府性基金或者行政事业性收费,不得开具增值税专用发票。
(5) Financial leasing and financing sale and leaseback.	5.融资租赁和融资性售后回租业务。

Continued

English Translation	Chinese Version
(a) Where a pilot taxpayer engaged in financial leasing as approved by the People's Bank of China, the China Banking Regulatory Commission, or the Ministry of Commerce provides the services of financial leasing, the sales amount of such services shall be the balance of the full prices and ex-price charges obtained by the taxpayer minus the paid loan interest (including interest on both foreign exchange loans and RMB loans), interest on bonds issued, and vehicle purchase tax.	(1)经人民银行、银监会或者商务部批准从事融资租赁业务的试点纳税人,提供融资租赁服务,以取得的全部价款和价外费用,扣除支付的借款利息(包括外汇借款和人民币借款利息)、发行债券利息和车辆购置税后的余额为销售额。
(b) Where a pilot taxpayer engaged in financial leasing as approved by the People's Bank of China, the China Banking Regulatory Commission, or the Ministry of Commerce provides financing services of sale and lease-back, the sales amount of such services shall be the balance of the full prices and ex-price charges (excluding the principle) obtained by the taxpayer minus the loan interest paid (including interest on both foreign exchange and RMB loans) and interest on bonds issued.	(2)经人民银行、银监会或者商务部批准从事融资租赁业务的试点纳税人,提供融资性售后回租服务,以取得的全部价款和价外费用(不含本金),扣除对外支付的借款利息(包括外汇借款和人民币借款利息)、发行债券利息后的余额作为销售额。
(c) Where a pilot taxpayer provides financing services of sale and leaseback of tangible personal property prior to the expiry of the contract on the financing sale and leaseback of the tangible personal property concluded before April 30, 2016, it may continue to pay VAT according to the rate of services of financial leasing of tangible personal property.	(3)试点纳税人根据 2016 年 4 月 30 日前签订的有形动产融资性售后回租合同,在合同到期前提供的有形动产融资性售后回租服务,可继续按照有形动产融资租赁服务缴纳增值税。
Where a pilot taxpayer continuing to pay VAT according to the rate of services of financial leasing of tangible personal property is engaged in financial leasing as approved by the People's Bank of China, the China Banking Regulatory Commission, or the Ministry of Commerce, for the financing services of sale and leaseback of tangible personal property provided by the pilot taxpayer prior to the expiry of the contract on the financing sale and leaseback of the tangible personal property concluded before April 30, 2016, the sales amount shall be calculated under the any of the following methods:	继续按照有形动产融资租赁服务缴纳增值税的试点纳税人,经人民银行、银监会或者商务部批准从事融资租赁业务的,根据 2016 年 4 月 30 日前签订的有形动产融资性售后回租合同,在合同到期前提供的有形动产融资性售后回租服务,可以选择以下方法之一计算销售额:

Continued

English Translation	Chinese Version
（ⅰ）The sales amount of such services shall be the balance of the full prices and ex-price charges collected from the lessee minus the purchase price collected from the lessee, and the paid loan interest (including interest on both foreign exchange and RMB loans) and interest on bonds issued.	①以向承租方收取的全部价款和价外费用,扣除向承租方收取的价款本金,以及对外支付的借款利息(包括外汇借款和人民币借款利息)、发行债券利息后的余额为销售额。
Where a taxpayer provides financing services of sale and leaseback of tangible personal property, the purchase price for tangible personal property that may be deducted in the calculation of the sales amount during the current period shall be the principal to be collected during the current period as agreed upon in a written contract. Where there is no written contract or there is no agreement in the written contract, it shall be the principal actually collected during the current period.	纳税人提供有形动产融资性售后回租服务,计算当期销售额时可以扣除的价款本金,为书面合同约定的当期应当收取的本金。无书面合同或者书面合同没有约定的,为当期实际收取的本金。
Where the pilot taxpayer provides financing services of sale and leaseback of tangible personal property, no special VAT invoice shall be issued for the purchase price for tangible personal property collected from a lessee, but plain voices may be issued.	试点纳税人提供有形动产融资性售后回租服务,向承租方收取的有形动产价款本金,不得开具增值税专用发票,可以开具普通发票。
（ⅱ）The sales amount of such services shall be the balance of the full prices and ex-price charges collected from the lessee minus the externally paid loan interest (including interest on both foreign exchange and RMB loans) and interest on bonds issued.	②以向承租方收取的全部价款和价外费用,扣除支付的借款利息(包括外汇借款和人民币借款利息)、发行债券利息后的余额为销售额。
(d)If the paid-in capital of a pilot taxpayer engaged in financing leasing as approved by a provincial commerce department or a state-level economic and technological development zone authorized by the Ministry of Commerce reaches 170 million yuan before May 1, 2016, the above items (a), (b) and (c) shall apply from the current month when the paid-in capital reaches the threshold; if the paid-in capital thereof has not reached 170 million yuan but the registered capital thereof reaches 170 million yuan after May 1, 2016, the above items (a), (b) and (c) shall apply before July 31, 2016, but the financial leasing and financing sale and leaseback business conducted after August 1, 2016 shall not be governed by the above items (a), (b) and (c).	(4)经商务部授权的省级商务主管部门和国家经济技术开发区批准的从事融资租赁业务的试点纳税人,2016 年 5 月 1 日后实收资本达到 1.7 亿元的,从达到标准的当月起按照上述第(1)、(2)、(3)点规定执行;2016 年 5 月 1 日后实收资本未达到 1.7 亿元但注册资本达到 1.7 亿元的,在 2016 年 7 月 31 日前仍可按照上述第(1)、(2)、(3)点规定执行,2016 年 8 月 1 日后开展的融资租赁业务和融资性售后回租业务不得按照上述第(1)、(2)、(3)点规定执行。

Continued

English Translation	Chinese Version
(6) The sales amount of an air transportation enterprise shall exclude the airport construction fees collected by it as an agent and passenger ticket prices of other air transportation enterprises collected by it as an agent, which are transferred to the principal after collection.	6.航空运输企业的销售额,不包括代收的机场建设费和代售其他航空运输企业客票而代收转付的价款。
(7) Where a pilot taxpayer which is a general taxpayer (hereinafter referred to as a general taxpayer) provides passenger terminal services, the sales amount of such services shall be the balance of the full prices andex-price charges it obtained minus the freight paid to the carrier.	7.试点纳税人中的一般纳税人(以下称一般纳税人)提供客运场站服务,以其取得的全部价款和价外费用,扣除支付给承运方运费后的余额为销售额。
(8) Where a pilot taxpayer provides tourist services, the sales amount of such services may be the balance of the full prices and ex-price charges it obtained minus the costs of accommodations, meals, transportation, visa, and admission tickets collected from the purchaser of tourist services and paid to other entities or individuals and the travel expenses paid to other tourist enterprises receiving tours.	8.试点纳税人提供旅游服务,可以选择以取得的全部价款和价外费用,扣除向旅游服务购买方收取并支付给其他单位或者个人的住宿费、餐饮费、交通费、签证费、门票费和支付给其他接团旅游企业的旅游费用后的余额为销售额。
Where a pilot taxpayer chooses to calculate the sales amount by the aforesaid method, no special VAT invoices shall be issued for the aforesaid costs collected from and paid on behalf of the purchaser of tourist services, but plain invoices may be issued for such costs.	选择上述办法计算销售额的试点纳税人,向旅游服务购买方收取并支付的上述费用,不得开具增值税专用发票,可以开具普通发票。
(9) Where a pilot taxpayer calculates tax by the simple tax computation method on its provision of construction services, the sales amount of such services shall be the balance of the full prices and ex-price charges it obtained minus the subcontracting fees paid.	9.试点纳税人提供建筑服务适用简易计税方法的,以取得的全部价款和价外费用扣除支付的分包款后的余额为销售额。
(10) A real estate developer which is a general taxpayer sells any real estate project it develops (excluding any old real estate project for which it choose to calculate tax by the simple tax computation method), the sales amount of such a project shall be the balance of the full prices and ex-price charges it obtained minus the land price paid to a government department when the land is assigned.	10.房地产开发企业中的一般纳税人销售其开发的房地产项目(选择简易计税方法的房地产老项目除外),以取得的全部价款和价外费用,扣除受让土地时向政府部门支付的土地价款后的余额为销售额。

Continued

English Translation	Chinese Version
An "old construction project" means a construction project for which the Construction Permit for Construction Projects indicates that the commencement date of the contract is before 30 April 2016.	房地产老项目,是指《建筑工程施工许可证》注明的合同开工日期在2016年4月30日前的房地产项目。
(11) To deduct any payments from the full prices and ex-price charges in accordance with the above items (4) through (10), a pilot taxpayer shall obtain valid vouchers issued in accordance with laws, administrative Regulation, and the relevant provisions of the State Administration of Taxation; otherwise, no deduction is allowed.	11.试点纳税人按照上述4—10款的规定从全部价款和价外费用中扣除的价款,应当取得符合法律、行政法规和国家税务总局规定的有效凭证。否则,不得扣除。
The aforesaid "vouchers" means:	上述凭证是指:
(a) For payments made to entities or individuals within China, invoices are the legal and valid vouchers.	(1)支付给境内单位或者个人的款项,以发票为合法有效凭证。
(b) For payments made to entities or individuals outside China, the receipts signed by such entities or individuals are the legal and valid vouchers, but the tax authorities may require such entities or individuals to provide confirmation certificates issued by overseas notary offices if any doubt is raised on such receipts.	(2)支付给境外单位或者个人的款项,以该单位或者个人的签收单据为合法有效凭证,税务机关对签收单据有疑异的,可以要求其提供境外公证机构的确认证明。
(c) For tax payments, tax payment vouchers are the legal and valid vouchers.	(3)缴纳的税款,以完税凭证为合法有效凭证。
(d) For the deduction of contributions to a governmental fund, administrative charges or land prices paid to a government, the financial receipts of which the production is supervised (printed) by a public finance department at or above the provincial level are the legal and valid vouchers.	(4)扣除的政府性基金、行政事业性收费或者向政府支付的土地价款,以省级以上(含省级)财政部门监(印)制的财政票据为合法有效凭证。
(e) Other vouchers prescribed by the State Administration of Taxation.	(5)国家税务总局规定的其他凭证。
Where the aforesaid vouchers obtained by taxpayers are VAT credit vouchers, the input tax shall be credited against the output VAT.	纳税人取得的上述凭证属于增值税扣税凭证的,其进项税额不得从销项税额中抵扣。
4. Input tax	(四)进项税额

103

Continued

English Translation	Chinese Version
(1) For the pilot taxpayers to which the general tax computation method applies, the input tax on the immovable properties which are acquired after May 1, 2016 and accounted as fixed assets under the accounting system as well as the immovable property projects under construction which are acquired after May 1, 2016 shall be credited against output tax over a two-year period from the date when the immovable properties are acquired at the proportions of 60% in the first year and 40% in the second year, respectively.	1.适用一般计税方法的试点纳税人,2016 年 5 月 1 日后取得并在会计制度上按固定资产核算的不动产或者 2016 年 5 月 1 日后取得的不动产在建工程,其进项税额应自取得之日起分 2 年从销项税额中抵扣,第一年抵扣比例为 60%,第二年抵扣比例为 40%。
The "immovable property acquired" includes the immovable properties acquired by various means such as direct purchase, acceptance of donations, acceptance of equity investment, self-building, and debt repayment, excluding real estate projects independently developed by real estate developers.	取得不动产,包括以直接购买、接受捐赠、接受投资入股、自建以及抵债等各种形式取得不动产,不包括房地产开发企业自行开发的房地产项目。
The input tax on an immovable property leased by financing or a temporary building or structure built and maintained at the construction site shall not be governed by the provisions on the credit over a two-year period.	融资租入的不动产以及在施工现场修建的临时建筑物、构筑物,其进项税额不适用上述分 2 年抵扣的规定。
(2) Where any fixed asset, intangible asset or immovable property on which no input tax shall be credited and is credited as prescribed in Item (1) of Article 27 of the Measures for Implementing the Pilot Program is changed for other purposes and used for any project on which the input tax is allowed to be credited, the input tax allowed to be credited shall be calculated in the month after the change of the purposes thereof under the following formula:	2.按照《试点实施办法》第二十七条第(一)项规定不得抵扣且未抵扣进项税额的固定资产、无形资产、不动产,发生用途改变,用于允许抵扣进项税额的应税项目,可在用途改变的次月按照下列公式计算可以抵扣的进项税额:
Input tax allowed to be credited = Net worth of the fixed asset, intangible asset, or immovable property / (1 + Applicable tax rate) × Applicable tax rate	可以抵扣的进项税额=固定资产、无形资产、不动产净值/(1+适用税率)×适用税率
For the aforesaid input tax allowed to be credited, a legal and valid VAT credit voucher shall be acquired.	上述可以抵扣的进项税额应取得合法有效的增值税扣税凭证。
(3) The input tax on the advisory fees, handing charges, consulting fees and other fees for investment and financing as paid to the creditor by the taxpayer for acceptance of loan services and directly related to the loan shall not be credited against the output tax.	3.纳税人接受贷款服务向贷款方支付的与该笔贷款直接相关的投融资顾问费、手续费、咨询费等费用,其进项税额不得从销项税额中抵扣。

Continued

English Translation	Chinese Version
5. Registration as a general taxpayer	（五）一般纳税人资格登记
The threshold for the annual taxable sales amount as prescribed in Article 3 of the Measures for Implementing the Pilot Program is 5 million yuan or more. The Ministry of Finance and the State Administration of Taxation may adjust the threshold for the annual taxable sales amount.	《试点实施办法》第三条规定的年应税销售额标准为 500 万元（含本数）。财政部和国家税务总局可以对年应税销售额标准进行调整。
6. Tax Computation Methods	（六）计税方法
A general taxpayer may calculate his taxes by the simple tax computation method when the aforesaid taxable activities are conducted：	一般纳税人发生下列应税行为可以选择适用简易计税方法计税：
（1）Public Transport Services.	1.公共交通运输服务
"Public transportation services" includes ferry boat and passenger ship transportation，public passenger transportation，subway，urban light rail，taxi，long-haul passenger transportation，and regular bus.	公共交通运输服务，包括轮客渡、公交客运、地铁、城市轻轨、出租车、长途客运、班车。
"Regular bus" means the land transportation to transport passengers on a fixed route，on a fixed schedule，and with fixed stops.	班车，是指按固定路线、固定时间运营并在固定站点停靠的运送旅客的陆路运输服务。
（2）An animation enterprise as determined may calculate its taxes by the simple tax computation method on animation script compilation，image design，background design，animation design，storyboarding，animation production，shooting，tracing，coloring，picture synthesis，dubbing，scoring，sound mixing，film editing，subtitling，and compression and transcoding (adapted to both network animation and mobile animation formats) provided by it for development of animation products，as well as the transfer within China of animation copyrights (including the licensing and re-licensing of animation brands，images，or contents).	2.经认定的动漫企业为开发动漫产品提供的动漫脚本编撰、形象设计、背景设计、动画设计、分镜、动画制作、摄制、描线、上色、画面合成、配音、配乐、音效合成、剪辑、字幕制作、压缩转码（面向网络动漫、手机动漫格式适配）服务，以及在境内转让动漫版权（包括动漫品牌、形象或者内容的授权及再授权）。
The standards and procedures for the determination of animation enterprises and independently developed and produced animation products shall be governed by the Notice of the Ministry of Culture, the Ministry of Finance and the State Administration of Taxation on Issuing the Measures for the Determination of Animation Enterprises （for Trial Implementation）（No. 51 [2008]，Ministry of Culture）.	动漫企业和自主开发、生产动漫产品的认定标准和认定程序，按照《文化部 财政部 国家税务总局关于印发＜动漫企业认定管理办法（试行）＞的通知》（文市发〔2008〕51 号）的规定执行。

Continued

English Translation	Chinese Version
(3) Movie projection services, warehousing services, loading/unloading handling services, collection and delivery services, and cultural and sports services.	3.电影放映服务、仓储服务、装卸搬运服务、收派服务和文化体育服务。
(4) Operating and leasing services provided with the subject matter being tangible personal property obtained by it before it is included in the pilot program.	4.以纳入营改增试点之日前取得的有形动产为标的物提供的经营租赁服务。
(5) A lease contract for tangible personal property which was signed by it but has not been completely performed before it is included in the pilot program.	5.在纳入营改增试点之日前签订的尚未执行完毕的有形动产租赁合同。
7. Construction Services	(七)建筑服务
(1) A general taxpayer may choose to calculate its taxes with the simple tax computation method on its provision of construction services in the form of contract for labor.	1.一般纳税人以清包工方式提供的建筑服务,可以选择适用简易计税方法计税。
"Construction services provided in the form of contract for labor" means the construction services in which the builder does not pay for the materials to be used on the construction project, or only pays for the auxiliary materials and collect labor costs, management fees or other costs thereof.	以清包工方式提供建筑服务,是指施工方不采购建筑工程所需的材料或只采购辅助材料,并收取人工费、管理费或者其他费用的建筑服务。
(2) A general taxpayer may choose to calculate its taxes with the simple tax computation method on its provision of construction services for a project with materials supplied by the contract giver.	2.一般纳税人为甲供工程提供的建筑服务,可以选择适用简易计税方法计税。
"A project with materials supplied by the contract giver" means a construction project of which all or part of the equipment, materials, and power is independently purchased by the contract giver of the project.	甲供工程,是指全部或部分设备、材料、动力由工程发包方自行采购的建筑工程。
(3) A general taxpayer may choose to calculate its taxes with the simple tax computation method on its provision of construction services for an old construction project.	3.一般纳税人为建筑工程老项目提供的建筑服务,可以选择适用简易计税方法计税。
An "old construction project" means:	建筑工程老项目,是指:
(a) A construction project for which the Construction Permit for Construction Projects indicates that the commencement date of the contract is before 30 April 2016.	(1)《建筑工程施工许可证》注明的合同开工日期在2016年4月30日前的建筑工程项目;

106

Continued

English Translation	Chinese Version
(b) A construction project of which the commencement date indicated in the construction project contract is before 30 April 2016, where no Construction Permit for Construction Projects has been obtained.	(2)未取得《建筑工程施工许可证》的,建筑工程承包合同注明的开工日期在 2016 年 4 月 30 日前的建筑工程项目。
(4) Where a general taxpayer calculates its taxes with the general tax computation method on its provision of construction services in two or more counties (cities or districts), it shall calculate the tax payable with the full prices and ex-price charges it obtained as the sales amount. The taxpayer shall, at the pre-levy rate of 2% on the basis of the balance of the full prices and ex-price charges it obtained minus the subcontracting fees paid, prepay taxes at the place where the construction services are provided, and then file its tax returns with the competent tax authority at the place where the taxpayer is located.	4.一般纳税人跨县(市)提供建筑服务,适用一般计税方法计税的,应以取得的全部价款和价外费用为销售额计算应纳税额。纳税人应以取得的全部价款和价外费用扣除支付的分包款后的余额,按照 2% 的预征率在建筑服务发生地预缴税款后,向机构所在地主管税务机关进行纳税申报。
(5) Where a general taxpayer calculates its taxes with the simple tax computation method on its provision of construction services in two or more counties (cities), it shall calculate the tax payable at the levy rate of 3%, with the balance of the full prices and ex-price charges it obtained minus the subcontracting fees paid as the sales amount. The taxpayer shall prepay taxes by the aforesaid tax computation method at the place where the construction services are provided, and then file its tax returns with the competent tax authority at the place where the taxpayer is located.	5.一般纳税人跨县(市)提供建筑服务,选择适用简易计税方法计税的,应以取得的全部价款和价外费用扣除支付的分包款后的余额为销售额,按照 3% 的征收率计算应纳税额。纳税人应按照上述计税方法在建筑服务发生地预缴税款后,向机构所在地主管税务机关进行纳税申报。
(6) A pilot taxpayer which is a small-scale taxpayer (hereinafter referred to as a "small-scale taxpayer") providing construction services in two or more counties (cities) shall calculate the tax payable at the levy rate of 3%, with the balance of the full prices and ex-price charges it obtained minus the subcontracting fees paid as the sales amount. The taxpayer shall prepay taxes by the aforesaid tax computation method at the place where the construction services are provided, and then file its tax returns with the competent tax authority at the place where the taxpayer is located.	6.试点纳税人中的小规模纳税人(以下称小规模纳税人)跨县(市)提供建筑服务,应以取得的全部价款和价外费用扣除支付的分包款后的余额为销售额,按照 3% 的征收率计算应纳税额。纳税人应按照上述计税方法在建筑服务发生地预缴税款后,向机构所在地主管税务机关进行纳税申报。
8. Sale of Immovable Properties	(八)销售不动产

Continued

English Translation	Chinese Version
(1)A general taxpayer may choose to calculate its taxes with the simple tax computation method on its sale of any immovable property（excluding self-built properties）it acquired before April 30，2016，and calculate the tax payable at the levy rate of 5％ with the balance of the full prices and ex-price charges it obtained minus the original purchase price of the immovable property or the value when the immovable property is acquired as the sales amount. The taxpayer shall prepay taxes by the aforesaid tax computation method at the place where the immovable property is located，and then file its tax returns with the competent tax authority at the place where the taxpayer is located.	1.一般纳税人销售其 2016 年 4 月 30 日前取得（不含自建）的不动产，可以选择适用简易计税方法，以取得的全部价款和价外费用减去该项不动产购置原价或者取得不动产时的作价后的余额为销售额，按照 5％ 的征收率计算应纳税额。纳税人应按照上述计税方法在不动产所在地预缴税款后，向机构所在地主管税务机关进行纳税申报。
(2)A general taxpayer may choose to calculate its taxes with the simple tax computation method on its sale of any immovable property it builds by itself before April 30，2016，and calculate the tax payable at the levy rate of 5％ with the full prices and ex-price charges it obtained as the sales amount. The taxpayer shall prepay taxes by the aforesaid tax computation method at the place where the immovable property is located，and then file tax returns with the competent tax authority at the place where the taxpayer is located.	2.一般纳税人销售其 2016 年 4 月 30 日前自建的不动产，可以选择适用简易计税方法，以取得的全部价款和价外费用为销售额，按照 5％ 的征收率计算应纳税额。纳税人应按照上述计税方法在不动产所在地预缴税款后，向机构所在地主管税务机关进行纳税申报。
(3)A general taxpayer shall calculate its taxes with the general tax computation method on its sale of any immovable property（excluding self-built properties）it acquired after May 1，2016，and calculate the tax payable with the full prices and ex-price charges it obtained as the sales amount. The taxpayer shall，at the pre-levy rate of 5％ on the basis of the balance of the full prices and ex-price charges it obtained minus the original purchase price of the immovable property or the value when the immovable property is acquired，prepay taxes at the place where the immovable property is located，and then file its tax returns with the competent tax authority at the place where the taxpayer is located.	3.一般纳税人销售其 2016 年 5 月 1 日后取得（不含自建）的不动产，应适用一般计税方法，以取得的全部价款和价外费用为销售额计算应纳税额。纳税人应以取得的全部价款和价外费用减去该项不动产购置原价或者取得不动产时的作价后的余额，按照 5％ 的预征率在不动产所在地预缴税款后，向机构所在地主管税务机关进行纳税申报。

Continued

English Translation	Chinese Version
(4)A general taxpayer shall calculate its taxes with the general tax computation method on its sale of any immovable property it builds by itself after May 1, 2016, and calculate the tax payable with the full prices and ex-price charges it obtained as the sales amount. The taxpayer shall, at the pre-levy rate of 5% on the basis of the full prices and ex-price charges it obtained, prepay tax at the place where the immovable property is located, and then file its tax returns with the competent tax authority at the place where the taxpayer is located.	4.一般纳税人销售其 2016 年 5 月 1 日后自建的不动产,应适用一般计税方法,以取得的全部价款和价外费用为销售额计算应纳税额。纳税人应以取得的全部价款和价外费用,按照 5% 的预征率在不动产所在地预缴税款后,向机构所在地主管税务机关进行纳税申报。
(5) Except for individual industrial and commercial households that sell the residential property purchase or other individuals who sell their immovable property, a small-scale taxpayer that sells any immovable property (excluding self-built property) it acquires shall calculate the tax payable at the levy rate of 5%, with the balance of the full prices and ex-price charges it obtained minus the original purchase price of the immovable property or the value when the immovable property is acquired as the sales amount. The taxpayer shall prepay taxes by the aforesaid tax computation method at the place where the immovable property is located, and then file its tax returns with the competent tax authority at the place where the taxpayer is located.	5.小规模纳税人销售其取得(不含自建)的不动产(不含个体工商户销售购买的住房和其他个人销售不动产),应以取得的全部价款和价外费用减去该项不动产购置原价或者取得不动产时的作价后的余额为销售额,按照 5% 的征收率计算应纳税额。纳税人应按照上述计税方法在不动产所在地预缴税款后,向机构所在地主管税务机关进行纳税申报。
(6) A small-scale taxpayer who sells any immovable property it builds by itself shall calculate the tax payable at the levy rate of 5%, with the full prices and ex-price charges it obtained as the sales amount. The taxpayer shall prepay taxes by the aforesaid tax computation method at the place where the immovable property is located, and then file its tax returns with the competent tax authority at the place where the taxpayer is located.	6.小规模纳税人销售其自建的不动产,应以取得的全部价款和价外费用为销售额,按照 5% 的征收率计算应纳税额。纳税人应按照上述计税方法在不动产所在地预缴税款后,向机构所在地主管税务机关进行纳税申报。
(7)A real estate developer which is a general taxpayer may choose to calculate its taxes at the levy rate of 5% by the simple tax computation method on its sale of any its self-developed old real estate project.	7.房地产开发企业中的一般纳税人,销售自行开发的房地产老项目,可以选择适用简易计税方法按照 5% 的征收率计税。
(8)A real estate developer which is a small-scale taxpayer shall calculate its taxes at the levy rate of 5% on its sale of any its self-developed real estate project.	8.房地产开发企业中的小规模纳税人,销售自行开发的房地产项目,按照 5% 的征收率计税。

Continued

English Translation	Chinese Version
(9) A real estate developer who sells its self-developed real estate project by means of collecting prepayments shall prepay VAT at the pre-levy rate of 3% upon receipt of prepayments.	9.房地产开发企业采取预收款方式销售所开发的房地产项目,在收到预收款时按照3%的预征率预缴增值税。
(10) The VAT on residential properties purchased by an individual industrial and commercial household shall be levied or exempted in accordance with Article 5 of the Provisions on the Transitional Policies for the Pilot Program of Replacing Business Tax with value-added tax (Annex 3). The taxpayer shall prepay taxes by the aforesaid tax computation method at the place where the immovable property is located, and then file its tax returns with the competent tax authority at the place where the taxpayer is located.	10.个体工商户销售购买的住房,应按照附件3《营业税改征增值税试点过渡政策的规定》第五条的规定征免增值税。纳税人应按照上述计税方法在不动产所在地预缴税款后,向机构所在地主管税务机关进行纳税申报。
(11) Any other individual who sells immovable properties (excluding self-built properties) it acquires except for the residential properties it purchases shall calculate the tax payable at the levy rate of 5%, with the balance of the full prices and ex-price charges it obtained minus the original purchase price of the immovable property or the value when the immovable property is acquired as the sales amount.	11.其他个人销售其取得(不含自建)的不动产(不含其购买的住房),应以取得的全部价款和价外费用减去该项不动产购置原价或者取得不动产时的作价后的余额为销售额,按照5%的征收率计算应纳税额。
9. Operational and Leasing Services for Immovable Property	(九)不动产经营租赁服务
(1) A general taxpayer may choose to calculate the tax payable at the levy rate of 5% by the simple tax computation method on its leasing of any immovable property it acquired before April 30, 2016. Where the taxpayer leases any immovable property it acquired before April 30, 2016 which is not located in the same county (or city) as the place where the taxpayer is located, it shall prepay taxes by the aforesaid tax computation method at the place where the taxpayer is located, and then file its tax returns with the competent tax authority at the place where the taxpayer is located.	1.一般纳税人出租其2016年4月30日前取得的不动产,可以选择适用简易计税方法,按照5%的征收率计算应纳税额。纳税人出租其2016年4月30日前取得的与机构所在地不在同一县(市)的不动产,应按照上述计税方法在不动产所在地预缴税款后,向机构所在地主管税务机关进行纳税申报。
(2) For the vehicle tolls of an expressway which is commenced before the implementation of the pilot program as collected by a highway management enterprise which is a general taxpayer, the tax payable may be calculated at the reduced rate of 3% by the simple tax computation method.	2.公路经营企业中的一般纳税人收取试点前开工的高速公路的车辆通行费,可以选择适用简易计税方法,减按3%的征收率计算应纳税额。

Continued

English Translation	Chinese Version
An "expressway which is commenced before the implementation of the pilot program" means an expressway for which the relevant construction permit indicates that the commencement date of the contract is before 30 April 2016.	试点前开工的高速公路,是指相关施工许可证明上注明的合同开工日期在 2016 年 4 月 30 日前的高速公路。
(3) Where a general taxpayer leases any immovable property it acquired before May 1, 2016 which is not located in the same county (or city) as the place where the taxpayer is located, it shall prepay tax at the pre-levy rate of 3% at the place where the immovable property is located, and then file its tax returns with the competent tax authority at the place where the taxpayer is located.	3.一般纳税人出租其 2016 年 5 月 1 日后取得的、与机构所在地不在同一县(市)的不动产,应按照 3%的预征率在不动产所在地预缴税款后,向机构所在地主管税务机关进行纳税申报。
(4) A small-scale taxpayer shall calculate the tax payable at the levy rate of 5% on its leasing of any immovable property it acquires (excluding the residential property leased by individuals). Where the taxpayer leases any immovable property which is not located in the same county (or city) as the place where the taxpayer is located, it shall prepay tax by the aforesaid tax computation method at the place where the taxpayer is located, and then file its tax returns with the competent tax authority at the place where the taxpayer is located.	4.小规模纳税人出租其取得的不动产(不含个人出租住房),应按照 5%的征收率计算应纳税额。纳税人出租与机构所在地不在同一县(市)的不动产,应按照上述计税方法在不动产所在地预缴税款后,向机构所在地主管税务机关进行纳税申报。
(5) Any other individual shall calculate the tax payable at the levy rate of 5% on his or her leasing of any immovable property (excluding any residential property) he or she acquires.	5.其他个人出租其取得的不动产(不含住房),应按照 5%的征收率计算应纳税额。
(6) Any individual shall pay the tax payable at the reduced levy rate of 1.5% from 5% on his or her leasing of any residential property he or she acquires.	6.个人出租住房,应按照 5%的征收率减按 1.5%计算应纳税额。

Continued

English Translation	Chinese Version
10. Where a general taxpayer calculates its taxes by the general tax computation method on its sale of an immovable property （excluding self-built ones） it acquired before April 30，2016，it shall calculate the tax payable with the full prices and ex-price charges it obtained as the sales amount. The aforesaid taxpayer shall，at the pre-levy rate of 5％ on the basis of the balance of the full prices and ex-price charges it obtained minus the original purchase price of the immovable property or the value when the immovable property is acquired，prepay taxes at the place where the immovable property is located，and then file its tax returns with the competent tax authority at the place where the taxpayer is located.	（十）一般纳税人销售其 2016 年 4 月 30 日前取得的不动产（不含自建），适用一般计税方法计税的，以取得的全部价款和价外费用为销售额计算应纳税额。上述纳税人应以取得的全部价款和价外费用减去该项不动产购置原价或者取得不动产时的作价后的余额，按照 5％ 的预征率在不动产所在地预缴税款后，向机构所在地主管税务机关进行纳税申报。
Where a real estate developer which is a general taxpayer calculates its taxes by the general tax computation method on its sale of any old real estate project or a general taxpayer calculate tax by the aforesaid method on its leasing of any immovable property it acquired before April 30，2016，it shall，at the pre-levy rate of 3％ on the basis of the full prices and ex-price charges it obtained，prepay taxes at the place where the immovable property is located，and then file its tax returns with the competent tax authority at the place where the taxpayer is located.	房地产开发企业中的一般纳税人销售房地产老项目，以及一般纳税人出租其 2016 年 4 月 30 日前取得的不动产，适用一般计税方法计税的，应以取得的全部价款和价外费用，按照 3％ 的预征率在不动产所在地预缴税款后，向机构所在地主管税务机关进行纳税申报。
A general taxpayer may calculate its taxes by the general tax computation method on its sale of an immovable property it builds by itself before April 30，2016，it shall calculate the tax payable with the full prices and ex-price charges it obtained as the sales amount. The taxpayer shall，at the pre-levy rate of 5％ on the basis of the full prices and ex-price charges it obtained，prepay taxes at the place where the immovable property is located，and then file its tax returns with the competent tax authority at the place where the taxpayer is located.	一般纳税人销售其 2016 年 4 月 30 日前自建的不动产，适用一般计税方法计税的，应以取得的全部价款和价外费用为销售额计算应纳税额。纳税人应以取得的全部价款和价外费用，按照 5％ 的预征率在不动产所在地预缴税款后，向机构所在地主管税务机关进行纳税申报。

Continued

English Translation	Chinese Version
11. For a general taxpayer who provides construction services in two or more provinces (provinces, autonomous regions, municipalities directly under the Central Government, or cities under separate state planning) or sells or leases any immovable property it acquired which is not located in a same province (or autonomous region, municipality directly under the Central Government, or city under separate state planning) as the place where the taxpayer is located, when it files its tax returns with the competent tax authority at the place where the taxpayer is located, if the tax payable calculated is much less than the tax prepaid, the State Administration of Taxation shall advise the provincial tax authority at the place where the construction services are provided or that at the place where the immovable property is located to suspend the prepayment of VAT for a period of time.	(十一)一般纳税人跨省(自治区、直辖市或者计划单列市)提供建筑服务或者销售、出租取得的与机构所在地不在同一省(自治区、直辖市或者计划单列市)的不动产,在机构所在地申报纳税时,计算的应纳税额小于已预缴税额,且差额较大的,由国家税务总局通知建筑服务发生地或者不动产所在地省级税务机关,在一定时期内暂停预缴增值税。
12. Place of VAT Payment.	(十二)纳税地点
If the head office and the branch offices of a pilot taxpayer which is a locally registered business are not in the same county (or city) but are in the same province (or autonomous region, municipality directly under the Central Government, or city under separate state planning), the head office may, with the approval of the public finance department (or bureau) and the state taxation bureau of the province (or autonomous region, municipality directly under the Central Government, or city under separate state planning), file a VAT return on a consolidated basis with the competent tax authority at the place where the head office is located.	属于固定业户的试点纳税人,总分支机构不在同一县(市),但在同一省(自治区、直辖市、计划单列市)范围内的,经省(自治区、直辖市、计划单列市)财政厅(局)和国家税务局批准,可以由总机构汇总向总机构所在地的主管税务机关申报缴纳增值税。
13. Business Occurred Before the Implementation of the Pilot Program.	(十三)试点前发生的业务

Continued

English Translation	Chinese Version
(1) Where a pilot taxpayer conducts taxable activities subject to balance-based business tax according to the relevant business tax policies of the state, if the full prices and ex-price charges received by the pilot taxpayer are less than the amount of deductibles, the part which has not been deducted by the date when it is included in the pilot program shall not be deducted in the computation of the amount of VAT taxable sales of the pilot taxpayer, and the pilot taxpayer shall apply to the original competent local tax authority for business tax refund.	1.试点纳税人发生应税行为,按照国家有关营业税政策规定差额征收营业税的,因取得的全部价款和价外费用不足以抵减允许扣除项目金额,截至纳入营改增试点之日前尚未扣除的部分,不得在计算试点纳税人增值税应税销售额时抵减,应当向原主管地税机关申请退还营业税。
(2) Where a pilot taxpayer conducting taxable activities has paid business tax thereon before the date when it is included in the pilot program, and its turnover is reduced as a result of any refund after the implementation of the pilot program, the taxpayer shall apply to the original competent local tax authority for refund of the business tax paid.	2.试点纳税人发生应税行为,在纳入营改增试点之日前已缴纳营业税,营改增试点后因发生退款减除营业额的,应当向原主管地税机关申请退还已缴纳的营业税。
(3) Where a pilot taxpayer needs to pay any tax in arrears on any taxable activities conducted before the date when it is included in the pilot program for tax inspection and other reasons, it shall pay the business tax in arrears according to the current business tax policies.	3.试点纳税人纳入营改增试点之日前发生的应税行为,因税收检查等原因需要补缴税款的,应按照营业税政策规定补缴营业税。
14. Sale of Used Fixed Assets	(十四)销售使用过的固定资产
Where a general taxpayer sells any fixed asset it uses by itself and acquired before the date when it is included in the pilot program, the current VAT policies on used goods shall apply.	一般纳税人销售自己使用过的、纳入营改增试点之日前取得的固定资产,按照现行旧货相关增值税政策执行。
"Used fixed assets" means fixed assets the depreciation of which has been calculated and recorded by a taxpayer in accordance with Article 28 of the Measures for Implementing the Pilot Program and under the financial accounting standards.	使用过的固定资产,是指纳税人符合《试点实施办法》第二十八条规定并根据财务会计制度已经计提折旧的固定资产。
15. Tax Rate Applicable to VAT Withheld	(十五)扣缴增值税适用税率
Where a purchaser within China withholds VAT for an entity or individual outside China, the VAT shall be withheld at the applicable tax rate.	境内的购买方为境外单位和个人扣缴增值税的,按照适用税率扣缴增值税。
16. Other Provisions	(十六)其他规定

Continued

English Translation	Chinese Version
(1) Where a pilot taxpayer sells telecommunications services along with user identification cards, telecommunications terminals or other goods or telecommunications services as a compliment, the full prices and ex-price charges obtained by the taxpayer shall be calculated separately and VAT shall be paid separately at the applicable rate.	1.试点纳税人销售电信服务时,附带赠送用户识别卡、电信终端等货物或者电信服务的,应将其取得的全部价款和价外费用进行分别核算,按各自适用的税率计算缴纳增值税。
(2) The taxable activities conducted by oil and gas field enterprises shall be taxed at the VAT rates as set out in the Measures for Implementing the Pilot Program and no longer taxed at the VAT rates as mentioned in the Notice of the Ministry of Finance and the State Administration of Taxation on Issuing the Measures for the Administration of value-added tax on Oil and Gas Field Enterprises (No. 8 [2009], Ministry of Finance).	2.油气田企业发生应税行为,适用《试点实施办法》规定的增值税税率,不再适用《财政部 国家税务总局关于印发＜油气田企业增值税管理办法＞的通知》(财税〔2009〕8 号)规定的增值税税率。
Ⅱ. Relevant policies on original VAT taxpayers [which means taxpayers which pay VAT in accordance with the Interim Regulation of the People's Republic of China on value-added tax (Order No. 538, State Council, hereinafter referred to as the " Interim VAT Regulation ")]	二、原增值税纳税人[指按照《中华人民共和国增值税暂行条例》(国务院令第 538 号)(以下称《增值税暂行条例》)缴纳增值税的纳税人]有关政策
1. Input Tax	(一)进项税额
(1) Where an original VAT general taxpayer purchases services, intangible assets or immovable properties, the input tax shall be the VAT amount indicated on a special VAT invoice obtained, and may be credited against the output tax	1.原增值税一般纳税人购进服务、无形资产或者不动产,取得的增值税专用发票上注明的增值税额为进项税额,准予从销项税额中抵扣。
The input tax on the immovable properties which are acquired after May 1, 2016 and accounted as fixed assets in the accounting books as well as the immovable property projects under construction which are acquired after May 1, 2016 shall be credited against output tax over a two-year period from the date when the immovable properties are acquired at the proportions of 60% in the first year and 40% in the second year, respectively.	2016 年 5 月 1 日后取得并在会计制度上按固定资产核算的不动产或者 2016 年 5 月 1 日后取得的不动产在建工程,其进项税额应自取得之日起分 2 年从销项税额中抵扣,第一年抵扣比例为 60%,第二年抵扣比例为 40%。
The input tax on an immovable property leased by financing or a temporary building or structure built and maintained at the construction site shall not be governed by the restriction of credit over a two-year period.	融资租入的不动产以及在施工现场修建的临时建筑物、构筑物,其进项税额不适用上述分 2 年抵扣的规定。

Continued

English Translation	Chinese Version
(2) The input tax on a motorcycle, automobile, or yacht subject to consumption tax for the original VAT general taxpayer's own use may be credited against the output tax.	2.原增值税一般纳税人自用的应征消费税的摩托车、汽车、游艇,其进项税额准予从销项税额中抵扣。
(3) Where an original VAT general taxpayer that purchases services provided by an entity or individual outside China shall withhold VAT as legally required, the input tax which may be credited against the output tax shall be the VAT amount indicated on the taxation payment voucher for payment of withholding tax obtained from the tax authority or the withholding agent.	3.原增值税一般纳税人从境外单位或者个人购进服务、无形资产或者不动产,按照规定应当扣缴增值税的,准予从销项税额中抵扣的进项税额为自税务机关或者扣缴义务人取得的解缴税款的完税凭证上注明的增值税额。
Where a taxpayer deducts the input tax on the basis of the taxation payment voucher, there shall be a written contract, a payment certificate, and an account statement or invoice issued by the entity outside China. If the required information is incomplete, the input tax shall not be deducted from the output tax.	纳税人凭完税凭证抵扣进项税额的,应当具备书面合同、付款证明和境外单位的对账单或者发票。资料不全的,其进项税额不得从销项税额中抵扣。
(4) Where the goods purchased or processing, repair, or maintenance services received by an original VAT general taxpayer are used for the items listed in the Explanatory Notes on the Sale of Services, Intangible Assets or Immovable Properties, it is not within the meaning of "used for non-VAT taxable items" as mentioned in Article 10 of the Interim VAT Regulation, and the input tax thereon may be credited against the output tax.	4.原增值税一般纳税人购进货物或者接受加工修理修配劳务,用于《销售服务、无形资产或者不动产注释》所列项目的,不属于《增值税暂行条例》第十条所称的用于非增值税应税项目,其进项税额准予从销项税额中抵扣。
(5) Where an original VAT general taxpayer purchases services, intangible assets or immovable assets, the input tax for the following items may not be credited against the output tax:	5.原增值税一般纳税人购进服务、无形资产或者不动产,下列项目的进项税额不得从销项税额中抵扣:
(a) Those used for the taxable items to which the simple tax computation method applies, the VAT exemption items or the items for collective welfare or individual consumption. In particular, the term "intangible assets or immovable property involved therein" only refers to those intangible assets (excluding other intangible equity assets) or immovable property exclusively used for the above items.	(1)用于简易计税方法计税项目、免征增值税项目、集体福利或者个人消费。其中涉及的无形资产、不动产,仅指专用于上述项目的无形资产(不包括其他权益性无形资产)、不动产。
"Individual consumption" includes entertainment consumption of a taxpayer.	纳税人的交际应酬消费属于个人消费。

Continued

English Translation	Chinese Version
(b) Purchased goods recorded as abnormal losses, as well as related processing, repair, and maintenance labor services and transportation services.	(2)非正常损失的购进货物,以及相关的加工修理修配劳务和交通运输服务。
(c) Purchased goods (excluding fixed assets), processing, repair, and maintenance labor services and transportation services used on products in process or finished products and recorded as abnormal losses.	(3)非正常损失的在产品、产成品所耗用的购进货物(不包括固定资产)、加工修理修配劳务和交通运输服务。
(d) Immovable properties as well as purchased goods, design services and architectural services used on products in process or finished products and recorded as abnormal losses.	(4)非正常损失的不动产,以及该不动产所耗用的购进货物、设计服务和建筑服务。
(e) Purchased goods, design services and architectural services consumed by immovable property projects under construction and recorded as abnormal losses.	(5)非正常损失的不动产在建工程所耗用的购进货物、设计服务和建筑服务。
The new construction, renovation, expansion, repair, or decoration of any immovable property by a taxpayer is an immovable property project under construction.	纳税人新建、改建、扩建、修缮、装饰不动产,均属于不动产在建工程。
(f) Purchased passenger transportation services, loan services, catering services, daily services for residents and entertainment services.	(6)购进的旅客运输服务、贷款服务、餐饮服务、居民日常服务和娱乐服务。
(g) Other circumstances as prescribed by the Ministry of Finance and the State Administration of Taxation.	(7)财政部和国家税务总局规定的其他情形。
"Goods" as mentioned in above sub-items (d) and (f) means the materials and equipment constituting immovable properties, including building and decoration materials, as well as water supply and drainage, heating, sanitation, ventilation, lighting, communication, gas, fire protection, central air conditioning, elevator, electrical and intelligent building equipment and supporting facilities.	上述第(4)点、第(5)点所称货物,是指构成不动产实体的材料和设备,包括建筑装饰材料和给排水、采暖、卫生、通风、照明、通讯、煤气、消防、中央空调、电梯、电气、智能化楼宇设备及配套设施。
The input tax on the advisory fees, handing charges, consulting fees and other fees for investment and financing which are paid to the creditor by the taxpayer for acceptance of loan services and are directly related to the loan shall not be credited against the output tax.	纳税人接受贷款服务向贷款方支付的与该笔贷款直接相关的投融资顾问费、手续费、咨询费等费用,其进项税额不得从销项税额中抵扣。

117

Continued

English Translation	Chinese Version
(6) Where the services purchased on which the input tax has been credited against the output tax falls under any of the circumstance as set out in Item (5) herein (excluding taxable items to which the simple tax computation method applies and the VAT exemption items), the input tax shall be credited against the input tax of the current period; and if such input tax cannot be determined, the input tax to be deducted shall be calculated according to the actual cost in the current period.	6.已抵扣进项税额的购进服务，发生上述第5点规定情形(简易计税方法计税项目、免征增值税项目除外)的，应当将该进项税额从当期进项税额中扣减；无法确定该进项税额的，按照当期实际成本计算应扣减的进项税额。
(7) Where any immovable property on which the input tax has been credited against the output tax falls under any circumstance as set out in above item (5), the input tax prohibited from credit shall be calculated under the following formula：	7.已抵扣进项税额的无形资产或者不动产,发生上述第5点规定情形的,按照下列公式计算不得抵扣的进项税额：
Input tax prohibited from credit＝Net worth of the intangible property or the immovable property×Applicable tax rate	不得抵扣的进项税额＝无形资产或者不动产净值×适用税率
(8) Where any fixed asset, intangible asset or immovable property on which no input tax shall be credited and is credited in accordance with Article 10 of the Interim VAT Regulation and the aforesaid Item (5) is changed for other purposes and used for any project on which the input tax is creditable, the creditable input tax shall be calculated in the month after the change of the purposes thereof in accordance legal and valid VAT credit vouchers under the following formula：	8.按照《增值税暂行条例》第十条和上述第5点不得抵扣且未抵扣进项税额的固定资产、无形资产、不动产,发生用途改变,用于允许抵扣进项税额的应税项目,可在用途改变的次月按照下列公式,依据合法有效的增值税扣税凭证,计算可以抵扣的进项税额：
Creditable input tax＝Net worth of the fixed asset, intangible asset, or immovable property / (1＋Applicable tax rate)×Applicable tax rate	可以抵扣的进项税额＝固定资产、无形资产、不动产净值/(1＋适用税率)×适用税率
For the aforesaid input tax allowed to be credited, legal and valid VAT credit vouchers shall be acquired.	上述可以抵扣的进项税额应取得合法有效的增值税扣税凭证。
2. Remaining End-of-period VAT Credit.	(二)增值税期末留抵税额
Where an original VAT general taxpayer is concurrently engaged in the sale of services, intangible assets or immovable property, its remaining end-of-period VAT credit by the date when the taxpayer is included in the pilot program shall not be credited against the output tax on the sale of services, intangible assets or immovable property.	原增值税一般纳税人兼有销售服务、无形资产或者不动产的,截止到纳入营改增试点之日前的增值税期末留抵税额,不得从销售服务、无形资产或者不动产的销项税额中抵扣。

Continued

English Translation	Chinese Version
3. Mixed Sale	(三)混合销售
A sale involving both goods and services shall be regarded as a mixed sale. A mixed sale by an entity or individual industrial and commercial household engaged in the production, wholesale or retail of goods shall be regarded as a sale of goods subject to VAT; a mixed sale by any other entity or individual industrial and commercial household shall be regarded as a sale of services subject to VAT.	一项销售行为如果既涉及货物又涉及服务,为混合销售。从事货物的生产、批发或者零售的单位和个体工商户的混合销售行为,按照销售货物缴纳增值税;其他单位和个体工商户的混合销售行为,按照销售服务缴纳增值税。
The aforesaid entity or individual industrial and commercial household engaged in the production, wholesale or retail of goods shall include an entity or individual industrial and commercial household that is mainly engaged in the production, wholesale or retail of goods and concurrently engaged in the sale of services.	上述从事货物的生产、批发或者零售的单位和个体工商户,包括以从事货物的生产、批发或者零售为主,并兼营销售服务的单位和个体工商户在内。
Annex 3:	附件3:
Provisions on Transitional Policies concerning the Pilot Program of Replacing Business Tax with value-added tax	营业税改征增值税试点过渡政策的规定
Ⅰ. The following items shall be exempted from the value-added tax (VAT)	一、下列项目免征增值税
(1)Nursing and teaching services provided by nurseries and kindergartens.	(一)托儿所、幼儿园提供的保育和教育服务。
"Nurseries or kindergartens" means the institutions for the preschool education of kids between zero and six years old, which are formed upon the approval of education departments at or above the county level and have obtained a license for running nurseries or kindergartens, including public and private nurseries, kindergartens, preschool classes, nursery classes, child care schools and nursery schools.	托儿所、幼儿园,是指经县级以上教育部门审批成立、取得办园许可证的实施0～6岁学前教育的机构,包括公办和民办的托儿所、幼儿园、学前班、幼儿班、保育院、幼儿院。
The "income of public nurseries or kindergartens that are exempted from VAT" means the teaching and nursing fees collected at the charging rates reviewed by the provincial public finance departments and price departments and approved by provincial people's governments.	公办托儿所、幼儿园免征增值税的收入是指,在省级财政部门和价格主管部门审核报省级人民政府批准的收费标准以内收取的教育费、保育费。

Continued

English Translation	Chinese Version
The "income of private nurseries or kindergartens that are exempted from VAT" means the teaching and nursing fees collected at the charging rates registered with and publicized by relevant local departments.	民办托儿所、幼儿园免征增值税的收入是指,在报经当地有关部门备案并公示的收费标准范围内收取的教育费、保育费。
The income from the fees collected by exceeding the prescribed charging rates, the fees additionally collected from holding experimental classes, specialty training classes and hobby lessons, etc., as well as sponsorship funds, educational support fees and other income beyond the prescribed scope that arise from the entry to kindergartens are not the income that shall be exempted from the VAT.	超过规定收费标准的收费,以开办实验班、特色班和兴趣班等为由另外收取的费用以及与幼儿入园挂钩的赞助费、支教费等超过规定范围的收入,不属于免征增值税的收入。
(2)Elderly Care Services Provided by Elderly Care Institutions.	(二)养老机构提供的养老服务
"Elderly care institutions" mean various types of elderly care institutions formed in accordance with the Measures for Licensing the Formation of Elderly Care Institutions (Order No. 48, Ministry of Civil Affairs) issued by the Ministry of Civil Affairs and registered in accordance with the law to provide centralized residence and care services to senior citizens. "Elderly care services" mean daily care, rehabilitation nursing, mental care, cultural, entertainment, and other services provided by the aforesaid elderly care institutions to the senior people accepted in accordance with the provisions of the Measures for the Administration of Elderly Care Institutions (Order No. 49, Ministry of Civil Affairs).	养老机构,是指依照民政部《养老机构设立许可办法》(民政部令第 48 号)设立并依法办理登记的为老年人提供集中居住和照料服务的各类养老机构;养老服务,是指上述养老机构按照民政部《养老机构管理办法》(民政部令第 49 号)的规定,为收住的老年人提供的生活照料、康复护理、精神慰藉、文化娱乐等服务。
(3)Nursing Services Provided by Charity Agencies for the Disabled.	(三)残疾人福利机构提供的育养服务
(4)Matrimonial Agency Services.	(四)婚姻介绍服务
(5)Funeral and Interment Services.	(五)殡葬服务
"Funeral and interment services" means the services such as the receipt and transport (including carriage and disinfection), makeup, anti-corrosion, storage (including refrigeration), and cremation, deposit of bone ash, leasing of condolence facilities and equipment, and rental and management of graves, of which the charging rates assessed by all local price departments together with the relevant departments, or which are subject to the administration of government-guided pricing.	殡葬服务,是指收费标准由各地价格主管部门会同有关部门核定,或者实行政府指导价管理的遗体接运(含抬尸、消毒)、遗体整容、遗体防腐、存放(含冷藏)、火化、骨灰寄存、吊唁设施设备租赁、墓穴租赁及管理等服务。

Continued

English Translation	Chinese Version
(6)Services Provided by Disabled Persons to the Society	(六)残疾人员本人为社会提供的服务
(7)Medical Services Provided by Medical Institutions.	(七)医疗机构提供的医疗服务
"Medical institutions" mean the institutions that are registered in accordance with the provisions of the Regulation on the Administration of Medical Institutions (Order No. 149，State Council) issued by the State Council，the Detailed Rules on the Implementation of the Regulation on the Administration of Medical Institutions (Order No. 35，Ministry of Health) issued by the Ministry of Health，and have obtained a Practicing License of Medical Institutions upon registration，as well as all types of medical institutions of armies and armed forces at all levels，which specifically include: all kinds of hospitals，outpatient departments (stations)，community health service centers (stations)，emergency medical centers (stations)，urban and rural health centers，nursing home (places)，sanitariums，and clinic inspection centers at all levels，sanitation and epidemic prevention stations (epidemic disease control centers) and various specialized disease prevention and control centers (stations) launched by governments at all levels and related departments，maternal and child care centers (stations)，maternal and infant care institutions，and child health institutions launched by governments at all levels，and blood stations (blood centers) and other medical institutions launched by governments at all levels.	医疗机构,是指依据国务院《医疗机构管理条例》(国务院令第149号)及卫生部《医疗机构管理条例实施细则》(卫生部令第35号)的规定,经登记取得《医疗机构执业许可证》的机构,以及军队、武警部队各级各类医疗机构。具体包括:各级各类医院、门诊部(所)、社区卫生服务中心(站)、急救中心(站)、城乡卫生院、护理院(所)、疗养院、临床检验中心,各级政府及有关部门举办的卫生防疫站(疾病控制中心)、各种专科疾病防治站(所),各级政府举办的妇幼保健所(站)、母婴保健机构、儿童保健机构,各级政府举办的血站(血液中心)等医疗机构。
For the purpose of this item，"medical services" means the various kinds of services listed in the Rules on National Medical Service Price Items ，which are provided by medical institutions to patients at the guided medical service prices (including government-guided prices and the prices determined by both the supplier and the demander through consultation) determined by competent price departments at or above the prefecture (city) level together with competent health departments at the same level and other relevant departments，as well as health and epidemic prevention services provided by medical institutions to the public.	本项所称的医疗服务,是指医疗机构按照不高于地(市)级以上价格主管部门会同同级卫生主管部门及其他相关部门制定的医疗服务指导价格(包括政府指导价和按照规定由供需双方协商确定的价格等)为就医者提供《全国医疗服务价格项目规范》所列的各项服务,以及医疗机构向社会提供卫生防疫、卫生检疫的服务。
(8)Educational services provided by schools that provide education for academic credentials.	(八)从事学历教育的学校提供的教育服务。

Continued

English Translation	Chinese Version
(a) "Education for academic credentials" means the teaching form whereby the education recipients study at the schools as approved by relevant departments of the state or other educational institutions after passing the national education examination or by any other admission method as prescribed by the state and obtain the academic credentials recognized by the state，which specifically includes：	1.学历教育，是指受教育者经过国家教育考试或者国家规定的其他入学方式，进入国家有关部门批准的学校或者其他教育机构学习，获得国家承认的学历证书的教育形式。具体包括：
（ⅰ）primary education：regular primary schools and adult primary schools；	(1)初等教育:普通小学、成人小学。
（ⅱ）junior secondary school education：regular junior secondary schools，vocational junior secondary schools and adult junior secondary schools；	(2)初级中等教育:普通初中、职业初中、成人初中。
（ⅲ）senior secondary school education：regular senior secondary schools，adult senior secondary schools and vocational senior secondary schools（including regular technical secondary schools，adult technical secondary schools，vocational senior secondary schools and skilled worker schools）；and	(3)高级中等教育:普通高中、成人高中和中等职业学校(包括普通中专、成人中专、职业高中、技工学校)。
（ⅳ）higher education：regular colleges and universities，adult colleges and universities，Internet colleges and universities，institutions for graduate degrees（doctor degrees and master degrees），self-taught higher education examinations as well as examinations of higher education of academic credentials.	(4)高等教育:普通本专科、成人本专科、网络本专科、研究生(博士、硕士)、高等教育自学考试、高等教育学历文凭考试。
(b) The "schools that provide education for academic credentials" means：	2.从事学历教育的学校，是指：
（ⅰ）regular schools；	(1)普通学校。
（ⅱ）various types of schools formed with the approval of people's governments at or above the prefecture (city) level or education administrative departments of governments at the same level，and the academic credentials they confer are recognized by the state；	(2)经地(市)级以上人民政府或者同级政府的教育行政部门批准成立、国家承认其学员学历的各类学校。
（ⅲ）technical training schools and senior technical training schools formed with the approval of administrative departments of human resources and social security at or above the provincial level；and	(3)经省级及以上人力资源社会保障行政部门批准成立的技工学校、高级技工学校。

Continued

English Translation	Chinese Version
(ⅳ) technical colleges formed with the approval of provincial people's governments.	（4）经省级人民政府批准成立的技师学院。
The aforesaid schools include private schools that provide education for academic credentials according to the relevant provisions, but exclude vocational training institutions and other educational institutions and academic credentials they confer are not recognized by the state.	上述学校均包括符合规定的从事学历教育的民办学校，但不包括职业培训机构等国家不承认学历的教育机构。
(c) The "income from the provision of educational services that is exempted from the VAT" means the income from the provision of services of education for academic credentials to students enrolled within the prescribed admission plans, which specifically includes the income from tuition, accommodation expenses, textbook fees, exercise-book fees, and exam registration fees, as well as the income of boarding fees obtained by dining halls of schools from dining services, that are reviewed and approved by relevant departments and collected at the prescribed rates. Other income including sponsorship fees and school selection fees, etc., collected by schools in any name falls outside the scope of income that shall be exempted from the VAT.	3.提供教育服务免征增值税的收入，是指对列入规定招生计划的在籍学生提供学历教育服务取得的收入，具体包括：经有关部门审核批准并按规定标准收取的学费、住宿费、课本费、作业本费、考试报名费收入，以及学校食堂提供餐饮服务取得的伙食费收入。除此之外的收入，包括学校以各种名义收取的赞助费、择校费等，不属于免征增值税的范围。
"Dining halls of schools" means the dining halls managed in accordance with the Provisions on the Administration of Hygiene of School Dining Halls and Collective Meals for Students (Order No. 14, Ministry of Education)".	学校食堂是指依照《学校食堂与学生集体用餐卫生管理规定》（教育部令第 14 号）管理的学校食堂。
(9) Services provided by students participating in work-study programs.	（九）学生勤工俭学提供的服务。
(10) Agricultural mechanical ploughing, irrigation and drainage, prevention and treatment of plant diseases and insect pests, plant protection, agriculture and animal husbandry insurance, and related technical training, and breeding as well as the prevention and treatment of diseases of poultry, livestock and aquatic animals.	（十）农业机耕、排灌、病虫害防治、植物保护、农牧保险以及相关技术培训业务，家禽、牲畜、水生动物的配种和疾病防治。

Continued

English Translation	Chinese Version
"Agricultural mechanical ploughing" means cultivation (including ploughing and weeding, planting, harvesting, threshing, and plant protection, etc.) conducted with agricultural machinery in agriculture, forestry and husbandry. "Irrigation and drainage" means farmland irrigation or drainage of flooded farmlands. "Prevention and treatment of plant diseases and insect pests" means the prediction, reporting, prevention and control of plant diseases and insect pests in agriculture, forestry, husbandry and fishery. "Agriculture and animal husbandry insurance" means the provision of insurance for animals and plants in the planting industry, breeding industry and husbandry. "Related technical training" means technical training relating to agricultural mechanical ploughing, irrigation and drainage, prevention and treatment of plant diseases and insect pests, and plant protection as well as technical training making farmers acquire knowledge of agriculture and husbandry insurance. The tax exemption scope of breeding and the prevention and treatment of diseases of poultry, livestock and aquatic animals includes the provision of drugs and medical appliances related to such services.	农业机耕,是指在农业、林业、牧业中使用农业机械进行耕作(包括耕耘、种植、收割、脱粒、植物保护等)的业务;排灌,是指对农田进行灌溉或者排涝的业务;病虫害防治,是指从事农业、林业、牧业、渔业的病虫害测报和防治的业务;农牧保险,是指为种植业、养殖业、牧业种植和饲养的动植物提供保险的业务;相关技术培训,是指与农业机耕、排灌、病虫害防治、植物保护业务相关以及为使农民获得农牧保险知识的技术培训业务;家禽、牲畜、水生动物的配种和疾病防治业务的免税范围,包括与该项服务有关的提供药品和医疗用具的业务。
(11) Income obtained from selling tickets at the first entrance admission in the provision of cultural and sports services by memorial halls, museums, cultural centers, governing bodies of protected historic and cultural sites, art galleries, exhibition halls, academies of painting and calligraphy, and libraries in their own places.	(十一)纪念馆、博物馆、文化馆、文物保护单位管理机构、美术馆、展览馆、书画院、图书馆在自己的场所提供文化体育服务取得的第一道门票收入。
(12) Income obtained from selling tickets for cultural and religious activities held in Buddha temples, Taoist temples, mosques and churches.	(十二)寺院、宫观、清真寺和教堂举办文化、宗教活动的门票收入。
(13) Government funds and administrative charges collected by entities other than administrative entities in compliance with the conditions prescribed in Article 10 of the Measures for the Implementation of the Pilot Program.	(十三)行政单位之外的其他单位收取的符合《试点实施办法》第十条规定条件的政府性基金和行政事业性收费。
(14) Individuals' transfer of copyright.	(十四)个人转让著作权。
(15) Individuals' sale of housing units built and used by themselves.	(十五)个人销售自建自用住房。

Continued

English Translation	Chinese Version
（16）Public rental housing units leased by business management entities of public rental housing units before December 31，2018.	（十六）2018 年 12 月 31 日前，公共租赁住房经营管理单位出租公共租赁住房。
"Public rental housing units" means the public rental housing units that are included in the development planning and annual plans for public rental housing units as approved by people's governments of provinces，autonomous regions，municipalities directly under the Central Government，cities under separate state planning，and Xinjiang Production and Construction Corps and are managed in accordance with the Guiding Opinions on Accelerating the Development of Public Rental Housing Units（No. 87 [2010]，Ministry of Housing and Urban-Rural Development）and the specific administrative measures developed by people's governments of cities and counties.	公共租赁住房，是指纳入省、自治区、直辖市、计划单列市人民政府及新疆生产建设兵团批准的公共租赁住房发展规划和年度计划，并按照《关于加快发展公共租赁住房的指导意见》（建保〔2010〕87 号）和市、县人民政府制定的具体管理办法进行管理的公共租赁住房。
（17）Transport income obtained in the Mainland by Taiwan shipping companies and airline companies from the direct shipping and direct air transport services across the Taiwan Strait.	（十七）台湾航运公司、航空公司从事海峡两岸海上直航、空中直航业务在大陆取得的运输收入。
"Taiwan shipping companies" means the shipping companies which have obtained a "License for Cross-Strait Water Transport" issued by the Ministry of Transport，on which the company's registered address is in Taiwan.	台湾航运公司，是指取得交通运输部颁发的"台湾海峡两岸间水路运输许可证"且该许可证上注明的公司登记地址在台湾的航运公司。
"Taiwan airline companies" means airline companies registered in Taiwan and approved to engage in the non-regular（or chartered airplane）transport for cross-strait passengers，cargo，and mails based on a "business license" issued by the Civil Aviation Administration of China or under the Cross-Straits Air Transport Agreement and the Supplementary Agreement on Cross-Straits Air Transport.	台湾航空公司，是指取得中国民用航空局颁发的"经营许可"或者依据《海峡两岸空运协议》和《海峡两岸空运补充协议》规定，批准经营两岸旅客、货物和邮件不定期（包机）运输业务，且公司登记地址在台湾的航空公司。
（18）Direct or indirect international cargo transport agency services provided by taxpayers.	（十八）纳税人提供的直接或者间接国际货物运输代理服务。
（a）All international cargo transport agency service income collected from the principal and international transport costs paid to an international transportation carrier by a taxpayer from the provision of direct or indirect international cargo transport agency services must be settled through a financial institution.	1.纳税人提供直接或者间接国际货物运输代理服务，向委托方收取的全部国际货物运输代理服务收入，以及向国际运输承运人支付的国际运输费用，必须通过金融机构进行结算。

Continued

English Translation	Chinese Version
(b) The provisions on international cargo transport agency services shall apply, mutatis mutandis, to cargo transport agency services provided by taxpayers for cargo transport between the Mainland and Hong Kong, Macao, or Taiwan region.	2.纳税人为大陆与香港、澳门、台湾地区之间的货物运输提供的货物运输代理服务参照国际货物运输代理服务有关规定执行。
(c) Where the principal requests an invoice, the taxpayer shall issue a general VAT invoice in full amount to the principal for the international cargo transport agency service income.	3.委托方索取发票的,纳税人应当就国际货物运输代理服务收入向委托方全额开具增值税普通发票。
(19) Interest income as follows.	(十九)以下利息收入。
(a) Small loans of financial institutions for farmer households before December 31, 2016.	1.2016 年 12 月 31 日前,金融机构农户小额贷款。
"Small loans" means single loans, of which the total balance of the farmer household is not more than 100,000 yuan.	小额贷款,是指单笔且该农户贷款余额总额在 10 万元(含本数)以下的贷款。
"Farmer households" means the resident households living in the administrative areas of villages or towns (excluding county towns) for a long period (one year or longer), the residents living within the administrative villages under the jurisdiction of county towns for a long period, the residents who have not registered permanent residence of a locality but have lived in the locality for one year or longer, the employees of state-owned farms and rural individual industrial and commercial households. The collective households of government organs, social organizations, schools, enterprises and public institutions of the state-owned economy in the administrative areas of villages or towns (excluding county towns) and within the administrative villages under the jurisdiction of county towns; and the residents who have registered permanent residence of a locality, but have left hometown with the whole family and have been seeking a livelihood elsewhere for one year or longer are not farmer households, no matter whether they keep the contracted land or not. Farmer households shall be calculated on the basis of household, and they may engage in both agricultural and non-agricultural production and business operation. The loans for a farmer household shall be determined on the basis of whether the borrower is a farmer household when loans are granted.	所称农户,是指长期(一年以上)居住在乡镇(不包括城关镇)行政管理区域内的住户,还包括长期居住在城关镇所辖行政村范围内的住户和户口不在本地而在本地居住一年以上的住户,国有农场的职工和农村个体工商户。位于乡镇(不包括城关镇)行政管理区域内和在城关镇所辖行政村范围内的国有经济的机关、团体、学校、企事业单位的集体户;有本地户口,但举家外出谋生一年以上的住户,无论是否保留承包耕地均不属于农户。农户以户为统计单位,既可以从事农业生产经营,也可以从事非农业生产经营。农户贷款的判定应以贷款发放时的承贷主体是否属于农户为准。

Continued

English Translation	Chinese Version
(b) National student loans.	2.国家助学贷款。
(c) National debts, and debts of local governments.	3.国债、地方政府债。
(d) Loans granted by the PBC to financial institutions.	4.人民银行对金融机构的贷款。
(e) Individual housing loans granted by housing provident fund management centers with housing provident funds at designated authorized banks.	5.住房公积金管理中心用住房公积金在指定的委托银行发放的个人住房贷款。
(f) Foreign exchange loans granted by financial institutions as authorized by foreign exchange administrative departments in the business operation of state foreign exchange reserves.	6.外汇管理部门在从事国家外汇储备经营过程中,委托金融机构发放的外汇贷款。
(g) Interest charged by an enterprise group or any core enterprise of the enterprise group from the enterprise group or entities subordinated to the group at a rate not higher than the interest rate of loans paid to financial institutions or the nominal interest rate of paid bonds in the uniform lending and repayment business.	7.统借统还业务中,企业集团或企业集团中的核心企业以及集团所属财务公司按不高于支付给金融机构的借款利率水平或者支付的债券票面利率水平,向企业集团或者集团内下属单位收取的利息。
VAT shall be paid in full amount if the interest charged by the fund user in uniform lending is higher than the interest rate of loans or the nominal interest rate of bonds paid to the financial institution.	统借方向资金使用单位收取的利息,高于支付给金融机构借款利率水平或者支付的债券票面利率水平的,应全额缴纳增值税。
Uniform borrowing and repayment business means:	统借统还业务,是指:
(a) business in which an enterprise group or any core enterprise of the enterprise group, after borrowing funds from a financial institution or issuing bonds, allocates the borrowed funds to affiliated entities (including independent accounting entities and non-independent accounting entities, hereafter the same) and collects funds from affiliated entities to repay the principal and interest of the financial institution or bond purchasers; and	(1)企业集团或者企业集团中的核心企业向金融机构借款或对外发行债券取得资金后,将所借资金分拨给下属单位(包括独立核算单位和非独立核算单位,下同),并向下属单位收取用于归还金融机构或债券购买方本息的业务。
(b) business in which an enterprise group, after borrowing funds from a financial institution or issuing bonds, the finance company affiliated to the group signs a uniform loan borrowing and repayment contract with an enterprise group or an entity affiliated to the group and allocates funds, and collects the principal and interest from the enterprise group or entity affiliated to the group, and makes transfer payment to the enterprise group, and the enterprise group uniformly repays the financial institution or bond purchasers.	(2)企业集团向金融机构借款或对外发行债券取得资金后,由集团所属财务公司与企业集团或者集团内下属单位签订统借统还贷款合同并分拨资金,并向企业集团或者集团内下属单位收取本息,再转付企业集团,由企业集团统一归还金融机构或债券购买方的业务。

Continued

English Translation	Chinese Version
(20) Revoked financial institutions pay off debts with goods, immovable properties, intangible assets, negotiable securities, negotiable instruments and other properties.	（二十）被撤销金融机构以货物、不动产、无形资产、有价证券、票据等财产清偿债务。
"Revoked financial institutions" means financial institutions as well as their local branch offices revoked based on the decision of the PBC and the China Banking Regulatory Commission ("CBRC") in accordance with the law, including commercial banks, trust investment companies, finance companies, financial leasing companies, and urban and rural credit cooperatives revoked in accordance with the law. Unless it is otherwise provided for, enterprises affiliated or subordinated to the revoked financial institutions shall not enjoy the VAT exemption policies for revoked financial institutions.	被撤销金融机构，是指经人民银行、银监会依法决定撤销的金融机构及其分设于各地的分支机构，包括被依法撤销的商业银行、信托投资公司、财务公司、金融租赁公司、城市信用社和农村信用社。除另有规定外，被撤销金融机构所属、附属企业，不享受被撤销金融机构增值税免税政策。
(21) Premium income derived from personal insurance products with a term of one year or more launched by an insurance company.	（二十一）保险公司开办的一年期以上人身保险产品取得的保费收入。
"Personal insurance with a term of one year or more" means the life insurance and pension annuity insurance with a term of one year or more that returns principal and interest, and health insurance with a term of one year or more.	一年期以上人身保险，是指保险期间为一年期及以上返还本利的人寿保险、养老年金保险，以及保险期间为一年期及以上的健康保险。
"Life insurance" means the personal insurance with the life of a person as the subject matter insured.	人寿保险，是指以人的寿命为保险标的的人身保险。
"Pension annuity insurance" means the personal insurance for old-age security under which the payment of insurance benefit is conditioned on the survival of the insured and the survival benefit is paid by installments at agreed intervals. Pension annuity insurance shall concurrently meet the following conditions:	养老年金保险，是指以养老保障为目的，以被保险人生存为给付保险金条件，并按约定的时间间隔分期给付生存保险金的人身保险。养老年金保险应当同时符合下列条件：
(a) The age stipulated in the insurance contract for paying survival benefit to the insured is not lower than the retiring age prescribed by the state.	1.保险合同约定给付被保险人生存保险金的年龄不得小于国家规定的退休年龄。
(b) The interval between two consecutive payments does not exceed one year.	2.相邻两次给付的时间间隔不得超过一年。
"Health insurance" means the personal insurance under which the payment of insurance benefit is conditioned on the losses incurred for health reasons.	健康保险，是指以因健康原因导致损失为给付保险金条件的人身保险。

Continued

English Translation	Chinese Version
The aforesaid tax exemption policies shall be subject to recordation administration，and the specific measures for recordation administration shall be governed by the provisions of *the Announcement of the State Administration of Taxation on Relevant Administration Issues after the Cancellation of the Approval Item of Exemption of Business Tax on Refundable Personal Insurance Products with a Term of One Year or More* (Announcement No. 65〔2015〕, SAT).	上述免税政策实行备案管理,具体备案管理办法按照《国家税务总局关于一年期以上返还性人身保险产品免征营业税审批事项取消后有关管理问题的公告》(国家税务总局公告 2015 年第 65 号)规定执行。
(22)Income from the transfer of the following financial commodities.	(二十二)下列金融商品转让收入。
(a)the trading of securities by domestic companies upon the entrustment of qualified foreign investors (QFII) in China.	1.合格境外投资者(QFII)委托境内公司在我国从事证券买卖业务。
(b)the trading of A shares by investors on the Hong Kong market (including entities and individuals) listed on the Shanghai Stock Exchange through the Shanghai-Hong Kong Stock Connect.	2.香港市场投资者(包括单位和个人)通过沪港通买卖上海证券交易所上市 A 股。
(c)Trading of fund shares in the Mainland with investors on the Hong Kong market (including entities and individuals) through mutual fund recognition.	3.对香港市场投资者(包括单位和个人)通过基金互认买卖内地基金份额。
(d)Trading of stocks and bonds by management institutions of securities investment funds (closed-end securities investment funds and open-end securities investment funds) using funds.	4.证券投资基金(封闭式证券投资基金,开放式证券投资基金)管理人运用基金买卖股票、债券。
(e)Individuals' transfer of financial commodities.	5.个人从事金融商品转让业务。
(23)Interest income from the inter-bank business of financial institutions.	(二十三)金融同业往来利息收入。
(a)Fund transfer between financial institutions and the PBC, including loans granted by the PBC to general financial institutions，and rediscount of the PBC to commercial banks，etc.	1.金融机构与人民银行所发生的资金往来业务。包括人民银行对一般金融机构贷款,以及人民银行对商业银行的再贴现等。
(b) Business with associated banks. Fund transfer among different branches and divisions of the same banking system.	2.银行联行往来业务。同一银行系统内部不同行、处之间所发生的资金账务往来业务。

Continued

English Translation	Chinese Version
(c) Fund transfer among financial institutions, which means short-term unsecured financing (not more than one year) conducted through the nationwide unified interbank lending network with the approval of the PBC between financial institutions in the national interbank lending market.	3.金融机构间的资金往来业务,是指经人民银行批准,进入全国银行间同业拆借市场的金融机构之间通过全国统一的同业拆借网络进行的短期(一年以下含一年)无担保资金融通行为。
(4) Rediscount business among financial institutions.	4.金融机构之间开展的转贴现业务。
Financial institutions means:	金融机构是指:
(a) banks: including the PBC, commercial banks and policy banks;	(1)银行:包括人民银行、商业银行、政策性银行。
(b) credit cooperatives;	(2)信用合作社。
(c) securities companies;	(3)证券公司。
(d) financial leasing companies, securities fund management companies, finance companies, trust investment companies, and securities investment funds;	(4)金融租赁公司、证券基金管理公司、财务公司、信托投资公司、证券投资基金。
(e) insurance companies; and	(5)保险公司。
(f) other institutions that are formed upon the approval of the PBC, the CBRC, the CSRC or the CIRC and engage in the financial insurance business.	(6)其他经人民银行、银监会、证监会、保监会批准成立且经营金融保险业务的机构等。
(24) The income obtained by a guarantee institution concurrently meeting the following conditions from the credit guarantee or re-guarantee business for small and medium-sized enterprises (excluding the income from credit ratings, consulting, and training, etc.) shall be exempted from VAT for a period of three years.	(二十四)同时符合下列条件的担保机构从事中小企业信用担保或者再担保业务取得的收入(不含信用评级、咨询、培训等收入)3年内免征增值税:
(a) It has obtained a business permit of a financing guarantee institution issued by the regulatory department, has been registered as an enterprise (or a public institution) in accordance with the law, and has a paid-in capital of more than 20 million yuan.	1.已取得监管部门颁发的融资性担保机构经营许可证,依法登记注册为企(事)业法人,实收资本超过2000万元。
(b) The average annual guarantee rate does not exceed 50% of the bank's benchmark loan interest rate over the same period. The average annual guarantee rate = income from guarantee fees of the current period / (guarantee balance at the beginning of the period + guarantee amount increased during the current period) × 100%.	2.平均年担保费率不超过银行同期贷款基准利率的50%。平均年担保费率=本期担保费收入/(期初担保余额+本期增加担保金额)×100%。

Continued

English Translation	Chinese Version
(c) It has conducted business operation in compliance with Regulation for two consecutive years or more, with its funds used primarily for the guarantee business, has sound internal management rules and the capacity for providing guarantee for small and medium-sized enterprises, has prominent business performance, and has a sound mechanism for ex ante evaluation, in-process monitoring and ex-post recourse and disposal for guaranteed projects.	3.连续合规经营 2 年以上,资金主要用于担保业务,具备健全的内部管理制度和为中小企业提供担保的能力,经营业绩突出,对受保项目具有完善的事前评估、事中监控、事后追偿与处置机制。
(d) The amount of accumulated guarantee loans it provides to small and medium-sized enterprises accounts for 80% or more of the total amount of its accumulative guarantee business for the recent two years, and the amount of its accumulated guarantee loans each of which is worth less than 8 million yuan accounts for 50% or more of the total amount of its accumulative guarantee business.	4.为中小企业提供的累计担保贷款额占其两年累计担保业务总额的 80%以上,单笔 800 万元以下的累计担保贷款额占其累计担保业务总额的 50%以上。
(e) The guarantee balance provided for a single guaranteed enterprise accounts for not more than 10% of the total amount of the paid-in capital of the guarantee institution, and the average guarantee liability amount in a single deal is not more than 30 million yuan.	5.对单个受保企业提供的担保余额不超过担保机构实收资本总额的 10%,且平均单笔担保责任金额最多不超过 3000 万元人民币。
(f) Its guarantee liability balance is not less than three times its net assets, and its compensatory rate is not more than 2%.	6.担保责任余额不低于其净资产的 3 倍,且代偿率不超过 2%。
The recordation administration method shall be employed in the exemption of VAT on guarantee institutions. An eligible guarantee institution shall undergo recordation formalities with the competent tax authority of the county (city) at the place where it is located and the administrative department of small and medium-sized enterprises at the same level, and may enjoy the VAT exemption for three years as of the day when it completes recordation formalities. After the expiration of the three-year VAT exemption period, the eligible guarantee institution may continue the status after undergoing recordation formalities under the prescribed procedures.	担保机构免征增值税政策采取备案管理方式。符合条件的担保机构应到所在地县(市)主管税务机关和同级中小企业管理部门履行规定的备案手续,自完成备案手续之日起,享受 3 年免征增值税政策。3 年免税期满后,符合条件的担保机构可按规定程序办理备案手续后继续享受该项政策。

Continued

English Translation	Chinese Version
The specific measures for recordation administration shall be governed by the Announcement of the State Administration of Taxation on Relevant Administrative Issues after the Cancellation of the Approval Item of Exemption of Business Tax on Credit Guarantee Institutions for Small and Medium-Sized Enterprises (Announcement No. 69〔2015〕, SAT), the recordation administrative departments of tax authorities shall be uniformly changed to county (city) state taxation bureaus.	具体备案管理办法按照《国家税务总局关于中小企业信用担保机构免征营业税审批事项取消后有关管理问题的公告》(国家税务总局公告 2015 年第 69 号)规定执行,其中税务机关的备案管理部门统一调整为县(市)级国家税务局。
(25) Interest subsidy income and price margin subsidy income obtained from the Central Treasury or local public finance departments by national commodity reserves management entities and their directly subordinated enterprises undertaking commodity reserves.	(二十五)国家商品储备管理单位及其直属企业承担商品储备任务,从中央或者地方财政取得的利息补贴收入和价差补贴收入。
"National commodity reserves management entities and their directly subordinated enterprises" means the commodity reserves enterprises that accept the authorization of relevant departments of the government of the four levels: the Central, province, city and county levels (or management entities designated by the government) to undertake the task of reserving six kinds of commodities, including cereals (including soybeans), edible oil, cotton, sugar, meat and salt (limited to central reserves), reserve and sell the aforesaid six kinds of reserved commodities in accordance with relevant policies and have obtained the fiscal funds or subsidies for reserves. "Interest subsidy income" means the interest income obtained by national commodity reserves management entities and their directly subordinated enterprises from the Central Treasury or local public finance departments for repaying the interest on loans from financial institutions for undertaking the task of reserving the aforesaid commodities. "Price margin subsidy income" includes sales price margin subsidy income and rotation price margin subsidy income. "Sales price margin subsidy income" means the full price margin subsidy income obtained from the Central Treasury or local public finance departments when the aforesaid reserved commodities are sold based on the order of the Central Government or local governments due to the fact that the sales income is less than the inventory cost. "Rotation price margin subsidy income" means the income of subsidies for price margin caused by different quality of old and new commodities, which is obtained from the Central Treasury or local public finance departments for organizing the rotation of policy-oriented reserved commodities on a periodical basis as required.	国家商品储备管理单位及其直属企业,是指接受中央、省、市、县四级政府有关部门(或者政府指定管理单位)委托,承担粮(含大豆)、食用油、棉、糖、肉、盐(限于中央储备)等 6 种商品储备任务,并按有关政策收储、销售上述 6 种储备商品,取得财政储备经费或者补贴的商品储备企业。利息补贴收入,是指国家商品储备管理单位及其直属企业因承担上述商品储备任务从金融机构贷款,并从中央或者地方财政取得的用于偿还贷款利息的贴息收入。价差补贴收入包括销售价差补贴收入和轮换价差补贴收入。销售价差补贴收入,是指按照中央或者地方政府指令销售上述储备商品时,由于销售收入小于库存成本而从中央或者地方财政获得的全额价差补贴收入。轮换价差补贴收入,是指根据要求定期组织政策性储备商品轮换而从中央或者地方财政取得的商品新陈品质价差补贴收入。

Continued

English Translation	Chinese Version
(26)Technology transfer and technical development andrelated technical consulting and technical services provided by taxpayers.	(二十六)纳税人提供技术转让、技术开发和与之相关的技术咨询、技术服务。
(a)"Technology transfer and technical development" means business activities within the scope of "transfer of technologies" and "research and development services" in the Notes to Sales Services, Intangible Assets and Real Estate. "Technical consulting" means the business activities of providing feasibility studies, technical forecast, special-topic technical investigation, and analysis and evaluation reports, etc., for specific technical projects.	1.技术转让、技术开发,是指《销售服务、无形资产、不动产注释》中"转让技术"、"研发服务"范围内的业务活动。技术咨询,是指就特定技术项目提供可行性论证、技术预测、专题技术调查、分析评价报告等业务活动。
"Technical consulting and technical services relating to technical transfer and technical development" means technical consulting and technical services provided by a transferor (or authorized developer) to assist the transferee (or client) in understanding the transferred (or developed) technology according to the provisions of the technological transfer or development contract. The payment for the technical consulting and technical services and the payment for technical transfer or technical development shall be indicated on the same invoice.	与技术转让、技术开发相关的技术咨询、技术服务,是指转让方(或者受托方)根据技术转让或者开发合同的规定,为帮助受让方(或者委托方)掌握所转让(或者委托开发)的技术,而提供的技术咨询、技术服务业务,且这部分技术咨询、技术服务的价款与技术转让或者技术开发的价款应当在同一张发票上开具。
(b)Recordation procedures. To apply for VAT exemption, a pilot taxpayer shall undergo determination by the provincial department of science and technology at the place where the pilot taxpayer is located on the basis of a written technical transfer or development contract, and submit to the competent tax authority the certification documents on the written contract and the review opinion of the competent department of science and technology for future reference.	2.备案程序。试点纳税人申请免征增值税时,须持技术转让、开发的书面合同,到纳税人所在地省级科技主管部门进行认定,并持有关的书面合同和科技主管部门审核意见证明文件报主管税务机关备查。
(27)Energy management contracting (EMC) services concurrently meeting the following conditions:	(二十七)同时符合下列条件的合同能源管理服务:
(a) The relevant technologies adopted by an energy service company in implementing EMC projects satisfy the technical requirements of the General Technical Rules for Energy Performance Contracting (GB/T 24915-2010) as issued by the General Administration of Quality Supervision, Inspection and Quarantine and the Standardization Administration of the People's Republic of China.	1.节能服务公司实施合同能源管理项目相关技术,应当符合国家质量监督检验检疫总局和国家标准化管理委员会发布的《合同能源管理技术通则》(GB/T24915-2010)规定的技术要求。

Continued

English Translation	Chinese Version
(b) The format and content of the savings sharing contract entered into by and between the energy service company and an energy consumption enterprise shall comply with the Contract Law of the People's Republic of China, the General Technical Rules for Energy Performance Contracting (GB/T 24915-2010) and other provisions.	2.节能服务公司与用能企业签订节能效益分享型合同,其合同格式和内容,符合《中华人民共和国合同法》和《合同能源管理技术通则》(GB/T24915-2010)等规定。
(28) The ticket proceeds of popular science publicity entities and the ticket proceeds arising from popular science activities carried out by Party and government departments and associations for science and technology at or above the county level before December 31, 2017.	(二十八)2017年12月31日前,科普单位的门票收入,以及县级及以上党政部门和科协开展科普活动的门票收入。
"Popular science publicity entities" means science and technology museums, museums of natural history, planetariums (observatories), meteorological observatories (stations), and seismic stations that are open to the public, as well as popular science publicity bases of institutions of higher learning and scientific research institutions that are open to the public.	科普单位,是指科技馆、自然博物馆,对公众开放的天文馆(站、台)、气象台(站)、地震台(站),以及高等院校、科研机构对公众开放的科普基地。
"Science popularization activities" means the activities of introducing to the general public the knowledge on natural science and social science, popularizing the application of science and technologies, advocating scientific methods, spreading scientific ideologies and advancing the scientific spirit by all media forms that the public can easily understand, accept and participate in.	科普活动,是指利用各种传媒以浅显的、让公众易于理解、接受和参与的方式,向普通大众介绍自然科学和社会科学知识,推广科学技术的应用,倡导科学方法,传播科学思想,弘扬科学精神的活动。
(29) Income gained from giving classes of advanced study or training classes by colleges and universities, secondary schools and elementary schools (excluding their subordinated entities) funded by governments which is fully attributable to the school.	(二十九)政府举办的从事学历教育的高等、中等和初等学校(不含下属单位),举办进修班、培训班取得的全部归该学校所有的收入。
"The income is fully attributable to the schools" means that the income from giving classes of advanced study or training classes shall be deposited into the uniform account of a school, be included in the budget, and be turned over in full amount to a special fiscal account for management. The school shall uniformly manage them and issue relevant vouchers at the same time.	全部归该学校所有,是指举办进修班、培训班取得的全部收入进入该学校统一账户,并纳入预算全额上缴财政专户管理,同时由该学校对有关票据进行统一管理和开具。

Continued

English Translation	Chinese Version
The income from giving classes of advanced study or training classes that are deposited into an account opened by the department of the school itself shall not be exempted from the VAT.	举办进修班、培训班取得的收入进入该学校下属部门自行开设账户的,不予免征增值税。
(30) Income obtained from the provision of "modern services" (excluding financial leasing services, advertising services and other modern services) and "life services" (excluding cultural and sports activities, other life services, sauna, and oxygen bars), which are formed by vocational schools launched by the government mainly for the purpose of providing place of practice for in-school students, funded, run and managed by such schools, and the business income of which is owned by the schools.	(三十)政府举办的职业学校设立的主要为在校学生提供实习场所、并由学校出资自办、由学校负责经营管理、经营收入归学校所有的企业,从事《销售服务、无形资产或者不动产注释》中"现代服务"(不含融资租赁服务、广告服务和其他现代服务)、"生活服务"(不含文化体育服务、其他生活服务和桑拿、氧吧)业务活动取得的收入。
(31) Income obtained from the provision of home care services by home care service staff members subject to the staffing system of home care service enterprises.	(三十一)家政服务企业由员工制家政服务员提供家政服务取得的收入。
"home care service enterprise" means an enterprise of which home care services are included in the business scope prescribed in the enterprise's business license.	家政服务企业,是指在企业营业执照的规定经营范围中包括家政服务内容的企业。
"Home care service staff member subject to the staffing system" means a home care service staff member concurrently meeting the following three conditions:	员工制家政服务员,是指同时符合下列3个条件的家政服务员:
(a) He or she has concluded a labor contract or service agreement with a term of half a year or longer with a home care service enterprise in accordance with the law, and actually works in the enterprise.	1.依法与家政服务企业签订半年及半年以上的劳动合同或者服务协议,且在该企业实际上岗工作。

Continued

English Translation	Chinese Version
(b) The home care service enterprise has paid for him or her the basic endowment insurance, basic medical insurance, work injury insurance, unemployment insurance or any other social insurance prescribed by the people's government at the place where the enterprise is located according to the policies of the state in full amount on a monthly basis. For a home care service staff member who has claimed any new-type rural endowment insurance, new-type rural cooperative medical insurance or other social insurance or for whom the entity where the laid-off worker worked continues to pay social insurance for him or her, if he or she has submitted a written request on non-payment of corresponding social insurance prescribed by the people's government at the place where the enterprise is located according to the provisions of policies of the state, and issued a certificate on the payment of relevant insurance issued by the town (township) where he or she is located or the entity where he or she worked with, it shall be deemed that the home care service enterprise has paid corresponding social insurance for him or her in full amount on a monthly basis.	2.家政服务企业为其按月足额缴纳了企业所在地人民政府根据国家政策规定的基本养老保险、基本医疗保险、工伤保险、失业保险等社会保险。对已享受新型农村养老保险和新型农村合作医疗等社会保险或者下岗职工原单位继续为其缴纳社会保险的家政服务员,如果本人书面提出不再缴纳企业所在地人民政府根据国家政策规定的相应的社会保险,并出具其所在乡镇或者原单位开具的已缴纳相关保险的证明,可视同家政服务企业已为其按月足额缴纳了相应的社会保险。
(c) The home care service enterprise has actually paid wage of the minimum standard applicable to the place where the enterprise is located and approved by the provincial people's government to him or her through a financial institution.	3.家政服务企业通过金融机构向其实际支付不低于企业所在地适用的经省级人民政府批准的最低工资标准的工资。
(32) Income from the issuance of welfare lotteries and sports lotteries.	(三十二)福利彩票、体育彩票的发行收入。
(33) Income from the rental of surplus real properties of the army.	(三十三)军队空余房产租赁收入。
(34) Income from the sale of housing units by enterprises and administrative institutions at the cost price or at the standard price in support of the housing system reform of the state.	(三十四)为了配合国家住房制度改革,企业、行政事业单位按房改成本价、标准价出售住房取得的收入。
(35) Transfer of the right to use land to agricultural producers for agricultural production.	(三十五)将土地使用权转让给农业生产者用于农业生产。
(36) Individuals' free transfer of real estate and the right to use land involved in the division of housing property.	(三十六)涉及家庭财产分割的个人无偿转让不动产、土地使用权。

Continued

English Translation	Chinese Version
The division of housing property covers the following circumstances: the division of property due to divorce; a grant as gift to his/her spouse, parent, child, grandparent, grandchild, brother or sister; a grant as gift to a person who directly performs the obligation of fostering or supporting the individual; or a statutory heir, a heir by testament or a devisee who acquires a housing property pursuant to law after the housing property's owner dies.	家庭财产分割,包括下列情形:离婚财产分割;无偿赠与配偶、父母、子女、祖父母、外祖父母、孙子女、外孙子女、兄弟姐妹;无偿赠与对其承担直接抚养或者赡养义务的抚养人或者赡养人;房屋产权所有人死亡,法定继承人、遗嘱继承人或者受遗赠人依法取得房屋产权。
(37)The land owner sells the right to use land and the land user returns the right to use land to the land owner.	(三十七)土地所有者出让土地使用权和土地使用者将土地使用权归还给土地所有者。
(38)The assignment, transfer or recovery of the right to use natural resources (excluding the right to use land) by local people's governments at or above the county level or natural resources administrative departments.	(三十八)县级以上地方人民政府或自然资源行政主管部门出让、转让或收回自然资源使用权(不含土地使用权)。
(39)Employment of family members living with military service members.	(三十九)随军家属就业。
(a)The taxable services provided by an enterprise newly formed for the employment of family members living with military service members shall be exempted from the VAT for three years from the date when the enterprise obtains its tax registration certificate.	1.为安置随军家属就业而新开办的企业,自领取税务登记证之日起,其提供的应税服务 3 年内免征增值税。
The family members of military service members employed by an enterprise enjoying preferential tax policies must account for 60% or more of the total number of employees of the enterprise, as proved by a certificate issued by the political and logistics organ at or above the corps level.	享受税收优惠政策的企业,随军家属必须占企业总人数的 60% (含)以上,并有军(含)以上政治和后勤机关出具的证明。
(b)The taxable services provided by a family member of a military service member in the form of operating an individual industrial and commercial household business shall be exempted from the VAT for three years as of the day when the family member undergoes tax registration formalities.	2.从事个体经营的随军家属,自办理税务登记事项之日起,其提供的应税服务 3 年内免征增值税。
A family member of a military service member must have a certificate issued by the political organ at or above the division level to show his or her identity.	随军家属必须有师以上政治机关出具的可以表明其身份的证明。

Continued

English Translation	Chinese Version
According to the aforesaid provisions, each family member of a military service member may enjoy tax exemption policies once.	按照上述规定,每一名随军家属可以享受一次免税政策。
(40)Employment of demobilized military officers.	(四十)军队转业干部就业。
(a)The taxable services provided by a demobilized military officer in the form of operating an individual industrial and commercial household business shall be exempted from the VAT for three years as of the day when the demobilized military officer obtains a tax registration certificate.	1.从事个体经营的军队转业干部,自领取税务登记证之日起,其提供的应税服务 3 年内免征增值税。
(b)The taxable services provided by an enterprise newly formed for the employment of demobilized military officers choosing independent employment shall be exempted from the VAT for three years from the date when the enterprise obtains a tax registration certificate, provided that the demobilized military officers choosing independent employment account for 60% or more of the total number of employees of the enterprise.	2.为安置自主择业的军队转业干部就业而新开办的企业,凡安置自主择业的军队转业干部占企业总人数 60%(含)以上的,自领取税务登记证之日起,其提供的应税服务 3 年内免征增值税。
A demobilized military officer choosing independent employment who enjoys the aforesaid preferential policies must have a demobilization certificate issued by the army at or above the division level.	享受上述优惠政策的自主择业的军队转业干部必须持有师以上部队颁发的转业证件。
Ⅱ. Immediate VAT Refund after Payment	二、增值税即征即退
(1)For pipeline transportation services provided by a general taxpayer, the VAT policy of refund immediately after payment shall apply to the portion of actual VAT burden on the taxpayer in excess of 3%.	(一)一般纳税人提供管道运输服务,对其增值税实际税负超过 3%的部分实行增值税即征即退政策。

Continued

English Translation	Chinese Version
(2)For the services of financial leasing of tangible personal property and sale and leaseback financing of tangible personal property provided by a general taxpayer among pilot taxpayers engaged in financial leasing as approved by the PBC, the CBRC, or the Ministry of Commerce, the VAT policy of refund immediately after payment shall apply to the portion of actual tax burden on the pilot taxpayer in excess of 3%. If the paid-in capital of a general taxpayer among pilot taxpayers engaged in financial leasing and sale and leaseback financing as approved by a provincial commerce department or a state economic and technological development zone authorized by the Ministry of Commerce reaches 170 million yuan after May 1, 2016, the aforesaid provisions shall apply from the month when the paid-in capital reaches the threshold, or if the paid-in capital fails to reach 170 million yuan but the registered capital reaches 170 million yuan after May 1, 2016, the aforesaid provisions may also apply from the first day of the next month before July 31, 2016. The financial leasing of tangible personal property and sale and leaseback financing of tangible personal property conducted after August 1, 2016 shall no longer be governed by the aforesaid provisions.	（二）经人民银行、银监会或者商务部批准从事融资租赁业务的试点纳税人中的一般纳税人，提供有形动产融资租赁服务和有形动产融资性售后回租服务，对其增值税实际税负超过3%的部分实行增值税即征即退政策。商务部授权的省级商务主管部门和国家经济技术开发区批准的从事融资租赁业务和融资性售后回租业务的试点纳税人中的一般纳税人，2016年5月1日后实收资本达到1.7亿元的，从达到标准的当月起按照上述规定执行；2016年5月1日后实收资本未达到1.7亿元但注册资本达到1.7亿元的，在2016年7月31日前仍可按照上述规定执行，2016年8月1日后开展的有形动产融资租赁业务和有形动产融资性售后回租业务不得按照上述规定执行。
(3)For the purpose of these Provisions, "actual VAT burden" means the portion of VAT actually paid by a taxpayer on taxable services provided for the current period to the total price and additional fees obtained by the taxpayer from providing taxable services during the current period.	（三）本规定所称增值税实际税负，是指纳税人当期提供应税服务实际缴纳的增值税额占纳税人当期提供应税服务取得的全部价款和价外费用的比例。
Ⅲ. Provisions on VAT Deduction	三、扣减增值税规定
(1)Business start-up and employment of retired soldiers.	（一）退役士兵创业就业。

Continued

Continued

English Translation	Chinese Version
(a) A self-employed retired soldier that conducts business operation in the form of an individual industrial and commercial household may enjoy a credit up to 8,000 yuan for each household per year against, by turns, the VAT, urban maintenance and construction tax, educational surtax, local education surtax and individual income tax actually payable for the current year for a period of three years. The credit limit may be raised by 20% at a maximum, and the people's government of a province, an autonomous region or a municipality directly under the Central Government may, according to the actual circumstances of its local area, determine the specific credit limit within the said range, and report it to the Ministry of Finance and the State Administration of Taxation ("SAT") for recordation.	1.对自主就业退役士兵从事个体经营的,在3年内按每户每年8000元为限额依次扣减其当年实际应缴纳的增值税、城市维护建设税、教育费附加、地方教育附加和个人所得税。限额标准最高可上浮20%,各省、自治区、直辖市人民政府可根据本地区实际情况在此幅度内确定具体限额标准,并报财政部和国家税务总局备案。
Where the amount of annual taxes payable by a taxpayer is less than the aforesaid credit limit, the amount shall be limited to the actual taxes payable. If the amount of annual taxes payable is more than the aforesaid credit limit, the aforesaid limit shall apply. If the taxpayer has actually conducted business operation for less than one year, it shall compute the tax reduction or exemption limit according to actual months. The computing formula is: Tax reduction or exemption limit = Annual tax reduction or exemption limit ÷ 12 × Actual months of business operation.	纳税人年度应缴纳税款小于上述扣减限额的,以其实际缴纳的税款为限;大于上述扣减限额的,应以上述扣减限额为限。纳税人的实际经营期不足一年的,应当以实际月份换算其减免税限额。换算公式为:减免税限额=年度减免税限额÷12×实际经营月数。
The taxpayer shall, during the current month when enjoying preferential tax policies, undergo recordation formalities with the competent tax authority based on the Certificate of Retirement from Active Duty of Compulsory Serviceman of the Chinese People's Liberation Army or the Certificate of Retirement from Active Duty of Non-Commissioned Officer of the Chinese People's Liberation Army and relevant materials required by the tax authority.	纳税人在享受税收优惠政策的当月,持《中国人民解放军义务兵退出现役证》或《中国人民解放军士官退出现役证》以及税务机关要求的相关材料向主管税务机关备案。

中国涉外税法

Continued

English Translation	Chinese Version
(b) Where a processing enterprise which is also a commercial and trade enterprise, service enterprise, or labor employment service enterprise or a small enterprise (entity) of processing nature of a sub-district or residential community enters into labor contracts for a term of one year or more with newly recruited self-employed retired soldiers to fill the newly created job vacancies in the current year and pays social insurance premiums for them in accordance with the law, the enterprise may, for three years, enjoy a fixed credit against, by turns, the VAT, urban maintenance and construction tax, educational surtax, local education surtax and enterprise income tax preferences according to the number of actually employed persons. The fixed credit shall be 4,000 yuan per person each year and may be raised by 50% at a maximum. The people's government of a province, an autonomous region or a municipality directly under the Central Government shall, according to the actual circumstances of its local area, determine the specific credit limit within the said range, and report it to the Ministry of Finance and the SAT for recordation.	2.对商贸企业、服务型企业、劳动就业服务企业中的加工型企业和街道社区具有加工性质的小型企业实体,在新增加的岗位中,当年新招用自主就业退役士兵,与其签订1年以上期限劳动合同并依法缴纳社会保险费的,在3年内按实际招用人数予以定额依次扣减增值税、城市维护建设税、教育费附加、地方教育附加和企业所得税优惠。定额标准为每人每年4000元,最高可上浮50%,各省、自治区、直辖市人民政府可根据本地区实际情况在此幅度内确定具体定额标准,并报财政部和国家税务总局备案。
For the purpose of this Article, "service enterprises" means enterprises that conduct business activities within the scope of "real estate lease services", "commercial assistance services" (excluding goods transport agency and agency customs declaration services), and "life services" (excluding cultural and sports services) in the Notes to Sales Services, Intangible Assets and Real Estate and private non-enterprise entities registered and formed in accordance with the Interim Regulation on the Registration and Administration of Private Non-Enterprise Entities (Order No. 251, State Council).	本条所称服务型企业是指从事《销售服务、无形资产、不动产注释》中"不动产租赁服务"、"商务辅助服务"(不含货物运输代理和代理报关服务)、"生活服务"(不含文化体育服务)范围内业务活动的企业以及按照《民办非企业单位登记管理暂行条例》(国务院令第251号)登记成立的民办非企业单位。

Continued

English Translation	Chinese Version
The taxpayer shall assess the sum of tax reduced or exempted of the enterprise according to the number of persons recruited by the enterprise and the length of the signed labor contract, and by turns, deduct the VAT, urban maintenance and construction tax, educational surtax, and local educational surtax on a monthly basis within the assessed sum of tax reduced or exempted. If the amount of VAT, urban maintenance and construction tax, educational surtax, and local educational surtax that shall be actually paid by the taxpayer is less than the assessed sum of tax reduced or exempted, the actually payable VAT, urban maintenance and construction tax, educational surtax, and local educational surtax shall be taken as the limit; and if the amount of actually payable VAT, urban maintenance and construction tax, educational surtax, and local educational surtax is more than the assessed sum of tax reduced or exempted, the assessed sum of tax reduced or exempted shall be taken as the limit.	纳税人按企业招用人数和签订的劳动合同时间核定企业减免税总额,在核定减免税总额内每月依次扣减增值税、城市维护建设税、教育费附加和地方教育附加。纳税人实际应缴纳的增值税、城市维护建设税、教育费附加和地方教育附加小于核定减免税总额的,以实际应缴纳的增值税、城市维护建设税、教育费附加和地方教育附加为限;实际应缴纳的增值税、城市维护建设税、教育费附加和地方教育附加大于核定减免税总额的,以核定减免税总额为限。
Where the amount of VAT, urban maintenance and construction tax, educational surtax, and local educational surtax actually reduced or exempted of the enterprise is less than the assessed sum of tax reduced or exempted at the end of a tax year, the enterprise shall deduct the enterprise income tax at the time of final settlement and payment of the enterprise income tax. If the amount is not fully deducted in the current year, the remainder of the amount shall not be carried forward to the following year.	纳税年度终了,如果企业实际减免的增值税、城市维护建设税、教育费附加和地方教育附加小于核定的减免税总额,企业在企业所得税汇算清缴时扣减企业所得税。当年扣减不足的,不再结转以后年度扣减。
The computing formula is: Sum of tax reduced or exempted of the enterprise $= \Sigma$ working months of each self-employed retired worker in the enterprise in the current year $\div 12 \times$ Credit limit	计算公式为:企业减免税总额$=\Sigma$每名自主就业退役士兵本年度在本企业工作月份$\div 12 \times$定额标准。
The enterprise shall enjoy preferential tax policies as of the month immediately after recruiting self-employed retired soldiers, and on the current month when it enjoys preferential tax policies, undergo recordation formalities with the competent tax authority based on the following materials:	企业自招用自主就业退役士兵的次月起享受税收优惠政策,并于享受税收优惠政策的当月,持下列材料向主管税务机关备案:

Continued

English Translation	Chinese Version
(a)Certificate of Retirement from Active Duty of Compulsory Serviceman of the Chinese People's Liberation Army or the Certificate of Retirement from Active Duty of Non-Commissioned Officer of the Chinese People's Liberation Army of newly recruited self-employed retired soldiers.	(1)新招用自主就业退役士兵的《中国人民解放军义务兵退出现役证》或《中国人民解放军士官退出现役证》。
(b)Labor contracts (duplicates) entered into by the enterprise and newly recruited self-employed retired soldiers, and records of the enterprise's payment of social insurance premiums for the employees.	(2)企业与新招用自主就业退役士兵签订的劳动合同(副本),企业为职工缴纳的社会保险费记录。
(c)Schedule on the work of self-employed retired soldiers at the enterprise in the current year.	(3)自主就业退役士兵本年度在企业工作时间表。
(d)Other relevant materials as required by the competent tax authority.	(4)主管税务机关要求的其他相关材料。
(3) "Self-employed retirement soldiers" as mentioned above means retired soldiers who have been discharged from active service and settled in the self-employment form in accordance with the Regulation on the Settlement of Retired Soldiers (Order No. 608, State Council and Central Military Commission).	3.上述所称自主就业退役士兵是指依照《退役士兵安置条例》(国务院、中央军委令第 608 号)的规定退出现役并按自主就业方式安置的退役士兵。
(4) The aforesaid preferential tax policies shall be implemented from May 1, 2016, to December 31, 2016. If a taxpayer has not enjoyed the policies for three years by December 31, 2016, the taxpayer may continue enjoying the policies until the expiration of the three-year period.	4.上述税收优惠政策的执行期限为 2016 年 5 月 1 日至 2016 年 12 月 31 日,纳税人在 2016 年 12 月 31 日未享受满 3 年的,可继续享受至 3 年期满为止。
A taxpayer who has enjoyed preferential business tax policies in accordance with the provisions of the Notice of the Ministry of Finance, the State Administration of Taxation and the Ministry of Civil Affairs on Adjusting Relevant Tax Policies to Improve Support to Self-Employed Retired Soldiers in Business Start-up and Employment (No. 42 [2014], MOF) shall enjoy preferential VAT policies according to the aforesaid provisions as of May 1, 2016, and may continue enjoying the policies until the expiration of the three-year period if the taxpayer has not enjoyed the policies for three years by December 31, 2016.	按照《财政部 国家税务总局 民政部关于调整完善扶持自主就业退役士兵创业就业有关税收政策的通知》(财税〔2014〕42 号)规定享受营业税优惠政策的纳税人,自 2016 年 5 月 1 日起按照上述规定享受增值税优惠政策,在 2016 年 12 月 31 日未享受满 3 年的,可继续享受至 3 年期满为止。

Continued

English Translation	Chinese Version
The implementation of the VAT exemption policy for the employment of urban retired soldiers as mentioned in item（12），Article 1 of Annex 3 to the Notice of the Ministry of Finance and the State Administration of Taxation on Including Railway Transport and Postal Service Sectors in the Pilot Program of Replacing Business Tax with value-added tax（No. 106〔2013〕，MOF）shall be terminated on January 1，2014. The said personnel may continue enjoying the policy until the expiration of the three-year period if they have not enjoyed the policy for three years by June 30，2014.	《财政部 国家税务总局关于将铁路运输和邮政业纳入营业税改征增值税试点的通知》（财税〔2013〕106 号）附件 3 第一条第（十二）项城镇退役士兵就业免征增值税政策，自 2014 年 7 月 1 日起停止执行。在 2014 年 6 月 30 日未享受满 3 年的，可继续享受至 3 年期满为止。
（2）Business start-up and employment of key groups.	（二）重点群体创业就业。
（a）A holder of an Employment and Business Start-up Certificate（which indicates "tax policies on self-employment" or "tax policies for self-employment within the graduation year"）or an Employment and Unemployment Registration Certificate（which indicates "tax policies for self-employment" or is accompanied by a Self-Employment Certificate for College Graduates）obtained before January 27，2015 who conducts business operation in the form of individual industrial and commercial households may enjoy a credit up to 8,000 yuan for each household per year against，by turns，the VAT，urban maintenance and construction tax，educational surtax，local educational surtax and individual income tax actually payable for the current year for a period of three years. The credit limit may be raised by 20% at a maximum. The people's government of a province，an autonomous region or a municipality directly under the Central Government may，according to the actual circumstances of its local area，determine the specific credit limit within the said range，and report it to the Ministry of Finance and the SAT for recordation.	1.对持《就业创业证》（注明"自主创业税收政策"或"毕业年度内自主创业税收政策"）或 2015 年 1 月 27 日前取得的《就业失业登记证》（注明"自主创业税收政策"或附着《高校毕业生自主创业证》）的人员从事个体经营的，在 3 年内按每户每年 8000 元为限额依次扣减其当年实际应缴纳的增值税、城市维护建设税、教育费附加、地方教育附加和个人所得税。限额标准最高可上浮 20%，各省、自治区、直辖市人民政府可根据本地区实际情况在此幅度内确定具体限额标准，并报财政部和国家税务总局备案。
Where the amount of annual taxes payable by a taxpayer is less than the aforesaid credit limit，the credit shall be limited to the actual taxes payable. If the amount of annual taxes payable is more than the aforesaid credit limit，the aforesaid credit limit shall apply.	纳税人年度应缴纳税款小于上述扣减限额的，以其实际缴纳的税款为限；大于上述扣减限额的，应以上述扣减限额为限。
The aforesaid person means：	上述人员是指：

Continued

English Translation	Chinese Version
（ⅰ）a person who has registered his or her unemployment with the public employment service agency of the human resources and social security department for half a year or longer;	（1）在人力资源社会保障部门公共就业服务机构登记失业半年以上的人员。
（ⅱ）a registered unemployed person of working age from a zero-employment family or from an urban resident family under the minimum living standard guarantee program; or	（2）零就业家庭、享受城市居民最低生活保障家庭劳动年龄内的登记失业人员。
（ⅲ）a college graduate during the year of graduation. The term "college graduates" means students graduating from ordinary institutions of higher learning or institutions of higher learning for adults which offer higher education credentials. The year of graduation is the calendar year of graduation, namely, from January 1 to December 31.	（3）毕业年度内高校毕业生。高校毕业生是指实施高等学历教育的普通高等学校、成人高等学校毕业的学生；毕业年度是指毕业所在自然年，即 1 月 1 日至 12 月 31 日。
（b）Where a processing enterprise which is also a commercial and trade enterprise, service enterprise or labor employment service enterprise and a small enterprise (entity) of processing nature of a sub-district or residential community enters into labor contracts for a term of one year or more with newly employed persons who have registered their unemployment with public employment service agencies of human resources and social security departments for half a year or more and hold an Employment and Unemployment Registration Certificate or have obtained an Employment and Unemployment Registration Certificate obtained before January 27, 2015 (which indicates "tax policies for enterprises absorbing the unemployed") to fill the newly created job vacancies in the current year and pays social insurance premiums for them in accordance with the law, the enterprise may enjoy, for three years, a fixed credit against, by turns, the VAT, urban maintenance and construction tax, educational surtax, local education surtax and enterprise income tax preferences according to the number of actually employed persons. The fixed credit shall be 4,000 yuan per person each year and may be raised by 30% at a maximum. The people's government of a province, an autonomous region or a municipality directly under the Central Government may, according to the actual circumstances of its local region, determine the specific fixed credit within the said range, and report it to the Ministry of Finance and the SAT for recordation.	2.对商贸企业、服务型企业、劳动就业服务企业中的加工型企业和街道社区具有加工性质的小型企业实体，在新增加的岗位中，当年新招用在人力资源社会保障部门公共就业服务机构登记失业半年以上且持《就业创业证》或 2015 年 1 月 27 日前取得的《就业失业登记证》（注明"企业吸纳税收政策"）人员，与其签订 1 年以上期限劳动合同并依法缴纳社会保险费的，在 3 年内按实际招用人数予以定额依次扣减增值税、城市维护建设税、教育费附加、地方教育附加和企业所得税优惠。定额标准为每人每年 4000 元，最高可上浮 30%，各省、自治区、直辖市人民政府可根据本地区实际情况在此幅度内确定具体定额标准，并报财政部和国家税务总局备案。

Continued

English Translation	Chinese Version
The amount of tax credit calculated according to the aforesaid standard shall be deductible from the VAT, urban maintenance and construction tax, educational surtax, local educational surtax and enterprise income tax actually payable by the enterprise for the current year. If the said amount is not fully deducted in the current year, the remainder thereof may not be carried forward to the following year.	按上述标准计算的税收扣减额应在企业当年实际应缴纳的增值税、城市维护建设税、教育费附加、地方教育附加和企业所得税税额中扣减，当年扣减不足的，不得结转下年使用。
For the purpose of this Article, the term "service enterprise" means an enterprise that conducts business activities within the scope of "real estate lease services", "commercial assistance services" (excluding goods transport agency and agency customs declaration service), and "life services" (excluding cultural and sports services) in the Notes to Sales Services, Intangible Assets and Real Estate, or a private non-enterprise entity registered and formed in accordance with the Interim Regulation on the Administration of Registration of Private Non-Enterprise Entities (Order No. 251, State Council).	本条所称服务型企业是指从事《销售服务、无形资产、不动产注释》中"不动产租赁服务"、"商务辅助服务"(不含货物运输代理和代理报关服务)、"生活服务"(不含文化体育服务)范围内业务活动的企业以及按照《民办非企业单位登记管理暂行条例》(国务院令第 251 号)登记成立的民办非企业单位。
(3) Persons enjoying the aforesaid preferential policies shall apply for an Employment and Business Start-up Certificate according to the following provisions:	3.享受上述优惠政策的人员按以下规定申领《就业创业证》：
(a) According to the provision of Article 63 of the Provisions on Employment Services and Employment Management (Order No. 28, Ministry of Labor and Social Security), an unemployed urban permanent resident who is of the statutory working age, is able to work and needs a job may register his or her unemployment with the public employment service agency, and apply for an Employment and Unemployment Registration Certificate. In particular, a rural migrant worker or any other non-local permanent resident who has been employed for six consecutive months at the place of his or her habitual residence may conduct unemployment registration at the place of his or her place of habitual residence after he or she becomes unemployed.	(1)按照《就业服务与就业管理规定》(劳动和社会保障部令第 28 号)第六十三条的规定，在法定劳动年龄内，有劳动能力，有就业要求，处于无业状态的城镇常住人员，在公共就业服务机构进行失业登记，申领《就业创业证》。其中，农村进城务工人员和其他非本地户籍人员在常住地稳定就业满 6 个月的，失业后可以在常住地登记。

Continued

English Translation	Chinese Version
(b)A person from a zero-employment family or a person from a family receiving urban minimum living standard guarantee shall register his or her unemployment with a public employment service agency, and apply for an Employment and Business Start-Up Certificate upon the strength of a certificate issued by the residential community or a certificate on minimum living standard guarantee, where applicable.	(2)零就业家庭凭社区出具的证明,城镇低保家庭凭低保证明,在公共就业服务机构登记失业,申领《就业创业证》。
(c)A college graduate during the year of graduation shall, before graduation, apply to the public employment service agency for an Employment and Business Start-Up Certificate as required upon the strength of his or her student's identity card, or authorize the career center of the college where he or she studies to apply to the public employment service agency for an Employment and Business Start-Up Certificate on his or her behalf. After graduation, a college graduate shall directly apply to the public employment service agency for an Employment and Business Start-Up Certificate as required.	(3)毕业年度内高校毕业生在校期间凭学生证向公共就业服务机构按规定申领《就业创业证》,或委托所在高校就业指导中心向公共就业服务机构按规定代为其申领《就业创业证》;毕业年度内高校毕业生离校后直接向公共就业服务机构按规定申领《就业创业证》。
(d)After any of the aforesaid personnel has applied for and obtained the relevant certificate, the human resources and social security department at the place of employment or business start-up shall verify and determine his or her eligibility, employment and unemployment status and enjoyment of policies, and indicate "tax policies for self-employment", "tax policies for self-employment in the graduation year" or "tax policies for enterprises absorbing the employment" on his or her Employment and Business Start-Up Certificate or indicate both if the conditions for both tax policies are satisfied. The competent tax authority shall affix its official seal to the Employment and Business Start-Up Certificate, and indicate the period of tax deduction or exemption.	(4)上述人员申领相关凭证后,由就业和创业地人力资源社会保障部门对人员范围、就业失业状态、已享受政策情况进行核实,在《就业创业证》上注明"自主创业税收政策"、"毕业年度内自主创业税收政策"或"企业吸纳税收政策"字样,同时符合自主创业和企业吸纳税收政策条件的,可同时加注;主管税务机关在《就业创业证》上加盖戳记,注明减免税所属时间。
(4)The aforesaid preferential tax policies shall be implemented from May 1, 2016 to December 31, 2016. If a taxpayer has not enjoyed the policies for three years, the taxpayer may continue enjoying the policies until the expiration of the three-year period.	4.上述税收优惠政策的执行期限为 2016 年 5 月 1 日至 2016 年 12 月 31 日,纳税人在 2016 年 12 月 31 日未享受满 3 年的,可继续享受至 3 年期满为止。

Continued

English Translation	Chinese Version
A taxpayer who has enjoyed preferential business tax policies in accordance with the provisions of the Notice of the Ministry of Finance, the State Administration of Taxation and the Ministry of Human Resources and Social Security on Continuing the Implementation of Relevant Tax Policies for Supporting and Promoting the Business Start-up and Employment of Key Groups (No. 39〔2014〕, MOF) shall enjoy preferential VAT policies according to the aforesaid provisions as of May 1, 2016, and may continue enjoying the policies until the expiration of the three-year period if it has not enjoyed the policies for three years by December 31, 2016.	按照《财政部 国家税务总局 人力资源社会保障部关于继续实施支持和促进重点群体创业就业有关税收政策的通知》(财税〔2014〕39 号)规定享受营业税优惠政策的纳税人,自 2016 年 5 月 1 日起按照上述规定享受增值税优惠政策,在 2016 年 12 月 31 日未享受满 3 年的,可继续享受至 3 年期满为止。
The implementation of the preferential VAT policies for unemployed personnel as mentioned in item (13), Article 1 of Annex 3 to the Notice of the Ministry of Finance and the State Administration of Taxation on Including Railway Transport and Postal Service Sectors in the Pilot Program of Levying value-added tax in Lieu of Business Tax (No. 106〔2013〕, MOF) shall be terminated on January 1, 2014. The said personnel may continue enjoying the policies until the expiration of the three-year period if they have not enjoyed the policies for three years by December 31, 2013.	《财政部 国家税务总局关于将铁路运输和邮政业纳入营业税改征增值税试点的通知》(财税〔2013〕106 号)附件 3 第一条第(十三)项失业人员就业增值税优惠政策,自 2014 年 1 月 1 日起停止执行。在 2013 年 12 月 31 日未享受满 3 年的,可继续享受至 3 年期满为止。
Ⅳ. A financial enterprise shall pay VAT according to the existing provisions on the receivable but unreceived loan interest within 90 days as of the interest settlement date after granting a loan, is not required to pay the VAT for the receivable but unreceived loan interest for 90 days after the interest settlement date, and pay the VAT as required when it actually receives the interest.	四、金融企业发放贷款后,自结息日起 90 天内发生的应收未收利息按现行规定缴纳增值税,自结息日起 90 天后发生的应收未收利息暂不缴纳增值税,待实际收到利息时按规定缴纳增值税。
The term "financial enterprises" as mentioned above means banks (including state-owned, collective, shareholding, equity cooperative, foreign-funded banks and banks of other forms of ownership), urban credit cooperatives, rural credit cooperatives, trust investment companies and finance companies.	上述所称金融企业,是指银行(包括国有、集体、股份制、合资、外资银行以及其他所有制形式的银行)、城市信用社、农村信用社、信托投资公司、财务公司。

Continued

English Translation	Chinese Version
V. Where an individual sells a housing unit held for less than two years after the date of purchase, he or she shall pay VAT in full amount at the 5% levy rate; if an individual sells a housing unit held for two years or more after the date of purchase, he or she shall be exempted from the VAT thereon. The aforesaid policies shall apply to the regions other than Beijing Municipality, Shanghai Municipality, Guangzhou Municipality and Shenzhen Municipality.	五、个人将购买不足 2 年的住房对外销售的,按照 5%的征收率全额缴纳增值税;个人将购买 2 年以上(含 2 年)的住房对外销售的,免征增值税。上述政策适用于北京市、上海市、广州市和深圳市之外的地区。
An individual who sells a housing unit held for less than two years after the date of purchase shall pay VAT in full amount at the 5% levy rate; if an individual sells a non-ordinary housing unit held for two years or more after the date of purchase, he or she shall pay VAT at the 5% levy rate on the basis of the balance between the sales price and the purchase price of the unit; and if an individual sells an ordinary housing unit held for two years or more after the date of purchase, he or she shall be exempted from the VAT thereon. The aforesaid policies shall only apply to the regions other than Beijing Municipality, Shanghai Municipality, Guangzhou Municipality and Shenzhen Municipality.	个人将购买不足 2 年的住房对外销售的,按照 5%的征收率全额缴纳增值税;个人将购买 2 年以上(含 2 年)的非普通住房对外销售的,以销售收入减去购买住房价款后的差额按照 5%的征收率缴纳增值税;个人将购买 2 年以上(含 2 年)的普通住房对外销售的,免征增值税。上述政策仅适用于北京市、上海市、广州市和深圳市。
The specific procedures for handling tax exemption, the time of purchasing a housing unit, the issuance of invoices, the acquisition of a housing unit in a way other than purchase and other relevant taxation administration provisions shall be governed by the relevant provisions of the Notice of the General Office of the State Council on Forwarding the Opinions of the Ministry of Construction and Other Departments on Effectively Stabilizing Housing Prices (No. 26〔2005〕, General Office of the State Council), the Notice of the State Administration of Taxation, the Ministry of Finance and the Ministry of Construction on Strengthening the Administration of Real Estate Taxes (No. 89〔2005〕, SAT) and the Notice of the State Administration of Taxation on Several Specific Issues concerning the Implementation of Real Estate Tax Policies (No. 172〔2005〕, SAT).	办理免税的具体程序、购买房屋的时间、开具发票、非购买形式取得住房行为及其他相关税收管理规定,按照《国务院办公厅转发建设部等部门关于做好稳定住房价格工作意见的通知》(国办发〔2005〕26 号)、《国家税务总局 财政部 建设部关于加强房地产税收管理的通知》(国税发〔2005〕89 号)和《国家税务总局关于房地产税收政策执行中几个具体问题的通知》(国税发〔2005〕172 号)的有关规定执行。

Continued

English Translation	Chinese Version
VI. The aforesaid preferential VAT policies with the exception of the items of the time limit has been prescribed and the policies in Article 5, other items shall all be implemented during the period of the pilot program of replacing business tax with VAT. If a pilot taxpayer has enjoyed business tax preferences according to the relevant policies before the date of implementation of the pilot program, it shall enjoy relevant VAT preferences according to these Provisions during the remaining term of the preferential tax policies.	六、上述增值税优惠政策除已规定期限的项目和第五条政策外，其他均在营改增试点期间执行。如果试点纳税人在纳入营改增试点之日前已经按照有关政策规定享受了营业税税收优惠，在剩余税收优惠政策期限内，按照本规定享受有关增值税优惠。
Annex 4	附件4：
Provisions on the Application of Zero VAT Rate and VAT Exemption Policy to Cross-Border Taxable Activities	跨境应税行为适用增值税零税率和免税政策的规定
I. The VAT zero rate shall apply to the following services and intangible assets sold by entities or individuals within the territory of the People's Republic of China (hereinafter referred to as "within China"):	一、中华人民共和国境内（以下称境内）的单位和个人销售的下列服务和无形资产，适用增值税零税率：
1. International Transportation Services	（一）国际运输服务
"International transportation services" means:	国际运输服务，是指：
(1) transporting passengers or cargo from China to abroad;	1.在境内载运旅客或者货物出境。
(2) transporting into China passengers or cargo from abroad; and	2.在境外载运旅客或者货物入境。
(3) transporting passengers or cargo outside China.	3.在境外载运旅客或者货物。
2. Air transport Services	（二）航天运输服务
3. The following services provided for foreign entities that are fully consumed outside China:	（三）向境外单位提供的完全在境外消费的下列服务：
(1) R&D services;	1.研发服务。
(2) energy management contracting services;	2.合同能源管理服务。
(3) design services;	3.设计服务。
(4) production and distribution services of radio, film, and television programs (or works);	4.广播影视节目（作品）的制作和发行服务。
(5) software services;	5.软件服务。
(6) circuit design and testing services;	6.电路设计及测试服务。

Continued

English Translation	Chinese Version
（7）information system services；	7.信息系统服务。
（8）business process management services；	8.业务流程管理服务。
（9）offshore service outsourcing business；	9.离岸服务外包业务。
Offshore service outsourcing business includes information technology outsourcing (ITO), technical business process outsourcing (BPO), and technical knowledge process outsourcing service (KPO). The specific business activities involved therein shall be governed by the corresponding business activities in the Explanatory Notes on Sales Services, Intangible Assets, and Real Estate.	离岸服务外包业务,包括信息技术外包服务(ITO)、技术性业务流程外包服务(BPO)、技术性知识流程外包服务(KPO),其所涉及的具体业务活动,按照《销售服务、无形资产、不动产注释》相对应的业务活动执行。
（10）Transfer of technologies.	10.转让技术。
4. Other services as prescribed by the Ministry of Finance and the State Administration of Taxation.	(四)财政部和国家税务总局规定的其他服务。
Ⅱ. The following services and intangible assets sold by entities or individuals within China shall be exempted from VAT, unless it is prescribed by the Ministry of Finance and the State Administration of Taxation that zero VAT rate is applicable：	二、境内的单位和个人销售的下列服务和无形资产免征增值税,但财政部和国家税务总局规定适用增值税零税率的除外：
1. The "following services" means：	(一)下列服务：
（1）construction services of engineering projects located outside China；	1.工程项目在境外的建筑服务。
（2）engineering supervision services for engineering projects located outside China；	2.工程项目在境外的工程监理服务。
（3）engineering prospecting and exploration services for projects and mineral resources located outside China；	3.工程、矿产资源在境外的工程勘察勘探服务。
（4）conference and exhibition services for conferences and exhibitions located outside China；	4.会议展览地点在境外的会议展览服务。
（5）warehousing services for warehouses located outside China；	5.存储地点在境外的仓储服务。
（6）tangible personal property rental services with the subject matter used outside China；	6.标的物在境外使用的有形动产租赁服务。
（7）broadcasting services provided outside China for radio, film, and television programs (or works); and	7.在境外提供的广播影视节目(作品)的播映服务。
（8）culture and sports services, education and medical services, and tourism services provided outside China.	8.在境外提供的文化体育服务、教育医疗服务、旅游服务。

Continued

English Translation	Chinese Version
2. Postal services，receipt and delivery services，and insurance services provided for export cargo	（二）为出口货物提供的邮政服务、收派服务、保险服务。
Insurance services provided for export cargo include insurance for export cargo and insurance for export credit.	为出口货物提供的保险服务，包括出口货物保险和出口信用保险。
3. The following services and intangible assets provided for foreign entities that are fully consumed outside China include：	（三）向境外单位提供的完全在境外消费的下列服务和无形资产：
（1）telecommunications services；	1.电信服务。
（2）intellectual property services；	2.知识产权服务。
（3）logistics support services（excluding warehousing services and receipt and delivery services）；	3.物流辅助服务（仓储服务、收派服务除外）。
（4）authentication and consultation services；	4.鉴证咨询服务。
（5）professional technical services；	5.专业技术服务。
（6）business support services；	6.商务辅助服务。
（7）advertising services with advertisements released outside China；and	7.广告投放地在境外的广告服务。
（8）intangible assets.	8.无形资产。
4. International transportation services provided in the mode of carriage without means of transport.	（四）以无运输工具承运方式提供的国际运输服务。
5. Direct paid financial services provided for monetary financing and other financial services among foreign entities，and such services are irrelevant to the cargo, intangible assets，and real estate within China.	（五）为境外单位之间的货币资金融通及其他金融业务提供的直接收费金融服务，且该服务与境内的货物、无形资产和不动产无关。
6. Other services as prescribed by the Ministry of Finance and the State Administration of Taxation.	（六）财政部和国家税务总局规定的其他服务。
Ⅲ. For international transportation service items for which corresponding qualification should be obtained in accordance with the relevant provisions of the state, where the taxpayer has obtained the corresponding qualification, the zero VAT rate policy shall apply; and if the taxpayer fails to obtain the corresponding qualification, the VAT exemption policy shall apply.	三、按照国家有关规定应取得相关资质的国际运输服务项目，纳税人取得相关资质的，适用增值税零税率政策，未取得的，适用增值税免税政策。

Continued

English Translation	Chinese Version
Where an entity or individual within China provides voyage charter services，if the leased means of transport is used for international transportation services and Hong Kong，Macao，and Taiwan transportation services，the lessor shall apply for the application of zero VAT rate as required.	境内的单位或个人提供程租服务，如果租赁的交通工具用于国际运输服务和港澳台运输服务，由出租方按规定申请适用增值税零税率。
Where an entity or individual within China provides the entity or individual within China with time charter services or wet-lease services，if the lessee provides any other entity or individual with international transportation services and Hong Kong，Macao，and Taiwan transportation services by using the leased means of transport，the lessee shall apply for the application of zero VAT rate. Where an entity or individual within China provides any foreign entity or individual with voyage charter services or wet-lease services，the lessor shall apply for the application of zero VAT rate.	境内的单位和个人向境内单位或个人提供期租、湿租服务，如果承租方利用租赁的交通工具向其他单位或个人提供国际运输服务和港澳台运输服务，由承租方适用增值税零税率。境内的单位或个人向境外单位或个人提供期租、湿租服务，由出租方适用增值税零税率。
Where an entity or individual within China provides international transportation services in the mode of carriage without means of transport，the actual carrier within China shall apply for the application of zero VAT rate；and the business operator of the business of carriage without means of transport shall apply for the application of VAT exemption policy.	境内单位和个人以无运输工具承运方式提供的国际运输服务，由境内实际承运人适用增值税零税率；无运输工具承运业务的经营者适用增值税免税政策。
Ⅳ. For services or intangible assets provided by an entity or individual within China to which zero VAT rate applies，if the simple tax computation method is applicable，the method of VAT exemption shall apply. If the general VAT computation method is applicable，the method of tax exemption，deduction，and refund shall apply to production enterprises. The method of tax exemption and refund shall apply to foreign trade enterprises that export the outsourced services or intangible assets. Foreign trade enterprises that directly export their services or intangible assets under their independent R&D shall be deemed as production enterprises for purposes of uniformly applying the method of tax exemption，deduction，and refund.	四、境内的单位和个人提供适用增值税零税率的服务或者无形资产，如果属于适用简易计税方法的，实行免征增值税办法。如果属于适用增值税一般计税方法的，生产企业实行免抵退税办法，外贸企业外购服务或者无形资产出口实行免退税办法，外贸企业直接将服务或自行研发的无形资产出口，视同生产企业连同其出口货物统一实行免抵退税办法。

Continued

English Translation	Chinese Version
The tax refund rate of services and intangible assets shall be the applicable VAT rate as prescribed in items (1) to (3) of Article 15 of *the Measures for Implementing the Pilot Program*. For services and intangible assets to which the method of tax refund (exemption) is applicable, if the competent tax authority thinks that the export price is unusually high, it shall have the authority to compute the amount of tax refund (or exemption) at the assessed export price; and if the assessed export price is lower than the purchase price of a foreign trade enterprise, the input tax on the deficit may not be refunded, and shall be converted into costs.	服务和无形资产的退税率为其按照《试点实施办法》第十五条第(一)至(三)项规定适用的增值税税率。实行退(免)税办法的服务和无形资产,如果主管税务机关认定出口价格偏高的,有权按照核定的出口价格计算退(免)税,核定的出口价格低于外贸企业购进价格的,低于部分对应的进项税额不予退税,转入成本。
Ⅴ. Where an entity or individual within China sells services or intangible assets to which zero VAT rate applies, the entity or individual may waive the application of zero VAT rate, choose the application of VAT exemption policy, or pay VAT as required. After an entity or individual waives the application of zero VAT rate, such entity or individual may not apply for the application of zero VAT rate within 36 months.	五、境内的单位和个人销售适用增值税零税率的服务或无形资产的,可以放弃适用增值税零税率,选择免税或按规定缴纳增值税。放弃适用增值税零税率后,36个月内不得再申请适用增值税零税率。
Ⅵ. Where an entity or individual within China sells services or intangible assets to which zero VAT rate applies, the entity or individual shall, on a monthly basis, apply for handling VAT refund (exemption) formalities with the competent tax authority in charge of tax refund. The specific administrative measures shall be separately developed by the State Administration of Taxation with consultation with the Ministry of Finance.	六、境内的单位和个人销售适用增值税零税率的服务或无形资产,按月向主管退税的税务机关申报办理增值税退(免)税手续。具体管理办法由国家税务总局商财政部另行制定。
Ⅶ. The term "fully consumed outside China" as mentioned in these Provisions refers to the following circumstances:	七、本规定所称完全在境外消费,是指:
1. The actual recipients of services are located outside China and such services are irrelevant to the cargo or real estate within China.	(一)服务的实际接受方在境外,且与境内的货物和不动产无关。
2. Intangible assets are fully used outside China and such intangible assets are irrelevant to the cargo or real estate within China.	(二)无形资产完全在境外使用,且与境内的货物和不动产无关。
3. Other circumstances as prescribed by the Ministry of Finance and the State Administration of Taxation.	(三)财政部和国家税务总局规定的其他情形。

154

Continued

English Translation	Chinese Version
Ⅷ. Taxable activities related to Hong Kong，Macao，and Taiwan that are conducted by an entity or individual within China shall be governed by the aforesaid provisions，unless it is otherwise provided for in this Notice.	八、境内单位和个人发生的与香港、澳门、台湾有关的应税行为，除本文另有规定外，参照上述规定执行。
Ⅸ. For contracts that have been concluded before April 30，2016 and meet the requirements of zero VAT rate or VAT exemption policy as prescribed in Annex 4 to the Notice of the Ministry of Finance and the State Administration of Taxation on Including the Railway Transportation and Postal Industries in the Pilot Program of Replacing Business Tax with value-added tax (No. 106〔2013〕，Ministry of Finance)，and the Notice of the Ministry of Finance and the State Administration of Taxation on the Application of the Zero value-added tax Rate Policy to Film and Television and Other Export Services (No. 118〔2015〕，Ministry of Finance)，taxpayers may continue to enjoy zero VAT rate or VAT exemption policy before the expiration of such contracts.	九、2016 年 4 月 30 日前签订的合同，符合《财政部 国家税务总局关于将铁路运输和邮政业纳入营业税改征增值税试点的通知》(财税〔2013〕106 号)附件 4 和《财政部 国家税务总局关于影视等出口服务适用增值税零税率政策的通知》(财税〔2015〕118号)规定的零税率或者免税政策条件的，在合同到期前可以继续享受零税率或者免税政策。

Appendix Ⅲ：Practice Questions

1. Who are the taxpayers of VAT in China?

2. What activities are subject to VAT in China?

3. What's the difference between business tax and VAT?

4. What different treatments are applicable to the general VAT payers and the small-scale taxpayers?

5. What's the difference between the VAT exemption and the zero rate (0)?

6. Which executive institutions are in charge of VAT collections in China?

7. Case Study

• Facts:

Kayco Company Ltd. is a trading company incorporated in Shanghai and is a general VAT payer subject to the Provisional Regulation of the VAT. On 11 January, 2021, Kayco Company Ltd. sells 20 computers to W Company Ltd. which is a general VAT payer at a price of RMB 20,000 (excluding taxes); and then on 12 January, 2021, W Company Ltd. sells these 20 computers to K Company Ltd. which is a general VAT payer at a price of RMB 30,000 (excluding taxes). On 11 January, 2021, Kayco Company Ltd. sells 30 computers to A Company Ltd. which is a small-sale VAT payer at a price of RMB 20,000 (excluding taxes); and then on 12 January, 2021, A Company Ltd. sells these 20 computers to K Company Ltd. which is a general VAT payer at a price of RMB 30,000 (excluding taxes). K Company Ltd. then sells the computers to B Company, which is a general VAT payer at a price of RMB 40,000 (excluding taxes). Then K Company Ltd. sells these 20 computers to B Company Ltd. a general VAT payer at a price of RMB 40,000 (excluding taxes).

• Questions:

(1) How much W Company Ltd. should pay to Kayco Company Ltd. for buying these computers?

(2) How much K Company Ltd. should pay to W Company Ltd. for buying these computers?

(3) How much VAT should W Company Ltd. pay to the Chinese tax authorities?

(5) How much A Company Ltd. should pay to Kayco Company Ltd. for buying these computers?

(6) How much K Company Ltd. should pay to A Company Ltd. for buying these computers?

(7) How much of VAT should A Company Ltd. pay to the Chinese tax authorities?

(8) How much of VAT should K Company Ltd. pay to the Chinese tax authorities?

CHAPTER 4   EXCISE TAX

4.1   Introduction

Excise tax was introduced into China in 1994 in a name of the "Consumption Tax". The governing law of such tax as of 2021 is still the Provisional Regulation of the People's Republic of China on Consumption Tax (the "Consumption Tax Provisional Regulation"), enacted by the State Council in December 1993 and came into force on 1 January 1994. The basic mechanism of China's excise tax remains the same as the commonly accepted concept of the "Pigou tax", which is an additional tax to be levied when consuming certain goods, for example, tobacco, alcoholic drinks, cars, motorcycles, yachts, expensive watches, and refined oil products.

4.2   Structure of the Consumption Tax Provisional Regulation

The Consumption Tax Provisional Regulation, after latest amendments by the State Council in 2008, has 17 articles, which could be divided into the following parts according to the covered issues.

Table 4-1   Structure of the Consumption Tax Provisional Regulation

Covered Issues	Consumption Tax Provisional Regulation
Taxpayers	Art. 1
Taxable goods and rates	Arts. 2-3
Taxable Timing	Art. 4
Calculation	Arts. 5-10
Exemption	Art. 11
Tax Administration	Arts. 12-16
Supplementary Provisions	Art. 17

4.3   Taxpayers

All entities and individuals, who are engaged in producing, consigned processing within China, or importing the taxable goods, shall be subject to excise tax in China, in addition to being subject to the VAT and other turnover taxes if any.

4.4   Taxable Goods and Tax Rates

The Consumption Tax Provisional Regulation list the following types of goods as the taxable goods of excise tax in China:

Table 4-2

1. Tobacco	
A class cigarettes	56% plus RMB 150 per 50,000 cigarettes
B class cigarettes	36% plus RMB 150 per 50,000 cigarettes

Continued

(A class cigarettes are those which cost more than RMB 70 per 200 cigarettes, and B class cigarettes are those which cost less than that).	
cigars	36%
cut tobacco	30%
2. Alcoholic beverages and alcohol	
spirits	20% plus RMB 0.5 per 500 ml
rice/millet wine	RMB 240 per ton
A class beer	RMB 250 per ton
B class beer	RMB 220 per ton
others	10%
3. pure alcohol	5%
4. High-grade cosmetics	30%
5. Jewelry	
gold or silver jewelry	5%
other jewelry	10%
6. Fireworks	15%
7. Oil products	
gasoline	RMB 1.52 per litre
diesel oil	RMB 1.2 per litre
aviation coal oil	RMB 1.2 per litre
naphtha	RMB 1.52 per litre
solvent oil	RMB 1.52 per litre
lubricating oil	RMB 1.52 per litre
fuel oil	RMB 1.2 per litre
8. Motorcycles	
cylinder of 250ml	3%
cylinder more than 250ml	10%
9. Cars	
Cylinder capacity:	
— up to 1 litre	1%

Continued

—	over 1 and up to 1.5 litre	3%
—	over 1.5 and up to 2 litre	5%
—	over 2 and up to 2.5 litre	9%
—	over 2.5 and up to 3 litre	12%
—	over 3 and up to 4 litre	25%
—	over 4	40%
commercial bus		5%
10. Golf clubs and equipment		10%
11. High-class watches		20%
12. Yachts		10%
13. Wood chopsticks		5%
14. Wood floor		5%

The State Council, MOF and SAT have revised the applicable tax rates on a number of taxable goods several times and also have replaced certain taxable goods with some new goods. For example, starting from 1 December 2014, no consumption tax is imposed on motorcycles with low carbon emissions and a cylinder capacity below 250 ml.[①] And with effect from 1 February 2015, the production, processing and import of batteries and coatings are subject to consumption tax at a rate of 4%.[②] With effect from 10 May 2015, the tax rate for cigarette wholesaling is increased from 5% to 11% and an additional consumption tax of RMB 0.005 per cigarette is imposed. Furthermore, the taxpayers engaged in both cigarette wholesaling and retailing currently are required to calculate their sales volume and sale proceeds separately for wholesaling and retailing activities.[③] Such changes of tax rates and taxable goods probably will continue in the next years, especially when demands for an excise tax law have already been brought out to the National People's Congress.

① Circular 〔2014〕 No. 93
② Circular 〔2015〕 No. 16
③ Circular 〔2015〕 No. 60

4.5   Tax Timing

Excise tax shall be paid at the time of sales of taxable consumables. However, the taxable goods manufactured for self-consumption or continuous manufacturing of taxable consumables shall be exempted from excise tax.

The entity to which the taxable goods are entrusted for processing shall collect excise tax at the time of delivery of the goods to the entrusting party. Where taxable goods under entrusted processing are used by the entrusting party for continuous manufacturing of taxable goods, the excise tax paid shall be allowed to offset pursuant to the provisions. Excise tax shall be paid for imported taxable goods at the time of Customs declaration for imports.

Appendix: Consumption Tax Provisional Regulation (2008 Amendment)[①]

English Translation	Chinese Version
Provisional Regulations of the People's Republic of China on Consumption Tax	中华人民共和国消费税暂行条例
(Enacted by State Council of the People's Republic of China Order No. 135 on 13 December 1993; Revised and passed by the 34th Session of the Standing Committee of the State Council on 5 November 2008) State Council of the People's Republic of China Order No. 539	(1993 年 12 月 13 日中华人民共和国国务院令第 135 号发布 2008 年 11 月 5 日国务院第 34 次常务会议修订通过) 国务院令第五百三十九号

[①]   The version was translated with a reference of the translations on the website of www.pkulaw.com.

Continued

English Translation	Chinese Version
Article 1 Organisations and individuals engaging in production, entrusted processing and importation of consumables stipulated in these Regulations in the People's Republic of China, and other organisations and individuals engaging in sale of consumables stipulated in these Regulations as determined by the State Council shall be taxpayers of consumption tax and shall pay consumption tax pursuant to these Regulations.	**第一条** 在中华人民共和国境内生产、委托加工和进口本条例规定的消费品的单位和个人，以及国务院确定的销售本条例规定的消费品的其他单位和个人，为消费税的纳税人，应当依照本条例缴纳消费税。
Article 2 The tax items and tax rates for consumption tax shall be implemented pursuant to the "Table of Tax Items and Tax Rates for Consumption Tax" in the Appendix of these Regulations. Adjustment of tax items and tax rates for consumption tax shall be decided by the State Council.	**第二条** 消费税的税目、税率，依照本条例所附的《消费税税目税率表》执行。 消费税税目、税率的调整，由国务院决定。
Article 3 A taxpayer whose business involves consumables subject to payment of consumption tax (hereinafter referred to as the "taxable consumables") under different tax rates shall carry out separate accounting of sales amounts and sales quantities of taxable consumables under different tax rates; where the taxpayer failed to carry out separate accounting of sales amounts and sales quantities or where the taxpayer has sold packages comprising taxable consumables subject to different tax rates, the higher tax rate shall apply.	**第三条** 纳税人兼营不同税率的应当缴纳消费税的消费品（以下简称应税消费品），应当分别核算不同税率应税消费品的销售额、销售数量；未分别核算销售额、销售数量，或者将不同税率的应税消费品组成成套消费品销售的，从高适用税率。

Continued

English Translation	Chinese Version
Article 4 Tax shall be paid at the time of sale of taxable consumables manufactured by a taxpayer. Taxable consumables manufactured by a taxpayer for self-consumption or continuous manufacturing of taxable consumables shall be exempted from consumption tax; tax shall be paid at the time of delivery of taxable consumables for usage for other purposes. Except where an entrusted party is an individual, the entrusted party to whom taxable consumables are entrusted for processing shall collect consumption tax at the time of delivery of the goods by the entrusting party to the entrusted party. Where taxable consumables under entrusted processing are used by the entrusting party for continuous manufacturing of taxable consumables, the consumption tax paid shall be allowed to offset pursuant to the provisions. Consumption tax shall be paid for imported taxable consumables at the time of Customs declaration for imports.	**第四条** 纳税人生产的应税消费品,于纳税人销售时纳税。纳税人自产自用的应税消费品,用于连续生产应税消费品的,不纳税;用于其他方面的,于移送使用时纳税。 委托加工的应税消费品,除受托方为个人外,由受托方在向委托方交货时代收代缴税款。委托加工的应税消费品,委托方用于连续生产应税消费品的,所纳税款准予按规定抵扣。 进口的应税消费品,于报关进口时纳税。
Article 5 Amount of consumption tax payable shall be computed using the ad valorem method, specific duty method or compound tax method which combines both the ad valorem method and the specific duty method (hereinafter referred to as the "compound tax method"). The formula for computation of tax amount payable shall be: Tax amount payable computed using the ad valorem method = Sales amount × Proportional tax rate Tax amount payable computed using the specific duty method = Sales quantity × Fixed tax rate Tax amount payable computed using the compound tax method = Sales amount × Proportional tax rate + Sales quantity × Fixed tax rate Sales amounts of taxable consumables sold by a taxpayer shall be computed in Renminbi. Where a taxpayer makes settlement of sales amounts in any currency other than Renminbi, the amounts shall be converted to Renminbi for computation.	**第五条** 消费税实行从价定率、从量定额,或者从价定率和从量定额复合计税(以下简称复合计税)的办法计算应纳税额。应纳税额计算公式: 实行从价定率办法计算的应纳税额=销售额×比例税率 实行从量定额办法计算的应纳税额=销售数量×定额税率 实行复合计税办法计算的应纳税额=销售额×比例税率+销售数量×定额税率 纳税人销售的应税消费品,以人民币计算销售额。纳税人以人民币以外的货币结算销售额的,应当折合成人民币计算。

Continued

English Translation	Chinese Version
Article 6 The sales amount shall be the total price and out-of-pocket expenses collected from the buyer by a taxpayer engaging in sale of taxable consumables.	**第六条** 销售额为纳税人销售应税消费品向购买方收取的全部价款和价外费用。
Article 7 Tax amount payable for taxable consumables manufactured by a taxpayer for self-consumption shall be computed pursuant to the sale price of identical consumables manufactured by the taxpayer; where there is no sale price for identical consumables, the tax amount payable shall be computed pursuant to the constituent price for tax assessment. The formula for computation of constituent price for tax assessment using the ad valorem method shall be: Constituent price for tax assessment＝(Cost＋Profit)÷(1－Proportional tax rate) The formula for computation of constituent price for tax assessment using the compound tax method shall be: Constituent price for tax assessment＝(Cost＋Profit＋Quantity of self-consumption of self-produced consumables×Fixed tax rate)÷(1－Proportional tax rate)	**第七条** 纳税人自产自用的应税消费品,按照纳税人生产的同类消费品的销售价格计算纳税;没有同类消费品销售价格的,按照组成计税价格计算纳税。 实行从价定率办法计算纳税的组成计税价格计算公式: 组成计税价格＝(成本＋利润)÷(1－比例税率) 实行复合计税办法计算纳税的组成计税价格计算公式: 组成计税价格＝(成本＋利润＋自产自用数量×定额税率)÷(1－比例税率)
Article 8 Tax amount payable for taxable consumables under entrusted processing shall be computed pursuant to the sale price of identical consumables of the entrusted party; where there is no sale price for identical consumables, the tax amount payable shall be computed pursuant to the constituent price for tax assessment. The formula for computation of constituent price for tax assessment using the ad valorem method shall be: Constituent price for tax assessment＝(Material cost＋Processing fee)÷(1－Proportional tax rate) The formula for computation of constituent price for tax assessment using the compound tax method shall be: Constituent price for tax assessment＝(Material cost＋Processing fee＋Entrusted processing quantity×Fixed tax rate)÷(1－Proportional tax rate)	**第八条** 委托加工的应税消费品,按照受托方的同类消费品的销售价格计算纳税;没有同类消费品销售价格的,按照组成计税价格计算纳税。 实行从价定率办法计算纳税的组成计税价格计算公式: 组成计税价格＝(材料成本＋加工费)÷(1－比例税率) 实行复合计税办法计算纳税的组成计税价格计算公式: 组成计税价格＝(材料成本＋加工费＋委托加工数量×定额税率)÷(1－比例税率)

Continued

English Translation	Chinese Version
Article 9 Tax amount payable for imported taxable consumables shall be computed pursuant to the constituent price for tax assessment. The formula for computation of constituent price for tax assessment using the ad valorem method shall be: Constituent price for tax assessment = (Customs dutiable value + Customs duties) ÷ (1 − Proportional consumption tax rate) The formula for computation of constituent price for tax assessment using the compound tax method shall be: Constituent price for tax assessment = (Customs dutiable value + Customs duties + Imported quantity × Fixed consumption tax rate) ÷ (1 − Proportional consumption tax rate)	**第九条** 进口的应税消费品,按照组成计税价格计算纳税。 实行从价定率办法计算纳税的组成计税价格计算公式: 组成计税价格＝(关税完税价格＋关税)÷(1−消费税比例税率) 实行复合计税办法计算纳税的组成计税价格计算公式: 组成计税价格＝(关税完税价格＋关税＋进口数量×消费税定额税率)÷(1−消费税比例税率)
Article 10 Where the price for tax assessment for sale of taxable consumables by a taxpayer is obviously low and without a valid reason, the tax authorities in charge shall assess the price for tax assessment.	**第十条** 纳税人应税消费品的计税价格明显偏低并无正当理由的,由主管税务机关核定其计税价格。
Article 11 Taxable consumables exported by a taxpayer shall be exempted from consumption tax, unless otherwise stipulated by the State Council. The measures for tax exemption for exported taxable consumables shall be stipulated by the finance and tax authorities of the State Council.	**第十一条** 对纳税人出口应税消费品,免征消费税;国务院另有规定的除外。出口应税消费品的免税办法,由国务院财政、税务主管部门规定。
Article 12 Consumption tax shall be levied and collected by the tax authorities; consumption tax of imported taxable consumables shall be levied by the Customs on behalf of the tax authorities. Consumption tax on taxable consumables brought or mailed into China by an individual shall be computed and collected together with the Customs duties. The detailed measures shall be formulated by the Customs Tariff Commission of the State Council jointly with the relevant authorities.	**第十二条** 消费税由税务机关征收,进口的应税消费品的消费税由海关代征。 个人携带或者邮寄进境的应税消费品的消费税,连同关税一并计征。具体办法由国务院关税税则委员会会同有关部门制定。

Continued

English Translation	Chinese Version
Article 13 A taxpayer shall file tax return with and make tax payment to the tax authorities in charge at the location or place of residence of the taxpayer for taxable consumables sold by the taxpayer and taxable consumables manufactured by the taxpayer for self-consumption, unless otherwise stipulated by the finance and tax authorities of the State Council. Except where an entrusted party is an individual, the entrusted party shall turn over the consumption tax collected for taxable consumables under entrusted processing to the tax authorities in charge at the location or place of residence of the entrusted party. Tax return for imported taxable consumables shall be filed with and tax payment shall be made to the Customs at the place of Customs declaration.	**第十三条** 纳税人销售的应税消费品,以及自产自用的应税消费品,除国务院财政、税务主管部门另有规定外,应当向纳税人机构所在地或者居住地的主管税务机关申报纳税。 委托加工的应税消费品,除受托方为个人外,由受托方向机构所在地或者居住地的主管税务机关解缴消费税税款。 进口的应税消费品,应当向报关地海关申报纳税。
Article 14 The deadline for payment of consumption tax shall be one day, three days, five days, 10 days, 15 days, one month or one quarter respectively. The specific tax payment deadlines for a taxpayer shall be assessed respectively by the tax authorities in charge according to the tax amount payable of the taxpayer; a taxpayer who is unable to pay tax by fixed deadlines may pay tax for each transaction. A taxpayer who opts for a tax payment period of one month or one quarter shall file tax return and make tax payment within 15 days from the date of expiry of the tax payment period; a taxpayer who opts for the tax payment period of one day, three days, five days, 10 days or 15 days shall pre-pay tax within five days from the date of expiry of the tax payment period, and file tax return and make tax payment within 15 days from the 1st day of the following month as well as settle the tax amount payable for the preceding month fully.	**第十四条** 消费税的纳税期限分别为1日、3日、5日、10日、15日、1个月或者1个季度。纳税人的具体纳税期限,由主管税务机关根据纳税人应纳税额的大小分别核定;不能按照固定期限纳税的,可以按次纳税。 纳税人以1个月或者1个季度为1个纳税期的,自期满之日起15日内申报纳税;以1日、3日、5日、10日或者15日为1个纳税期的,自期满之日起5日内预缴税款,于次月1日起15日内申报纳税并结清上月应纳税款。
Article 15 A taxpayer importing taxable consumables shall make tax payment within 15 days from the date of issuance of the special letter of payment of consumption tax for Customs imports by the Customs.	**第十五条** 纳税人进口应税消费品,应当自海关填发海关进口消费税专用缴款书之日起15日内缴纳税款。

Continued

English Translation	Chinese Version
Article 16 Administration of levying and collection of consumption tax shall comply with the Administrative Law of the People's Republic of China on the Levying and Collection of Taxes and the relevant provisions of these Regulations.	**第十六条** 消费税的征收管理，依照《中华人民共和国税收征收管理法》及本条例有关规定执行。
Article 17 These Regulations shall be effective 1 January，2009.	**第十七条** 本条例自 2009 年 1 月 1 日起施行。

CHAPTER 5
INDIVIDUAL INCOME TAX

5.1   Introduction

The individual income tax (IIT) in China is governed by the Individual Income Tax Law (IIT Law), which was promulgated by the People's Congress in 1980 and has been amended 7 times since then on. These amendments were mainly to increase amounts of the allowable deductions, for the purpose of catching up the inflations and economic developments of China over the last 40 years. For example, the amount of the allowable deductions for calculating the IIT on salary and wages incomes was RMB 800 in the IIT Law of 1980, whereas such an amount was slowly increased to RMB 5,000 in the amendment in 2018. While the latest amendment in 2018 (the "2018 Amendment") introduced a number of new concepts into the Chinese individual income tax regime. For example, a 183-day rule was added into the criteria for determining a Chinese tax resident, a new type of income named the "contingent income" was introduced into the IIT regime to replace the type of "other incomes", and a concept named the "comprehensive income" was introduced to be a new category for calculating the IIT for incomes from salary and wages incomes, labor services, author's remuneration and royalties.

The source of law for IIT also includes the Implementation Regulations on the Individual Income Tax Law enacted by the State Council (the IIT Implementation Regulation), and many tax circulars issues by MOF and/or

SAT for the purpose of clarifying issues from the implementation of the IIT Law and the IIT Implementation Regulation.

The Chinese IIT regime essentially is schedular, which means that ① only the listed types of income are subject to tax; and ② each category of incomes is computed separately and there is no aggregation of the different categories. Some categories of income are taxed at progressive rates, for example the category of "comprehensive income", whereas some categories are taxed at a flat rate. For example, the category of the incomes dividends and interest. And there is no joint taxation for spouses or for family units, while the tax year for IIT in China starts from 1 January to 31 December each year.

5.2   Structure of the IIT Legislations

The IIT Law currently has 22 articles, which could be divided into the following parts according to their covered issues. And accordingly the IIT Implementation Regulation provide with implementation rules for the IIT Law.

Table 5-1   Structure of the IIT Legislations Law and Implementation Regulation

Covered Issues	IIT Law	IIT Implementation Regulation
Taxpayers	Art. 1	Arts. 2-3
Taxable Income	Art. 2	Arts. 6-8
Tax Rates	Art. 3	
Exemptions	Arts. 4-5	Arts. 4-5 and 9-13
Tax Payable	Art. 6	Arts. 14-19
Foreign Tax Credit	Art. 7	Arts. 20-22
Special Adjustments	Art. 8	
Tax Administration	Arts. 9-20	Arts. 23-34
Supplementary Provisions	Arts. 21-22	Art. 1 and Arts. 35-36

5.3   Taxpayers

An individual shall be subject to individual income tax in China, if he or she:

- is a Chinese tax resident; or
- is not a Chinese tax resident but has income sourced from China.

An individual being a Chinese tax resident shall be subject to individual income tax in China for his/her worldwide incomes; whereas an individual not being a Chinese tax resident shall be subject to individual income tax in China only for his/her income sourced from China. Therefore, two important rules under the IIT Law must apply when assessing the IIT burdens of an individual in China: (1) the resident rules, which test whether the individual is a Chinese tax resident; and (2) the source rules, which test where the income is sourced from?

5.3.1 Resident Rules

According to the resident rules provided in the Article 1 of the IIT Law, an individual is regarded as a Chinese tax resident if he/she domiciles in China or is not domiciled in China but has stayed in China in aggregation for 183 days or more of a tax year. Clearly, there are two tests for determining whether an individual is a Chinese resident: (1) the place of domicile; and (2) the length of stay in China.

The concept of "being domiciled in China", according to the IIT Implementation Regulation, means an individual habitually resides in China due to have a household registration, or having family or economic ties in China. While even if an individual is not domiciled in China, the 183-day rule shall still apply to the individual testing his/her length of stay in China in a tax year. This test requests the individual must physically present in China, regardless of the purpose of the stay.

Clearly, the resident rules in the IIT Law are board. An individual will become a Chinese resident if either of the two tests is satisfied. As a result, the issue of dual-residents may arise when an individual satisfies both the resident rules of China and the rules of the other tax jurisdictions. For example, an individual, who holds a U.S. passport while has stayed in China for 183 days in tax year, is regarded as a tax resident of both the U.S. and China according their domestic laws. In order to resolve such a dual-residents issue, China has included the tie-breaker rules into the Article 4 (resident) of all its bilateral tax treaties (see Chapter 7 of the book).

Then for not becoming a Chinese tax resident, an individual must not have any place of domicile in China and have not stayed in China for 183 days or more in a tax year.

5.3.2 Source Rules

The following income, regardless where the payment thereof is made, shall be treated as being sourced from inside China, unless MOF or SAT may provide otherwise:

(1)income derived from provision of labor services in China due to holding the posts, being employed or performing contracts, among others;

(2)income derived from lease of property to lessees for being used in China;

(3)income derived from granting franchises to be used in China;

(4)income derived from transfer of real properties which are located in China or transfer other properties in China; and

(5)income in forms of interest or dividends paid by enterprises, institutions, economic organizations which are located in China or by Chinese individual tax residents.

For a Chinese tax resident, his/her worldwide income shall be subject to individual income tax in China. The concept worldwide income refers to both the income sourced from inside of China and the income sourced from outside of China. Whereas for a non-Chinese tax resident, he/she shall be subject to individual income tax in China only for his/her income sourced from China.

5.4 Taxable Income

The forms of the incomes could be in cash, in kind, in securities and in any other form of economic benefits. With regard to the income in kind, the amount of taxable income shall be calculated according to the price indicated on the relevant certificates; and in case there is no certificate for such income in kind or in case the price indicated on the certificate is evidently low, the amount of the taxable income shall be assessed by reference to the market price. With regard to the income in a form of securities, the amount of taxable income shall be assessed based on the par value or market price. And with regard to the economic benefits in other forms, the amount of taxable income shall be assessed by reference to market price.

Under the schedular tax regime provided in the IIT Law, the following nine types of income are taxable unless the income is exempted according to the IIT Law. Therefore, the amount of the taxable income should be calculated as the total amount of the income to be deducted by the exempted incomes. The IIT Implementation Regulation and the tax circulars of SAT and MOF briefly elaborate the contents of these 9 types of income, forms of these income as well as the exempted incomes.

5.4.1 Nine Types of Income

5.4.1.1 Income from wages and salaries

This type of income refers to the income from wages, salaries, bonuses, year-end salary increases, labor dividends, and allowances obtained by an individual due to his/her job or employment, as well as subsidies and other income related to his/her job or employment.

5.4.1.2 Income from remuneration for labor services

This type of income refers to the income obtained by an individual from providing labor services, which includes but not limited to, income derived from services in designing, decoration, installation, drafting, chemical examination, testing, medical treatment, law practice, accounting, consulting, lecturing, translating, proof-reading, calligraphy and painting, sculpture, film and television, audio and video recording, performance, advertisement, exhibition, technical services, go-between service, brokerage service, commissioned services and other labor services.

5.4.1.3 Income from author's remunerations

This type of income refers to the income obtained by an individual from the publication of their works in the form of books, newspaper articles or periodical articles, and etc.

5.4.1.4 Income from royalties

This type of income refers to the income obtained by an individual from licensing the use right of patent, trademark, copyrights, know-how and other franchises.

5.4.1.5 Business income

This type of income is quite broad, referring to incomes obtained by an individual through carrying out business activities, including but not limited to the follows:

(1) income obtained by a household from carrying out production and business activities; income of an individual investor from his/her sole proprietorship enterprise registered in China; and an individual partner of a partnership registered in China;

(2) income obtained by an individual from providing paid services in accordance with law, for example, schooling, medical treatment, consultation, and etc.;

(3) income obtained by an individual from carrying out the contracted operation or the leased operation of enterprises or institutions, and income from subcontracting and subleasing enterprises or institutions; and

(4) income obtained by an individual from engaging in other production and business activities.

5.4.1.6 Income from interest and dividends

This type of income refers to the income obtained by an individual on the basis of his/her having creditor's rights or equity rights.

5.4.1.7 Income from lease of properties

This type of income refers to the income obtained by an individual through leasing out his/her real estate, machinery and equipment, motor vehicles and ships and other properties.

5.4.1.8 Income from conveyance of properties

This type of income refers to the income obtained by an individual through transferring his/her ownership on securities, equities, shares in partnerships, real estate, machinery and equipment, motor vehicles and ships, and other properties.

5.4.1.9 Contingent income

This type of income refers to the income obtained by an individual contingently from receiving awards, winning prizes in lotteries, and obtaining other windfalls. MOF and SAT issued a circular in June 2019[①], specifically listing out the following income which should belong to the type of contingent income:

(1)income derived by an individual from provision of guarantee for an entity or an individual;

(2)a gifted real propert received by an individual without consideration;

But the gifted real property derived under any of the following circumstances should not be subject to IIT under the type of contingent income:

①when the owner gifts the title of his/her real properties without consideration to his/her spouse, parents, grandparents, children, grandchildren, or siblings;

②when the owner gifts the title of his/her real property without consideration to a guardian or custodian who bears direct guardianship or custodianship over him/her; or

③when the owner of a real property passed away and his/her statutory heir or testamentary beneficiary or devisee obtains the property's title pursu-

_____

① The MOF and the SAT, The Announcement on Determination of Income Types subject to Individual Income Tax for Relevant Incomes Obtained by Individuals 〔Announcement〔2019〕No. 74〕issued on 13 June 2019 and came into force retroactively on 1 January, 2019.

ant to the law.

(3)a gift (including the online windfalls) received by an individual randomly from an enterprise in its carrying out business promotion and advertising activities, or carrying out annual meetings, forums, celebration events and other activities.

But if the gift received is in a form of spending vouchers, gift vouchers, discount vouchers or any other form with a function for price reduction or discount, then such a gift should not be subject to IIT under the type of contingent income.

5.4.2 Exempted Income

The following three categories of income are exempted from individual income tax, and thus they are allowed to be excluded from the amount of taxable income for IIT purpose in China.

5.4.2.1 Statutory exemption

(1)awards and prizes in the fields of science, education, technology, culture, health, sports and environmental protection awarded by the provincial level governments in China, by ministries or commissions under the State Council, by units of the People's Liberation Army at or above the army level, or by foreign organizations and international organizations;

(2)interest accruing from the treasury bonds issued by the MOF or from financial bonds approved for issuing by the State Council of China;

(3)subsidies or allowances paid to academies or other allowances being exempted in accordance with regulations enacted by the State Council of China;

(4)welfare benefits which are paid from the welfare funds of enterprises, institutions, public organs and social organizations, or which are paid as the living subsidies through using the funds of trade unions; and the conform payments or the relief payments, which refer to the subsidies paid by the civil affairs department to individuals suffering from living difficulties;

(5)remedies paid from insurance;

(6)severance pay, demobilization pay or retirement paid to military personnel;

(7) settling-in allowance, severance pay, pensions, and living allow-ances or subsidies for the retired according to the unified standards in China;

(8) incomes received by diplomatic representatives, consular officers and other personnel of foreign embassies and consulates in China, which are ex-empted from individual income tax in China in accordance with the Regula-tion of the People's Republic of China on Diplomatic Privileges and Immuni-ties and the Regulation of the People's Republic of China on Consular Privi-leges and Immunities;

(9) incomes which are exempt from individual income tax, according to the international conventions to which the Chinese government is a member or according to the agreement which the Chinese Government has signed; and

(10) other income being exempted by the State Council of China and be-ing filed with the Standing Committee of the National People's Congress of China;

(11) income being donated by an individual to public welfare and chari-table institutions for causes of education or poverty alleviation, that does not exceed 30% of the amount of taxable income declared by the taxpayer. The full amount of such donations may be exempted if the State Council provides otherwise;

(12) 30% of the income from author's remuneration.

5.4.2.2 Exemption by provincial governments on a case-by-case basis

Under any of the following circumstances, individual income tax may be reduced within a specific scope and time limit, which shall be prescribed by the provincial governments:

(1) income of the handicapped, the elderly who has no children, and members of martyrs' families; and

(2) an individual who suffers from heavy losses incurred due to severe natural disasters.

The exemption decisions must be filed with the standing committee of the people's congress at the same level, when a provincial government exer-cises the above described powers.

5.4.2.3 Exemption for individuals having no domicile in China

Notwithstanding the principal rule is that a non-Chinese tax resident should be subject to IIT in China for his/her income sourced from China, the IIT Implementation Regulation provides an exemption for the non-Chinese tax residents who has no domicile in China and has stayed in China for less than 90 days during a tax year. Such a non-Chinese tax resident shall be exempted from IIT on the part of his/her income derived from China, on a precondition that such income is paid by an employer outside China and not borne by any employer in China.

Furthermore, as for the Chinese tax resident who does not have a domicile in China but has stayed for 183 days or more in China in a calendar year, this Chinese tax resident could be exempted from IIT in China, after having filed the exemption application with the in-charge Chinese tax authority, on the part of his/her income which were sourced from outside of China and were paid by overseas entities or individuals. However, in order to enjoy this exemption, the Chinese tax resident must have stayed in China less than 6 consecutive years for 183 days or more in a calendar year. This pre-condition seems not be difficult satisfy, because as long as this Chinese tax resident had left China for 30 days or more in a single trip in any of the years in each of which he or she has stayed for a total of 183 days or more in China, the starting time of the specified consecutive years in each of which he or she has stayed for a total of 183 days or more in China shall be recounted.

5.5   Tax Payable

5.5.1 Calculation Methods

The above nine types of income shall be computed and taxed on a schedular basis, in the following six separate categories of income:

(1) the category of "comprehensive income", which consists of four

types of income, namely (ⅰ) the income from wages and salaries, (ⅱ) the income from remuneration for labor services, (ⅲ) the income from author's remuneration, and (ⅳ) the income from royalties;

(2) the category of "business income", which consists of only the type of business income;

(3) the category of "interest and dividends", which consists of only the type of income from interest and dividends;

(4) the category of "income from lease of property", which consists of only the type of income from lease of property;

(5) the category of "income from conveyance of property", which consists of only the type of income from conveyance of property; and

(6) the category of "contingent income", which consists of only the type of contingent income.

The tax rates applicable and the allowed deductions for each category are different. For example, the category of "comprehensive income" is taxed at progressive rates ranging from 3% to 45%, while the category of "business income" taxed at progressive rates ranging from 5% to 35%. As for the remaining four categories of income, a flat rate of 20% shall apply.

Therefore, a reasonable calculation approach is to firstly put the nine types of income into the correct categories of income, and then to calculate the amount of tax payable for each category separately. The following formula could be applied when calculating the amount of tax payable for each category of income:

"tax payable＝(taxable income of the category—allowed deductions) × the applicable tax rate"

After having worked out the amount of the tax payable for each category of income, then to add them up to calculate the total amount of the tax payable for the taxpayer. No tax credit is available for IIT purposes, except for foreign tax credits.

5.5.2 Tax Payable for the Category of "Comprehensive Income"

The category of "comprehensive income" was introduced into the IIT Law by the 2018 Amendment with an effect from 1 January 2019. This concept in fact refers to a calculation pool which must be used when calculating the tax payable for all the first four of the nine types of income[①]. Although the deductions allowed for these four types of income are different, all of them must be put into this one calculation pool (namely, the category of "comprehensive income"). The following formulas could be used when calculating the tax payable for the category of "comprehensive income":

• Tax payable for the category of "comprehensive income" = Taxable income × Tax rates

• Taxable income = Income from wages and salaries-allowed deductions + Income from remuneration for labor service-allowed deductions + Income from author's remuneration-allowed deductions + Income from royalties-allowed deductions

• Tax rates: progressive rates ranging from 3% to 45% (see the below Table 5-2)

Table 5-2   Tax Rates

Brackets	Amount of Annual Taxable Income	Tax Rate (%)
1	Up to RMB 36,000	3
2	Over RMB 36,000 nor more than RMB 144,000	10
3	Over RMB 144,000 nor more than RMB 300,000	20
4	Over 3 RMB 00,000 nor more than RMB 420,000	25
5	Over RMB 420,000 nor more than RMB 660,000	30
6	Over RMB 660,000 nor more than RMB 960,000	35
7	Over RMB 960,0000	45

---

① The first four of the nine types of income refer to the following types of income: (i) income from wages and salaries, (ii) income from remuneration for labor services, (iii) income from author's remuneration, and (iv) income from royalties.

The allowed deductions for each of these four types of income are different and need to be calculated separately. And no other cost or expenses are deductible than those described as follows.

5.5.2.1 allowed deductions for income from wages and salaries

If the taxpayer is a Chinese tax resident, both the fixed deductions and the additional special deductions are allowed to be deducted when calculating his/her taxable income from wages and salaries. Whereas that if the taxpayer is a non-Chinese tax resident, only a fixed deduction amounting to RMB 5,000 per month is allowed.

(1) the fixed deductions consist of ① the social contributions and annuities paid by the taxpayer if such paid contributions are within the limit prescribed by the relevant Chinese laws and regulations; and ② a fixed amount of RMB 60,000 per year;

(2) the additional special deductions refer to six types of deductions, namely ① the expenses for children's education, ② the expenses for continuing education, ③ the medical expenses for serious diseases, ④ interest paid for house loan, ⑤ rent for accommodations, and ⑥ the elderly care expenses. The taxpayer may deduct any or all of these additional special deductions (subject to certain caps on the deducible amount) when calculating his/her taxable income, only if having such kind of expenses occurred and the following conditions are satisfied[①]:

①expenses for children's education: the maximum deductible amount for such expenses is RMB 1,000 per month for each child, who is more than 3 years old and is in education up including postgraduate and doctoral education. The parents, as the taxpayers, may choose to deduct by either parent 100% of such fixed deduction, or deduct it as per 50% for the father and mother respectively.

②expenses for continuing education: the fixed amount of deduction is RMB 400 per month for a period of no longer than months when the taxpay-

---

① The State Council, Notice of the State Council on Issuing the Interim Measures for the Additional Special Deductions for Individual Income Tax (Guofa 〔2018〕 No. 41), enacted by the State Council on 13 December, 2018 and came into force on 1 January, 2019.

er participates into any continuing academic education in China. And if the continuing academic education is for a bachelor's degree or below, the taxpayer may choose to deduct this fixed amount of deduction from his/her own taxable income or from his/her parents' taxable income.

Whereas for a taxpayer taking any continuing education for occupation trainings or for specialized technique qualifications, the fixed amount of deduction shall be RMB 3,600 per year in the year when he/she obtains the relevant certificate.

③medical expenses for serious diseases: the maximum amount of deduction is RMB 80,000 per year, if the taxpayer's medical expenses in that year is more than RMB 15,000, which excludes the medical insurance coverage. The deduction must be made to the extent of based on the actual expenses incurred, but such a deduction may be made from the taxable income of the taxpayer or from the taxable income of his/her spouse. As for the medical expenses incurred by a child, such a deduction may be made from the taxable income of either parent.

④interest paid for house loan: the maximum amount of deduction is RMB1,000 per month in the year when the loan interest is actually incurred, up to a period of 240 months. The loan must be undertaken by the taxpayer, his/her spouse or both of them for purchasing their first residential property in China, and such a deduction may be deducted from the taxable income of either spouse.

⑤rent for accommodations: a fixed amount ranging form RMB 800 to RMB 1500 per month (according to the location of the rented accommodation) is deductible if the taxpayer does not own a residential property in the city where he/she works.

⑥the elderly care expenses: a fixed amount of RMB 2,000 per year is deductible if the taxpayer is the only child of his/her parents and is supporting either or both of his/her parents aged above 60. Where the taxpayer is not the only child, the deductible amount of RMB 2,000 per month shall be apportioned equally among the taxpayer and his/her siblings, with no more than RMB 1,000 per month apportioned to each person.

The above fixed deductions and additional special deductions shall be deductible within the limit of the taxpayer's taxable income in the tax year; for those deductions whose amounts are not deducted in full in the current tax year, it is not allowed to be carried forward to the subsequent years.

5.5.2.2 allowed deductions for income from remuneration for labor services, for income from author's remuneration, and for income from royalties

When calculating the taxable income for these three types of income, the allowed deduction is 20% of total amount of the income, when the taxpayer is a Chinese tax resident. No deduction is allowed for non-Chinese tax resident.

5.5.3 Tax Payable for the Category of "Business Income"

The category of "business income" consists of only one type of income, i.e. the business income, thus the formula to calculate the tax payable for this category is as follows:

Tax payable for the category of "business income" = Taxable income × Tax rates

The taxable income herein is calculated by the amount of the taxpayer's the annual gross income to less his/her costs, expenses and losses occurred. The scope of such "costs and expenses" is quite broad, including both various direct expenditures incurred in the process of production and business activities, and indirect expenses allocated to and included in costs, sales expenses, management expenses and financial expenses, etc. With regard to the "losses", it includes but not limited to the losses from the shortage, destruction or discard of fixed assets and inventories, losses from the conveyance of property, losses from bad debts, losses from natural disasters and other force majeure factors, and other losses incurred in the process of production and business activities.

The tax rates applicable herein are the progressive rates ranging from 5% to 35% .(see Table 5-3)

Table 5-3   Tax Rates

Brackets	Amount of Annual Taxable Income	Tax Rate (%)
1	Up to RMB 30,000	5
2	Over RMB 30,000 nor more than RMB 90,000	10
3	Over RMB 90,000 nor more than RMB 300,000	20
4	Over RMB 300,000 nor more than RMB 500,000	30
5	Over RMB 500,000	35

5.5.4 Tax Payable for the Category of "Interest and Dividends"

This category consists of only the type of income from interest and dividends, so the calculation formula for this category is as follows:

Tax payable for the category of "interest and dividends" = Taxable income × Tax rate

Calculating the amount of tax payable for this category is comparably simple, as the taxable amount shall be the total amount of the dividends or interest income obtained by the taxpayer each time and the applicable tax rate is a single rate of 20%.

5.5.5 Tax Payable for the Category of "Income from Lease of Property"

This category consists of only the type of income from lease of properties, and its calculation formula is quite straightforward:

Tax payable for the category of "income from lease of properties" = Taxable income × Tax rate

The amount of taxable income shall be the income received less a fixed amount of RMB 800 if such income received is less than RMB 4,000 each time; or the deduction 20% of the income if the income received is RMB 4,000 or more each time. While the tax rate applicable to this category is a single rate of 20%.

5.5.6 Tax Payable for the Category of "Income from Conveyance of Property"

This category consists of only the type of income from conveyance of property, so the calculation formula is straightforward too:

Tax payable for the category of "income from conveyance of property" = Taxable income × Tax rate

The tax rate applicable to this category is a single rate of 20%. And the taxable income shall be the amount of income obtained from conveyance of properties to be deducted by the original value of the properties and the reasonable expenses, for example, the relevant taxes and fees paid for selling the properties.

The "original value of the property" shall be determined differently as follows, according to the property conveyed.

(1) for securities, the original price shall be the purchasing price and the relevant expenses;

(2) for buildings, the original price shall be the construction fees or purchasing price of the buildings as well as other relevant expenses;

(3) for land use rights, the original price shall be the price paid for obtaining the land use rights, expenses for development of the land, and other relevant expenses;

(4) for machinery and equipment, motor vehicles or ships, the original price shall be the purchasing price, fees for transportation and installation, and other relevant expenses.

5.5.7 Tax Payable for the Category of "Contingent Income"

This category consists of only the type of contingent income, and calculating the tax payable for this category is comparably simple:

Tax payable for the category of "contingent income" = Taxable income × Tax rate

The taxable amount shall be the total amount of the contingent income and the applicable tax rate is a single rate of 20%.

5.6   Special Adjustments

One of the new concepts introduced by the 2018 Amendment to the IIT regime of China is the special adjustment power of Chinese tax authorities. Since 1 January 2019, Chinese tax authorities shall have the power to make tax payment adjustments in reasonable methods, under any of the following circumstances:

(1) Business transactions between an individual and his/her affiliates do not conform to the independent transaction principle, resulting in reduction of the amount of tax payable by the individual or his or her affiliates, which is not justified.

(2) An enterprise incorporated outside of China having an evidently low actual tax burden, which is controlled by a resident individual or is jointly controlled by a resident individual and a resident enterprise, fails to distribute or distributes a reduced amount of profits attributable to the resident individual without any reasonable operational need.

(3) An individual obtains inappropriate tax benefits from the implementation of any other arrangement without any reasonable commercial purpose.

5.7   Tax Administration

5.7.1 Withholding or Self-declaration

The tax administration of IIT shall be subject to both the IIT Law and the Law of the People's Republic of China on the Administration of Tax Collection. The tax filing and payment method can be carried out either in a

185

form of withholding by a withholding agent or in a form of self-declaration by the taxpayer.

Where there is a withholding agent, the agent shall be obliged to file tax returns for the taxpayers within the first 15 days of the next month, to withhold the tax from the payments to the taxpayer, as well as to provide the tax payment proof to the taxpayer. A service fee equivalent to 2% of the amount of tax withheld shall be paid by the Chinese tax authorities to the withholding agent.

The taxpayer shall self-declare his/her individual income tax in China through filing a tax return with the in-charge tax authorities, under any of the following circumstances:

(1)filing a tax return for his/her comprehensive income on a consolidated basis;

(2)no withholding agent for any taxable income obtained;

(3)failure by the withholding agent to withhold taxes on any taxable income;

(4)income sourced from outside of China;

(5)where the taxpayer's Chinese household registration has been cancelled due to his/her emigration;

(6)where a non-Chinese tax resident receives income from wages and salaries at two or more places in China; and

(7)any other circumstances prescribed by the State Council.

5.7.2 Tax Returns

The individual income tax on the comprehensive income shall be calculated annually; if there is a withholding agent, the withholding agent shall withhold and prepay taxes on a monthly or transaction-by-transaction basis, rather than filing a tax return on a consolidated basis. And the taxpayer shall file a tax return on a consolidated basis for annual assessment purpose from March 1 to June 30 of the next year after she/he receives income from wages and salaries, income from remuneration for labor services, income from author's remuneration, or income from royalties.

The individual income tax on the business income shall be calculated annually, and the taxpayer shall, within 15 days after the end of a month or quarter, file a tax return with and prepay taxes to the tax authority; and file a tax return on a consolidated basis before March 31 of the next year after obtaining the income.

For the income from interest and dividends, income from lease of property, income from conveyance of property, and contingent income, the individual income tax shall be calculated on a monthly or transaction-by-transaction basis, and if there is a withholding agent, the withholding agent shall withhold taxes on a monthly or transaction-by-transaction basis.

5.7.3 Annual Assessment

A taxpayer must file a tax return for annual assessment purpose with the in-charge Chinese tax authority from March 1 to June 30 of the next year, under any of the following circumstances:

(1) The taxpayer has obtained these incomes from two or more sources, and the balance after deducting special deductibles from the annual amount of the category of comprehensive income is RMB 60,000 or more;

(2) The taxpayer has obtained one or more sums of income from remuneration for labor services, income from author's remuneration, or income from royalties, and the balance after deducting special deductibles from the annual amount of comprehensive income is RMB 60,000 or more;

(3) The amount of tax prepaid in the tax year is lower than the amount of tax payable; or

(4) The taxpayer applies for tax refund.

Appendix Ⅰ:IIT Law (2018 Amendment)①

English Translation	Chinese Version
Individual Income Tax Law of the People's Republic of China	中华人民共和国个人所得税法
（Adopted by the Third Session of the Fifth National People's Congress on September 10, 1980, amended for the first time in accordance with the Decision of the Fourth Session of the Standing Committee of the Eighth National People's Congress Concerning Amendment to the Individual Income Tax Law of the People's Republic of China on October 31, 1993; and amended for the second time in accordance with the Decision of the 11th Session of the Standing Committee of the Ninth National People's Congress Concerning Amendment to the Individual Income Tax Law of the People's Republic of China on August 30, 1999; amended for the third time in accordance with the Decision of the 18th Session of the Standing Committee of the Tenth National People's Congress on Amending the Individual Income Tax Law of the People's Republic of China on October 27, 2005; amended for the fourth time in accordance with the Decision of the 28th Session of the Standing Committee of the Tenth National People's Congress on Amending the Individual Income Tax Law of the People's Republic of China on June 29, 2007; amended for the fifth time in accordance with the Decision of the 31st Session of the Standing Committee of the Tenth National People's Congress on Amending the Individual Income Tax Law of the People's Republic of China on December 29, 2007; amended for the sixth time in accordance with the Decision of the 21st Session of the Standing Committee of the Eleventh National People's Congress on Amending the Individual Income Tax Law of the People's Republic of China on June 30, 2011; and amended for the seventh time in accordance with the Decision of the fifth Session of the Standing Committee of the Thirteenth National People's Congress to Amend the Individual Income Tax Law of the People's Republic of China on August 31, 2018）	（1980 年 9 月 10 日第五届全国人民代表大会第三次会议通过 根据 1993 年 10 月 31 日第八届全国人民代表大会常务委员会第四次会议《关于修改〈中华人民共和国个人所得税法〉的决定》第一次修正 根据 1999 年 8 月 30 日第九届全国人民代表大会常务委员会第十一次会议《关于修改〈中华人民共和国个人所得税法〉的决定》第二次修正 根据 2005 年 10 月 27 日第十届全国人民代表大会常务委员会第十八次会议《关于修改〈中华人民共和国个人所得税法〉的决定》第三次修正 根据 2007 年 6 月 29 日第十届全国人民代表大会常务委员会第二十八次会议《关于修改〈中华人民共和国个人所得税法〉的决定》第四次修正 根据 2007 年 12 月 29 日第十届全国人民代表大会常务委员会第三十一次会议《关于修改〈中华人民共和国个人所得税法〉的决定》第五次修正 根据 2011 年 6 月 30 日第十一届全国人民代表大会常务委员会第二十一次会议《关于修改〈中华人民共和国个人所得税法〉的决定》第六次修正 根据 2018 年 8 月 31 日第十三届全国人民代表大会常务委员会第五次会议《关于修改〈中华人民共和国个人所得税法〉的决定》第七次修正）

---

① The version was translated with a reference of the translations on the website of www.pkulaw.com.

Continued

English Translation	Chinese Version
Article 1 A resident individual is an individual who is domiciled in China or who is not domiciled in China but has stayed in the aggregate for 183 days or more of a tax year in China. A resident individual shall, in accordance with the provisions of this Law, pay individual income tax on his or her income obtained inside and outside China.	**第一条**　在中国境内有住所，或者无住所而一个纳税年度内在中国境内居住累计满一百八十三天的个人，为居民个人。居民个人从中国境内和境外取得的所得，依照本法规定缴纳个人所得税。
A nonresident individual is an individual who neither is domiciled in China nor stays in China or who is not domiciled in China but has stayed in the aggregate for less than 183 days of a tax year in China. A nonresident individual shall, in accordance with the provisions of this Law, pay individual income tax on his or her income obtained inside China.	在中国境内无住所又不居住，或者无住所而一个纳税年度内在中国境内居住累计不满一百八十三天的个人，为非居民个人。非居民个人从中国境内取得的所得，依照本法规定缴纳个人所得税。
Tax year means the Gregorian calendar year that runs from January 1 to December 31.	纳税年度，自公历一月一日起至十二月三十一日止。
Article 2 Individual income tax shall be paid on the following individual income：	**第二条**　下列各项个人所得，应当缴纳个人所得税：
(1)Income from wages and salaries.	（一）工资、薪金所得；
(2)Income from remuneration for labor services.	（二）劳务报酬所得；
(3)Income from author's remuneration.	（三）稿酬所得；
(4)Income from royalties.	（四）特许权使用费所得；
(5)Business income.	（五）经营所得；
(6)Income from interest and dividends	（六）利息、股息、红利所得；
(7)Income from lease of property.	（七）财产租赁所得；
(8)Income from conveyance of property.	（八）财产转让所得；
(9)Contingent income.	（九）偶然所得。

Continued

English Translation	Chinese Version
Resident individuals shall calculate by tax year on a consolidated basis the individual income tax, and nonresident individuals shall calculate by itemization on a monthly or transaction-by-transaction basis the individual income tax, on the income obtained as set forth in subparagraphs (1) to (4) of the preceding paragraph (hereinafter referred to as the "comprehensive income"). The individual income tax on the income set forth in subparagraphs (5) to (9) of the preceding paragraph obtained by a taxpayer shall be calculated respectively in accordance with the provisions of this Law.	居民个人取得前款第一项至第四项所得(以下称综合所得),按纳税年度合并计算个人所得税;非居民个人取得前款第一项至第四项所得,按月或者按次分项计算个人所得税。纳税人取得前款第五项至第九项所得,依照本法规定分别计算个人所得税。
Article 3 Individual income tax rates:	**第三条** 个人所得税的税率:
(1) Progressive tax rates ranging from 3% to 45% (see the attached tax rate schedule) shall apply to comprehensive income.	(一)综合所得,适用百分之三至百分之四十五的超额累进税率(税率表附后);
(2) Progressive tax rates ranging from 5% to 35% (see the attached tax rate schedule) shall apply to business income.	(二)经营所得,适用百分之五至百分之三十五的超额累进税率(税率表附后);
(3) The proportional tax rate of 20% shall apply to income from interest and dividends, income from lease of property, income from conveyance of property, and contingent income.	(三)利息、股息、红利所得,财产租赁所得,财产转让所得和偶然所得,适用比例税率,税率为百分之二十。
Article 4 Individual incomes set forth below shall be exempt from individual income tax:	**第四条** 下列各项个人所得,免征个人所得税:
(1) prizes in the fields of science, education, technology, culture, health, sports and environmental protection awarded by the provincial level governments in China, by ministries or commissions under the State Council, by units of the People's Liberation Army at or above the army level, or by foreign organizations and international organizations;	(一)省级人民政府、国务院部委和中国人民解放军军以上单位,以及外国组织、国际组织颁发的科学、教育、技术、文化、卫生、体育、环境保护等方面的奖金;
(2) interest accruing from national treasury bonds or from financial bonds issued by the central government of China;	(二)国债和国家发行的金融债券利息;
(3) subsidies or allowances paid according to the unified standards in China;	(三)按照国家统一规定发给的补贴、津贴;

Continued

English Translation	Chinese Version
(4) welfare benefits, conform payment, or relief payment;	(四)福利费、抚恤金、救济金;
(5) remedies paid from insurance;	(五)保险赔款;
(6) severance pay, demobilization pay or retirement paid to military personnel;	(六)军人的转业费、复员费、退役金;
(7) settling-in allowance, severance pay, pensions, and living allowances or subsidies for the retired according to the unified standards in China;	(七)按照国家统一规定发给干部、职工的安家费、退职费、基本养老金或者退休费、离休费、离休生活补助费;
(8) incomes received by diplomatic representatives, consular officers and other personnel of foreign embassies and consulates in China, which are exempted from individual income tax in China pursuant to the relevant laws;	(八)依照有关法律规定应予免税的各国驻华使馆、领事馆的外交代表、领事官员和其他人员的所得;
(9) incomes which are exempted from individual income tax, according to the international conventions to which the Chinese government is a member or according to the agreement which the Chinese Government has signed; and	(九)中国政府参加的国际公约、签订的协议中规定免税的所得;
(10) other income being exempted by the State Council of China.	(十)国务院规定的其他免税所得。
The tax exemptions prescribed in subparagraph (10) of the preceding paragraph shall be filed by the State Council with the Standing Committee of the National People's Congress.	前款第十项免税规定,由国务院报全国人民代表大会常务委员会备案。
Article 5 Under any of the following circumstances, individual income tax may be reduced within a specific scope and time limit, which shall be prescribed by the provincial governments and be filed with the standing committee of the people's congress at the same level:	**第五条**　有下列情形之一的,可以减征个人所得税,具体幅度和期限,由省、自治区、直辖市人民政府规定,并报同级人民代表大会常务委员会备案:
(1) income of the handicapped, the elderly who has no children, and members of martyrs' families.	(一)残疾、孤老人员和烈属的所得;
(2) heavy losses incurred due to severe natural disasters.	(二)因自然灾害遭受重大损失的。

Continued

English Translation	Chinese Version
Other tax reductions may be prescribed by the State Council but shall be filed with the Standing Committee of the National People's Congress.	国务院可以规定其他减税情形，报全国人民代表大会常务委员会备案。
Article 6 Calculation of the amount of taxable income：	**第六条**　应纳税所得额的计算：
(1) For the comprehensive income of a resident individual，the amount of taxable income shall be the amount of income obtained in each tax year less expenses of 60,000 yuan, special deductibles, special additional deductibles, and other deductibles determined in accordance with the law.	（一）居民个人的综合所得，以每一纳税年度的收入额减除费用六万元以及专项扣除、专项附加扣除和依法确定的其他扣除后的余额，为应纳税所得额。
(2) For the income from wages and salaries of a non-resident individual，the amount of taxable income shall be the amount of monthly income less expenses of 5,000 yuan. For the income from remuneration for labor services，author's remuneration，and royalties，the amount of taxable income shall be the amount of income obtained each time.	（二）非居民个人的工资、薪金所得，以每月收入额减除费用五千元后的余额为应纳税所得额；劳务报酬所得、稿酬所得、特许权使用费所得，以每次收入额为应纳税所得额。
(3) For business income，the amount of taxable income shall be the gross income in each tax year less costs，expenses and losses.	（三）经营所得，以每一纳税年度的收入总额减除成本、费用以及损失后的余额，为应纳税所得额。
(4) For the income from lease of property，the amount of taxable income shall be the income less expenses of 800 yuan if the income is less than 4,000 yuan each time；and the amount of taxable income shall be the income less expenses at 20% of the income if the income is 4,000 yuan or more each time.	（四）财产租赁所得，每次收入不超过四千元的，减除费用八百元；四千元以上的，减除百分之二十的费用，其余额为应纳税所得额。
(5) For the income from conveyance of property，the amount of taxable income shall be the income from conveyance of property less the original value of the property and reasonable expenses.	（五）财产转让所得，以转让财产的收入额减除财产原值和合理费用后的余额，为应纳税所得额。
(6) For the income from interest and dividends and contingent income，the amount of taxable income shall be the amount of income obtained each time.	（六）利息、股息、红利所得和偶然所得，以每次收入额为应纳税所得额。

Continued

English Translation	Chinese Version
The amount of income from remuneration for labor services, author's remuneration, and royalties shall be reduced by subtracting expenses at 20% of the income obtained. The amount of income from author's remuneration shall be calculated at 70% of the income obtained.	劳务报酬所得、稿酬所得、特许权使用费所得以收入减除百分之二十的费用后的余额为收入额。稿酬所得的收入额减按百分之七十计算。
The part of income donated by an individual to public welfare and charitable causes such as education and poverty alleviation that does not exceed 30% of the amount of taxable income declared by the taxpayer may be deducted from the amount of taxable income, unless the State Council prescribes the pre-tax deduction in full amount of donations made to public welfare and charitable causes.	个人将其所得对教育、扶贫、济困等公益慈善事业进行捐赠,捐赠额未超过纳税人申报的应纳税所得额百分之三十的部分,可以从其应纳税所得额中扣除;国务院规定对公益慈善事业捐赠实行全额税前扣除的,从其规定。
As mentioned in Paragraph (1) of this article, special deductibles include but are not limited to contributions to the basic pension insurance, basic medical insurance, unemployment insurance, and other social insurance and housing provident funds paid by resident individuals in accordance with the scopes and standards specified by the state; and special additional deductibles include but are not limited to expenditures for education of children, continuing education, medical treatment of serious diseases, housing loan interest, housing rents and support for elderly parents. The specific scopes, standards and implementation procedures shall be determined by the State Council and filed with the Standing Committee of the National People's Congress.	本条第一款第一项规定的专项扣除,包括居民个人按照国家规定的范围和标准缴纳的基本养老保险、基本医疗保险、失业保险等社会保险费和住房公积金等;专项附加扣除,包括子女教育、继续教育、大病医疗、住房贷款利息或者住房租金、赡养老人等支出,具体范围、标准和实施步骤由国务院确定,并报全国人民代表大会常务委员会备案。
Article 7 For the income obtained by a resident individual from outside China, the amount of individual income tax already paid outside China by the individual may be deducted from the amount of tax payable by the individual, but the tax credit shall not exceed the amount of tax payable on the income obtained by the taxpayer from outside China as calculated in accordance with the provisions of this Law.	**第七条**　居民个人从中国境外取得的所得,可以从其应纳税额中抵免已在境外缴纳的个人所得税税额,但抵免额不得超过该纳税人境外所得依照本法规定计算的应纳税额。

Continued

English Translation	Chinese Version
Article 8 Under any of the following circumstances, tax authorities shall have the authority to make tax payment adjustments in reasonable methods:	**第八条** 有下列情形之一的,税务机关有权按照合理方法进行纳税调整:
(1)Business transactions between an individual and his or her affiliates do not conform to the independent transaction principle, resulting in reduction of the amount of tax payable by the individual or his or her affiliates, which is not justified.	(一)个人与其关联方之间的业务往来不符合独立交易原则而减少本人或者其关联方应纳税额,且无正当理由;
(2)An enterprise formed in a country (or region) with an evidently low actual tax burden, which is controlled by a resident individual or is jointly controlled by a resident individual and a resident enterprise, fails to distribute or distributes a reduced amount of profits attributable to the resident individual without any reasonable operational need.	(二)居民个人控制的,或者居民个人和居民企业共同控制的设立在实际税负明显偏低的国家(地区)的企业,无合理经营需要,对应当归属于居民个人的利润不作分配或者减少分配;
(3) An individual obtains inappropriate tax benefits from the implementation of any other arrangement without any reasonable commercial purpose.	(三)个人实施其他不具有合理商业目的的安排而获取不当税收利益。
Where tax authorities make tax payment adjustments under the preceding paragraph, which requires collection of taxes in arrears, such taxes in arrears shall be collected, together with interest thereon in accordance with the law.	税务机关依照前款规定作出纳税调整,需要补征税款的,应当补征税款,并依法加收利息。
Article 9 Individuals having income are the taxpayers of individual income tax, and the entities or individuals making payments from which the income is derived are the withholding agents.	**第九条** 个人所得税以所得人为纳税人,以支付所得的单位或者个人为扣缴义务人。
Where a taxpayer has a Chinese citizen identity number, the taxpayer's identification number shall be his or her Chinese citizen identity number; otherwise, the taxpayer shall be assigned a taxpayer's identification number by the tax authority. When a withholding agent withholds taxes, the taxpayers shall provide their taxpayer's identification numbers to the withholding agent.	纳税人有中国公民身份号码的,以中国公民身份号码为纳税人识别号;纳税人没有中国公民身份号码的,由税务机关赋予其纳税人识别号。扣缴义务人扣缴税款时,纳税人应当向扣缴义务人提供纳税人识别号。
Article 10 Under any of the following circumstances, a taxpayer shall file a tax return in accordance with the law:	**第十条** 有下列情形之一的,纳税人应当依法办理纳税申报:

194

Continued

English Translation	Chinese Version
(1) Filing a tax return on a consolidated basis is required for comprehensive income obtained.	（一）取得综合所得需要办理汇算清缴；
(2) There is no withholding agent for any taxable income obtained.	（二）取得应税所得没有扣缴义务人；
(3) The withholding agent fails to withhold taxes on any taxable income obtained.	（三）取得应税所得，扣缴义务人未扣缴税款；
(4) Income is obtained overseas.	（四）取得境外所得；
(5) Chinese household registration is cancelled as a result of emigration.	（五）因移居境外注销中国户籍；
(6) A nonresident individual obtains income from wages and salaries at two or more places inside China.	（六）非居民个人在中国境内从两处以上取得工资、薪金所得；
(7) Any other circumstances prescribed by the State Council.	（七）国务院规定的其他情形。
The withholding agent shall, in accordance with the provisions issued by the state, file withholding returns for all taxpayers in full amount, and provide the taxpayers with their individual incomes, taxes withheld, and other information.	扣缴义务人应当按照国家规定办理全员全额扣缴申报，并向纳税人提供其个人所得和已扣缴税款等信息。
Article 11 The individual income tax on the comprehensive income obtained by a resident individual shall be calculated annually; if there is a withholding agent, the withholding agent shall withhold and prepay taxes on a monthly or transaction-by-transaction basis; and if the filing of a tax return on a consolidated basis is needed, the return shall be filed from March 1 to June 30 of the next year after obtaining the income. The measures for withholding and prepayment shall be developed by the taxation department of the State Council.	第十一条　居民个人取得综合所得，按年计算个人所得税；有扣缴义务人的，由扣缴义务人按月或者按次预扣预缴税款；需要办理汇算清缴的，应当在取得所得的次年三月一日至六月三十日内办理汇算清缴。预扣预缴办法由国务院税务主管部门制定。
Where a resident individual provides the withholding agent with information on special additional deductibles, the withholding agent shall, when withholding and prepaying taxes on a monthly basis, make deductions as required, and shall not refuse to do so.	居民个人向扣缴义务人提供专项附加扣除信息的，扣缴义务人按月预扣预缴税款时应当按照规定予以扣除，不得拒绝。

Continued

English Translation	Chinese Version
Where there is a withholding agent for the income from wages and salaries, income from remuneration for labor services, income from author's remuneration, and income from royalties obtained by a nonresident individual, the withholding agent shall withhold taxes on a monthly or transaction-by-transaction basis, rather than filing a tax return on a consolidated basis.	非居民个人取得工资、薪金所得，劳务报酬所得，稿酬所得和特许权使用费所得，有扣缴义务人的，由扣缴义务人按月或者按次代扣代缴税款，不办理汇算清缴。
Article 12 The individual income tax on the business income obtained by a taxpayer shall be calculated annually, and the taxpayer shall, within 15 days after the end of a month or quarter, file a tax return with and prepay taxes to the tax authority; and file a tax return on a consolidated basis before March 31 of the next year after obtaining the income.	第十二条　纳税人取得经营所得，按年计算个人所得税，由纳税人在月度或者季度终了后十五日内向税务机关报送纳税申报表，并预缴税款；在取得所得的次年三月三十一日前办理汇算清缴。
For the income from interest and dividends, income from lease of property, income from conveyance of property, and contingent income obtained by a taxpayer, the individual income tax shall be calculated on a monthly or transaction-by-transaction basis, and if there is a withholding agent, the withholding agent shall withhold taxes on a monthly or transaction-by-transaction basis.	纳税人取得利息、股息、红利所得，财产租赁所得，财产转让所得和偶然所得，按月或者按次计算个人所得税，有扣缴义务人的，由扣缴义务人按月或者按次代扣代缴税款。
Article 13 Where there is no withholding agent for a taxpayer's taxable income obtained, the taxpayer shall, within the first 15 days of the next month after obtaining the income, file a tax return with and pay taxes to the tax authority.	第十三条　纳税人取得应税所得没有扣缴义务人的，应当在取得所得的次月十五日内向税务机关报送纳税申报表，并缴纳税款。
Where the withholding agent fails to withhold taxes on a taxpayer's taxable income obtained, the taxpayer shall pay taxes before June 30 of the next year after obtaining the income; or if the payment period is specified in a notice from the tax authority, the taxpayer shall pay taxes during the specified period.	纳税人取得应税所得，扣缴义务人未扣缴税款的，纳税人应当在取得所得的次年六月三十日前，缴纳税款；税务机关通知限期缴纳的，纳税人应当按照期限缴纳税款。
Where a resident individual obtains any income from outside China, the individual shall file a tax return from March 1 to June 30 of the next year after obtaining the income.	居民个人从中国境外取得所得的，应当在取得所得的次年三月一日至六月三十日内申报纳税。

Continued

English Translation	Chinese Version
Where a nonresident individual obtains any income from wages and salaries from two or more places inside China, the individual shall file a tax return with the tax authority within the first 15 days of the next month after obtaining the income.	非居民个人在中国境内从两处以上取得工资、薪金所得的,应当在取得所得的次月十五日内申报纳税。
Where a taxpayer's Chinese household registration is cancelled as a result of emigration, the taxpayer shall settle taxes before cancellation of his or her Chinese household registration.	纳税人因移居境外注销中国户籍的,应当在注销中国户籍前办理税款清算。
Article 14 The tax deducted in advance or withheld by a withholding agent each month or in each transaction shall be paid to the state treasury within the first 15 days of the next month, with an individual income tax withholding return filed with the tax authority.	**第十四条**　扣缴义务人每月或者每次预扣、代扣的税款,应当在次月十五日内缴入国库,并向税务机关报送扣缴个人所得税申报表。
Where a taxpayer claims any tax refund by filing a tax return on a consolidated basis or a withholding agent claims any tax refund by filing a tax return on a consolidated basis on behalf of a taxpayer, the tax authority shall, after verification, handle the tax refund in accordance with the provisions on the administration of the state treasury.	纳税人办理汇算清缴退税或者扣缴义务人为纳税人办理汇算清缴退税的,税务机关审核后,按照国库管理的有关规定办理退税。
Article 15 Public security, people's bank, financial regulation, and other relevant departments shall assist tax authorities in confirming the identity and financial account information of taxpayers. Education, health, medical insurance, civil affairs, human resources and social security, housing and urban-rural development, public security, people's bank, financial regulation, and other relevant departments shall provide tax authorities with information on special additional deductibles of taxpayers such as education of children, continuing education, medical treatment of serious diseases, housing loan interest, housing rents and support for elderly parents.	**第十五条**　公安、人民银行、金融监督管理等相关部门应当协助税务机关确认纳税人的身份、金融账户信息。教育、卫生、医疗保障、民政、人力资源社会保障、住房城乡建设、公安、人民银行、金融监督管理等相关部门应当向税务机关提供纳税人子女教育、继续教育、大病医疗、住房贷款利息、住房租金、赡养老人等专项附加扣除信息。

Continued

English Translation	Chinese Version
Where an individual conveys any real estate, the tax authority shall assess the individual income tax payable based on the real estate registration and other relevant information, and the registration agency shall, when handling transfer registration, verify the payment receipt of individual income tax related to the conveyance of real estate. Where an individual undergoes modification registration for transfer of equities, the registration authority of the market participant shall verify the payment receipt of individual income tax related to the equity transaction.	个人转让不动产的,税务机关应当根据不动产登记等相关信息核验应缴的个人所得税,登记机构办理转移登记时,应当查验与该不动产转让相关的个人所得税的完税凭证。个人转让股权办理变更登记的,市场主体登记机构应当查验与该股权交易相关的个人所得税的完税凭证。
The relevant departments shall, in accordance with the law, include information on the compliance of taxpayers and withholding agents with this Law in their credit information systems, and implement joint incentives or sanctions.	有关部门依法将纳税人、扣缴义务人遵守本法的情况纳入信用信息系统,并实施联合激励或者惩戒。
Article 16 All income shall be calculated in RMB. If income is obtained in a currency other than RMB, it shall be converted into RMB at the central parity of RMB exchange rate for purposes of tax payment.	第十六条 各项所得的计算,以人民币为单位。所得为人民币以外的货币的,按照人民币汇率中间价折合成人民币缴纳税款。
Article 17 A service fee equivalent to 2 per cent of the amount of tax withheld shall be paid to the withholding agent.	第十七条 对扣缴义务人按照所扣缴的税款,付给百分之二的手续费。
Article 18 The imposition, reduction, or suspension of collection of individual income tax on interest income from savings deposits and the specific measures shall be specified by the State Council and filed with the Standing Committee of the National People's Congress.	第十八条 对储蓄存款利息所得开征、减征、停征个人所得税及其具体办法,由国务院规定,并报全国人民代表大会常务委员会备案。
Article 19 Taxpayers, withholding agents, and tax authorities and their staff members that violate the provisions of this Law shall be held legally liable in accordance with the provisions of the Law of the People's Republic of China on the Administration of Tax Collection and relevant laws and regulations.	第十九条 纳税人、扣缴义务人和税务机关及其工作人员违反本法规定的,依照《中华人民共和国税收征收管理法》和有关法律法规的规定追究法律责任。

Continued

English Translation	Chinese Version
Article 20 The administration of individual income tax collection shall be governed by the provisions of this Law and the Law of the People's Republic of China on the Administration of Tax Collection.	第二十条　个人所得税的征收管理,依照本法和《中华人民共和国税收征收管理法》的规定执行。
Article 21 The State Council shall，pursuant to the provisions of this Law，formulate the regulation for its implementation.	第二十一条　国务院根据本法制定实施条例。
Article 22 This Law shall enter into force on the day of its promulgation.	第二十二条　本法自公布之日起施行。

Schedule 1 of Individual Income Tax Rates（applicable to comprehensive income）	个人所得税税率表一(综合所得适用)
See the Form(1)	参见附表(1)
(Notes：1. For purposes of this Schedule，"amount of annual taxable income" means the balance of comprehensive income obtained by a resident individual after subtracting expenses of 60,000 yuan，special deductibles，special additional deductibles，and other deductibles determined in accordance with the law from the amount of income in each tax year，in accordance with the provision of Article 6 of this Law.	(注 1:本表所称全年应纳税所得额是指依照本法第六条的规定,居民个人取得综合所得以每一纳税年度收入额减除费用六万元以及专项扣除、专项附加扣除和依法确定的其他扣除后的余额。
2. The amount of tax payable on the income from wages and salaries，income from remuneration for labor services，income from author's remuneration，and income from royalties obtained by a nonresident individual shall be calculated on a monthly basis after conversion in accordance with this Schedule.)	注 2:非居民个人取得工资、薪金所得,劳务报酬所得,稿酬所得和特许权使用费所得,依照本表按月换算后计算应纳税额。)

Appendix Ⅱ : Exercises

1.Which changes were made into the IIT Law by the 2018 Amendment?

2.What are the differences between the 2018 Amendment and the former six times of amendments to the IIT Law?

3.Who are taxpayers for IIT in China?

4.What's the tax base for Chinese tax residents in terms of paying IIT in China?

5.What's the tax base for non-Chinese tax residents in terms of paying IIT in China?

6.Which incomes could be exempted from paying IIT in China?

7.How to calculate IIT in China?

8.How to pay IIT in China?

9.Case Study One

• Facts：

Mr. Chen is a Chinese tax resident who received the following incomes in the year of 2020：

(1)Salaries paid by his employer (a German company) into Mr. Chen's bank account in Berlin, while Mr. Chen exercised his employment duties in Shanghai in January 2020.

(2)Service fees paid by Mr. Li a Chinese individual for Mr. Chen translated a paper of Mr. Li from Chinese into German language in Berlin in February 2020.

(3)Mr. Chen won USD 30,000 through gambling in a casino at Las Vegas, the United States in March 2020.

• Questions:

(1)Which incomes for which Mr. Chen should be subject to individual income tax in China?

(2)If Mr. Chen is non-Chinese tax resident, which incomes for which Mr. Chen should be subject to individual income tax in China?

10.Case Study Two

• Facts：

Jessie is a U.S. citizen who has no domicile in China. In the year 2020, Jessie traveled in China for tourism purpose from 1 January to 31 March, 2020, and then she went to Shanghai on 1 August, 2020 for taking a four-month program of learning Chinese language at Fudan University. Jessie left China on 31 December, 2020.

• Questions:

(1)Is Jessie a Chinese tax resident or a non-Chinese tax resident under the Chinese IIT Law?

(2)If Jessie had incomes sourced from the United States, should she be subject to the Chinese individual income tax for those incomes?

11.Case Study Three

Were Mr. Chen's following incomes sourced from China?

(1)Salaries paid by his employer (a German company) into Mr. Chen's bank account in Berlin, while Mr. Chen exercised his employment duties in Shanghai in January 2020.

(2)Service fees paid by Mr. Li a Chinese individual for Mr. Chen translated a paper of Mr. Li from Chinese into German language in Berlin in February 2020.

(3)Mr. Chen won USD 30,000 through gambling in a casino at Las Vegas, the United States in March 2020.

12.Case Study Four

• Facts:

Mr. Wang is a Chinese citizen studying at the National University of Singapore, while his family and his economic sources are all in China. Mr. Wang is the only son of his parents, who are 70 years old. Mr. Wang hasn't got married yet, and no children. He has no job in China and did not pay for any social contributions. He was quite healthy in 2020, and has no housing loan or rental paid in China.

Mr. Wang derived the following incomes in the year 2020:

(1)Mr. Wang worked as a part-time employee at a Sinco, a Singaporean trading company from 1 January 2020 to December 2020. Sinco paid Mr. Wang RMB 10,000 (before tax) every month into his bank account in Singapore.

(2)Lucia paid Mr. Wang RMB 5,000 in December 2020 for Mr. Wang translating her paper from English into Chinese.

(3)Mr. Wang published a paper on a law journal, which paid him RMB 5,000 into his bank account in Shanghai in January 2020.

(4)Mr. Wang has licensed a patent of his to Microsoft, which paid him

RMB 10,000 into his bank account in the U.S. in December 2020.

(5)Mr. Wang owns 30% the shares of a U.S. company, Kayco Company Ltd. which paid him RMB 10,000 as dividends distribution into his bank account in Shanghai in December 2020.

• Question:

How much individual income tax Mr. Wang should pay in China for his above incomes received in the year 2020?

CHAPTER 6
ENTERPRISE INCOME TAX

6.1   Introduction

The enterprise income tax regime in China is governed by the Enterprise Income Tax Law (the "EIT Law"), which was promulgated by the People's Congress on 16 March 2007, effective from 1 January 2008 and being latest amended in December 2018. In order to provide some detailed rules and guidance for implementing the EIT Law, the State Council enacted the Implementation Regulations (the "EIT Regulations") on the Enterprise Income Tax Law in December 2007, and the MOF and SAT have been issuing tax circulars since 2008.

The applicable scope of the EIT Law is quite broad, including all enterprise, public institutions, social units, and other forms of organizations, except for sole individual proprietorship enterprises and partnership enterprises. Furthermore, the EIT Law adopts a classical double tax system whereby profits distributed by an enterprise in the form of dividends are subject to individual income tax in the hands of individual shareholders. But subject to conditions, a resident enterprise is generally allowed to exclude dividends received from another resident enterprise from its taxable income.

6.2　Structure of the EIT Legislations

The EIT Law has 60 Articles, which are divided in the text into the eight chapters according to their covered issues, and accordingly the EIT Regulation provides with implementation rules for the EIT Law.

Table 6-1　Structure of the EIT Law and Regulation

Covered Issues	EIT Law	EIT Regulation
Ⅰ.General Principles (taxpayers and tax rate)	Arts. 1-4	Arts. 1-8
Ⅱ.Taxable Income	Arts. 5-21	Arts. 9-75
Ⅲ.Tax Payable	Arts. 22-24	Arts. 76-81
Ⅳ.Tax Incentives	Arts. 25-36	Arts. 82-102
Ⅴ.Withholding Obligations	Arts. 37-40	Arts. 103-108
Ⅵ.Special adjustment	Arts. 41-48	Arts. 109-123
Ⅶ.Tax Administration	Arts. 49-56	Arts. 124-129
Ⅷ.Supplementary Provisions	Arts. 57-60	Arts. 130-132

6.3　Taxpayers

Except for the sole proprietorship enterprises and the partnerships which are Chinese tax residents[①], all enterprises and other organizations shall be subject to the EIT Law for paying their enterprise income tax in

---

①　With respect to these sole proprietorship enterprises and the partnerships, they shall not pay the enterprise income tax for their profits, but their shareholders or partners shall be subject to the Chinese individual income tax in accordance with the Chinese Individual Income Tax. However, if the sole proprietorship enterprises and partnerships are non-Chinese tax residents, they shall be subject to the enterprise income tax at their own enterprise level.

China.

These taxpayers are divided into two categories, the Chinese tax residents and the non-Chinese tax residents. A Chinese tax resident enterprise is subject to the EIT on its worldwide income; in contrast a non-Chinese tax resident enterprise generally is subject to the EIT only for its income sourced from China, unless it has an "establishment" or an office in China. In the later situation, the non-Chinese tax resident enterprise shall be subject to the EIT for both the incomes it sourced from China and its income sourced from outside of China but which has "actual connections" with the said office or establishment.

Therefore, when determining the EIT liability of an enterprise, it is necessary to take the following three issues into account :

(1) Whether the enterprise is a Chinese tax resident?

(2) Whether a non-Chinese tax resident enterprise has an establishment or an office in China?

(3) Where the income of the enterprise is sourced from?

6.3.1 Chinese Tax Residents

The EIT Law adopts both the place of incorporation doctrine and the place of actual management doctrine, when defining a Chinese tax resident enterprise. Consequently, an enterprise shall become a Chinese tax resident according to the EIT Law, if

(1) the enterprise is incorporated in China in accordance with Chinese laws, or

(2) the enterprise is incorporated outside of China under foreign laws, but its place of actual management is inside China.

The "place of actual management" is interpreted by the EIT Regulation as the place where to factually exercise of the substantial and over-all management and control of the enterprise with regard to its production and business operations, personnel, finance, assets, etc. Clearly these factors are quite objective and thus would have to rely on tax authorities' discretion when applying them to determine the place of actual management of an enterprise. A Chinese tax resident enterprise is subject to the EIT on its world-wide income.

6.3.2 Non-Chinese Tax Residents

Then as for an non-Chinese tax resident enterprise, it must be an enterprise incorporated outside of China under the laws of a foreign country and with its place of actual management us also located outside China.

A non-Chinese tax resident enterprise generally is subject to the EIT only for its income sourced from China, unless it has an "establishment" or an office in China. In the later situation, the non-Chinese tax resident enterprise shall be subject to the EIT for both the incomes it sourced from China and its income sourced from outside of China but which has "actual connections" with the said office or establishment. The term "actual connections" herein means the connections whereby its an "establishment" or an office in China holds the equity or credit, or owns, manages or controls its property, etc.

6.3.3 Offices and Establishments

The EIT Law uses the terms "offices" and "establishment", which are defined by the EIT Regulation as the institutions and places where the non-Chinese tax resident enterprise engages in production activities and business operations within the territory of China, including

(1) management institutions, operational institutions, and offices;

(2) factories, farms, and places for the exploitation of natural resources;

(3) establishments for provision of labor services;

(4) establishments for engineering operations with respect to construction, installation, assembling, repairing, and surveying, etc.;

(5) other institutions and establishments where production activities and operations are carried out; and

(6) where a non-resident enterprise entrusts any agent to carry out pro-

duction activities or business operations within the territory of China, including the entrustment of any entity or individual to sign contracts on its behalf to handle the warehousing or delivery of goods, etc., such agent shall be regarded as an institution or establishment of the nonresident created within China.

In comparison with the concept "permanent establishment" (PE) used in the Chinese tax treaties, the above terms "offices" and "establishment" in the EIT Law obviously do not request for any fixity, permanent, or "at disposal" elements, and even do not expressly require the non-Chinese tax resident enterprise for having a physical presence in China. Therefore, the terms "offices" and "establishment" under the EIT Law are much broader than the concept "permanent establishment" used in the Chinese tax treaties.

6.4   Source Rules

The source of income shall be determined in accordance with the following rules, regardless of the place of payment:

(1)income from the sale of goods shall be determined according to the place where the transaction is carried out;

(2)income from provision of labor services shall be determined according to the place where labor services are provided;

(3)income from transfer of immovable properties shall be determined according to the place where such real property is situated;

(4)income from transfer of movable properties shall be determined according to the location of the seller;

(5)income from transfer of other properties in a form of equity investments shall be determined according to the place where the invested entity is located;

(6)income from equity investments, for example dividends, shall be determined according to the place where the enterprise that distributes the income is located;

(7)interest, rental, and royalties derived from franchising shall be determined according to the place where the institution payer is located or according to the place where the abode of the individual payer is located;

(8)other income shall be determined by the competent department of treasury or taxation of the State Council.

6.5　Calculation of EIT

6.5.1 Taxable Period

The EIT is levied on a current year basis and the tax year is the calendar year from 1 January to 31 December. If an enterprise starts or terminates its business operation within a tax year, its actual operating period in that year will be the enterprise's taxable period.

6.5.2 Calculation Formula

The formula for calculating the amount of tax payable for the EIT is as follows:

Tax payable = Taxable income × Applicable tax rate-tax exemption and deduction-tax credit

The following sections will describe the approaches for calculating the taxable income, the tax credit and the amount of the tax being exempted, as well as the approaches for determine the applicable tax rate.

6.5.3 Tax Rates

The standard tax rate for the enterprise income tax rate is 25%, but lower tax rates are commonly used as a form of tax incentives being provided by the EIT Law and the EIT Regulation and even by the SAT/MOF tax circulars from time to time. For example, a reduced tax rate of 15% shall apply to the high-and new-tech enterprises which are supported by Chinese governments, and a lower rate of 20% applies to those qualified micro-low-profit enterprises. In addition, the EIT Law grants the governments of autonomous regions for ethnic minorities with a power to decide the reduction or exemption of the EIT tax for the enterprises in the said autonomous regions.

6.6   Taxable Income

6.6.1 General Principle

The tax base for calculating an enterprise's EIT in China is called the "taxable income", which is the balance amount after deducting the tax-free income, tax-exempt income, allowable deductions and the losses of the previous years from the enterprise's total amount of incomes of the tax year. In other words, the following formula could be applied to calculate the taxable income of an enterprise's EIT for a tax year:

Taxable income = Total income − Tax-free income − Tax-exempt income-allowable deductions−Losses of previous years

The taxable income must be calculated on an accrual basis, thus income and costs and expenses relating to the current period must be included for the current period, regardless of whether the payment has been received or made. And for those income and costs and expenses that are not related to the current period, they shall not be treated as incurred in the current period even if the payment has been received or made within the current period.

6.6.2 Total Income

All incomes an enterprise from whatever sources should be included into the amount of total incomes of the enterprise, including but not limited to:

(1)income from sale of goods, for examples, commodities, products, raw materials, packaging materials, low-value perishables, and other inventories, etc;

(2)income from provision of labor services, for examples, construction, installation, reparation, fixing, transportation and traffic, warehousing and lease, finance and insurance, post and telecommunications, consultation and brokerage, cultural and sports activities, scientific research, technical services, educational trainings, catering and lodging, intermediary services, health and medical services, residential community services, travel, entertainment, processing, and other labor services, etc;

(3)income from transaction of properties, for examples, fixed assets, biological assets, intangible assets, equity, credits, etc;

(4)dividend and proceeds from equity investments;

(5)income from interests which obtained by the enterprise by providing capital to other persons for use without becoming an equity investment, for examples, interest of bank deposits, loan interest, debenture interest, arrearage interest, etc.;

(6) income from rentals obtained by the enterprise from granting the use-right of its fixed assets, packaging materials or other tangible properties;

(7)income from royalties obtained by the enterprise through providing the use-right of its patents, know-how, trademarks, copyrights, or other franchised rights;

(8)donations received in forms of monetary assets or non-monetary assets as being gratuitously donated by other enterprises, organizations or individuals; and

(9)other incomes which are not listed in the above (1) to (8) items, for examples, income from the excess assets of the enterprise, income from the overdue deposits for packaging materials that fails to be refunded, the payable items that cannot be paid, the receivables that are received after being treated as bad debt, income from the restructuring of debts, income from subsidies, income from damages, income from foreign exchange rates, etc.

The above incomes could be obtained by the enterprise in a monetary form ora non-monetary form. The monetary incomes include but not limited to cash, bank deposits, receivable accounts, receivable instruments, bond investment to be held until maturity, and relief of obligation, etc. While the non-monetary incomes include fixed assets, biological assets, intangible assets, equity investments, inventories, bond investments not to be held until maturity, labor services, and other relevant rights and interests, etc. The value of these non-monetary incomes shall be determined according to the arm's length value referring to their market price.

6.6.3 Tax-Free Income

The following three incomes are tax-free incomes which shall be excluded from the total amount of the taxable income:

(1)the fiscal appropriations (funding) by Chinese governments, which refer to the fiscal capital allotted by Chinese governments at various levels to public institutions, social unities, and organizations which are within the budgetary management of Chinese governments, unless it is otherwise provided for by the State Council or the competent department of treasury or taxation;

(2) the administrative charges and the governmental funds which are collected according to law and fall under the treasury administration;

The term "administrative charges" herein refers to the fees charged in the process of conducting social public management or providing specified public services to citizens, legal persons or other organizations in accordance to laws and regulations and such charges shall be subject to fiscal management by Chinese governments.

The term "governmental funds" refers to the fiscal capital that an enterprise collects on behalf of the Chinese governments for the use of specified purposes according to laws and regulations.

(3)other fiscal capital obtained by enterprises upon the approval of the State Council and to be used for the specified purposes as determined by the treasury or taxation ministries.

6.6.4 Tax-Exempt Income

The tax-exempt income means the income which should be included into the taxable income of an enterprise but is specifically exempted, wholly or partially, by a tax incentive policy provided. Generally, tax incentives may only be granted by law or the State Council. The State Council issued a decree Guo Fa [2015] No. 25 on the general policy on tax incentives that stresses the uniformity of the tax incentives regime and the validation of tax incentives granted by local governments. The State Council is authorized to announce other tax incentives to accommodate the needs of economic and social development. From time to time, notices are, under instructions of the State Council, issued by MOF and SAT to introduce new incentives, interpret, detail and implement the existing tax incentives. Taxpayers may apply tax incentives based on their own judgement as to whether they are entitled to the incentives concerned. The onerous pre-approval is no longer required. However, a taxpayer applying a tax incentive must submit a filing form and other required documents to the tax authorities. Taxpayers are responsible for the truthfulness of their filings, and must notify the tax authorities and undertake refiling if the circumstances or conditions under which tax incentives were granted have changed. The competent tax authorities have the right to initiate ex-post examinations.

6.6.4.1 Full-exemption

According to the EIT Law and the EIT Regulation, the following incomes shall be wholly exempted from paying the EIT in China:

(1)income from treasury bonds which refers to the interest income arising from the treasury bonds an enterprise holds issued by the MOF;

(2)dividends and other equity investment proceeds distributed between qualified resident enterprises, which refer to the investment proceeds obtained by a resident enterprise from its direct investment in any other resident enterprises. However, such tax-exempt income shall not include the investment proceeds from stock publicly issued and trade on a stock exchange which is consecutively held by a resident enterprise for not more than 12 months;

(3)dividends and other equity investment proceeds that a non-resident enterprise with offices or establishments in China obtains from a resident enterprise and which have actual connection with such institutions or establishments; and

(4)incomes of qualified non-profit organizations, including donations received, government subsidies and income received for provision of services to the government, member fees collected according to regulations issued by the civil affairs departments or the finance departments at the level higher than the provincial governments, interest on bank deposits of non-taxable/exempt income; and other types of income prescribed by the MOF and the SAT. Clearly that such tax-exempt income shall not include the income of a non-profit organizations arising from its profitable activities.

In order to become a "qualified non-profit organization" which could be exempted from the EIT for the above mentioned tax-exempt incomes, the non-profit organization must satisfy all of the following requirements and apply with the in-charge tax authority for recognizing it being a qualified non-profit organization[1]:

(1)having registered as a non-profit organization in China according to Chinese laws and regulations;

(2)engaging in public interest activities or non-profit activities;

(3)the incomes obtained by the non-profit organization, except for the reasonable expenses for the organization's operation, are all used for public interest or non-profit undertaking which are provided in its articles of association as registered and approved;

(4)the properties and proceeds of the non-profit organization are not distributable;

(5)pursuant to its articles of association as registered and approved, the remained properties of the non-profit organization upon its de-registration shall be used for public interest or non-profit events or shall be donated to other organizations in the same nature and with the same tenets by the in-charge registration and administration institutions. In the later situation,

---

[1] Circular [2018] No.13.

such a donation should be noticed to the public;

(6) the contributors shall not enjoy any property right or reserve any right on the properties which have been contributed into the non-profit organization;

(7) salaries and benefits of the staffs of the non-profit organization should be limited within the an allowed amount, and it is forbidden to distribute the organization's properties in any disguised manner.

6.6.4.2 Full or partial exemption

According to the EIT Law and EIT Regulation, the following incomes may be exempted wholly or partially from the EIT:

(1) The incomes incurred from project of agriculture, forestry, husbandry and fishery, unless the project is restricted or prohibited by Chinese governments. Such incomes are divided into the following two categories according to the amounts of the exempted incomes:

①Exempt the total amount of income derived by an enterprise from engaging in the following activities:

• planting of vegetables, cereals, potatoes, oil plants, beans, cotton, hemps, sugar plants, fruits, nuts, etc;

• breeding of new varieties of crops;

• planting of traditional Chinese medicinal herbs;

• cultivation and planting of forest trees;

• raising of animals and poultry;

• gathering of forest products;

• other agricultural, forest, animal raising and fishing projects such as irrigation, initial processing of agricultural products, veterinary science, promotion of agricultural techniques, operations and reparation of agricultural machines, etc.; and

• ocean fishing.

②Exempt half amount of the income from the EIT derived by an enterprise from engaging in the following activities:

• planting of flowers, teas, and other beverage plants and spicery plants;

• maritime aquaculture and inland aquaculture.

(2) The incomes incurred from business operations of the important public infrastructure projects supported by Chinese governments, which include ports, wharves, airports, railways, highways, municipal public transportation, electric power, water conservancy, etc. as listed in the Catalogue of Public Infrastructure Projects Entitled to Enterprise Income Tax Preferential Treatment.

The total amount of such income shall be exempted from the EIT for the first three years as of the year when the enterprise obtains its first revenue arising from production or operation; and then half amount of such income shall be exempted from the EIT for the fourth to the sixth year.

(3) The income derived from the projects of environmental protection, energy and water saving, which meet the relevant conditions set out by the MOF and the SAT. These projects include the processing of public sewage, the processing of public garbage, the comprehensive exploitation and utilization of firedamp, the renovation of technologies of saving energy or discharging wastes, the desalination of sea water, etc.

The total amount of income derived by an enterprise from engaging in the above mentioned projects shall be exempted from the EIT for the first three years as of the tax year it obtains the first business revenue, and then half amount of such income shall be exempted from the EIT for the fourth to the sixth year.

(4) The incomes derived from transfer of technologies, of which the portion not exceeding CNY 5 million shall be exempted from the EIT, and then for the remaining amount exceeding the CNY 5 million shall be subject to the EIT only for half of the amount.

6.6.5 Reduction of the Taxable Income

The EIT Law and the EIT Regulations also provide a number of tax exemption or deduction incentives to certain industrial sectors or enterprises, which are allowed to offset against the amount of taxable income.

For example, in order to encourage investment into small or medium-sized high and new technology enterprises, 70% of such equity investment

215

by the startup investment enterprise shall be allowed to set off the enterprise's taxable amount, as long as it holds such equity investment in the targeted enterprises for no less than two years. And if its taxable amount is not enough for setoff, the balance is allowed to be carried forward to subsequent years for setoff purpose.

Another example is to allow the enterprise to use 10% of its investment in purchasing the "special equipment" to set off its taxable income of the year. The "special equipment herein refers to those equipment used for environmental protection, energy and water saving and work safety purpose[①], and the enterprises must purchase and actually put into use these special equipments. If the amount of taxes is not sufficient for credit, the margin may be carried forward for credit in the following 5 tax years. However, if the enterprise transfers or leases any of the aforesaid special equipment within 5 years after its purchase, its preferential treatment shall be terminated and the enterprise shall pay the enterprise income tax accordingly.

6.7　Deductions

6.7.1 General Principle

Costs, expenses, (certain) taxes, losses and other expenditures are generally deductible to the extent that they are incurred in gaining or producing income and the amount to be deducted is evidenced and in accordance with the relevant laws and regulations.

[①]　These special equipments are listed in the Catalogue of Special Equipments Dedicated to Environmental Protection Entitled to Preferential Income Tax Treatment, the Catalogue of Special Equipments Dedicated to Conservation of Energy and Water Entitled to Preferential Income Tax Treatment, and the Catalogue of Special Equipments Dedicated to Work Safety Entitled to Preferential Income Tax Treatment.

Costs refer to manufacturing costs, sales costs, write-off costs, business expenditures and other expenditures incurred by an enterprise in its production activities and business operations. For example, cost of raw materials, cost of goods sold, business expenditures, other consumable expenditures, cost of services received, cost of fixed assets and cost of intangibles incurred by an enterprise in its production and business operations.

Expenses are defined as sales expenses, management expenses and financial expenses incurred by an enterprise in its production and business operations, with the exception of those business operations that have already been included in the cost.

Taxes that are deductible refer to the various taxes (other than the VAT and the EIT) paid by an enterprise, such as consumption tax, urban maintenance and construction fees, education fees, resource tax, customs duties, land value-added tax and stamp duty.

Deductible losses refers to the loss or destruction of fixed assets and inventories due to damages and loss from the transfer of property, loss from bad debt, loss from force majeure such as natural disaster, etc. and other kinds of loss, subject to restrictions and conditions imposed by the tax authorities.

And other deductible expenditures incurred by an enterprise in its production activities and business operations other than the costs, expenses, taxes paid, and losses.

The above deductible expenditures are either a capital or revenue nature. Therefore, the expenditures incurred in acquiring fixed assets or in developing intangible assets are called the "capital-related expenditures", which are not fully deductible in the year they are incurred but may be depreciated or amortized over a number of years. While the expenditures incurred in the course of carrying on business are called the "revenue-related expenditures", such as cost of goods sold, manufacturing costs, marketing expenses, administrative expenses, financial expenses and taxes on sales, which are deductible in the current tax year.

6.7.2 Revenue-Related Expenditures

The revenue-related expenses in general shall be deducted in the current accounts of the enterprise for the full amount or a portion of the expenses.

6.7.2.1 Employees' remuneration and expenses

Reasonable wages and salaries paid to employees are deductible. Wages and salaries are referred to as relevant cash or non-cash labour service remuneration paid by an enterprise during each year to its employees, including basic wages, bonus, allowances, subsidies, year-end salary, overtime payment and other appointment-related or employment-related expenditures.

Contributions made to the compulsory social security insurances of employees are also deductible. The deductible contributions to the compulsory social security insurances mentioned in the law are basic pension insurance, basic medical insurance, unemployment insurance, work injury insurance, maternity insurance and housing fund.

Contributions to supplementary old age pension insurance and medical insurance for employees are deductible, provided that such contributions do not exceed 5% of the total wages of employees.

Commercial insurance premiums that an enterprise pays for its employees are not deductible, except for the personal security insurance premiums which are paid its employees engaging in special occupations under the relevant provisions of the state and other commercial insurance premiums that are deductible under the relevant provisions of the competent departments of treasury and taxation of the State Council.

The expenses for the education of staff members incurred by an enterprise are deductible to the extent that they do not exceed 2.5% of the total amount of salaries and wages unless it is otherwise different provided for by the State Council. The excess may be carried forward to future years for deduction.

The employee welfare expenses incurred by an enterprise are deductible to the extent that it does not exceed 14% of the total amount of salaries and wages.

The labor union funds allocated by an enterprise are deductible to the extent that they do not exceed 2% of the total amount of salaries and wages.

Reasonable expenses for labor protection incurred by an enterprise shall be deductible.

6.7.2.2 Interest

Financial costs incurred by an enterprise during its production and business operations are generally deductible if they are not to be capitalized. Where an enterprise borrows any loan for purposes of purchasing or creating fixed assets or intangible assets and inventories that cannot enter into the scheduled marketability state until 12 months later or more, the reasonable expenses arising from such loans in the process of purchasing or creating relevant assets shall be treated as capital expenditure and be included into the cost of relevant capital for deduction purpose.

Deductible interest includes:

(1) interest expenses for the loans borrowed by a non-financial enterprise from a financial enterprise, the interest expenses for the various deposits of financial enterprises, the interest expenses for inter-bank loans, and the expenses for the debentures issued by an enterprise upon approval;

(2) the portion of interest expenses for the loans borrowed by a non-financial enterprise from another non-financial enterprise that do not exceed the amount calculated at the interest rates for an identical kind and identical term of a financial enterprise;

(3) the foreign exchange losses incurred by enterprise in monetary exchanges from the conversion of any non-renminbi monetary assets or obligations into current renminbi at the term-end medium exchange rate are deductible, except for the portion that has already been incorporated into the relevant capital costs and the portion that relates to the profit distribution to owners.

6.7.2.3 Rental and lease expenses

Rental paid for fixed assets by an enterprise for its production activities and business operations are deductible as follows:

(1) The rental expenses incurred from the renting of fixed assets by means of operational lease shall be evenly deducted in proportion to the term of lease;

(2) the rental expenses incurred from the renting of fixed assets by means of financing lease shall be deducted by installments to the extent of

the portion of financing that forms a part of the fixed asset value for which depreciation shall be reserved;

(3)in a sale and leaseback financial lease transaction, the part of the payment that is categorized as interest is a deductible expense for the lessee[1]. Rental payments paid by a branch to another branch (business unit) of the same enterprise are not deductible.

6.7.2.4 Expenses for business entertainment

The expenses for business entertainment incurred by an enterprise relating to its production activities and business operations shall be deducted to the extent of 60% of the actually incurred amount but not more than 5‰ of the sales revenue of the current year.

6.7.2.5 Advertisement and promotion expenses

The expenses for advertising and promotion incurred by an enterprise are deductible up to 15% of the turnover of the enterprise of the current year. However, advertisement and promotion expenses incurred by tobacco industries are not deductible for EIT purposes[2].

6.7.2.6 Donations

The charitable donations to the approved public welfare social organizations[3]are deductible, within the amount limited to 12% of the enterprise's

---

[1]　(SAT Public Notice [2010]No. 13)

[2]　Circular [2017] No. 41

[3]　The "public welfare social organization" herein means a charity organization or any other social organization that satisfies all the following conditions: (i) It is registered in accordance with the law and has the legal person status; (ii) it serves the purpose of promoting public welfare undertakings and does not take profit making as the purpose; (iii) all the assets and the appreciation thereof are owned by the legal person; (iv) it mainly uses its income and working balance for the undertaking in line with the purpose of formation of the legal person; (v) the remaining property after its termination does not belong to any individual or profit-making organization; (vi) it does not engage in any business irrelevant to the purpose of its formation; (vii) it has sound financial accounting rules; (viii) the donator does not participate in the distribution of the property of the legal person in any form; and (ix) it meets other conditions prescribed by the public finance department and competent tax department of the State Council together with the civil affairs department of the State Council and other registration administrative departments.

total annual profits. The qualified donations in excess of 12% of the annual profit may be carried forward to the subsequent 3 years.

The charitable donations are defined as donations made by an enterprise through the people's governments and their departments at the county or higher levels or through charitable organizations recognized by the provincial or higher governments for the purposes prescribed by the "Law of the People's Republic of China on Donation for Charitable Activities".

A charitable organization must fulfill all of the following conditions:

(1) It is legally registered as a legal person;

(2) it is non-profit seeking and aims at the development of public interests;

(3) the total assets and their increase are owned by the organization as a legal person;

(4) its revenue and positive operation results are mainly used for activities that are in line with the objectives of the organization;

(5) the remaining assets after liquidation may not be transferred to any individual or profit-making organization;

(6) it is not engaged in any activities that are not related to the objectives of the organization;

(7) it has a sound and complete financial and accounting system;

(8) donors may not in any form be involved in the distribution of the organization's assets; and

(9) other conditions prescribed by the State Council and the tax authorities.

The Civil Affairs Department is responsible for the qualification of charitable organizations and, together with the Finance Department and the Tax Bureau, for determining the deductibility of the donations. The list of qualified organizations is published annually.

6.7.2.7 Service and management fees

Service fees are deductible if they are considered to be "reasonable". Reasonable fees paid by a Chinese establishment or place of business of a foreign enterprise to its head office in the course of production and business operations are deductible if they are at arm's length and the payments can be substantiated.

6.7.2.8 Environmental protection funds

The funds an enterprise draws for the special use of environmental protection, ecological recovery pursuant to the relevant provisions of the laws and administrative regulations shall be deductible. The aforesaid special funds shall not be deductible if their purpose of use is changed after being drawn.

6.7.2.9 Properties insurance payment

The insurance premiums that an enterprise pays according to the prescribed rates for the insurance of property shall be deductible.

6.7.3 Capital-Related Expenditures

Capital-related expenditures may not be deducted in the current year but should be included into the cost of the relevant capital and then to be deducted by installments (namely to be depreciated or amortized) over a number of years. Accelerated depreciation or amortizations is available for certain assets as a tax incentive.

6.7.3.1 Depreciation

Depreciation for fixed assets is computed annually on a straight-line basis on the assumption that there will be a reasonable residual value. A fixed asset for depreciation purposes refers to buildings, structures, machines, means of transportation and other equipment, appliances and tools, which are used for production, provision of services, leasing and management with a useful life of more than 12 months.

In general, a fixed asset may only be depreciated if it has been brought into use. The taxpayer must be the legal owner of the fixed asset or the lessee under a financial lease is entitled to claim the depreciation allowances. In addition, a purchaser under a hire purchasing contract and the person having usufruct have the right to claim depreciation if certain conditions are satisfied. Under a financial leasing contract, the lessee may claim depreciation.

Depreciation of fixed assets is computed on an annual basis and the fixed assets to be depreciated must be valued at historical costs. The depreciable assets are grouped into classes and the minimum period over which each class may be written down is as follows:

(1) 20 years for buildings and structures;

(2) 10 years for aircrafts, trains, vessels, machinery, mechanical equipment and other production equipment;

(3) 5 years for appliances, tools and furniture used for production and business operations;

(4) 4 years for transportation means other than aircrafts, trains and vessels; and

(5) 3 years for electronic/digital equipment.

Expenditures incurred for renovations of written-off fixed assets, leased fixed assets and for extensive renovation to fixed assets may be amortized over the period of the new useful life after the renovation if the expenditure exceeds 50% of the book value of the fixed asset and its useful life after the renovation is more than 2 years.

The minimum depreciation periods for various types of production-nature biological assets are respectively 10 years for production-nature biological asset in the nature of forestry and 3 years for production-nature biological asset in the nature of livestock.

6.7.3.2 Amortization

The intangibles assets must be amortized over a minimum period of 10 years on a straight-line basis, if the intangibles are used for the taxpayer's business operation. The intangible asset refers to the non-monetary long-term assets without a physical form which are held by an enterprise for purposes of producing products, providing labor services, lease or operational management, including patent rights, trademark rights, copyrights, land use rights, know-how, good-will, etc.

The depreciation bases are as follows:

(1) purchase price plus other charges and taxes paid if the intangible is acquired;

(2) the expenditures incurred if the intangible is self-developed; and

(3) the fair market value plus the related charges and taxes if the intangible is obtained in the form of donation, capital contribution, exchange of

non-monetary assets and debt structuring, etc.

Other expenditures should be amortized over no less than 3 years.

Self-created goodwill is not allowed to be amortized or deducted, but ac-quired goodwill may be deducted in the event of liquidation or transfer of the whole enterprise.

6.7.4 Super-Deductions

A number of expenditures are allowed not only for deduction of their full amounts but also allowing to an additional deductions of certain amounts, which are called the "super-deductions". The function of these su-per-deductions is clearly a kind of tax incentive policies which China intends to use for encouraging a number of business sectors or actives. For exam-ples, an additional 50% deduction of the expenses incurred from research and development of new technologies, new products and new techniques is granted by the EIT Law for the purpose of promoting new technologies; and an additional 100% deduction of the salaries and wages paid to the disabled employees are granted for the purpose of encouraging hiring the disables.

Furthermore, allowing to accelerate the depreciation of certain fixed as-sets is also a kind of tax incentive for the purpose of promoting technological progress or production efficiency. One method used in this tax incentive is to shorten the depreciation period of the fixed assets, for example, shortening the depreciation period to only 60% of the years. Another main method used to apply the double-declining balance method or the sum-of-the-years-digits method when calculating the depreciation amounts.

6.7.5 Non-deductible Expenses

The following disbursements are disallowed for deduction for the EIT purpose, even if an enterprise has already incurred such disbursements in the tax year:

(1) dividend, profit distributions and other returns on equity investment;

(2) payment of enterprise income tax;

(3) surcharge for defaulted tax payment;

(4) fines and penalties and losses caused by confiscation;

(5) donations in excess of 12% of the total profits;

(6) sponsorship payment[①];

(7) non-approved reserved expenditures[②];

(8) goodwill, except for acquired goodwill in the case of liquidation or transfer of the whole enterprise;

(9) management fees paid by one enterprise to another, the rentals and franchise royalties paid among the operational institutions within an enterprise, and the interest paid among the business offices of a non-financial enterprise shall not be deductible;

(10) other disbursements for non-business purposes; and

(11) costs and expenses incurred for or the properties used for deriving the tax-free incomes.

6.8   Losses of Previous Years

Losses occur if the costs and expenses exceed the revenue generated from business operations. Losses from an equity investment may be deducted on a one-off basis in the tax year in which the losses are recognized. However, the losses incurred by a company's overseas business establishment may

---

① The sponsorship payment refers to the various non-advertising expenditures incurred by an enterprise that have nothing to do with its production activities or business operations.

② Reserves and provisions, for example, the depreciation reserves or the risk reserves for the various assets, are generally not deductible in computing taxable income. And except for financial institutions, no reserves for bad debts arising from trading may be formed. Taxpayers may claim an annual reserve for bad debts if they are engaged in banking, insurance services or other similar businesses. According to Circular [2015] No. 9, state banks, commercial banks, financial companies, urban and rural credit cooperatives, and financial leasing companies may apply the deductible provision to losses incurred by ordinary loans.

not be offset against the profits of its domestic business establishments.

The losses, which cannot be fully set-off in the current tax year, are allowed to be carried forward for 5 years for off-setting purpose in the process of calculation of taxable income. But no carry-back is allowed.

In the case of a merger or division, losses that were suffered by companies or an establishment prior to the merger and have not been utilized may be set off against the taxable income of the consolidated company after the merger and carried forward for a period of a maximum of 5 years.

6.9 Tax Exemption and Deduction

The tax exemption and reduction refer to the amount of the EIT payable, which are reduced or exempted wholly or partially under the tax incentive policies provided by the EIT Law and the EIT Regulation. In addition, the National People's Congress in the EIT Law granted the State Council with a legislative power of enacting tax incentive policies in the cases of where the national economic and social development so requires or business operations of enterprises have been seriously affected by emergencies and other factors.

6.10 Foreign Tax Credit

The foreign income tax paid by a Chinese resident enterprise for its income sourced from outside of China is allowed to be deducted from its tax payable for the EIT purpose. This method is called the "credit method", which is provided in the EIT Law for the purpose to relief of double taxation for Chinese resident enterprises. However, this credit method is also eligible for those non-Chinese tax resident enterprises, which derived incomes outside of China but these incomes have no actual connection with their offices or establishments in China.

The limit of tax credit shall be the payable amount of taxes on such incomes computed according to this Law. The portion exceeding the limit of tax credit may, during the five subsequent years, be offset by way of deducting the limit of tax credit of each year from the balance after the deduction of the limit of tax credit of the current year.

6.11   Tax Administration

6.11.1 Tax Registration

The Chinese resident enterprises are required to conduct tax registration with the in-charge Chinese tax authorities of the place of its incorporation (for those enterprises incorporated in China) or the place of actual management (for those enterprises incorporated outside of China).

6.11.2 Monthly or Quarterly Advance Filing

The Chinese resident enterprises are required to make provisional assessments and file provisional EIT returns on a monthly or quarterly basis and make advance tax payments. The returns are generally prepared on a self-assessment basis and the advance payments are reconciled after the end of a tax year in the annual filing for final tax settlement. The advance payments should be made on a monthly or quarterly basis within 15 days after the end of each month or quarter.

6.11.3 Annual Filing

A Chinese resident enterprise must file with the in-charge Chinese tax authority its annual return and the annual financial statements within 5 months after the end of each tax year. The returns may be filed on paper or electronically but must be filed in the Chinese language, or in both the Chinese and foreign languages.

A final annual tax settlement follows after the annual filing for the purpose to calculate the amount of the underpaid tax or the overpaid tax. Any underpaid tax shall be paid within 5 months, and any tax overpayment may be refunded upon approval of tax authorities.

6.11.4 Surcharge and Penalties

Those who fail to complete tax registration procedures, change or cancel tax registrations, or file income or withholding tax returns in time may be subject to a fine of up to CNY 2,000. If the taxpayer or withholding agent fails to fulfill the registration or filing obligations after a renewed time limit, the penalty could be increased to CNY 10,000.

The late payment surcharge is 0.05% of the unpaid tax balance for each day the income tax unpaid. Generally, the tax authorities are authorized to impose a penalty of 50% to 500% of the amount of tax unpaid or underpaid. If the taxpayer fails to file a tax return or to pay the tax due on time, additional fines are imposed. And a criminal investigation and prosecution could be initiated if the amount of taxes evaded, by non-filing or filing of a false tax return, exceeds CNY 50,000 or more. A withholding tax agent may face a criminal investigation and prosecution as well, if the withheld taxes not paid to the tax authorities due to fraud or concealment are more than CNY 10,000.

If it is the taxpayer or withholding agent who fails to pay or underpays tax, the statute of limitations is 10 years. But in the case of tax fraud, evasion or refusal to pay tax, no limitation is set for tax collection.

6.12   Special Rules for Non-Chinese Tax Residents

With regard to income which the non-Chinese tax resident enterprises sourced from China and has no actual connections with their offices or establishments in China, there is no withholding tax imposed in China, but such incomes shall be subject to the EIT in accordance of certain many special rules provided the EIT Law. Such incomes generally are in forms of dividends, interest, rental, royalties or capital gains, etc.

The first notable special rule is about the tax rate, which is not the standard rate of 20% as being provided in the EIT Law, but is a reduced rate of 10% which is provided by the EIT Regulation as a tax incentive policy for non-Chinese tax resident enterprises unless a reduced rate is provided under a tax treaty between China and residence state of the non-Chinese tax resident enterprise.

The second special rule is about the tax base, which needn't be calculated as complicated as the Chinese tax resident following the above described formulas, but will take the full amount of the income (a gross basis) sourced from China as its taxable income.

The third special rule is to impose a withholding obligation on the Chinese payer, who, regardless an individual or a legal person, must withhold the amount of the EIT payable from the incomes, file the withholding tax return with the in-charge Chinese tax authority, make the tax payments within 7 days, and then provide tax payment evidence to the recipient.

Appendix Ⅰ: EIT Law (2018 Amendment)①

English Translation	Chinese Version
Enterprise Income Tax Law of the People's Republic of China	中华人民共和国企业所得税法
(Adopted at the 5th Session of the 10th National People's Congress of the People's Republic of China on March 16, 2007, amended for the first time in accordance with the Decision of the Standing Committee of the National People's Congress on Amending the Enterprise Income Tax Law of the People's Republic of China at the 26th session of the Standing Committee of the Twelfth National People's Congress of the People's Republic of China on February 24, 2017; and amended for the second time in accordance with the Decision of the Standing Committee of the National People's Congress to Amend Four Laws Including the Electric Power Law of the People's Republic of China on December 29, 2018)	(2007 年 3 月 16 日第十届全国人民代表大会第五次会议通过 根据 2017 年 2 月 24 日第十二届全国人民代表大会常务委员会第二十六次会议《关于修改〈中华人民共和国企业所得税法〉的决定》第一次修正 根据 2018 年 12 月 29 日第十三届全国人民代表大会常务委员会第七次会议《关于修改〈中华人民共和国电力法〉等四部法律的决定》第二次修正)
Chapter Ⅰ General Provisions	**第一章　总　　则**
Article 1 Within the territory of the People's Republic of China, the enterprises and other organizations that have incomes (hereinafter referred to as the enterprises) shall be payers of the enterprise income tax and shall pay their enterprise income taxes in accordance with this Law.	**第一条**　在中华人民共和国境内,企业和其他取得收入的组织(以下统称企业)为企业所得税的纳税人,依照本法的规定缴纳企业所得税。
This Law does not apply to the sole individual proprietorship enterprises and partnership enterprises.	个人独资企业、合伙企业不适用本法。
Article 2 Enterprises are classified into resident and nonresident enterprises.	**第二条**　企业分为居民企业和非居民企业。

---

①　The English version was translated with a reference of the translations on the website of www.pkulaw.com.

Continued

English Translation	Chinese Version
The term "resident enterprise" as mentioned in this Law refers to an enterprise that is established inside China, or which is established under the law of a foreign country (region) but whose actual office of management is inside China.	本法所称居民企业,是指依法在中国境内成立,或者依照外国(地区)法律成立但实际管理机构在中国境内的企业。
The term "non-resident enterprise" as mentioned in this Law refers to an enterprise established under the law of a foreign country (region), whose actual institution of management is not inside China but which has offices or establishments inside China; or which does not have any offices or establishments inside China but has incomes sourced in China.	本法所称非居民企业,是指依照外国(地区)法律成立且实际管理机构不在中国境内,但在中国境内设立机构、场所的,或者在中国境内未设立机构、场所,但有来源于中国境内所得的企业。
Article 3 A resident enterprise shall pay the enterprise income tax on its incomes derived from both inside and outside China.	**第三条** 居民企业应当就其来源于中国境内、境外的所得缴纳企业所得税。
For a non-resident enterprise having offices or establishments inside China, it shall pay enterprise income tax on its incomes derived from China as well as on incomes that it earns outside China but which has real connection with the said offices or establishments.	非居民企业在中国境内设立机构、场所的,应当就其所设机构、场所取得的来源于中国境内的所得,以及发生在中国境外但与其所设机构、场所有实际联系的所得,缴纳企业所得税。
For a non-resident enterprise having no office or establishment inside China, or for a non-resident enterprise whose incomes have no actual connection to its institution or establishment inside China, it shall pay enterprise income tax on the incomes derived from China.	非居民企业在中国境内未设立机构、场所的,或者虽设立机构、场所但取得的所得与其所设机构、场所没有实际联系的,应当就其来源于中国境内的所得缴纳企业所得税。
Article 4 The enterprise income tax rate shall be 25%.	**第四条** 企业所得税的税率为 25%。
The tax rate that applies to a non-resident enterprise's incomes as mentioned in Paragraph 3, Article 3 of this Law shall be 20%.	非居民企业取得本法第三条第三款规定的所得,适用税率为 20%。

Continued

English Translation	Chinese Version
Chapter Ⅱ Taxable Amount of Income	**第二章 应纳税所得额**
Article 5 The balance after deducting the tax-free incomes, tax-exempt incomes, all deduction items as well as the permitted remedies for losses of the previous year(s) from an enterprise's total amount of incomes of each tax year shall be the taxable amount of incomes.	**第五条** 企业每一纳税年度的收入总额，减除不征税收入、免税收入、各项扣除以及允许弥补的以前年度亏损后的余额，为应纳税所得额。
Article 6 An enterprise's monetary and non-monetary incomes from various sources shall be the total amount of incomes，including：	**第六条** 企业以货币形式和非货币形式从各种来源取得的收入，为收入总额。包括：
(1)income from sale of goods；	(一)销售货物收入；
(2)income from provision of labor services；	(二)提供劳务收入；
(3)income from transaction of properties；	(三)转让财产收入；
(4)dividend and other proceeds from equity investments；	(四)股息、红利等权益性投资收益；
(5)income from interests；	(五)利息收入；
(6)income from rentals；	(六)租金收入；
(7)income from royalties；	(七)特许权使用费收入；
(8)donations received；and	(八)接受捐赠收入；
(9)other incomes.	(九)其他收入。
Article 7 The following incomes included in the total amount of incomes shall be tax-free incomes：	**第七条** 收入总额中的下列收入为不征税收入：
(1)Fiscal appropriations；	(一)财政拨款；
(2)administrative charges and the governmental funds that are collected according to the law and fall under the treasury administration；and	(二)依法收取并纳入财政管理的行政事业性收费、政府性基金；
(3) Other tax-free incomes as prescribed by the State Council.	(三)国务院规定的其他不征税收入。
Article 8 The reasonable disbursements that are actually incurred and in which have actual connection with the business operations of an enterprise，including the costs，expenses，taxes，losses and other expenditures，may be deducted in the calculation of the taxable amount of incomes.	**第八条** 企业实际发生的与取得收入有关的、合理的支出，包括成本、费用、税金、损失和其他支出，准予在计算应纳税所得额时扣除。

Continued

English Translation	Chinese Version
Article 9 Of an enterprise's charitable donation expenditures, the part which is not more than 12% of its total annual profits shall be deductible in the calculation of its taxable income; and the excess over 12% of its total annual profits may be carried forward for three years in the calculation of its taxable income.	**第九条**　企业发生的公益性捐赠支出，在年度利润总额12%以内的部分，准予在计算应纳税所得额时扣除；超过年度利润总额12%的部分，准予结转以后三年内在计算应纳税所得额时扣除。
Article 10 None of the following disbursements may be deducted in the calculation of the taxable amount of incomes:	**第十条**　在计算应纳税所得额时，下列支出不得扣除：
(1) Dividendand other equity investment proceeds paid to the investors;	（一）向投资者支付的股息、红利等权益性投资收益款项；
(2) payment for enterprise income tax;	（二）企业所得税税款；
(3) late fee for taxes;	（三）税收滞纳金；
(4) pecuniary punishment, fines, and losses of properties confiscated;	（四）罚金、罚款和被没收财物的损失；
(5) disbursements for donations other than those provided for in Article 9;	（五）本法第九条规定以外的捐赠支出；
(6) sponsorship disbursements;	（六）赞助支出；
(7) unverified reserve disbursements;	（七）未经核定的准备金支出；
(8) other disbursements that have nothing to do with the obtainment of revenues;	（八）与取得收入无关的其他支出。
Article 11 When calculating the taxable amount of incomes, an enterprise is allowed to deduct the depreciations of fixed assets calculated under the relevant provisions.	**第十一条**　在计算应纳税所得额时，企业按照规定计算的固定资产折旧，准予扣除。
No depreciation may be calculated for any of the following fixed assets:	下列固定资产不得计算折旧扣除：
(1) The fixed assets that have not yet been put into use, excluding houses and buildings;	（一）房屋、建筑物以外未投入使用的固定资产；
(2) the fixed assets rented in by way of commercial lease;	（二）以经营租赁方式租入的固定资产；
(3) the fixed assets rented out by way of finance leasing;	（三）以融资租赁方式租出的固定资产；

Continued

English Translation	Chinese Version
(4)the fixed assets for which depreciation has been allocated in full amount but which remain in use;	(四)已足额提取折旧仍继续使用的固定资产;
(5)the fixed assets that have nothing to do with the business operations;	(五)与经营活动无关的固定资产;
(6)the land that is separately appraised and entered into account as an item of fixed asset; and	(六)单独估价作为固定资产入账的土地;
(7)other fixed assets for which no depreciation may be calculated.	(七)其他不得计算折旧扣除的固定资产。
Article 12 When calculating the taxable amount of incomes, an enterprise is allowed to deduct the amortized expenses of intangible assets calculated according to the relevant provisions.	**第十二条** 在计算应纳税所得额时,企业按照规定计算的无形资产摊销费用,准予扣除。
No amortized expense may be calculated for the following intangible assets:	下列无形资产不得计算摊销费用扣除:
(1)The intangible assets, for which the self-development expenses have been deducted in the calculation of the taxable amount of incomes;	(一)自行开发的支出已在计算应纳税所得额时扣除的无形资产;
(2)the self-created business reputation;	(二)自创商誉;
(3)the intangible assets that have nothing to do with the business operations; and	(三)与经营活动无关的无形资产;
(4)other intangible assets for which no amortized expense may be calculated.	(四)其他不得计算摊销费用扣除的无形资产。
Article 13 The following expenses incurred by an enterprise shall, in the calculation of the taxable amount of incomes, be treated as long-term deferred expenses. Those amortized under the relevant provisions are allowed to be deducted:	**第十三条** 在计算应纳税所得额时,企业发生的下列支出作为长期待摊费用,按照规定摊销的,准予扣除:
(1)the expenses for the rebuilding of a fixed asset, for which depreciation has been prepared in full amount;	(一)已足额提取折旧的固定资产的改建支出;
(2)the expenses for the rebuilding of a rented fixed asset;	(二)租入固定资产的改建支出;
(3)the expenses for the heavy repair of a fixed asset; and	(三)固定资产的大修理支出;

Continued

English Translation	Chinese Version
(4)other expenses that shall be treated as long-term deferred expenses.	(四)其他应当作为长期待摊费用的支出。
Article 14 During the period of external investment, an enterprise shall not deduct the costs of the investment assets when it calculates the taxable amount of incomes.	**第十四条**　企业对外投资期间,投资资产的成本在计算应纳税所得额时不得扣除。
Article 15 Where an enterprise uses or sells its inventories, it is allowed to deduct the costs of the inventories calculated according to the relevant provisions in the calculation of the taxable amount of incomes.	**第十五条**　企业使用或者销售存货,按照规定计算的存货成本,准予在计算应纳税所得额时扣除。
Article 16 Where an enterprise transfers an asset, it is allowed to deduct the net value of the asset in the calculation of the taxable amount of incomes.	**第十六条**　企业转让资产,该项资产的净值,准予在计算应纳税所得额时扣除。
Article 17 When an enterprise calculates its enterprise income taxes on a consolidated basis, it shall not offset the losses of its overseas business institutions against the profits of its domestic business institutions.	**第十七条**　企业在汇总计算缴纳企业所得税时,其境外营业机构的亏损不得抵减境内营业机构的盈利。
Article 18 The losses incurred by an enterprise during a tax year may be carried forward and subtracted from the incomes during subsequent years for a maximum carry-forward period of 5 years.	**第十八条**　企业纳税年度发生的亏损,准予向以后年度结转,用以后年度的所得弥补,但结转年限最长不得超过五年。
Article 19 Where a non-resident enterprise obtains incomes as described in Paragraph 3, Article 3 of this Law, it shall calculate the taxable amount of income through following approaches:	**第十九条**　非居民企业取得本法第三条第三款规定的所得,按照下列方法计算其应纳税所得额:
(1)the taxable amount of incomes from dividends and other equity investment proceeds, interests, rentals and royalties shall be based on the total amount of incomes;	(一)股息、红利等权益性投资收益和利息、租金、特许权使用费所得,以收入全额为应纳税所得额;
(2)the taxable amount of incomes from the assignment of property shall be the balance of the total amount of incomes less the net value of the property; and	(二)转让财产所得,以收入全额减除财产净值后的余额为应纳税所得额;
(3)the taxable amount of any other income shall be calculated by reference to the approaches as mentioned in the preceding items.	(三)其他所得,参照前两项规定的方法计算应纳税所得额。

Continued

English Translation	Chinese Version
Article 20 The specific measures for the scope and criterions of revenues and deductions, as well as the tax treatment of assets as provided for in the present Chapter shall be formulated by the treasury and tax administrative departments of the State Council.	第二十条　本章规定的收入、扣除的具体范围、标准和资产的税务处理的具体办法，由国务院财政、税务主管部门规定。
Article 21 When calculating the taxable amount of incomes, if the enterprise's financial or accounting treatment method does not conform to any tax law or administrative regulation, the taxable amount shall be calculated in accordance with the tax law or administrative regulation.	第二十一条　在计算应纳税所得额时，企业财务、会计处理办法与税收法律、行政法规的规定不一致的，应当依照税收法律、行政法规的规定计算。
Chapter Ⅲ Amount of Payable Taxes	**第三章　应纳税额**
Article 22 The amount of payable taxes shall be the balance of the taxable amount multiplied by the applicable tax rate minus the tax amounts deducted and exempted as provided for in this Law.	第二十二条　企业的应纳税所得额乘以适用税率，减除依照本法关于税收优惠的规定减免和抵免的税额后的余额，为应纳税额。
Article 23 An enterprise may deduct from the taxable amount of incomes of the current period the amount of income tax that the enterprise has already paid overseas for the following incomes. The limit of tax credit shall be the payable amount of taxes on such incomes computed according to this Law. The portion exceeding the limit of tax credit may, during the five subsequent years, be offset by way of deducting the limit of tax credit of each year from the balance after the deduction of the limit of tax credit of the current year:	第二十三条　企业取得的下列所得已在境外缴纳的所得税税额，可以从其当期应纳税额中抵免，抵免限额为该项所得依照本法规定计算的应纳税额；超过抵免限额的部分，可以在以后五个年度内，用每年度抵免限额抵免当年应抵税额后的余额进行抵补：
(1)A resident enterprise's taxable incomes derived outside China; and	（一）居民企业来源于中国境外的应税所得；
(2)taxable incomes earned outside China by a non-resident enterprise having offices or establishments in China, but which have no actual connection with the said offices or establishments.	（二）非居民企业在中国境内设立机构、场所，取得发生在中国境外但与该机构、场所有实际联系的应税所得。

Continued

English Translation	Chinese Version
Article 24 For the dividends and other equity investment proceeds derived outside China，which a resident enterprise obtains from its directly or indirectly controlled foreign enterprise，the portion of income tax on this income paid by the foreign enterprise outside China may be treated as the allowable tax credit of overseas income tax amount of the resident enterprise and be deducted within the limit of tax credit as prescribed in Article 23 of this Law.	第二十四条　居民企业从其直接或者间接控制的外国企业分得的来源于中国境外的股息、红利等权益性投资收益,外国企业在境外实际缴纳的所得税税额中属于该项所得负担的部分,可以作为该居民企业的可抵免境外所得税税额,在本法第二十三条规定的抵免限额内抵免。
Chapter Ⅳ Preferential Tax Treatments	**第四章　税收优惠**
Article 25 Preferential in enterprise income tax treatments are granted to the important industries and projects whose development is supported and encouraged by the state.	第二十五条　国家对重点扶持和鼓励发展的产业和项目,给予企业所得税优惠。
Article 26 The following incomes of an enterprise shall be tax-free incomes：	第二十六条　企业的下列收入为免税收入：
（1）the income from treasury bonds；	（一）国债利息收入；
（2）dividends and other equity investment proceeds distributed between qualified resident enterprises；	（二）符合条件的居民企业之间的股息、红利等权益性投资收益；
（3）dividends and other equity investment proceeds that a non-resident enterprise with offices or establishments in China obtains from a resident enterprise and which have actual connection with such institutions or establishments；and	（三）在中国境内设立机构、场所的非居民企业从居民企业取得与该机构、场所有实际联系的股息、红利等权益性投资收益；
（4）incomes of qualified non-profit organizations.	（四）符合条件的非营利组织的收入。
Article 27 The enterprise income tax on the following incomes may be exempted or reduced：	第二十七条　企业的下列所得,可以免征、减征企业所得税：
（1）the incomes incurred from projects of agriculture，forestry，husbandry and fishery；.	（一）从事农、林、牧、渔业项目的所得；
（2）the incomes incurred from business operations of the important public infrastructure investment projects supported by the state；	（二）从事国家重点扶持的公共基础设施项目投资经营的所得；

Continued

English Translation	Chinese Version
(3) the incomes incurred from the projects of environmental protection, energy and water saving, which meet the relevant requirements;	(三)从事符合条件的环境保护、节能节水项目的所得;
(4) the incomes incurred from the transfer of technologies, which meet the relevant requirements; and	(四)符合条件的技术转让所得;
(5) the incomes as prescribed in Paragraph 3, Article 3 of this Law.	(五)本法第三条第三款规定的所得。
Article 28 The enterprise income tax on a small meagre-profit enterprise that meets the prescribed conditions shall be levied at a reduced tax rate of 20%.	**第二十八条** 符合条件的小型微利企业,减按 20%的税率征收企业所得税。
The enterprise income tax on important high-and new-tech enterprises that are necessary to be supported by the state shall be levied at the reduced tax rate of 15%.	国家需要重点扶持的高新技术企业,减按 15%的税率征收企业所得税。
Article 29 The autonomous organ of an autonomous region of ethnic minorities may decide the reduction or exemption of the local portion of the enterprise income tax to be paid by enterprises within the said autonomous region. The decisions of deduction or exemption made an autonomous prefecture or county shall be submitted to the people's government of the province, autonomous region, or municipality directly under the Central Government for approval.	**第二十九条** 民族自治地方的自治机关对本民族自治地方的企业应缴纳的企业所得税中属于地方分享的部分,可以决定减征或者免征。自治州、自治县决定减征或者免征的,须报省、自治区、直辖市人民政府批准。
Article 30 The following expenses of an enterprise may be additionally calculated and deducted:	**第三十条** 企业的下列支出,可以在计算应纳税所得额时加计扣除:
(1) the expenses for the research and development of new technologies, new products and new techniques; and	(一)开发新技术、新产品、新工艺发生的研究开发费用;
(2) the wages paid to the disabled employees or other employees whom the state encourages to hire.	(二)安置残疾人员及国家鼓励安置的其他就业人员所支付的工资。
Article 31 A startup investment enterprise engaged in important startup investments that are necessary to be supported and encouraged by the state may deduct from the taxable amount of incomes a certain proportion of the amount of investment.	**第三十一条** 创业投资企业从事国家需要重点扶持和鼓励的创业投资,可以按投资额的一定比例抵扣应纳税所得额。

Continued

English Translation	Chinese Version
Article 32 Where it is surely necessary to accelerate the depreciation of any fixed asset of an enterprise because of technological progress or due to any other cause, it may shorten the term of depreciation or adopt an approach to accelerate the depreciation.	**第三十二条** 企业的固定资产由于技术进步等原因,确需加速折旧的,可以缩短折旧年限或者采取加速折旧的方法。
Article 33 The incomes generated by an enterprise from producing products conforming to the industrial policies of the state in the way of comprehensive utilization of resources may be downsized in the calculation of the amount of taxable incomes.	**第三十三条** 企业综合利用资源,生产符合国家产业政策规定的产品所取得的收入,可以在计算应纳税所得额时减计收入。
Article 34 The amount of an enterprise's investment in the purchase of special equipment for environmental protection, energy and water saving, work safety, etc. may be deducted from the tax amount at a certain rate.	**第三十四条** 企业购置用于环境保护、节能节水、安全生产等专用设备的投资额,可以按一定比例实行税额抵免。
Article 35 The specific measures for the preferential tax treatments as mentioned in this Law shall be formulated by the State Council.	**第三十五条** 本法规定的税收优惠的具体办法,由国务院规定。
Article 36 Where the national economic and social development so requires, or the business operations of enterprises have been seriously affected by emergencies and other factors, the State Council may formulate special preferential policies concerning the enterprise income tax and submitted them to the Standing Committee of the National People's Congress for archival purposes.	**第三十六条** 根据国民经济和社会发展的需要,或者由于突发事件等原因对企业经营活动产生重大影响的,国务院可以制定企业所得税专项优惠政策,报全国人民代表大会常务委员会备案。
Chapter V Withholding by Income Sources	**第五章　源泉扣缴**
Article 37 The payable income taxes on the incomes as described in Paragraph 3, Article 3 of this Law that a non-resident enterprise earns shall be withheld by income sources, with the payer acting as the obligatory withholder. The tax amount shall be withheld by the obligatory withholder from each payment or payment due.	**第三十七条** 对非居民企业取得本法第三条第三款规定的所得应缴纳的所得税,实行源泉扣缴,以支付人为扣缴义务人。税款由扣缴义务人在每次支付或者到期应支付时,从支付或者到期应支付的款项中扣缴。

Continued

English Translation	Chinese Version
Article 38 For the payable income taxes on the incomes that a non-resident enterprise obtains from undertaking an engineering project or providing labor services inside China, the tax organ may designate the payer of the project price or remuneration as the obligatory withholder.	**第三十八条** 对非居民企业在中国境内取得工程作业和劳务所得应缴纳的所得税,税务机关可以指定工程价款或者劳务费的支付人为扣缴义务人。
Article 39 For the income tax that shall be withheld under Articles 37 and 38 of this Law but the obligatory withholder has failed to withhold or is unable to perform the withholding obligation, the taxpayer shall pay them at the place where the income has occurred. If the taxpayer fails to do so, the tax organ may recover the payable tax of the enterprise from its other income items inside China for which the payer should pay.	**第三十九条** 依照本法第三十七条、第三十八条规定应当扣缴的所得税,扣缴义务人未依法扣缴或者无法履行扣缴义务的,由纳税人在所发生地缴纳。纳税人未依法缴纳的,税务机关可以从该纳税人在中国境内其他收入项目的支付人应付的款项中,追缴该纳税人的应纳税款。
Article 40 An obligatory withholder shall turn over the withheld taxes to the state treasury within 7 days after the date of withholding and submit to the local tax organ a form of report on the withheld enterprise income taxes.	**第四十条** 扣缴义务人每次代扣的税款,应当自代扣之日起七日内缴入国库,并向所在地的税务机关报送扣缴企业所得税报告表。
Chapter VI Special Adjustments to Tax Payments	**第六章 特别纳税调整**
Article 41 With regard to a transaction between an enterprise and its affiliate, if the taxable revenue or income of the enterprise or its affiliate decreases due to inconformity with the arms length principle, the tax organ may make an adjustment through a reasonable method.	**第四十一条** 企业与其关联方之间的业务往来,不符合独立交易原则而减少企业或者其关联方应纳税收入或者所得额的,税务机关有权按照合理方法调整。
The costs of an enterprise and its affiliate for joint development or accepting the assignment of intangible assets, or jointly providing or accepting labor services shall, according to the arms length principle, be apportioned in the calculation of the taxable amount of incomes.	企业与其关联方共同开发、受让无形资产,或者共同提供、接受劳务发生的成本,在计算应纳税所得额时应当按照独立交易原则进行分摊。

Continued

English Translation	Chinese Version
Article 42 An enterprise may file with the tax organ the pricing principles and computation approaches for the transactions between it and its affiliates, the tax organ and the enterprise shall enter into an advance pricing arrangement upon negotiations and confirmation.	**第四十二条**　企业可以向税务机关提出与其关联方之间业务往来的定价原则和计算方法,税务机关与企业协商、确认后,达成预约定价安排。
Article 43 When an enterprise submits to the tax organ its annual enterprise income tax returns, the enterprise shall enclose an annual report on the related transactions with its affiliates.	**第四十三条**　企业向税务机关报送年度企业所得税纳税申报表时,应当就其与关联方之间的业务往来,附送年度关联业务往来报告表。
When the tax organ investigates into the affiliated transactions, the enterprise and its affiliates, as well as other enterprises relating to the affiliated transactions under investigation, shall provide the pertinent materials according to the relevant provisions.	税务机关在进行关联业务调查时,企业及其关联方,以及与关联业务调查有关的其他企业,应当按照规定提供相关资料。
Article 44 Where any enterprise refuses to provide the materials of transactions with its affiliates, or provides any false or incomplete materials that cannot reflect the true information about the affiliated transactions, the tax organ may decide a taxable income after an investigation.	**第四十四条**　企业不提供与其关联方之间业务往来资料,或者提供虚假、不完整资料,未能真实反映其关联业务往来情况的,税务机关有权依法核定其应纳税所得额。
Article 45 With regard to an enterprise that is established by a resident enterprise, controlled by a resident enterprise, or by a Chinese resident who is located in a country (region) where the actual tax burden is obviously lower than the tax rate as prescribed in Paragraph 1 of Article 4 of this Law, if the profits are not distributed or are distributed partially for a cause that is not a reasonable business operation, the portion of the aforesaid profits attributable to this resident enterprise shall be included in its incomes of the current period.	**第四十五条**　由居民企业,或者由居民企业和中国居民控制的设立在实际税负明显低于本法第四条第一款规定税率水平的国家(地区)的企业,并非由于合理的经营需要而对利润不作分配或者减少分配的,上述利润中应归属于该居民企业的部分,应当计入该居民企业的当期收入。
Article 46 The interest disbursement for any debt investments and equity investments, which an enterprise accepts from its affiliates, in excess of the prescribed criterion shall not be deducted in the calculation of the taxable amount of income.	**第四十六条**　企业从其关联方接受的债权性投资与权益性投资的比例超过规定标准而发生的利息支出,不得在计算应纳税所得额时扣除。

Continued

English Translation	Chinese Version
Article 47 Where an enterprise makes any other arrangement not for any reasonable business purpose, if its taxable revenue or income decreases, the tax organ has the power to make an adjustment through a reasonable method.	第四十七条 企业实施其他不具有合理商业目的的安排而减少其应纳税收入或者所得额的,税务机关有权按照合理方法调整。
Article 48 If the tax organ makes an adjustment to a tax payment under the provisions of this Chapter and if it is necessary to recover the tax payment in arrears, it shall do so and charge an additional interest under the provisions of the State Council.	第四十八条 税务机关依照本章规定作出纳税调整,需要补征税款的,应当补征税款,并按照国务院规定加收利息。
Chapter Ⅶ Administration of Tax Collection	**第七章 征收管理**
Article 49 The administration of the collection of enterprise income taxes shall be governed by the Law of the People's Republic of China on the Administration of Tax Collection in addition to this Law.	第四十九条 企业所得税的征收管理除本法规定外,依照《中华人民共和国税收征收管理法》的规定执行。
Article 50 Unless it is otherwise provided for in any tax law or administrative regulation, the tax payment place of a resident enterprise shall be the registration place of the said enterprise. But if its registration place is outside China, the tax payment place shall be the place where its office of actual management is located.	第五十条 除税收法律、行政法规另有规定外,居民企业以企业登记注册地为纳税地点;但登记注册地在境外的,以实际管理机构所在地为纳税地点。
A resident enterprise that has established an operational institution that has no legal person status in China shall calculate and pay its enterprise income taxes on a consolidated basis.	居民企业在中国境内设立不具有法人资格的营业机构的,应当汇总计算并缴纳企业所得税。
Article 51 Where a non-resident enterprise obtains any income as described in Paragraph 2, Article 3 of this Law, the tax payment place shall be the place where the institution or establishment is located. Where a non-resident enterprise has two or more institutions or establishments inside China, if it meets the conditions as specified by the taxation department of the State Council, choose to have its main institution or establishment pay the enterprise income tax on a consolidated basis.	第五十一条 非居民企业取得本法第三条第二款规定的所得,以机构、场所所在地为纳税地点。非居民企业在中国境内设立两个或者两个以上机构、场所,符合国务院税务主管部门规定条件的,可以选择由其主要机构、场所汇总缴纳企业所得税。
For a non-resident enterprise that obtains any income as described in Paragraph 3, Article 3 of this Law, the place where the obligatory withholder is located shall be the place for the payment of enterprise income taxes.	非居民企业取得本法第三条第三款规定的所得,以扣缴义务人所在地为纳税地点。

Continued

English Translation	Chinese Version
Article 52 Unless it is otherwise provided for by the State Council, enterprises shall not pay their enterprise income taxes on a consolidated basis.	**第五十二条**　除国务院另有规定外,企业之间不得合并缴纳企业所得税。
Article 53 Enterprise income taxes shall be calculated on the basis of a tax year. A tax year commences on January 1 and ends on December 31 of the Gregorian calendar year.	**第五十三条**　企业所得税按纳税年度计算。纳税年度自公历 1 月 1 日起至 12 月 31 日止。
Where an enterprise starts or terminates its business operations in the middle of a tax year so that its actual business operation period in this tax year is shorter than 12 months, its actual business operation period shall constitute its tax year.	企业在一个纳税年度中间开业,或者终止经营活动,使该纳税年度的实际经营期不足十二个月的,应当以其实际经营期为一个纳税年度。
At the time of liquidation of an enterprise, the liquidation period shall be the tax year for the enterprise.	企业依法清算时,应当以清算期间作为一个纳税年度。
Article 54 Enterprise income taxes shall be paid in advance on the monthly or quarterly basis.	**第五十四条**　企业所得税分月或者分季预缴。
An enterprise shall, within 15 days after the end of a month or quarter, submit to the tax organ an enterprise income tax return for advance payment and pay the tax in advance.	企业应当自月份或者季度终了之日起十五日内,向税务机关报送预缴企业所得税纳税申报表,预缴税款。
An enterprise shall, within 5 months after the end of each year, submit to the tax organ an annual enterprise income tax return for the settlement of tax payments and settle the payable or refundable amount of taxes.	企业应当自年度终了之日起五个月内,向税务机关报送年度企业所得税纳税申报表,并汇算清缴,结清应缴应退税款。
When an enterprise submits an enterprise income tax return, it shall attach to it the financial statements and other relevant materials according to the relevant provisions.	企业在报送企业所得税纳税申报表时,应当按照规定附送财务会计报告和其他有关资料。
Article 55 When an enterprise terminates its business operation in the middle of a year, it shall, within 60 days after the actual date of termination of its business operations, apply to the tax organ for calculating and paying the enterprise income taxes of the current period.	**第五十五条**　企业在年度中间终止经营活动的,应当自实际经营终止之日起六十日内,向税务机关办理当期企业所得税汇算清缴。

Continued

English Translation	Chinese Version
Before an enterprise goes through the deregistration formalities, it shall make a declaration to the tax organ on the liquidation and shall pay the enterprise income taxes.	企业应当在办理注销登记前,就其清算所得向税务机关申报并依法缴纳企业所得税。
Article 56 Enterprise income taxes to be paid under this law shall be calculated on the basis of RMB. For any income calculated on the basis of a currency other than RMB, the amount of taxes shall be calculated and paid after this income is converted into RMB.	**第五十六条** 依照本法缴纳的企业所得税,以人民币计算。所得以人民币以外的货币计算的,应当折合成人民币计算并缴纳税款。
Chapter Ⅷ Supplementary Provisions	**第八章 附 则**
Article 57 For the enterprises that were established prior to the promulgation of this Law and enjoyed lower tax rates according to the provisions of the previous tax laws and administrative regulations, their income tax rates shall, according to the provisions of the State Council, be gradually transferred to the tax rate provided in this Law within five years after this Law is promulgated. The enterprises that have enjoyed the preferential treatment of tax exemption for a fixed term may, according to the provisions of the State Council, continue to enjoy such treatment after the promulgation of this Law until the fix term expires. However, for those that have failed to enjoy the preferential treatment due to failure to make profits, the term of preferential treatment may be counted as of the year when this Law is promulgated.	**第五十七条** 本法公布前已经批准设立的企业,依照当时的税收法律、行政法规规定,享受低税率优惠的,按照国务院规定,可以在本法施行后五年内,逐步过渡到本法规定的税率;享受定期减免税优惠的,按照国务院规定,可以在本法施行后继续享受到期满为止,但因未获利而尚未享受优惠的,优惠期限从本法施行年度起计算。
The high-and new-tech enterprises that need the key support of the state newly established in the particular areas established by law for developing foreign economic cooperation and technological exchanges or in the areas where the State Council has provided for the implementation of the abovementioned special policies may continue to enjoy transitional preferential tax treatments, according to the specific measures to be formulated by the State Council.	法律设置的发展对外经济合作和技术交流的特定地区内,以及国务院已规定执行上述地区特殊政策的地区内新设立的国家需要重点扶持的高新技术企业,可以享受过渡性税收优惠,具体办法由国务院规定。
Other enterprises falling in the encouraged category as already determined by the State Council may enjoy the preferential treatment of tax reduction or exemption according to the provisions of the State Council.	国家已确定的其他鼓励类企业,可以按照国务院规定享受减免税优惠。

Continued

English Translation	Chinese Version
Article 58 Where any provision in a tax treaty concluded between the government of the People's Republic of China and a foreign government is different from the provisions in this Law, the provision in the treaty shall prevail.	**第五十八条**　中华人民共和国政府同外国政府订立的有关税收的协定与本法有不同规定的,依照协定的规定办理。
Article 59 The State Council shall formulate a regulation on the implementation of this Law.	**第五十九条**　国务院根据本法制定实施条例。
Article 60 This law shall come into force as of August 1, 2008. The Income Tax Law of the People's Republic of China on Foreign-funded Enterprises and Foreign Enterprises adopted at the 4th Session of the Standing Committee of the 7th National People's Congress on April 9, 1991 and the Interim Regulation of the People's Republic of China on Enterprise Income Tax promulgated by the State Council on December 13, 1993 shall be repealed simultaneously.	**第六十条**　本法自 2008 年 1月 1 日起施行。1991 年 4 月 9 日第七届全国人民代表大会第四次会议通过的《中华人民共和国外商投资企业和外国企业所得税法》和 1993 年 12 月 13 日国务院发布的《中华人民共和国企业所得税暂行条例》同时废止。

Appendix Ⅱ: Exercises

1. Who are taxpayers for EIT in China?

2. What's the tax base for Chinese tax residents in terms of paying EIT in China?

3. What's the tax base for non-Chinese tax residents in terms of paying EIT in China?

4. Which incomes could be exempted from paying EIT in China?

5. How to calculate EIT in China?

6. How to pay EIT in China?

7. Were the EIT incentives before 2008 the same as the present one? Why?

8. Air pollution is a critical issue in China right now. Chinese government intends to control the pollution through using tax instruments. What

would be your tax policy advice to Chinese government? How your tax policy advice will impact on doing business in China?

9.China is implementing a strategy of encouraging Chinese companies to invest abroad. What would be your tax policy advice to Chinese government for strengthening the competitiveness of Chinese companies' outbound investment on overseas market?

10.Case Study

• Fact

A Chinese resident enterprise X is going to pay dividend amount of CNY 100,000.00 to its investor Y, which is a non-Chinese tax resident enterprise having no offices or establishments in China. And there is no tax treaty between China and the residence state of Y.

• Questions

(1)Who is the EIT taxpayer for such dividends income?

(2)How much the EIT should be?

(3)Who is going to pay the EIT for such dividends income to the Chinese tax authority?

CHAPTER 7
RELIEF OF DOUBLE TAXATION①

7.1　Introduction

Double taxation may arise when carrying cross-border transactions involving in China, because Chinese tax residents are subject to income taxes in China on their worldwide income basis and while non-Chinese tax residents are in general subject to income taxes for their incomes sourced from China too. Both China and other jurisdictions involved may impose income

---

①　The content of this chapter is based on the publications of Dr. Li on journals, books and international conferences, for example, her papers "Tax Treaty and Policy: Development and Updates-China", co-authored with Tianlong Hu, in Yariv Brauner and Pasquale Pistone(eds.), *BRICS and the Emergence of International Tax Coordination*, Amsterdam: IBFD, 2015; "Taxation of Intellectual Property Under Domestic Law, EU Law and Tax Treaties: China (People's Rep.)", in Guglielmo Maisto (ed.), *Taxation of Intellectual Property Under Domestic Law, EU Law and Tax Treaties*, Amsterdam: IBFD, 2017; "Tax Sparing: Use It, But Not as a Foreign Aid Tool", *Intertax*, 2017, Vol.45, No.8/9, pp.546-555; "Taxation of Shipping and Air Transportation: Chinese Mainland and Hong Kong SAR", in Guglielmo Maisto (ed.), *Taxation of Shipping and Air Transport in Domestic Law, EU Law and Tax Treaties*, Amsterdam: IBFD, 2017; "The China-Pakistan Avoidance of Double Taxation Agreement and the China-Pakistan Economic Corridor", co-authored with Muhammad Ashfaq Ahmed and Peter Mellor, *International Tax Bulletin*, 2018, Vol.72, No.8; "New Trends in the Definition of Permanent Establishment: China (People's Rep.)", in Guglielmo Maisto (ed.), *New Trends in the Definition of Permanent Establishment*, Amsterdam: IBFD, 2019; and "*The Tax Sparing Mechanism and Foreign Direct Investment*", Amsterdam: IBFD, 2019.

taxes on the same taxpayer in respect of the same income in the same period. This is called the "juridical double taxation".

Juridical double taxation normally may arise from one of the following three conflicts of tax jurisdictions:

(1)Source-source conflict

Both China and the jurisdictions involved assert that, in terms of their respective domestic tax laws, that it is the source of the taxpayer's income, and thus each country contends that it is entitled to impose tax on the taxpayer's income derived from the source. For example, the IIT Law of China provides that income for provision of services in China is sourced from China, while the domestic law of Country B may state that income of service shall be sourced in Country B if the payment is made inside of Country B. In that case, both China and the Country B contend to be the source state which is entitled to impose income taxes on the service provider according to the domestic laws.

(2)Residence-residence conflict

Both China and the jurisdictions involved assert, in terms of their respective domestic tax laws, that it is the country of residence of the taxpayer. In these circumstances, the taxpayer is described as a "dual resident". For example, Country A may consider a company as its resident for tax purposes because the company is incorporated in Country A, while China may consider the same company a resident of China for tax purposes because the actual management place of the company is in China. Then each country contends that it is the resident state, which is entitled to impose income taxes on the taxpayer's worldwide income according to the domestic law.

(3)Source-residence conflict

In the case that, one country asserts the right to tax a taxpayer's income as the taxpayer's country of residence and the other country asserts its right to tax taxpayer's income as the country of source, then the source-residence conflict will arise. For example, China may assert its right under its EIT Law to tax the worldwide income of a company which is a tax resident of China; while Country S may assert its right under its domestic law to tax the company for its income sourced from Country S. Vice versa. In that case, the company will be taxed twice by both the residence state and the source state.

7.2   Unilateral Approach: The Credit Method in Domestic Law

China adopts a "foreign tax credit method" in both the IIT Law and the EIT Law to relieve the double taxation imposed on its tax residents' income sourced from outside of China, when China is in the position of a residence state. The foreign tax credit method allows Chinese tax residents to credit their foreign tax paid in the source state, up to the limit of the amount of tax payable for IIT/EIT in respect of such foreign income in China. The creditable foreign tax herein must be the income taxes which should be and have been actually paid by the taxpayer in accordance with the law of the source state.

The credit method adopted by China is an ordinary tax credit, which does not allow a full credit of tax paid at source state where the tax rate is higher than that in China. For example, if a source state is going to collect a tax of 30% on the income sourced from its jurisdiction by a Chinese tax resident, while the EIT rate in China is only 25% on the same income, China will allow the amount of the foreign tax credit up to the amount of the tax that China would otherwise have collected on the foreign source income.

The ordinary tax credit is normally calculated by way of allocating aproportionate share of the taxpayer's total income tax liability in China on its worldwide income (before allowing for the foreign tax credit) to its foreign source income. This means pro-rating the total income tax liability in China between foreign source and domestic source income in the respective ratios of: (1) foreign source income as a proportion of total income; and (2) domestic source income as a proportion of total income.

The foreign tax credit limitation imposed by the ordinary tax credit method is then determined by applying the ratio calculated under (1) above to the taxpayer's total income tax liability in China on its worldwide income (before allowing for the foreign tax credit).

Clearly, the limit on foreign tax credits imposed by the ordinary credit method is relevant only when the Chinese domestic tax rate is less than the foreign tax rate, i.e. China's tax rate is lower than the source state' tax rate. If the domestic tax rate is equal to or greater than the foreign tax rate, the ordinary tax credit method allows a full credit for foreign tax paid. In that case, the domestic tax payable on foreign source income is higher than the foreign tax payable such that China is not required to give up any tax to which it is independently entitled to collect on domestic source income, in order to remove the double taxation of foreign source income.

Furthermore, the above credit must be carried out in a quarantine approach of country by country. That means the amount of tax payable on all foreign sourced income of a taxpayer shall be calculated together but separately for each different tax jurisdiction. Where the amount of the foreign tax paid by the taxpayer at a source state is lower than the tax payable for that income in China, the taxpayer shall be the difference in China; while if the former exceeds the latter, the excessive part cannot not be used to credit against the tax payable for the income sourced from other source states in the same tax year. The excess amount is allowed to carry forward up to the subsequent 5 tax year, for a purpose to credit against any tax payable for foreign sourced income derived from that source state.

7.3 Bilateral Approach: Tax Treaties

The bilateral "double tax agreements" (the "DTAs") which China concluded with 107 countries and the bilateral arrangements which Chinese Mainland signed with Hong Kong SAR, Macao SAR and Taiwan respectively will also play a role in relief of double taxation. The structure and the provisions of these DTAs are quite similar to the OECD Model Convention and the UN Model Convention, although the SAT has never published its own-model convention which it has referred when negotiating these DTAs. Therefore, the articles of a Chinese DTA in general can be divided into the following four parts:

Table 7-1

Content	Articles①

I .General Provisions
  • Persons Covered
  • Taxes Covered
  • Definition and Interpretation
	Art.1, Art.4
	Art.2
	Art.3

II .Distributive Rules	Arts.6-21
III .Methods of Relief of Double Taxation	Art.22
IV .Others (non-discrimination, exchange of information, disputes resolution, etc.)	Arts.23-29.

7.3.1 Persons Covered

The Chinese DTAs in general shall apply to "the persons who are residents of either or both Contracting States".It requires that the persons covered by the Chinese DTAs must be residents of China, of the contracting state or of both. The term "person" herein includes an individual, a company and any other body of persons, which has a broad meaning, including various associations, foundations, etc..

7.3.1.1 Residents

The term "resident" herein shall be determined according to the domestic tax laws of China and the Contracting States. Such a resident must be subject to full tax in China or in the contacting state. The term "being subject to tax" mentioned herein is not equivalent to a defacto tax, for example, the foundations or charitable organizations meeting certain conditions may be exempt from tax in a State. However, if they fall under the scope of being li-

---

①   The articles reference herein is the DTA between the Government of the People's Republic of China and the Government of the Republic of Singapore for the Avoidance of Double Taxation and the Prevention of Fiscal Evasion with Respect to Taxes on Income, concluded on 11 July, 2007.

able to tax as prescribed in the tax law of that State and are regulated by the tax law of that State, they shall still be deemed as liable to tax, and may be regarded as residents for the purpose of the DTA.

In terms of the definition of the "residents" under the Chinese tax law, the individual resident and the enterprise resident shall be subject to the provisions of the IIT Law and the EIT Law respectively:

(1)Individual Residents

In accordance with the IIT Law, an individual is regarded as a Chinese tax resident if he/she is domiciled in China or is not domiciled in China but has stayed in China in aggregation for 183 days or more of a tax year. Clearly, there are two tests for determining whether an individual is a Chinese resident: ① the place of domicile; and ② the length of stay in China.

(b)Enterprise Residents

The EIT Law adopts both the place of incorporation doctrine and the place of actual management doctrine, when defining a Chinese tax enterprise resident. Consequently, an enterprise shall become a Chinese tax resident according to the EIT Law, if ①the enterprise is incorporated in China in accordance with Chinese laws, or ②the enterprise is incorporated outside of China under foreign laws, but its place of actual management is inside China.

7.3.1.2 Dual-Residents

A situation of "dual-residents" may occur when the same person is determined as a"resident" both by the domestic laws of China and the Contracting States. Then Article 4 of the Chinese DTAs shall be applied to determine the resident status of the person for the purpose of the DTAs.

(1)In the case of an individual dual-resident, the following tie-breaker rule shall be applied in sequence:

①Permanent home: a permanent home shall include any form of domicile, such as a house or apartment rented by an individual and a rented room, but such domicile must be permanent, that is, the individual plans to live in it on a long-term instead of temporarily for reasons of travel, business or others.

②Center of vital interests: the center of vital interests shall be comprehensively determined by referring to the family and social relations of the individual, occupational, political, cultural and other activities, business places, the place of management of property and other factors. Particular attention shall be paid to the individual's behavior, that is, the State where the individual has been living and working, and has a family and property is usually the place where the center of vital interests is situated.

③Habitual abode: if the individual has a permanent home available to him in both China and the Contracting States and his/her centre of vital economic interests cannot be determined in the above test, then the habitual abode of this person shall become the testing criteria. When determining the habitual abode, it shall assess how long the individual has stayed in China and in the contracting state, regardless of the reasons for his/her stay.

④Nationality: if an individual has a habitual abode in both Contracting States or in neither of them, his/her nationality shall determine his resident status.

⑤Mutual Agreement Procedure: if the status of the individual still cannot be determined by using the aforesaid criterions, the competent authorities of the Contracting States shall settle the question by mutual agreement in accordance with the procedures as prescribed in the DTA.

(2)In the case of an enterprise (a company or any other body of persons) dual-resident, most of the Chinese DTAs provided the "place of effective management" as the determinant criteria. If the competent authorities of China and the Contracting States cannot reach a consensus due to different criterions for determining the place of effective management, they shall settle the question by mutual agreement in accordance with the procedures as prescribed in the DTA. However, it is notable that some DTAs provided the place of head office or the place of incorporation as the determinant factor. Hence it is necessary to examine the specific factor of the particular DTA when looking into a cross-border transaction involving China.

7.3.2 Taxes Covered

The taxes covered by the Chinese DTAs are only the taxes levied on incomes. It means that only the income taxes of China and the Contracting

States can be covered by the DTAs, unless it is otherwise specified in the DTAs by the Contracting States. From China's perspective, such income taxes shall include both the IIT and the EIT.

The Chinese DTAs shall apply also to any identical or substantially similar taxes which are imposed after the date of signature of the DTAs in addition to, or in place of, the existing taxes. But in that case, the competent authority of the party to which changes have occurred shall timely notify the other party of the relevant changes, and if the significant changes in the domestic laws will affect the obligations in the DTA, the laws shall not apply until the competent authorities of both parties have mutually recognized the changes thereof in general.

7.3.3 Definition and Interpretation

Article 3 of the DTAs define some terms frequently used in the DTAs, while there are also some important terms being defined in the other relevant articles of DTAs such as Article 4 (residents), Article 5 (permanent establishment), Article 10 (dividends), Article 11 (interest), and Article 12 (royalties).

While for the terms not defined in the DTAs, interpretation of such terms shall be subject to the domestic laws of China and the Contracting States, and the relevant terms under the domestic tax laws shall prevail over the interpretation given to the terms under other laws. As a consequence, the SAT plays a predominant role in interpretation of the terms in the Chinese DTAs. The SAT enacted 30-plus circulars addressing specifically to the implementation and interpretation of the terms of the Chinese DTAs[1], in-

---

① For example, Notice on Implementing and Interpreting Some Provisions of the Avoidance of Double Taxation Agreement (Caishuixiezi 〔1986〕 No. 15), Notice on Implementing and Interpreting Some Provisions of the China-U.S. Avoidance of Double Taxation Agreement (Caishuixiezi 〔86〕 No. 033), Notice on Implementing and Interpreting Some Provisions of the China-Netherland Avoidance of Double Taxation Agreement (Guoshuiwaizi 〔89〕 No. 038), Notice on Implementing and Interpreting Some Provisions of the China-Singapore. Avoidance of Double Taxation Agreement (Guoshuihan 〔2008〕 No. 1212).

cluding the definition and interpretation of certain terms which are not defined in the DTAs, for example, "beneficial owners", "capital gains" and "indirect shares transfer", and etc.[①]Amongst these SAT circulars, the Circular GuoShuiFa [2010] No.75 on the Interpretation of Articles and Protocol of the Tax Treaty between China and Singapore, issued on 26 July, 2010, provides the detailed guidelines on the application and interpretation of the Chinese DTA with Singapore (signed on 11 July, 2007) and its protocol (signed on 24 August, 2009). This circular No. 75 also serves as guidelines for the application and interpretation of other Chinese DTAs, as long as their articles are identical with those of the DTA with Singapore.

7.3.4 Distributive Rules

In general, Articles 6 to 21 of the Chinese DTAs provide with the conflict rules, which are usually called the "distributive rules", to resolve the conflicts of tax jurisdiction between China and the Contracting States. Although each state has a jurisdiction to tax and this is recognized by public international law, the states may agree to restrict their substantive tax rights through concluding DTAs when their tax jurisdictions are overlapping on the same income. The basic mechanism of these distributive rules is to allocate taxing power between China and the Contracting States with regarding to the particular type of incomes. For example, with regarding to business profits, the residence state shall have exclusive taxing power unless the person covered has a permanent establishment at the source state; while with regard to dividends, interest and royalties, the source state may have priority to tax,

---

① For example, Tax Issues for Equity Transfers by Non-China Tax Resident Enterprises (Guoshuihan No. 698 [2009]), issued on 15 December, 2009 and effective on 1 January, 2008; Interpretation Notes on the Double Tax Agreement Concluded between China and Singapore (Guoshuifa No. 75 [2010]), issued and effective on 26 July, 2010. Announcement on Several Issues Concerning the Administration of Income Tax on Non-resident Enterprises (Bulletin [2011] No. 24), issued on 28 March, 2011 and effective on 1 April, 2011; Announcement on Issues Concerning Capital Gains Provision under the Tax Treaties (Bulletin [2012] No. 59), issued and effective on 31 December, 2012.

although the tax rate it may apply shall be limited by the rate agreed by the contacting states in the DTAs.

7.3.4.1 Income from immovable property

The distributive rules for incomes from Immovable Property are provided in the article 6 of the Chinese DTAs. In general, the state where the immovable property is situated may have the right to tax such income, although the residence state of the income receiver shall also have right to tax. Such incomes refer to the gains derived from the use of immovable property provided that the ownership of the immovable property is not alienated, including income derived from the direct use, lease, or use in any other form of the immovable property. In the meanwhile, the definition of the term "immovable property" shall be subject to the domestic law of China and the contracting states, unless the contracting state may agree otherwise.

7.3.4.2 Business profit

Article 7 is the distributive rule for business profits derived from business activities carried on by an enterprise of a Contracting State in the other Contracting State. This article provides that residence state shall have an exclusive tax power to such business profit, unless the enterprise carrying out such business activities constitutes a permanent establishment at the source state.

1.Permanent establishment

Obviously, according to Article 7, the "permanent establishment" is the key factor determining whether the source state may have a taxing power over the business profits of the enterprise-resident of the other state. The definition of the term "permanent establishment" is provided in Article 5 of the Chinese DTAs, referring to a fixed place of business through which the business of an enterprise is wholly or partly carried on. According to the Circular 75, the SAT requires a permanent establishment to include the following features:

(1)The place of business is a physical existence, but these places are not limited in scale or scope, such as machinery, warehouses and booths notwithstanding whether they are owned or leased by the enterprise or whether the houses, places, facilities or equipment are partly used for other activities. A place may be a small corner of a market, or a part of a long-term rented warehouse (for the storage of taxable commodities), or is established within another enterprise, etc., as long as there is a certain disposable space, it may be regarded as a place of business.

(2) The place of business is relatively fixed, and somewhat permanent in terms of time. ① the fixed places of business herein include the offices, branches and other fixed places registered and established at the source state, and even the facilities used to provide services at the source state, for example, a hotel room rented for a long term. ② for some business activities which frequently move between adjacent locations, although the place of business seems to be unfixed, but if such move within a certain area is the inherent nature of such business activities, it may be generally determined that there exists a single fixed place. For example, an office rented in different hotel rooms or different floors of a hotel according to its needs, the said hotel may be regarded as a place of business. And when setting up booths at different locations in a same shopping mall or market, the shopping mall or market can also constitute a fixed place of business. ③ the place of business must be permanent rather than temporary in time to a certain extent. Meanwhile, temporary interruption or suspension of business activities does not affect the permanent nature of the place.

(3) The business activities must be, entirely or partly, carried on through such place of business at the source state. The meaning of the term "business" shall not only include production and business activities, but also the business activities carried on by non-profit organizations, excluding the preparatory or auxiliary activities for such organizations. In the meanwhile, carrying on activities "through" the place of business shall be construed in the broad sense, which shall include all circumstances under which an enterprise carries on activities at any disposable location.

Paragraph 2 of Article 5 lists the specific places which will be deemed as a permanent establishment, including (1) a place of management, (2) a branch, (3) an office, (4) a factory, (5) a workshop; and (6) a mine, an oil or gas well, a quarry or any other place of extraction of natural resources.

Meanwhile Paragraph 3 generally provides the following two situations where services provided by an enterprise at the source sate may also constitute a permanent establishment at the source state:

①a building site, a construction, assembly or installation project or supervisory activities in connection therewith, but only where such site, project or activities continue for a period of more than 6 months;

②the furnishing of services, including consultancy services, by an enterprise through employees or other personnel engaged by the enterprise for such purpose, but only if such activities of that nature continue (for the same or a connected project) for a period or periods aggregating more than 6 months within any twelve-month period.

One notable issue is that above continuing period for the services provided in the Chinese DTAs used to follow more with the provisions in the UN Model Convention, i.e. a shorter term of service period, for the purpose of assuring the source state may excise its taxing power on the business profits. While in DTAs China concluded in recent years, such service period often is more like the provisions in the OECD Model Convention, i.e. a term longer than 6 months or 183 days. Such a change in terms of the service period might reflect China's treaty policy change from a source state to a residence state over the past forty years.

Then the Chinese DTAs, following the OECD Model Convention and the UN Model Convention, often exclude certain activities at the source state from being constituting a permanent establishment, for examples:

(1)the use of facilities solely for the purpose of storage, display or delivery of goods or merchandise belonging to the enterprise;

(2)the maintenance of a stock of goods or merchandise belonging to the enterprise solely for the purpose of storage, display or delivery;

(3)the maintenance of a stock of goods or merchandise belonging to the enterprise solely for the purpose of processing by another enterprise;

(4)the maintenance of a fixed place of business solely for the purpose of purchasing goods or merchandise or of collecting information, for the enterprise;

(5)the maintenance of a fixed place of business solely for the purpose of carrying on, for the enterprise, any other activity of a preparatory or auxiliary character;

(6) the maintenance of a fixed place of business solely for any combination of activities mentioned in Sub-paragraphs (1) to (5), provided that the overall activity of the fixed place of business resulting from this combination is of a preparatory or auxiliary character.

Lastly, Article 5 of the Chinese DTAs often provides the situations where a dependant agent or an independent agent can also constitute a permanent establishment for the enterprise at the source state. Normally such an agent must have, and habitually exercise, at the source state, an authority to conclude contracts in the name of the enterprises. However, the Chinese DTAs, which followed the UN Model Convention, often provide a broader scope of the work committed by the agent, for example, insurance company collecting premium at the source state, or a person without authority to conclude contracts but to maintain a stock of goods or deliver on behalf of the enterprise, these agents are deemed as the permanent establishment of the enterprise as well.

2. Profits attributable to the permanent establishment

Once the enterprise has a permanent establishment at the source state, then the source state shall have right to tax the profits attributable to such a permanent establishment. The profit taxable herein shall include not only the profits derived from the source state by such permanent establishment, but also various other types of income derived in and out of the source state which are effectively connected with such permanent establishment, including dividends, interest, rents, royalties and other income. The phrase "effectively connected with" as mentioned herein generally means having direct ownership, or actual business operation and management and other relations with the shares, claims, industrial property, equipment and related activities, etc.

If the enterprise carries on the same business at different locations of the source state, it shall be deemed to have only a single permanent establishment, and the profits arising from its business activities at different locations shall be attributable to such permanent establishment for tax purpose at the source state.

The DTAs usually do not provide a specific method for the computation of business profits, instead it provides several principles to be followed in computation. For example, a permanent establishment shall be treated as an independent tax entity, and as to the business transactions of a permanent establishment, no matter they are conducted with the head office or with other permanent establishments of the enterprise, the profits attributable to such permanent establishment shall be computed on the basis of the fair market value under the arm's length principle. And in computing the profits of a permanent establishment, the expenses which are incurred for the purposes of the permanent establishment should be deductible, no matter where they are incurred, including some expenses which do not directly reflect the actual expenses of the permanent establishment, such as the executive expenses, general administrative expenses, etc. as apportioned by the head office to the permanent establishment. However, these expenses must be incurred for the purpose of the permanent establishment, and the apportionment ratio shall be within a reasonable range. In practical implementation, the enterprise shall provide the scope of apportionment of expenses, quota of expenses, distribution basis and methods, and other materials so to prove the reasonableness of the expenses.

Generally speaking, if the separate account of a permanent establishment can reflect the true level of its profits, the profits to be attributed to the permanent establishment shall be computed according to such account. However, when it is difficult to determine the profits attributable to the permanent establishment on the basis of the separate account, the total profits of the enterprise may be apportioned according to a formula and thereby the profits to be attributed to the permanent establishment can be determined. The result from such a method shall be different from that computed according to the separate account, and both the adoption of formula and the apportionment method may involve the problem of how to compute and determine the total profits of the enterprise.

7.3.4.3 Shipping and air transport

Article 8 of Chinese DTAs provides the distributive rules for incomes derived from carrying on shipping or air transportation activities. The enterprises usually shall be exempt from tax at the source state, and consequently the residence state of the enterprise shall have an exclusive taxing power. Such incomes shall also include those income closely related to the international traffic, including: income from the sale of tickets on a commission basis for other international traffic enterprises; income from the transport of passengers from downtown to airports; income from the transport from a warehouse to an airport or a dock or from an airport or a dock to a purchaser, and from direct delivery of goods to the purchaser through trucks; and income from the hotels established by the enterprise only to provide interim accommodation for the passengers who it carries.

7.3.4.4 Dividends

Article 10 of Chinese DTAs provides a distributive rule for allocating the taxing power on dividends. The term "dividends" refer to the profits distributed by a company to its shareholders and shall include not only the profit distribution determined each year by the shareholders' meeting, but also the distribution of currencies or proceeds with monetary value, such as bonus shares, bonuses, liquidation income and other disguised profit distribution. When it is difficult to determine a payment is dividend or interest, the SAT intends to apply the principle of substance over form. For example, in general, the income from various types of bonds shall not be regarded as dividends; however, if a lender does bear the risk of the company of the debtor, the interest may be regarded as dividends.

The Chinese DTAs usually provide that dividends may be taxed by the residence state of the beneficial owner, but such right to tax is not exclusive because the source state (i.e. the state where the company paying the dividends is situated) may also tax. However, the source state's right to tax shall be limited to up to a certain tax rate agreed by the contacting states in the DTA. For example, Singapore and China agreed in their DTA in 2007 that the tax rate is limited to 5 per cent of the dividends if the beneficial owner of dividends is a company which holds directly at least 25 per cent of the equity of the company paying the dividends; and the tax rate is limited to 10 per cent of the dividends in all other cases. In terms of the definition of the term "beneficial owners", the SAT issued several circulars to define and interpret this term under the Chinese DTAs.

If the beneficial owner of the dividends has a permanent establishment at the source state, or performs independent personal services at the source state through a fixed base, and the shareholding in respect of which dividends are paid constitutes part of the permanent establishment or fixed base, or is effectively connected with such permanent establishment or fixed base, the source state from which the dividends are derived may tax the dividends by incorporating them into the profits of the permanent establishment. But in order to excise such a taxing power, the relevant business activities from which the dividends are derived are carried on through a permanent establishment and the shareholding is effectively connected with the permanent establishment.

The above mentioned distributive rules and the preferential provisions of the DTAs shall not apply to the transactions or arrangements of which the main purpose is to obtain favorable tax status. Where a taxpayer improperly enjoys the treatment in the DTAs, the competent tax authorities of China and the Contracting States shall have the right to make adjustment. In that case, the tax adjustment methods for anti-tax avoidance under Chinese domestic laws shall be taken into account.

7.3.4.5 Interest

Article 11 of Chinese DTAs provides a distributive rule for allocating the taxing power on interest. The term "interest" as defined by this article to be the income from debt-claims of every kind, whether or not secured by mortgage and whether or not carrying a right to participate in the debtor's profits, and in particular, income from government securities and income from bonds or debentures, including premiums and prizes attaching to such securities, bonds or debentures. While penalty charges for late payment shall not be regarded as interest for the purpose of the DTA. According to the Circular 75, the SAT paid particular attentions to the following factors when determine an income being "interest":

(1)Interest generally refers to the income derived from various kinds of debt-claims. "Various debt-claims" shall include negotiable securities in the form of cash or currency, as well as government securities, bonds or debentures.

(2) As to whether other income related to interest belongs to the category of "interest", it shall be treated differently according to the character of such income:

① the income attaching to bonds, for example, the premiums and prizes from issuing bonds shall constitute interest, but the profits and losses which have been incurred in the sale of bonds by the bondholders shall not be interest.

② the income which is related to the loan business and is attached to a debt-claim may be regarded as interest, but the income which has been incurred independently from the creditor, such as guarantee fees charged separately, shall not be regarded as interest in principle.

The same as the distributive rule for dividends, the residence state of the beneficial owner may tax the interest, while the source state (i. e. the state where the one paying the interest is situated) also has right to tax limited to a certain tax rate agreed by the contacting states in the DTA. For example, the China-Singapore DTA (2007) provides that when the beneficial owner is a bank or a financial institution, the maximum tax rate imposed by the source state shall be 7 per cent; and the tax rate of interest shall be 10 per cent in all other cases. Certain interest derived by state-owned financial institutions as agreed and listed by the Contracting States in the DTAs shall be exempted from tax at the source state. The determination of beneficial owners shall be governed by the tax circulars issued by the SAT. While in determining the beneficial owner of interest, particular regard shall be given to whether there are other loan or deposit contracts between the creditor and a third party which are similar to the said loan contract in amount, interest rate, conclusion date, etc. in addition to the loan contract in respect of which the interest arises and is paid.

Similarly, if the beneficial owner of interest, being a resident of a Contracting State, has a permanent establishment at the source state, or performs independent personal services at the source state from a fixed base, and the debt-claim in respect of which the interest is paid constitutes part of the assets of the permanent establishment or fixed base or is effectively connected with such permanent establishment or fixed base in other aspects, the source state from which the interest is derived may tax the interest by incorporating it into the profits of the permanent establishment. This distributive rule will apply only when the relevant business activities from which the interest is derived are carried on through a permanent establishment and the debt-claim is effectively connected with the permanent establishment as described above. The above distributive rule shall not apply if one alienates the loans to the permanent establishment which provides preferential tax treatment for interest only for the purpose of abusing the DTA.

The above mentioned distributive rules shall not apply if the interest is overpaid by reason of a special relationship between the payer and the beneficial owner or between both of them and some other person. In that case, the part of the excess payment which should be paid according to the arm's length price shall not enjoy the preferential treatment in the DTA. In addition, the same as the anti-tax avoidance provisions in the above dividend article, the above mentioned distributive rules and the preferential provisions of the DTAs shall not apply to the transactions or arrangements of which the main purpose is to obtain favorable tax status. Where a taxpayer improperly enjoys the treatment in the DTAs, the competent tax authorities of China and the Contracting States shall have the right to make adjustment. In that case, the tax adjustment methods for anti-tax avoidance under Chinese domestic laws shall be taken into account.

7.3.4.6 Royalties

Article 12 of Chinese DTAs provides a distributive rule for allocating the taxing power on royalties. The term "royalties" as defined in most of Chinese DTAs is following the UN Model Convention, which refers to the "payments of any kind received as a consideration for the use of, or the right to use, any copyright of literary, artistic or scientific work including cinematograph films, or films or tapes for radio or television broadcasting, any computer software, patent, trade mark, design or model, plan, secret formula or process, or for the use of, or the right to use, industrial, commercial or scientific equipment or for information concerning industrial, commercial or scientific experience." While some Chinese DTAs concluded in recent years defined the term of royalties without providing the last sentence "for the use of, or the right to use, industrial, commercial or scientific equipment or for information concerning industrial, commercial or scientific experience", which reflects the definition of "royalties" in the current OECD Model Convention,

According to the Circular 75, the SAT interprets the definition of "royalties" from the following perspectives:

(1) The "royalties" shall firstly be related to the use of, or the right to use, the following rights: various forms of literature and art constituting rights and property, and intellectual property determined in the relevant text and information concerning industrial, commercial or scientific experience, regardless of whether these rights have been registered or must be registered at the specified departments. It shall also be noted that this definition includes not only the payments made under permission but also the payment of compensation made for tort.

(2) The royalties shall also include the income from the use of, or the right to use, industrial, commercial or scientific equipment, i.e., rental of equipment, but shall exclude the part regarded as interest for the payments involved in the relevant finance lease agreement in which the ownership of the equipment is ultimately alienated to the user; and also exclude the income from the use of immovable property, and Article 6 of the DTA shall apply to such income.

(3) The royalties shall also include the income from the use of, or the right to use, the information concerning industrial, commercial or scientific experiences. Such income shall be construed as arising from proprietary technology, which generally refers to the information or materials which are necessary for the production of certain products or process reproduction, and are unpublicized and have the character of proprietary technology. The royalties relevant to proprietary technology usually involves that the technology licensing party agrees to license its technology which is not disclosed to the other party, so the other party can freely use the technology, the technology licensing party usually does not personally participate in the specific application of the licensed technology by the technology alienee and does not guarantee the results of application. The licensed technology has been usually in

existence already, but also includes the technology which is licensed for use after being researched upon the requirements of the technology alienee, and restriction on the use of which such as confidentiality is contained in the contract.

(4)If, in a service contract, a service provider uses some expertise and technologies during the course of providing services, but does not license the right to use these technologies, payments for such services shall not be royalties. If the fruit arising from the services provided by the service provider falls within the scope of the definition of royalties, and the service provider still retains the ownership of such fruit, and the service recipient only has the right to use such fruit, then the income arising from such services shall be royalties.

(5)If, during the course of alienating or licensing the right to use the proprietary technology, the technology licensing party sends personnel to provide relevant support, guidance and other services for the application of such technology, and charges a service fee, such service fee shall be regarded as royalty no matter it is charged separately or by being included in the price of technology, and this Article shall apply. However, if the services provided by the aforesaid personnel have constituted a permanent establishment, the service income attributable to the permanent establishment shall be governed by the provisions on business profits of Article 7 of the DTA, and the personnel providing the service shall be governed by the provisions on dependent personal services of Article 15 of the DTA. The income from services which do not constitute a permanent establishment or the service income not attributable to the permanent establishment shall still be governed by the provisions on royalties.

(6) The consideration for after-sales service under the item of simple trade of goods, the consideration received by a seller for providing services to the buyer in the product warranty period, and the income derived from the services provided by an institution or individual specializes in engineering, management, consultancy and other professional services are not royalties and shall be regarded as income from services and be governed by the provisions of Article 7 of the DTA on business profits.

　　Most of the Chinese DTAs provide the distributive rule for allocating the taxing power on royalties in accordance with the provisions of the UN Model Convention. The residence state of the beneficial owner may tax the royalties, while the source state (i.e. the state where the one paying the royalties is situated) also has right to tax limited to a certain tax rate agreed by the Contacting States in the DTA. For example, the China-Singapore DTA (2007) provided that the right of the source state to tax is limited to a maximum tax rate of 10 per cent. But then the Protocol of the DTA further provides a preferential treatment for the royalties paid for the use of or the right to use any industrial, commercial or scientific equipment, i.e. only 60 per cent of the gross amount of royalties paid shall be taken as the taxable base.

　　The same as the interpretation approach for the term "beneficial owner" in the articles for dividends and interest, the definition of "beneficial owner" for this royalties article shall be subject to the tax circulars issued by the SAT. According to Circular 75, the SAT, in determining the beneficial owner, shall pay special attention to examining, in addition to the alienation contract on the right to use copyright, patent, technology, etc. for which royalties arise and are paid, whether there are alienation contracts in terms of the right to use or ownership of copyright, patent, technology, etc. between the applicant and a third party.

　　Similar to the distributive rules of interest, if the beneficial owner of the royalties has a permanent establishment at the source state, or performs independent personal services from a fixed base at the source state, and the right or property in respect of which the royalties are paid constitutes part of the assets of the permanent establishment or fixed base or is effectively connected with such permanent establishment or fixed base in other aspects, the source state then may tax the royalties by incorporating them into the profits of the permanent establishment. However, such a distributive rule shall apply only when the relevant business activities from which the royalties are derived are carried on through a permanent establishment, and the right or property in respect of which the royalties arise is effectively connected with the permanent establishment as described above. It shall not apply if someone alienates the right or property to the permanent establishment providing preferential tax treatment for the royalties only for the purpose of abusing the DTA.

The anti-tax avoidance rules similar to the interest article are also provided in this article for royalties. If the royalties are overpaid by reason of a special relationship between the payer and the beneficial owner or between both of them and some other person, the part of the excess payment which should be paid according to the arm's length price shall not enjoy the preferential treatment in the DTA. In addition, the above mentioned distributive rules and the preferential provisions of the DTAs shall not apply to the transactions or arrangements of which the main purpose is to obtain favorable tax status. Where a taxpayer improperly enjoys the treatment in the DTAs, the competent tax authorities of China and the Contracting States shall have the right to make adjustment. In that case, the tax adjustment methods for anti-tax avoidance under Chinese domestic laws shall be taken into account.

7.3.4.7 Capital gains

Article 13 of Chinese DTAs provides the distributive rules for the tax on the gains derived from the alienation of property, including gains from the alienation of various kinds of movable property, immovable property and rights. The DTA itself does not define the "capital gains", but in general the term "capital gains" refers to the gains arising from the change in legal ownership of property, including the gains from the sale or exchange of property, and also the gains from partial alienation, requisition or sale of rights, etc.

(1)Gains derived from the alienation of immovable property

The Chinese DTAs usually provides that gains derived from the alienation of immovable property may be taxed in the State in which the immovable property is situated. Therefore, both the source state and the residence state will share taxing right over such gains. For example, Article 13(1) of the China-Singapore Tax Treaty (2007) provides that "gains derived by a resident of a Contracting State from the alienation of immovable property referred to in Article 6 and situated in the other Contracting State may be taxed in that other State."

(2)Gains derived from the alienation of movable property to the business property of the permanent establishment

The Chinese DTAs usually provides that the state where the permanent establishment is situated and the residence state will share taxing right over such gains. For example, Article 13(2) of the China-Singapore tax treaty (2007) provides that "gains from the alienation of movable property forming part of the business property of a permanent establishment which an enterprise of a Contracting State has in the other Contracting State or of movable property pertaining to a fixed base available to a resident of a Contracting State in the other Contracting State for the purpose of performing independent personal services, including such gains from the alienation of such a permanent establishment (alone or with the whole enterprise) or of such fixed base, may be taxed in that other State."

(3)Gains derived from the alienation of ships or aircrafts operated in international traffic

The Chinese DTAs usually provides an exclusive taxing right to the residence state of the enterprise which operates the ships or aircrafts operated in international traffic, or movable property pertaining to the operation of the aforesaid ships or aircrafts. For example, Article 13(3) of the China-Singapore Tax Treaty (2007) provides that "gains derived by a resident of a Contracting State from the alienation of ships or aircraft operated in international traffic, or movable property pertaining to the operation of such ships or aircraft, shall be taxable only in that State."

(4)Gains derived from the alienation of shares

The Chinese DTAs provide different distributive rules for the gains derived from alienation of different shares.

①Where alienated shares of a company which has more than 50 per cent of their value directly or indirectly from an immovable property, the state where the immovable property located may also tax on the gain.

For example, Article 13(4) of the China-Singapore Tax Treaty (2007) provides that "Gains derived by a resident of a Contracting State from the alienation of shares deriving more than 50 per cent of their value directly or indirectly from immovable property situated in the other Contracting State may be taxed in that other State." Hence where a resident of Singapore holds shares in a company of China (or purchases shares of a company of China listed in Singapore), if the shares of the company of China derive more than 50 per cent of their value directly or indirectly from an immovable property situated in China, then China may tax the gains derived by such resident of Singapore from the alienation of its shares in the company, regardless of the proportion of equity held by the resident of Singapore in the company of China.

It is notable that the notion "the company's shares derive more than 50 per cent of their value directly or indirectly from an immovable property situated in China" means that, at any time during the period preceding the alienation of shares of the company (so far, the DTA does not specify the specific time, and the period may be temporarily deemed as three years in the implementation of the DTA), the value of the immovable property situated in China held, directly or indirectly, by the company of which the shares are alienated accounts for more than 50 per cent of the value of the total assets of the company.

②Where alienated shares of a company at any time during the twelve-month period preceding the alienation of the shares had a participation, directly or indirectly, of at least 25 per cent in the capital of that company of the other state, then the other state may also tax on the gain. For example, Article 13(5) of the China-Singapore Tax Treaty (2007) provides that "Subject to Paragraph 4, gains derived by a resident of a Contracting State from the alienation of shares, participation, or other rights in the capital of a company or other legal person which is a resident of the other Contracting State may be taxed in that other Contracting State if the recipient of the gains, at any time during the twelve-month period preceding such alienation, had a participation, directly or indirectly, of at least 25 per cent in the capital of that company or other legal person." According to this article, for gains derived by a resident of Singapore from the alienation of shares, participation, or other rights in the equity of a company or other legal person which is a resident of China, China shall have the right to tax such gains if the recipient of the gains, at any time during the twelve-month period preceding such alienation, had a participation, directly or indirectly, of at least

25 per cent in the equity of that company or other legal person.

Attentions should be given to the issue of being "held, indirectly" when implementing the above provisions. In addition to considering the property constitution of the company of which the shares are alienated, attention shall also be paid to whether the company of which the shares are alienated has held shares of any other company and the composition of property value of that company. For example, when a resident of Singapore derives gains from the alienation of its shares in a company of China, it is likely to make a claim for exemption from the tax on its gains derived from the alienation as provided for in the DTA on the ground that the value of the immovable property is less than 50 per cent of the asset value of such Chinese company (and such resident of Singapore holds less than 25 per cent of equity in the company which is a resident of China). In this regard, if the aforesaid company of China holds shares in any other company of China, and the property of that other company of China derives its value mainly from the immovable property situated in China, then the property value of the company of China in which the shares are held shall be partially (computed according to the shareholding percentage) belong to the company of China as mentioned heretofore, and in computing the property value of the company of which the shares are alienated, the amount of the value of immovable property of the latter controlled company which is attributable to the first-mentioned company and is computed according to the shareholding percentage shall be considered together so as to find out whether the proportion of the value of immovable property in the property value of the company which is a resident of China and of which the shares are alienated has reached 50 per cent.

For example, Company A which is a resident of Singapore holds 20 per cent of shares in Company B which is a resident of China, the property value of Company B is 100 (unit omitted), amongst which the value of immovable property is 40. If Company B holds 80 per cent of the shares of Company C which is a resident of China, if the property value of Company C is 100, amongst which, the value of immovable property is 90, then, when handling the treatment of the DTA in accordance with the provisions of this paragraph and computing the property value of Company B, 80 per cent of the property value of Company C shall be taken into consideration, that is, the value of property held directly or indirectly by Company B shall be $100 + 100 \times 80\% = 180$, amongst which, the value of immovable property shall be $40 + 90 \times 80\% = 112$, and the proportion of the value of immovable property shall be 62 per cent. The aforesaid example is based on the premise of eliminating the effect of the internal transactions between Company B and Company C. Therefore, when a company which is a resident of Singapore alienates its shares in Company B, which is a resident of China, China shall have the right to tax the gains from the alienation according to the DTA since the property of Company B has derived more than 50 per cent of its value directly or indirectly from the immovable property situated in China.

(5)Gains derived from the alienation of other assets

This is a catch-all distributive rule for the gains from the alienation of the various assets which are not listed in the above four distributive rules. In general, the Chinese DTAs provide an exclusive taxing power to the residence state of the alienator. For example, Article 13(6) of the China-Singapore Tax Treaty (2007) provides that "Gains from the alienation of any property other than that referred to in the preceding paragraphs of this Article shall be taxable only in the Contracting State of which the alienator is a resident."

7.3.4.8 Independent personal services

Many Chinese DTAs provide this distributive rule income derived from provision of independent personal services, in accordance with the provisions of the UN Model Convention. The term "independent personal services" herein refers to those professional services and other activities of an independent character. The DTAs usually provide some examples for such services, for examples, Article 14(2) of the China-Singapore Tax Treaty (2007) provides that the term "professional services" includes especially independent scientific, literary, artistic, educational or teaching activities as well as the independent activities of physicians, lawyers, engineers, architects, dentists and accountants. But these examples listed are not exhaustive. The difficulties of interpretation that may arise from some special circumstances may be settled by the competent authorities of China and the Contracting

States through mutual agreement procedures.

In the Circular 75, the SAT lists the following assessment factors for it determining whether an individual provided independent personal service under the DTA:

(1) Occupational certificates, including registration certificates and the certificates which can prove his identity, or descriptions of his present occupation in the resident identification certificate issued by the tax authority of the Contracting State of which he is a resident;

(2) The work contract signed by the individual with the relevant company indicating that the relationship between individual and the company is a labor service relationship rather than employment, including specifically:

①the individual does not enjoy the treatment of employees of the company in terms of medical insurance, social insurance, vocational pay, overseas allowances, etc.;

②the remuneration received by the individual from performance of services is computed and paid on the hourly, weekly or monthly basis or in a lump;

③the scope of the services performed by the individual is fixed or limited, and he is responsible for the quality of the work done; and

④the individual shall bear all the expenses incurred correspondingly from the performance of the services as stipulated in the contract.

The distributive rules under this article is that n principle, the income shall be taxable only in the residence state of the individual, but if any of the following conditions is met, the source state may also tax the income:

• The individual has a fixed base regularly available to him for the purpose of performing independent personal services. The standards for the determination of fixed bases shall be similar with that for permanent establishments, see Article 5 of the DTA for details. However, a fixed base is different from a permanent establishment, independent personal services are not required to be performed through a fixed base, but the business activities of an enterprise shall be required to be carried on partially or wholly through a permanent establishment.

• An individual has stayed at the source state for a period or periods amounting to or exceeding in the aggregate 183 days within any twelve-month period.

For example, Article 14(2) of the China-Singapore Tax Treaty (2007) provides that "Income derived by an individual who is a resident of a Contracting State from the performance of professional services or other activities of an independent character shall be taxable only in that State unless:

(1)he has a fixed base regularly available to him in the other Contracting State for the purpose of performing his activities; in that case, only so much of the income as is attributable to that fixed base may be taxed in that other Contracting State; or

(2)his stay in the other Contracting State is for a period or periods amounting to or exceeding in the aggregate 183 days within any twelve-month period; in that case, only so much of the income as is derived from his activities performed in that other State may be taxed in that other State."

Then according to the above distributive rules, an individual who is a resident of Singapore came to China on April 1st, 2008 to perform independent personal services, and stayed in China for 150 days in total within the twelve-month period until March 31st, 2009, and stayed in China for 210 days within the twelve-month period from August 1st, 2008 to July 31st, 2009. In this situation, the performance of independent personal services in China by such person in the tax years of 2008 and 2009 both made him subject to tax in China. But it needs to be clarified that, as China is the State from which the income is derived and thus has the right to tax the income derived by the individual who is a resident of Singapore from his performance of independent personal services in China, China shall only tax the income as is attributable to the aforesaid fixed base or the income as is derived by the Singaporean individual from the period of providing independent personal services in China.

7.3.4.9 Dependent personal services

The distributive rules under this article are applicable to the income derived by an individual from the performance of service activities with an employment (employee) status.

(1)In principle, the wages, salaries and remunerations derived by a resident of a Contracting State in respect of an employment shall be taxable on-ly at the residence state, unless the employment is exercised in the other Contracting State. If the employment is so exercised, such remuneration as is derived therefrom may be taxed in that other State. For example, Article 15(1) of the China-Singapore Tax Treaty (2007) provides that "subject to the provisions of Articles 16, 18 and 19, salaries, wages and other similar remuneration derived by a resident of a Contracting State in respect of an employment shall be taxable only in that State unless the employment is ex-ercised in the other Contracting State. If the employment is so exercised, such remuneration as is derived therefrom may be taxed in that other State." Accordingly, the remunerations derived by a resident of Singapore in respect of an employment in normal circumstances shall be taxable only in Singa-pore; however, his remuneration derived from the employment exercised in China may be taxed in China.

(2) The exception to the above distributive rule is that when the em-ployed individual may satisfy all of the following three conditions, the wa-ges, salaries and remunerations derived by a resident of a Contracting State in respect of an employment shall be taxable only at his/her residence state even if the employment is exercised in the other Contracting State:

①The individual is present at the other state for a period or periods ex-ceeding in the aggregate 183 days within any twelve-month period;

②such remuneration is paid by, or on behalf of, an employer who is not a resident of the other Contracting State; and

③the remuneration is not paid by the permanent establishment or fixed base which the employer has set up in the other Contracting State.

Only when all of the above three conditions are satisfied, the other Con-tracting State (i.e. the source state) shall be deprived of its taxing power o-ver the wages, salaries and remunerations derived by the employed person.

For example, according to Article 15(2) of the China-Singapore Tax Treaty (2007), if an individual of Singapore is designated to work in the per-manent establishment which the enterprise of Singapore has set up in China, or the enterprise of Singapore designates its employees or other personnel it employs to work in a contracted project or service project which has constituted a permanent establishment in China, the income derived by such personnel from the period of working in the permanent establishment situated in China shall be deemed to be paid by the permanent establishment, regardless of how long such personnel have worked in China or where their wages or salaries are paid.

(3) The exceptional rule to the above two distributive rules is applicable only to the remunerations derived by the personnel from the employment exercised aboard a ship or aircraft operated in international traffic. Under this Rule, such remunerations shall be taxable in the resident state of the enterprise operating such traffic.

It is notable that the SAT takes a position that the term "employer" shall be construed as one who has the right to the work results of the employees and assumes the relevant responsibilities and risks thereof. And it in the Circular 75 lists the following factors for attention when determining the employment of an individual:

①If an enterprise of China adopts the method of "international service employment" and employs personnel to perform the relevant service activities in China through any overseas agency, although these employed personnel may be apparently employees of the agency, if the enterprise in China which employs such personnel assumes the responsibilities and risks arising from the work of the aforesaid employed personnel, the enterprise of China shall be deemed to be the actual employer of the aforesaid employed personnel, and the remunerations derived by such personnel from the employment exercised in China shall be taxable in China. The actual employer may be determined by considering the following factors:

• The enterprise of China has command over the work exercised by the aforesaid personnel;

• the work place of the aforesaid personnel in China is under the control or charge of the enterprise of China;

• the remunerations paid by the enterprise of China to the agency are computed on the basis of the working hours of the aforesaid personnel, or is in certain connection with the wages of the aforesaid personnel. For example, the remunerations paid to the agency are determined according to a certain proportion of the total amount of the wages paid to the personnel;

• the tools and materials used by the aforesaid personnel for work are mainly provided by the enterprise of China; and

• the quantity and standards of the personnel to be employed by the enterprise of China are determined by the enterprise of China rather than the agency.

②Where an enterprise of Singapore designates its employees to work in an enterprise which is a resident of China, the actual employer shall be determined in consideration of the aforesaid factors and under the principle of substance over form. If the aforesaid employees are staff of the enterprise of China in name, but in substance perform the duties of the designating enterprise, then the aforesaid relevant standards shall be referred to, and it shall be determined whether the enterprise of Singapore has a permanent establishment in China according to Article 5 under the precondition of determining that the enterprise of Singapore is the actual employer of the employees. If the aforesaid staff are indeed employed by the enterprise of China during the period of working in China, but they also work for the designating enterprise at the same time, it shall be determined in accordance with Article 5 of the DTA whether the aforesaid enterprise of Singapore has a permanent establishment in China on the basis of the actual conditions of the work done by the personnel for their designating enterprise.

7.3.4.10 Director fees

Article 16 of the Chinese DTAs is a distributive rule applicable only to the directors' fees and the other similar payments derived by an individual in his/her capacity of being a member of the board of directors. The "other similar payments" shall include the benefits in kind derived by individuals as the members of the company's board of directors, such as stock options, accommodation or transport vehicles, health or life insurance and club membership. This distributive rule allows the resident state of the company, of which the individual is a member of the board of directors, to tax such director fees; and in the meanwhile, the residence state of the director shall also have right to tax the director fee.

7.3.4.11 Artistes and sportsmen

This Article provides the distributive rules applicable to the income derived by an artist or a sportsman from his personal activities exercised at the source state, and such income generally refers to the appearance fees derived from the performance activities and the advertising fees which are connected, directly or indirectly, with the performing activities. In principle, both the source state and the residence state of the artist or sportsman shall have right to tax such income, even if the income from the activities exercised by an artist or a sportsman is received by another person, such as a performance agent, company of stars or performance group. However, if the income allocated to the artists or sportsmen from the income derived from the sale of audio and video products recorded in the performing activities or the income which is related to the artists or sportsmen and is involved in other copyrights shall be dealt with in accordance with the relevant provisions on royalties of the DTA.

With regard to the artists covered by this Article could be an entertainer, the SAT in Circular 75 gave the following detailed constructions:

(1) the activities of artists shall include: the activities exercised by entertainers of stage, motion picture or television, music and other art forms; the activities of artists or sportsmen of a Contracting State who are invited to the other Contracting State to shoot advertising pictures for the enterprises because of their celebrity; the activities which are of entertainment nature and involve political, social, religious or charitable purposes. However, it should be noted that the scope of artists shall not be extended to the accompanying administrative and logistics personnel (such as photographers, producers, directors, choreographers, technicians and delivery personnel of road show groups).

(2) the activities of the sportsmen shall not be confined to participants of traditional sports (such as sportsmen of race, high jump and swimming), but also include sportsmen of activities such as golf, horse racing, football, cricket, tennis and racing. This Article shall also apply to the income derived from the activities of an entertainment nature, such as the income derived from competitions of billiards, Chinese chess and bridge.

7.3.4.12 Pensions

Article 18 is the distributive rule for pensions. In principle, the residence state of the person receiving the pension shall have the exclusive right to tax pensions, regardless of where the person receiving the pensions has worked previously. For example, Article 18 of the China-Singapore Tax Treaty (2007) provides that "subject to the provisions of Paragraph 2 of Article 19, pensions and other similar remuneration paid to a resident of a Contracting State in consideration of past employment shall be taxable only in that State." Obviously, the income covered by this Article shall include the pensions and other similar remuneration paid in consideration of past employment. The SAT in Circular 75 interpreted that the term "other similar remuneration" herein shall include the non-periodic payments which are similar to pensions, such as the pensions paid in a lump sum when or after the employment is terminated.

7.3.4.13 Government services

Article 19 provides with the distributive rules for incomes derived from provision Government Services. Such incomes shall include the salaries, wages and other similar remunerations, other than pension, including the various benefits in kind derived in respect of the services rendered to the government or statutory body of a Contracting State, for examples, the apartments, commuting vehicles, health and life insurance or club membership, etc.

In general, the Contracting State which makes the payment shall have the exclusive right to tax such income. For example, according to Article 19 (1)① of the China-Singapore Tax Treaty (2007), salaries, wages and other similar remuneration, other than a pension, paid by Singapore government to an individual in respect of services rendered to Singapore shall be taxable only in that State. Thus in case an office set up by the Singaporean government in China employs a resident of Singapore, the remunerations derived by the Singaporean resident during the period of working in the office shall be taxable only in Singapore.

Furthermore, Article 19 (1) ① of the China-Singapore Tax Treaty (2007) further provides that " such salaries, wages and other similar remuneration shall be taxable only in the other Contracting State if the services are rendered in that State and the individual is a resident of that State who: ① is a national of that State; or ② did not become a resident of that State solely for the purpose of rendering the services."Therefore, in case that an office set up by the Singaporean government in China employs a resident of China, who is either a national of China or who has already been residents of China before working for such office, then such remunerations shall be taxable only in China.

Article 19(2) is a special provision on pensions. Notwithstanding the distributive rule provided in the above Article 18 for pensions, if the pension paid by, or out of funds created by, a government department to an individual in respect of services rendered to that department regardless of where the person is living when the pension is paid, then in principle the state making the payment shall have the exclusive right to tax. However, if the individual is a resident of, and a national of, the other Contracting State, that other State shall have the exclusive right to tax.

However, if the remunerations derived by an individual in respect of the services rendered in connection with a business-related purpose (such as state-owned roads, post offices and state-owned theaters) carried on by the government or local authority, the above distributive rules under Article 19 shall not apply. Instead, the distributive rules under Articles 15, 16, 17 and 18 shall apply respectively according to the nature of such income.

7.3.4.14 Students

Article 20 provides with distributive rules for income received by a student or an apprentice for the purpose of his maintenance, education or training. When a student or an apprentice who is a resident of a Contracting State before arriving at the other Contracting State and then temporarily lives in the other Contracting State for the purpose of education or training or obtaining technical experience and receives income for the purpose of his maintenance and learning, such incomes shall not be taxed in that other Contracting State, provided that such income arises from sources outside that State.

For example, Article 20 of the China-Singapore Tax Treaty (2007) provides that "payments which a student or a business apprentice who is or was immediately before visiting a Contracting State resident of the other Contracting State and who is present in the first mentioned State solely for the purpose of his education or training receives for the purpose of his maintenance, education or training shall not be taxed in that State, provided that such payments arise from sources outside that State." Therefore, where an individual who is a resident of Singapore studies in China, the subsidies for tuitions, grants, scholarships, etc. received by him from the sources outside China shall not be taxed in China, provided that such payment does not exceed that for his maintenance, education or training. However, as the SAT interpreted in the Circular 75, if the student or trainee has income from work, the service remuneration and the payments received for the purpose of maintenance, education or training shall be differentiated. If the amount of remuneration is equivalent to the amount of remuneration received by the employees of enterprises who provide similar services, it may be indicated generally that such remuneration is service remuneration, and the provisions of Article 14 or Article 15 of the China-Singapore Tax Treaty (2007) shall apply respectively according to the nature of the services.

7.3.4.15 Other income

Article 21 provides a distributive rule for the incomes not deal with in the foregoing distributive rules of the Chinese DTAs. Most of the Chinese DTAs have adopted the provision from the UN Model Convention with regarding to this Article, providing that both the source state and the residence state shall have right to tax such income. For example, Article 21 of the China-Singapore Tax Treaty (2007) provides that "items of income not deal with in the foregoing Articles of this Agreement and arising in a Contracting State may be taxed in that State." Hence, China shall have the first right to tax other income which is derived by an enterprise or an individual which or who is a resident of Singapore and arises in or is derived from China. The SAT, as expressed in Circular 75 that the concept of the "other income" herein to be shall be interpreted according to the domestic laws of the Contracting States.

7.3.5 Methods of Relief of Double Taxation

Article 22 provides with the measures which the resident state shall pay for the purpose to either crediting the taxes paid by its residents at the other contracting state or to exempting the incomes sourced from the other Contacting States. Article 22 usually provides separate paragraphs which expressly provide the specific relief method for the Contracting States in the positions of a residence state. For example, Article 22(1) of the China-Singapore Tax Treaty (2007) provides with the relief method when China is in the position of the residence state; meanwhile Article 22(2) of the China-Singapore Tax Treaty (2007) provides with the relief method when Singapore is in the position of the residence state. All Chinese DTAs so far have provided only the credit method for China as a residence state, because the Chinese IIT Law and the EIT Law has only provided with the credit method for China to relieve foreign taxes from its tax residents. While for the relief method of the other Contacting States, some Chinese DTAs have provided with a credit method while some provided with an exemption method.

7.3.5.1 Direct tax credit

The method to relief of juridical double taxation has been provided in all Chinese DTAs. For example, Article 22(1)① of the China-Singapore Tax Treaty (2007) provides that "in China, double taxation shall be eliminated as follows: ① Where a resident of China derives income from Singapore the amount of tax on that income payable in Singapore in accordance with the provisions of this Agreement, may be credited against the Chinese tax imposed on that resident. The amount of the credit, however, shall not exceed the amount of the Chinese tax on that income computed." Clearly this is a credit method which China shall apply to credit the taxes paid by its resident in Singapore on the income derived from Singapore. When applying this credit method, the income derived by a resident of China from Singapore and the domestic income derived in China should be consolidated and the tax payable in China be computed according to the tax rate as prescribed in the taxation laws of China, and the amount of tax payable in Singapore to the extent of the amount of the tax computed in accordance with the domestic tax rate of China shall be creditable. Through applying this credit method, the Chinese government recognizes that Singapore shall have the first right to tax some income derived by a resident of China from Singapore, but does not recognize Singapore's exclusive right to tax. In other words, China shall still have jurisdiction over its residents and charge tax on the income derived by its ownresidents from Singapore, but shall allow the residents to credit the tax paid in Singapore against the tax payable in China.

The same as China, Singapore also committed to apply the credit method to relief of double taxation on the income derived by its residents in China. The first sentence of Article 22(2) of the China-Singapore Tax Treaty (2007) provides that "in Singapore, double taxation shall be avoided as follows: Where a resident of Singapore derives income from China which, in accordance with the provisions of this Agreement, may be taxed in China, Singapore shall, subject to its laws. Regarding the allowance as a credit against Singapore tax of tax payable in any country other than Singapore, allow the Chinese tax paid, whether directly or by deduction, as a credit against the Singapore tax payable on the income of that resident."

In contrast, in the China-Poland Tax Treaty (1988), Poland committed to adopt an exemption method for relief of double taxation on certain incomes derived by its residents in China, although China committed for a credit method. It is provided in Article 22(2)① of the China-Poland Tax Treaty (1988) that "in Poland, double taxation shall be eliminated as follows: ① Where a resident of Poland derives income which, in accordance with the provisions of this Agreement may be taxed in China, Poland shall, subject to the provisions of sub-paragraphs ② to ④ of this paragraph, exempt such income from tax."

7.3.5.2 Indirect tax credit

Some Chinese DTAs have furthermore provided an indirect tax credit method to implement a dividend imputation system for the purpose to relief of economic double taxation. Given that taxation of dividends in effect taxes corporate profits twice: once at the company level and again at the shareholder level when the company's after-tax profits are distributed by way of a dividend to its shareholders. This is known as "economic double taxation". The indirect tax credit method gives an income tax credit to a resident company that pays a dividend to foreign shareholders conditional upon the income tax credit being used to fund an additional "supplementary dividend" to be paid to the foreign shareholder. The rationale underlying this method is to reduce corporate tax paid by foreign investors (which is generally not creditable against the foreign investor's home country tax liability), and simultaneously to increase tax credits allowed in the foreign investor's home jurisdiction for the non-resident withholding tax that it pays in the country from which the dividends are sourced.

For example, Article 22 (1) ② of the China-Singapore Tax Treaty (2007) provides an indirect credit method that "In China, double taxation shall be eliminated as follows: ② Where the income derived from Singapore is a dividend paid by a company which is a resident of Singapore to a company which is a resident of China and which owns not less than 10 per cent of the shares of the company paying the dividend, the credit shall take into account the tax paid to Singapore by the company paying the dividend in respect of its income." Accordingly, with regard to the dividends derived by a company which is a resident of China from a company which is a resident of Singapore where the Chinese company owns not less than 20 per cent of the shares, not only the income tax paid to Singapore in respect of such dividend may be directly credited, but also the enterprise income tax of Singapore paid by the company which is a resident of Singapore paying the dividend in respect of the profits corresponding to the dividend may be computed and credited through the indirect credit method. However, the amount of tax that may be credited directly or indirectly shall be computed in accordance with the relevant provisions of the domestic laws of China.

7.3.5.3 Tax sparing

Some Chinese DTAs have additionally provided a Tax Sparing mechanism which is usually reflected in tax treaty provisions whereby one state commits to credit the taxes spared (i.e. not actually paid) at another. For example, Article 22(3) of the China-Singapore Tax Treaty (2007) provides a unilateral tax sparing credit as follows "for the purposes of the credit referred to in Paragraph 2 of this Article, Chinese tax payable shall be deemed to include the amount of Chinese tax which would have been paid if the Chinese tax had not been exempted, reduced or refunded in accordance with the Enterprise Income Tax Law of the People's Republic of China and the Detailed Rules and Regulations for the Implementation of such Law." According to this Tax Sparing provision, Singapore commits that the preference of tax reduction or exemption enjoyed by a resident of Singapore in accordance with the domestic laws of China shall be regarded as having been taxed according to the domestic laws of China and be creditable.

In contrast, some Chinese DTAs provide a reciprocal Tax Sparing mechanism. For example, Article 23 (4) of the China-Italy Tax Treaty (1986) provides that "for the purposes of Paragraphs 2 and 3 of this Article where a tax on business profits, dividends, interest or royalties arising in a Contracting State is exempted or reduced for a limited period of time in accordance with the laws and regulations of that State, such tax which has been exempted or reduced shall be deemed to have been paid at a full amount in the case of business profits and at an amount not exceeding: ① 10 per cent of the gross amount of the dividends and interest referred to under Articles 10 and 11; ② 15 per cent of the gross amount of the royalties referred to under Article 12."

One important function of the Tax Sparing mechanism is to ensure the tax incentives provided by the Contracting States of the DTAs. Some Contracting States may provide taxpayers with meanings of sparing certain taxes through providing tax incentives or as a result of implementing their tax treaty. As such spared taxes can reduce the global tax burden of the investors of foreign direct investment (FDI), they have been found to have positive effects on influencing the FDI's location. Tax Sparing mechanism has a function to preserve these spared taxes to benefit the FDI investors. Thus, this mechanism, in this sense, might also be able to contribute to influence the FDI's location decisions.

China was an advocate for tax sparing mechanism before 2009. China in its first tax treaty (i.e. the Japan-China Tax Treaty (1983)) already included a unilateral Tax Sparing mechanism under which Japan committed to both matching credit and contingent relief referring to specific Chinese tax incentives[1]. When the OECD reflected its negative attitude toward Tax Sparing mechanism in its 2000 MC, China made a reservation to add Tax Sparing provisions in relation to the tax incentives that are provided for under China national laws[2].However, following China shifting its position from a source state to a residence state, China slowly lost its motivation to initiate Tax Sparing negotiation for the purpose of preserving its tax incentives anymore. After the EIT Law abolished the tax incentives applicable to foreign investment into China, China became quite reluctant to sign Tax Sparing provisions, only a few DTAs having such a mechanism.[3]

7.3.6 Others

7.3.6.1 Non-discrimination

This Article set out a general principle that an individual who possesses the nationality of a Contracting State shall not be discriminated against in terms of tax, i.e., the nationals of a Contracting State shall be subject to the same tax treatment in the other Contracting State as that the nationals of that other Contracting State are subject to in the same circumstances. Furthermore, the taxes levied in a Contracting State on a permanent establishment which an enterprise of the other Contracting State set up in the Contracting State shall not be less favorably than the taxes levied on enterprises

---

① Article 23 of the Japan-China Tax Treaty (1983) and the Japan-China Exchange Note (1991), providing that Tax Sparing relief in forms of both matching credit for withholding taxes on royalty, dividends and interest and contingent relief of taxes on business income of the Japanese investment under specific Chinese tax incentives.

② Paragraphs 1, 3 and 4 of the Positions on Article 23 of the OECD MC (2010) provided as follows: "1. Albania, Argentina, Brazil, India, Ivory Coast, Malaysia, Morocco, the People's Republic of China, Serbia, Thailand, Tunisia and Vietnam reserve the right to add tax sparing provisions in relation to the tax incentives that are provided for under their respective national laws." OECD (2012), Model Tax Convention on Income and on Capital 2010 (updated 2010), OECD Publishing. http://dx.doi.org/10.1787/978926417517-en)

③ Na Li, *The Tax Sparing Mechanism and Foreign Direct Investment*, Amsterdam: IBFD, 2019.

of that Contracting State carrying on the same activities. Same treatment is mainly reflected in terms of tax rate, expense deduction, depreciation, carry-over of losses, capital gains, tax credits, etc. However, it should be noted that the activities carried on by the permanent establishment shall be similar with the activities carried on by the resident enterprise with which the permanent establishment is compared. In addition, a Contracting State shall not grant discriminatory tax treatment to the enterprises whose equity is wholly or partly owned or controlled, directly or indirectly, by one or more residents of the other Contracting State. For example, according to Article 23 of the China-Singapore Tax Treaty (2007), an enterprise which is a resident of China and invested in by a resident of Singapore shall be subject to the same tax treatment as that a similar enterprise which is a resident of China is subject to.

The exceptions to the above nondiscriminatory tax treatment include two situations. Firstly, the contracting state is obliged to grant to the individuals who are residents or nationals of the other Contracting State the reliefs, allowances, reductions and exemptions and other treatments for tax purposes which are equivalent to those the individuals residents or nationals of the first state can enjoy.Secondly, the tax incentives granted by each Contracting State to its nationals for the purpose of promoting social or economic development in accordance with its national policy and criteria shall not be construed as discrimination under this Article.

7.3.6.2 Mutual agreement procedure

All Chinese DTAs have an article providing the Mutual Agreement Procedure (MAP), which is the approach to resolve tax disputes arising from implementation and interpretation of Chinese DTAs. As of today, China has not accepted for any arbitration approach, therefore, disputes arising from or relating to the Chinese DTAs will be resolved either by domestic legal remedy approaches or by a mutual agreement mechanism between the competent authorities in accordance with the Mutual Agreement Procedure provided in this Article.

In general, the following conditions must be satisfied when initiating this MAP mechanism:

(1)A person considers that the actions of one or both of the Contracting States result or will result for him in taxation not in accordance with the provisions of the DTA;

(2) irrespective of the remedies provided by the domestic law of the Contracting States;

(3) the person may present his case to the competent authority of the Contracting State of which he is a resident or, if his case comes under Paragraph 1 of Article 23, to that of the Contracting State of which he is a national;

(4) the case must be presented within 3 years from the first notification of the action resulting in taxation not in accordance with the provisions of the DTAs.

After receiving the MAP application, the competent authority shall endeavor, if the objection appears to it to be justified and if it is not itself able to arrive at a satisfactory solution, to resolve the case by mutual agreement with the competent authority of the other Contracting State, with a view to the avoidance of taxation which is not in accordance with the DTA. Any agreement reached shall be implemented notwithstanding any time limits in the domestic law of the Contracting States.

In addition, even without receiving any MAP application, the competent authorities of the Contracting States shall also be obliged to endeavor to resolve by mutual agreement any difficulties or doubts arising as to the interpretation or application of the DTA. And they may also consult together for the elimination of double taxation in cases not provided for in the DTA.

7.3.6.3 Exchange of information

All Chinese DTAs have an article imposing an obligation on the Contracting States to exchange of tax information upon request. For example, Article 25 of the China-Singapore Tax Treaty (2007) provides that "the competent authorities of the Contracting States shall exchange such information as is foreseeably relevant for carrying out the provisions of this Agreement or to the administration or enforcement of the domestic laws concerning taxes covered by the Agreement imposed on behalf of the Contracting States or their local authorities, insofar as the taxation there under is not contrary to the Agreement."

This Article usually imposes a confidentiality obligation on the Contracting State with regarding to the information received. For example, the Contracting State should treat the information received as secret in the same manner as information obtained under its domestic laws, and such information shall be disclosed only to persons or authorities (including courts and administrative bodies) concerned with the assessment or collection of, the enforcement or prosecution in respect of, or the determination of appeals in relation to the taxes.

In addition, the state receiving the request for exchange of information shall not be obliged to conduct any of the following activities:

(1) to carry out administrative measures at variance with the laws and administrative practice of that or of the other contracting state;

(2) to supply information which is not obtainable under the laws or in the normal course of the administration of that or of the other contracting state;

(3) to supply information which would disclose any trade, business, industrial, commercial or professional secret or trade process, or information, the disclosure of which would be contrary to public orders.

7.3.6.4 Application of domestic anti-tax avoidance measures

Some Chinese DTAs have an article named the "miscellaneous rule", which generally provides that the domestic anti-tax avoidance laws and regulations of the Contracting States shall not be affected by the DTA. For example, Article 26 of the China-Singapore Tax Treaty (2007) provides that "nothing in this Agreement shall prejudice the right of each Contracting State to apply its domestic laws and measures concerning the prevention of tax avoidance, whether or not described as such, insofar as they do not give rise to taxation contrary to the Agreement." Accordingly, both Contracting States may implement their domestic anti-tax avoidance rules when application and interpretation of these Chinese DTAs. Such an article is very important under the current circumstance of anti-tax avoidance throughout of the world.

7.3.6.5 Members of diplomatic missions and consular posts

All Chinese DTAs have such an article reaffirming that nothing in the DTA shall affect the fiscal privileges of members of diplomatic missions or consular posts under the general rules of international law or under the provisions of special agreements.

Appendix Ⅰ: An Example of Relief of Double Taxation in China

We can use the following example to illustrate how to apply the foreign-tax credit method, in the form of both direct credit and indirect credit, for the purpose to relief of double taxation in China.

Assume a Chinese foreign direct investor has the following foreign direct investments in EU Member States; assume further that none of the EU subsidiaries qualifies for the exemption of withholding taxes for dividends paid across EU Member States under the EU Parent-Subsidiary Directive[①]:

1.Step 1: Identify which subsidiaries qualify for the three-tier subsidiaries threshold for application of the indirect credit method.

The China-France Income Tax Treaty (2013) and the Belgium-China Income Tax Treaty (2009) both provide a 20% shareholding ratio threshold for Chinese FDI subsidiaries in France and Belgium, respectively, for application of the indirect credit method. This threshold is the same as the Chinese domestic law requirement. Thus, for testing the three-tier subsidiaries in France and Belgium, the 20% threshold shall apply.

As for Bulgaria, a threshold of 10% shall apply, because the Bulgaria-China Income and Capital Tax Treaty (1988) provides a lower, 10% shareholding ratio threshold for Chinese FDI subsidiaries in Bulgaria for application of the indirect credit method(sees Figure 7-1).

(1)UK Subsidiary-B1, UK Subsidiary-B2, Germany Subsidiary-B3 and

---

① Council Directive 2011/96/EC of 30 November, 2011.

China

Chinese Foreign Direct Investor (a Chinese Resident Enterprise) – A

EU

50%   50%   100%   100%

| UK Subsidiary – B1 | UK Subsidiary – B2 | Germany Subsidiarv– B3 | Germany Subsidiary – B4 |

30%   50%   50%   50%

| France Subsidiary – C1 | France Subsidiary –C2 | Bulgaria Subsidiary –C3 | Bulgaria Subsidiary – C4 |

40%   25%

20%   15%

Belgium Subsidiary – D

100%

Belgium Subsidiary – E

Figure 7-1   Example

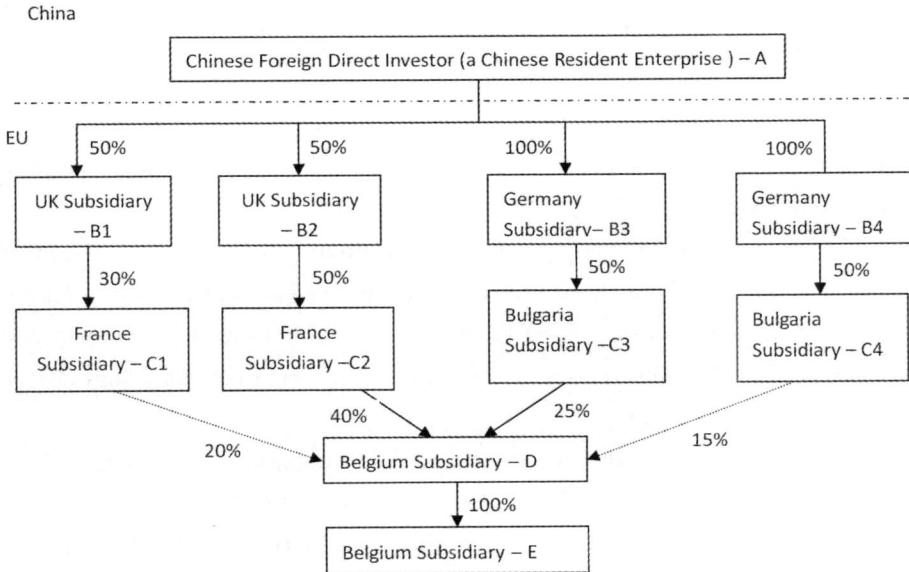

Germany Subsidiary-B4 all qualify for application of the direct credit method, because the Chinese resident foreign direct investor has a direct capital investment in these subsidiaries for more than 20%.

(2)France Subsidiary-C1 should not fall under the scope of the indirect credit method, because the Chinese foreign direct investor's indirect shareholding in C1 is only 15% (i.e. 50% × 30%), which is less than the 20% threshold.

(3) France Subsidiary-C2 should fall under the scope of the indirect credit method, because the Chinese foreign direct investor's indirect shareholding in C2 is 25% (i.e. 50% × 50%), which is more than the 20% threshold.

(4) Bulgaria Subsidiary-C3 should fall under the scope of the indirect credit method, because the Chinese foreign direct investor's indirect shareholding in C3 is 50% (i.e. 100% × 50%), which is more than the 10% threshold.

(5) Bulgaria Subsidiary-C4 should fall under the scope of the indirect credit method, because the Chinese foreign direct investor's indirect share-

holding in C4 is 50% (i. e. 100% × 50%), which is more than the 10% threshold.

(6) Belgium Subsidiary-D should fall under the scope of the indirect credit method, because the Chinese foreign direct investor's indirect shareholding in D is 33% (i.e. 3%＋10%＋12.5%＋7.5%), which is more than the 20% threshold.

(7)Belgium Subsidiary-E should not fall under the scope of the indirect credit method, although the Chinese foreign direct investor's indirect shareholding in E is 33% (i.e. 3%＋10%＋12.5%＋7.5%), which is more than the 20% threshold. The reason is that E is the fourth-tier subsidiary of the Chinese foreign direct investor.

2.Step 2: Calculate the tax attributable to the higher-tier enterprise under the indirect credit method (per each investment line).

(1)For UK Subsidiary-B1 and its subsidiaries: B1 shall be the only enterprise in its investment line for calculating indirect credit, because its subsidiary C1 does not qualify for the indirect credit method [sees 1(1)].

Assume that B1 has a total taxable income of EUR 10 million in the United Kingdom, which includes dividends amounting to EUR 3 million distributed by C1, and that B1 paid withholding tax at a rate of 10% (i.e. EUR 0.3 million) in France for this dividend income. Assume that the statutory corporate income tax rate to which B1 is subject in the United Kingdom is 30%, so B1 paid EUR 2.1 million in the United Kingdom (i.e. EUR 10 million-EUR 3 million, because the United Kingdom adopts the exemption method for income derived outside the United Kingdom). Thus, B1's after-tax profit for the current year is EUR 7.6 million (i.e. EUR 10 million-EUR 2.1 million-EUR 0.3 million), which B1 fully distributes to its shareholders as dividends for the current year. The Chinese foreign direct investor received half of B1's such dividends distribution (i.e. EUR 3.8 million), because the Chinese foreign direct investor holds 50% of the shares of B1.

Thus, according to the formula for calculating tax attributable to the higher-tier enterprise, $(A+B)\times C\div D$, where:

A＝tax paid on profits and investment income by the current-tier enterprises;

B=taxes paid by lower-tier enterprises but attributable to the current-tier enterprise;

C=dividends repatriated to the higher-tier enterprise; and

D=after-tax profit of the current-tier enterprise.

We can calculate that the tax attributable by B1 to the Chinese foreign direct investor is (EUR 2.1 million+EUR 0.3 million+0)×(EUR 3.8 million÷EUR 7.6 million)=EUR 1.2 million.

(2)For UK Subsidiary-B2 and its subsidiaries: B2 itself and both of its subsidiaries, C2 and D, qualify for the indirect credit method in this investment line.

Assume D's total taxable income is EUR 12.5 million, which is subject to a statutory corporate income tax rate of 20% in Belgium. Thus, D pays EUR 2.5 million (i.e. EUR 12.5 million × 20%) in Belgium and then distributes all after-tax dividends in the amount of EUR 10 million. Thus, its parent company C2 receives EUR 4 million, in accordance with its shareholding of 40% of the shares in D.

Then, according to the formula for calculating tax attributable to the higher-tier enterprise, (A+B)×C÷D, we can calculate that the tax attributable by D to C2 is (EUR 2.5 million+0+0)×(EUR 4 million÷EUR 10 million)=EUR 1 million.

Assume C2's total taxable income is EUR 20 million, including the EUR 4 million in dividends received from D. C2 paid EUR 0.4 million as withholding taxes in Belgium at a rate of 10% (i.e. EUR 4 million × 10%) and, according to our calculation in 2(2)①, we know that C2 has been attributed EUR 1 million in foreign taxes by D.

Assume further that C2 is subject to a statutory corporate income tax rate of 25% in France. It then paid EUR 3.6 million in income taxes in France after C2 applied both the direct credit and indirect credit method in France. Thus, C2's after-tax profit is EUR 16 million (i.e. EUR 20 million−EUR 3.6 million−EUR 0.4 million) for the current year. If C2 distributes half of its after-tax profits to its shareholders as dividends, B2 will receive EUR 4 million (i.e. EUR 16 million×50%×50%) for the current year in accordance with its shareholding of 50% of the shares in C2. In addition, assume that C2 had an after-tax profit in the amount of EUR 16 million (on which C2 paid French corporate income taxes of EUR 4 million) for the previous year, and C2 distributed all of it as dividends to its shareholders in the current year. From this distribution, B2 also received dividends in the amount of EUR 8 million (i.e. EUR 16 million×50%). In sum, in the current year, C2 distributed a total amount of EUR 12 million to B2 as dividends.

Then, according to the formula for calculating tax attributable to the higher-tier enterprise, $(A+B)\times C\div D$, we can calculate that the tax attributable by C2 to B2 for its dividends distribution for the current year is (EUR 3.6 million+EUR 0.4 million+EUR 1 million)×(EUR 4 million÷EUR 16 million)=EUR 1.25 million.

The tax attributable by C2 to B2 for its dividends distribution for the previous year is (EUR 4 million+0+0)×(EUR 8 million÷EUR 16 million)=EUR 2 million.

Assume B2's total taxable income is EUR 50 million, including the EUR 12 million in dividends received from C2. B2 paid EUR 1.2 million as withholding taxes in France at a rate of 10% (i.e. EUR 12 million×10%) and, according to our above calculation in 2(2)②, we know that B2 has been attributed EUR 3.25 million in foreign taxes by C2.

Assume further that B2 is subject to a statutory corporate income tax rate of 30% in the United Kingdom, so it paid EUR 1.14 million in the United Kingdom after exempting the foreign-source income from UK taxes. Thus, B2's after-tax profit for the current year is EUR 37.4 million (i.e. EUR 50 million-EUR 11.4 million-EUR 1.2 million), and B2 fully distributes this after-tax profit to its shareholders as dividends. The Chinese foreign direct investor receives EUR 18.74 million as dividends, because it holds 50% of the shares in B2.

Then, according to the formula for calculating tax attributable to the higher-tier enterprise, $(A+B)\times C\div D$, we can calculate that the tax attributable by B2 to the Chinese foreign direct investor is (EUR 11.4 million+EUR 1.2 million+EUR 3.25million)×(EUR 18.7 million÷EUR 37.4 million)=EUR 7.925 million.

(3)For Germany Subsidiary-B3 and its subsidiaries: B3 itself and both of its subsidiaries, C3 and D, qualify for the indirect credit method in this investment line.

Assume D's total taxable income is EUR 12.5 million, which is subject to a statutory corporate income tax rate of 20% in Belgium. Thus, D paid EUR 2.5 million (i.e. EUR 12.5 million×20%) in Belgium and then distributed all after-tax profits as dividends in the amount of EUR 10 million. Thus, its parent company C3 receives EUR 2.5 million in accordance with its shareholding of 25% of the shares in D.

Then, according to the formula for calculating tax attributable to the higher-tier enterprise, $(A+B) \times C \div D$, we can calculate that the tax attributable by D to C2 is (EUR 2.5 million+0+0)×(EUR 2.5 million÷EUR 10 million)=EUR 0.625 million.

Assume that C3's total taxable income is EUR 10 million, including the EUR 2.5 million in dividends received from D. C2 paid EUR 0.25 million in withholding taxes in Belgium at a rate of 10% (i.e. EUR 2.5 million×10%) and, according to our above calculation in 2(2)④, we know that C3 has been attributed EUR 0.625 million in foreign taxes by D.

Assume further that C3 is subject to a statutory corporate income tax rate of 30% in Bulgaria. It then paid EUR 2.45 million in income taxes in Bulgaria after C3 applied both the direct credit and indirect credit methods in Bulgaria. Thus, C3's after-tax profit is EUR 7.3 million (i.e. EUR 10 million−EUR 2.45 million−EUR 0.25 million) for the current year. If C3 distributes all of its after-tax profits to its shareholders as dividends, B3 will receive EUR 3.65 million (i.e. EUR 7.3 million×50%) for the current year, in accordance with its shareholding of 50% of the shares in C3.

Then, according to the formula for calculating tax attributable to the higher-tier enterprise, $(A+B) \times C \div D$, we can calculate that the tax attributable by C3 to B3 for its dividends distribution for the current year is (EUR 2.45 million+EUR 0.25 million+EUR 0.625 million)×(EUR 3.65 million ÷EUR 7.3 million)=EUR 1.6625 million.

Assume B3's total taxable income is EUR 20 million, including the EUR 3.65 million in dividends received from C3. B3 paid EUR 0.365 million as withholding taxes in Bulgaria at a rate of 10% (i.e. EUR 3.65 million×10%) and, according to our above calculation in 2(2)⑤, we know that B3 has been attributed EUR 1.6625 million in foreign taxes by C3.

Assume also that B3 is subject to a statutory corporate income tax rate of 30% in Germany. It then paid EUR 4.63 million in Germany after exemption of the foreign-source income from German taxes. Thus, B3's after-tax profit for the current year is EUR 15 million (i.e. EUR 20 million—EUR 4.635 million—EUR 0.365 million), and B3 fully distributed this after-tax profit to the Chinese foreign direct investor as dividends (because the Chinese foreign direct investor holds 100% of the shares in B3).

Then, according to the formula for calculating tax attributable to the higher-tier enterprise, $(A+B)\times C\div D$, we can calculate that the tax attributable by B3 to the Chinese foreign direct investor is (EUR 4.635 million+EUR 0.365 million+EUR 1.6625 million)×(EUR 15 million÷EUR 15 million)=EUR 6.6625 million.

(4) For Germany Subsidiary-B4 and its subsidiaries: Only B4 itself and C4 qualify for the indirect credit method in this investment line. D does not qualify for the indirect tax credit in this investment line, because its shares held by C4 are only 15%, which does not satisfy the 20% threshold of the shareholding test.

Assume C4's total taxable income is EUR 10 million, including the EUR 1.5 million in dividends received from D. C4 paid EUR 0.15 million in withholding taxes in Belgium at a rate of 10% (i.e. EUR 1.5 million×10%); however, it cannot attribute this Belgian taxation to B4, because D does not qualify for the indirect tax credit in this investment line.

Assume further that C4 is subject to a statutory corporate income tax rate of 25% in Bulgaria. It then paid EUR 2.35 million in income taxes in Bulgaria after C4 applied both the direct credit and indirect credit methods in Bulgaria. Thus, C4's after-tax profit is EUR 7.5 million (i.e. EUR 10 million—EUR 2.35 million—EUR 0.15 million) for the current year. If C4 distributes all of its after-tax profits to its shareholders as dividends, B4 will receive EUR 3.75 million (i.e. EUR 7.5 million×50%) for the current year, in accordance with its shareholding of 50% of the shares in C4.

Then, according to the formula for calculating tax attributable to the higher-tier enterprise, $(A+B) \times C \div D$, we can calculate that the tax attributable by C4 to B4 for its dividends distribution for the current year is (EUR 2.35 million + EUR 0.15 million + 0) × (EUR 3.75 million ÷ EUR 7.5 million) = EUR 1.25 million.

Assume B4's total taxable income is EUR 20 million, including the EUR 3.75 million in dividends received from C4. B4 paid EUR 0.375 million as withholding taxes in Bulgaria at a rate of 10% (i.e. EUR 3.75 million × 10%) and, according to our calculation in 2(2)⑦, we know that B3 has been attributed EUR 1.25 million in foreign taxes by C4.

Assume further that B4 is subject to a statutory corporate income tax rate of 30% in Germany, so it paid EUR 4.625 million in Germany after exemption of the foreign-source income from German taxes. Thus, B4's after-tax profit for this year is EUR 15 million (i.e. EUR 20 million—EUR 4.625 million—EUR 0.37 5 million), and B4 fully distributes this after-tax profit to the Chinese foreign direct investor as dividends (because the Chinese foreign direct investor holds 100% of the shares in B4).

Then, according to the formula for calculating tax attributable to the higher-tier enterprise, $(A+B) \times C \div D$, we can calculate that the tax attributable by B4 to the Chinese foreign direct investor = (EUR 4.625 million + EUR 0.375 million + EUR 1.25 million) × (EUR 15 million ÷ EUR 15 million) = EUR 6.25 million.

3.Step 3: Calculate the sum of the creditable foreign taxes under both the direct credit method and the indirect credit method (per country).

(1)From the calculations in Step 2, we know that the Chinese foreign direct investor's total foreign-source income that can be subject to the indirect tax credit method is EUR 52.5 million, which consists of income from the following two countries:

• From the United Kingdom: EUR 22.5 million, which is the sum of the dividends from UK Subsidiary-B1 (EUR 3.8 million) and the dividends from UK Subsidiary-B2 (EUR 18.7 million).

• From Germany: EUR 30 million, which is the sum of the dividends from Germany Subsidiary-B3 (EUR 15 million) and the dividends from Germany Subsidiary-B4 (EUR 15 million).

(2)In addition, from the calculations in Step 2, we know that the foreign tax attributable to the Chinese foreign direct investor for its foreign-source income is EUR 22.0375 million, which consists of the foreign tax attributable from the following two countries:

· From the United Kingdom: EUR 9.125 million, which is sum of the foreign tax attributable from UK Subsidiary-B1 (EUR 1.2 million) and the foreign tax attributable from UK Subsidiary-B2 (EUR 7.925 million).

· From Germany: EUR 12.9125 million, which is the sum of the foreign tax attributable from Germany Subsidiary-B3 (EUR 6.6625 million) and the foreign tax attributable from Germany Subsidiary-B4 (EUR 6.25 million).

(3)Calculating the direct taxes paid by the Chinese foreign direct investor in the United Kingdom and Germany for its dividends income:

If we assume that the withholding taxes imposed in the United Kingdom and in Germany were both at the rate of 10%, the total withholding taxes the Chinese foreign direct investor pays in the United Kingdom and Germany for its dividends income will be EUR 5.25 million, which consists of:

· Withholding tax paid in the United Kingdom of EUR 2.25 million (i.e. EUR 22.5 million × 10%).

· Withholding tax paid in Germany of EUR 3 million (i.e. EUR 30 million × 10%).

(4)Calculating the sum of the creditable taxes under both the direct credit method and the indirect credit method for the Chinese foreign direct investor:

· Creditable taxes from the United Kingdom are EUR 11.375 million, which consists of direct credit of EUR 2.25 million and indirect credit of EUR 9.125 million.

· Creditable taxes from Germany are EUR 15.9125 million, which consists of direct credit of EUR 3 million and indirect credit of EUR 12.9125 million.

4.Step 4: Calculate the foreign-tax credit limit (per country).

Assume that the total domestic and foreign income for the Chinese foreign direct investor in the current year is EUR 157.9625 million, which includes foreign-source income of EUR 52.50 million (as calculated in 3(1)⑨ and ⑩).

(1) Calculate the sum of the foreign-source income and the creditable foreign taxes attributed to it:

• Dividends from the United Kingdom and taxes attributed to such dividends are EUR 31.625 million, which consists of dividends of EUR 22.5 million and attributable foreign taxes of EUR 9.125 million.

• Dividends from Germany and taxes attributed to such dividends are EUR 42.9125 million, which consists of dividends of EUR 30 million and attributable foreign taxes of EUR 12.9125 million.

Thus, the sum of the Chinese foreign direct investor's foreign-source income and the creditable foreign taxes attributed to it is EUR 74.5375 million, which consists of the total foreign-source income (EUR 52.50 million) and the total creditable foreign taxes attributed to it (EUR 22.0375 million).

The sum of the domestic and foreign-source income and the creditable foreign taxes attributed to it is EUR 180 million, that is, the sum of the total domestic and foreign-source income for the Chinese foreign direct investor in the current year (EUR 157.9625 million) and the total creditable foreign taxes attributed to it (EUR 22.0375 million).

(2) Calculate the tax payable (before the foreign-tax credit) in China:

EUR 180 million $\times$ 25% = EUR 45 million.

(3) Calculate the foreign-tax credit limit (per country) according to the following formula:

Foreign-tax credit limit = A $\times$ B $\div$ C, where:

A = total Chinese enterprise income tax payable on worldwide taxable income;

B = taxable income sourced from a particular country; and

C = total worldwide taxable income.

Thus, we can calculate that:

• Foreign-tax credit limit for income from the United Kingdom = EUR 45 million $\times$ EUR 31.625 million $\div$ EUR 180 million = EUR 7.90625 million.

• Foreign-tax credit limit for income from Germany = EUR 45 million

×EUR 42.9125 million÷EUR 180 million＝EUR 10.728125 million.

(4)Calculate for any excess foreign-tax credit (per country):

We know from the calculations in 3(4)⑮ and ⑯ that the sum of the creditable taxes under both the direct credit method and the indirect credit method for the Chinese foreign direct investor for income from the United Kingdom is EUR 11.375 million, while the sum for the income from Germany is EUR 15.9125 million.

However, the foreign-tax credit limits for the current year, calculated in 4(3)⑲ and ⑳ are EUR 7.90625 million for the income from the United Kingdom and EUR 10.728125 million for the income from Germany. Thus, the Chinese foreign direct investor has excess foreign-tax credit for both the United Kingdom (EUR 3.46875 million) and Germany (EUR 5.184375 million), which it can carry forward in the following consecutive 5 years as credit for the income from the United Kingdom and Germany, respectively.

Appendix Ⅱ: Exercises

1.What are the situations for arising of double taxation in China?

2.Who are the persons covered by the Chinese DTAs?

3.Which taxes are covered by the Chinese DTAs ?

4.How to resolve the issue of dual-residents under the Chinese DTAs?

5.How to interpret the terms used by undefined in the Chinese DTAs?

6.What's the relationship between Chinese domestic laws and Chinese DTAs?

7.How to tax business profit under the Chinese DTAs?

8. How to tax shipping and air transport income under the Chinese DTAs?

9. How to tax dividends, interest and royalties under the Chinese DTAs?

10.How to tax capital gains under the Chinese DTAs?

11.How to tax personal services income under the Chinese DTAs?

12.Does China apply the credit method or the exemption method under the Chinese DTAs?

13.What's the function of the tax sparing mechanism?

14.How to relieve double taxation in China if there is no DTA between China and the involving jurisdiction?

15.Case Study

• Facts

Mr. Wu is a Chinese tax resident, who worked in State A which has no any bilateral tax treaty with China. Mr. Wu's employer paid him a monthly salary of 10,000 (before tax) from 1 January, 2020 to December 2020 into Mr. Wu's bank account in State A. For such salary income, Mr. Wu has paid his income tax of 50 in State A. For the meanwhile, Mr. Wu owns 30% the shares of Kayco Company Ltd. which is located in State B. Kayco Company Ltd. paid Mr. Wu 10,000 as dividends distribution into his bank account in Shanghai in December 2020. For such dividends income, Mr. Wu has paid the income tax of 8,000 in State B. There is no any bilateral tax treaty between State B and China.

• Question

(1)Shall Mr. Wu be subject to individual income tax in China for her above incomes?

(2)If yes, then how to relieve Mr. Wu's double taxation?

CHAPTER 8
TAX ADMINISTRATION^①

8.1　Introduction

Tax administrations in China are conducted by the following two executive institutions which both are reporting to the State Council.

(1)General Administration of Customs of China (GACC) administrates and collects customs duty, taxes and related charges on imported or exported goods, in accordance with the Customs Law, the Tax Administration Law and other relevant laws and regulations. The GACC is a ministerial-level government agency that directly reports to the State Council and oversees all the regional customs across the country.

(2)State Administration of Taxation of China (SAT) is in responsible for administration and collection of the remaining taxes as well as social contributions. The SAT is a ministerial-level government agency reporting directly to the State Council, and since 2018 has been consisting of a head office in Beijing and local offices at each provincial level and below across the country.

---

① 　The content of this chapter is based on the paper "24 Years Later: China Finally Centralizes Its Tax Administration", which Dr. Li co-authored with Richard Krever and was published on Tax Notes International, 2018, Vol.4, No.8, pp.539-544.

8.2   The Governing Law

The governing laws of tax administrations in China consist of both the domestic laws and the relevant tax treaties.

8.2.1 Domestic Law

Tax administration in China, on the one hand, is governed by the Law of the People's Republic of China on the Administration of Tax Collection (the "Tax Administration Law"), which was promulgated by the People's Congress in 1992 and has been amended seven times since then on. Accordingly, the State Council enacted the Implementation Rules for the Tax Administration Law (the "Implementation Rules") and amended these rules following each amendment to the Tax Administration Law. At the meanwhile, the laws and regulations applicable to specific taxes also provide a number of articles with regard to tax administration matters of a specific tax. Also SAT and GACC from time to time have issued circulars jointly or respectively to provide detailed guidance in their tax administration and collection work.

The Tax Administration Law currently has 94 articles, which could be divided into the following eight parts. (Table 8-1)

Table 8-1   **Structure of Tax Administration Law**

Covered Issues	Tax Administration Law
General provisions	Arts. 1-14
Taxable registration	Arts. 15-18
Accounting books and records	Arts. 19-24
Tax declaration	Arts. 25-27
Tax collection	Arts. 28-53
Tax inspection	Arts. 54-59
Legal liability	Arts. 60-88
Supplementary provisions	Arts. 89-94

8.2.2 Tax Treaties

The Chinese tax treaties which have provisions for or relating to tax administration matters are also a part of the governing laws for tax administration in China. For example, all the Chinese DTAs have a provision of"exchange of information" imposing an obligation for the competent authorities of China and the Contracting States to exchange of tax information. And the ten TIEAs which China signed with those low-tax or no-tax jurisdictions during the period from 2009 to 2014 were for the purpose solely to exchanging information relating to taxes.

In addition, through signing the multilateral tax treaties, which are the "Multilateral Convention on Mutual Administrative Assistance in Tax Matters as mended by the 2010 protocol" and the "Multilateral Competent Authority Agreement on Automatic Exchange of Financial Account Information", China committed to exchange of tax relevant information with the Contracting States on a multilateral basis. The details of the Chinese authorities implementing the above described exchange of information obligation shall be addressed in the Section 7 herein.

8.3　Collection of Taxes

Before the State Council implemented the miles-stone tax administration reform in 2018, tax administration by the SAT has been conducted in a dual central-provincial regime for 24 years in China. The national administration of taxation was responsible for administering the VAT and income tax for public companies listed on the stock exchange, meanwhile the local administrations of taxation was assigned the responsibility for administering personal income tax, company a national administration of taxation and local administrations of taxation. On paper, both administrations reported to the

SAT, with the offices of the local administrations of taxation also reporting to the relevant provincial governments. In practice, however, the ties between the local administration of taxation and the national administration of taxation were tenuous at best. The 2018 reform ended this dual regime by having the local administrations of taxation being integrated into the national administration of taxation. As a consequence, the SAT finally centralized its tax administration power to the central level.

8.4   Collection of Social Contributions

Starting from 1 January, 2019, the local offices of the SAT have been in charge of collection of social contributions too. Social contributions in China are also called the "social security insurances", which are generally divided between employers, employees and the government according to the Social Security Law adopted by the National People's Congress on 28 October, 2010. These social contributions cover the basic pensions, medical and unemployment insurances. Injury at work, maternity insurances and housing funds, which employers also are required to pay for employees, are regulated by the provincial governments.

Where a bilateral or multilateral social security agreement with a foreign country is in force, that agreement prevails. Thus, the social security insurances for foreigners from countries that have concluded a Social Security Agreement with China must be determined according to that agreement.

8.5   Tax Audit

Chinese tax authorities are authorized to examine the financial, accounting and tax documents and to check that withholding of taxes has been correctly carried out. Further, the tax authorities have the right to inspect the site of the business with or without the announcement in advance.

The tax audit processes can be lengthy and usually begin with the tax authorities' initial review of the questionnaires or forms completed by taxpayers at the request of tax authorities. Visits by the tax authorities are then made to the taxpayer's offices and discussions and negotiations on the issues raised in the course of the tax audit follow. After this, the tax authorities issue their findings in the form of a notice. Taxpayers may appeal against the findings of the tax authorities if they disagree.

8.6　Taxpayers' Rights

The history of protecting taxpayers' rights started from the year of 2001, when the Tax Collection and Administration Law codified 30 provisions as the legal basis for the protection of taxpayers' rights and the optimization of service delivery. In 2009, the SAT released the Announcement on Taxpayers' Rights and Obligations, which specified their rights and obligations in a stand-alone tax document. In 2013, the Guidelines on Protection of Taxpayers' Rights were circulated, which further clarified related regulations and standards and outlined the requirements on nine aspects: transparency in operational procedures, administration by law, effective communication, risk management, reduced compliance burden, information security, dispute resolution, administration of intermediaries and establishment of rights' protection organizations. In 2014, the SAT released the Notice on Standardizing Tax Attestation Service and Prohibiting Compulsory Procuration for Tax Attestation to standardize service delivery and working style.

In 2015, the SAT promulgated the Announcement on Revision of Complaints Handling concerning Taxpayer Service to standardize codes of conducts in dealing with taxpayers' complaints. This document highlighted the following issues: quick response to taxpayers' comments and complaints, various channels to accept the complaints, integrated actions to handle the complaints to enhance taxpayers' satisfaction and compliance level.

8.7   Exchange of Information

China has committed to exchange of tax information in all its DTAs, which please refer to the Chapter 7 herein for details. In addition, China, during the period from 2009 to 2011, has signed tax information exchange agreements (TIEAs) with Argentina, the Bahamas, Bermuda, the British Virgin Islands, Guernsey, the Isle of Man and Jersey. These TIEAs provide China with access to the income and capital information of individuals and corporations for the purpose of China's combating cross-border tax avoidance and evasion through low-tax jurisdictions.

However, barriers to effective use of the tax information exchanged still exist in China, because the domestic laws have not been updated to facilitate the implementation of the Convention or the TIEAs. Although the SAT already issued the working rules for the exchange of international tax information (the 2006 Working Rules)[1] in 2006, which still apply to the Chinese tax authorities' practice in the exchange of information as of today, some of the provisions of the 2006 Working Rules are needed to be detailed or amended to be used in the present global tax cooperation environment. For example, both Article 9 of the Convention and Article 6 of the TIEA which China signed with the British Virgin Islands and the Bahamas provide the mechanism of "tax examination abroad". However, neither the Convention nor the TIEAs specify how to implement this mechanism, and the 2006 Working Rules do not have any provisions regarding tax examination abroad. In addition, Article 11 and Article 12 of the Convention provide the rules for "recovery of tax claims" and "measures of conservancy", while Chinese domestic law does not have any provisions about these rules. Therefore, China would have to make a reservation on these two rules when ratifying the Con-

---

[1]   Working Rules for the Exchange of International Tax Information (Guoshuihan [2006] No. 70) issued by the SAT on 18 May, 2006.

vention, unless China can supplement the 2006 Working Rules or enact new regulations in its domestic law for implementing these two rules.

Following both the Multilateral Convention on Mutual Administrative Assistance in Tax Matters as mended by the 2010 protocol and the Multilateral Competent Authority Agreement on Automatic Exchange of Financial Account Information coming into force in China in 2017, Chinese tax authorities are exposed to an obligation of exchange of tax-related information automatically on a multilateral basis. It imposes significant challenges to Chinese tax administration. In order to implement the Standard for Automatic Exchange of Financial Account Information in Tax Matters developed by the OECD and endorsed by the G20, six Chinese government departments, including the SAT, the MOF, the Bank of China, the China Banking Regulatory Commission, the China Securities Regulatory Commission and the China Insurance Regulatory Commission issued Administrative Measures on Due Intelligence Investigation into Financial Accounts of Non-residents on 9 May, 2017. According this circular, Chinese domestic financial institutions are required to report financial accounts held by non-resident individuals and entities, including the name, address, jurisdiction of residence, tax identification number, account number, account balance, interest, dividends and total gross amount of other income generated with respect to the assets held in the account. The information will be exchanged automatically by the tax authorities with other jurisdictions on an annual basis.

Appendix Ⅰ: Tax Administration Law
(2015 Amendment)[①]

English Translation	Chinese Version
Law of the People's Republic of China on the Administration of Tax Collection	中华人民共和国税收征收管理法
(Adopted at the 27th Session of the Standing Committee of the Seventh National People's Congress on September 4, 1992; Amended for the first time in accordance with the Decision to Amend the Tax Collection Administration Law of the People's Republic of China made at the 12th meeting of the Standing Committee of the Eighth National People's Congress on February 28, 1995; Revised at the 21st Session of the Standing Committee of the Ninth National People's Congress on April 28, 2001; and amended for the second time in accordance with the Decision of Standing Committee of the National People's Congress on Amending the Cultural Relics Protection Law of the People's Republic of China and Other Eleven Laws as adopted at the Third Session of the Standing Committee of the Twelfth National People's Congress on June 29, 2013; and amended for the third time in accordance with the Decision on Amending the Seven Laws Including the Law of the People's Republic of China on Ports adopted at the Third Session of the Twelfth National People's Congress on April 24, 2015.)	(1992 年 9 月 4 日第七届全国人民代表大会常务委员会第二十七次会议通过。根据 1995 年 2 月 28 日第八届全国人民代表大会常务委员会第十二次会议《关于修改〈中华人民共和国税收征收管理法〉的决定》第一次修正。2001 年 4 月 28 日第九届全国人民代表大会常务委员会第二十一次会议修订根据 2013 年 6 月 29 日第十二届全国人民代表大会常务委员会第三次会议《关于修改〈中华人民共和国文物保护法〉等十二部法律的决定》第二次修正。根据 2015 年 4 月 24 日第十二届全国人民代表大会常务委员会第十四次会议《关于修改〈中华人民共和国港口法〉等七部法律的决定》第三次修正)

---

① The version was translated with a reference of the translations on the website of www.pkulaw.com.

Continued

English Translation	Chinese Version
Chapter 1 General Provisions **Article 1** The Law of the People's Republic of China on the Administration of Tax Collection (hereinafter the Law) is developed in order to improve the administration of tax collection, regulate tax collection and payment, ensure the tax revenues of the State, safeguard the lawful rights and interests of taxpayers and promote socio-economic development.	第一章　总则 第一条 为了加强税收征收管理,规范税收征收和缴纳行为,保障国家税收收入,保护纳税人的合法权益,促进经济和社会发展,制定本法。
Article 2 The Law applies to the administration of collection of all taxes levied by the taxation authorities by law.	第二条 凡依法由税务机关征收的各种税收的征收管理,均适用本法。
Article 3 The imposition, cessation, reduction, exemption and refund of taxes and payment of delinquent tax shall be carried out in accordance with applicable requirements of the laws. Where the State Council is authorized by law to formulate relevant regulations, such regulations shall be observed. No government agency, entity or individual may, in violation of the laws and/or administrative regulations, make any decision as to the imposition, cessation, reduction, exemption and refund of a tax and payment of delinquent taxes or any decision that is contrary to the tax laws and/or administrative regulations without authorization.	第三条 税收的开征、停征以及减税、免税、退税、补税,依照法律的规定执行;法律授权国务院规定的,依照国务院制定的行政法规的规定执行。 任何机关、单位和个人不得违反法律、行政法规的规定,擅自作出税收开征、停征以及减税、免税、退税、补税和其他同税收法律、行政法规相抵触的决定。
Article 4 Entities and individuals that are obligated to pay taxes pursuant to the laws and administrative regulations are taxpayers. Entities and individuals that are obligated to withhold and remit taxes, or collect and remit taxes pursuant to the laws and administrative regulations are withholding agents. All taxpayers and withholding agents shall pay taxes, withhold and remit taxes, or collect and remit taxes in accordance with applicable requirements of the laws and/or administrative regulations.	第四条 法律、行政法规规定负有纳税义务的单位和个人为纳税人。 法律、行政法规规定负有代扣代缴、代收代缴税款义务的单位和个人为扣缴义务人。 纳税人、扣缴义务人必须依照法律、行政法规的规定缴纳税款、代扣代缴、代收代缴税款。

Continued

English Translation	Chinese Version
Article 5 The competent department in charge of taxation under the State Council is in charge of the administration of tax collection across the country. The State tax bureaus and the local tax bureaus in different localities are in charge of administration of tax collection within the scope of administration of tax collection specified by the State Council respectively. The local people's governments at all levels shall strengthen their leadership over or coordination of the administration of tax collection within respective administrative regions, and support the taxation authorities in performing out their duties by law, calculating the amounts of taxes to be paid according to the statutory tax rates and collecting taxes by law. All related departments and entities shall support and assist the taxation authorities in performing their duties by law. No entity or individual may prevent the taxation authorities from performing their duties by law.	**第五条** 国务院税务主管部门主管全国税收征收管理工作。各地国家税务局和地方税务局应当按照国务院规定的税收征收管理范围分别进行征收管理。 地方各级人民政府应当依法加强对本行政区域内税收征收管理工作的领导或者协调,支持税务机关依法执行职务,依照法定税率计算税额,依法征收税款。 各有关部门和单位应当支持、协助税务机关依法执行职务。 税务机关依法执行职务,任何单位和个人不得阻挠。
Article 6 The State will equip the taxation authorities at all levels with modern information technologies, push forward the modernization of the information system for administration of tax collection, establish and improve the information-sharing system among taxation authorities and other administrative departments under the governments in a well-planned manner. Taxpayers, withholding agents and other relevant entities shall, in accordance with applicable requirements of the State, provide the taxation authorities with information relating to payment, withholding and remittance, or collection and remittance of taxes in a truthful manner.	**第六条** 国家有计划地用现代信息技术装备各级税务机关,加强税收征收管理信息系统的现代化建设,建立、健全税务机关与政府其他管理机关的信息共享制度。 纳税人、扣缴义务人和其他有关单位应当按照国家有关规定如实向税务机关提供与纳税和代扣代缴、代收代缴税款有关的信息。
Article 7 The taxation authorities shall carry out extensive publicity on the laws and administrative regulations on tax collection, popularize knowledge about payment of taxes and provide taxpayers with consulting services relating to payment of taxes free of charge.	**第七条** 税务机关应当广泛宣传税收法律、行政法规,普及纳税知识,无偿地为纳税人提供纳税咨询服务。

Continued

English Translation	Chinese Version
Article 8 Taxpayers and withholding agents have the right to inquire the taxation authorities about the requirements of the laws and administrative regulations of the State concerning taxation and the information relating to the tax payment procedures. Taxpayers and withholding agents have the right to require the taxation authorities to keep confidential the information of taxpayers and withholding agents. The taxation authorities shall keep confidential the information of taxpayers and withholding agents by law. Taxpayers have the right to apply for tax reduction, tax exemption and refund of taxes by law. Taxpayers and withholding agents have the right of statement and right of defense against the decisions made by the taxation authorities. They have the right to apply for administrative review, institute administrative proceedings and request State compensation, etc. in accordance with applicable requirements of laws. Taxpayers and withholding agents have the right to complain about and report the acts of the taxation authorities and their staff in violation of the laws and disciplines.	第八条 纳税人、扣缴义务人有权向税务机关了解国家税收法律、行政法规的规定以及与纳税程序有关的情况。 纳税人、扣缴义务人有权要求税务机关为纳税人、扣缴义务人的情况保密。税务机关应当依法为纳税人、扣缴义务人的情况保密。 纳税人依法享有申请减税、免税、退税的权利。 纳税人、扣缴义务人对税务机关所作出的决定,享有陈述权、申辩权;依法享有申请行政复议、提起行政诉讼、请求国家赔偿等权利。 纳税人、扣缴义务人有权控告和检举税务机关、税务人员的违法违纪行为。
Article 9 The taxation authorities shall improve team building so as to improve the political and professional quality of the staff. The taxation authorities and taxation officials shall be impartial in enforcing laws, devoted to their duties, honest and upright, treat people politely, provide them with services in good manners, respect and protect the rights of taxpayers and withholding agents and accept supervision by law. No taxation official may solicit or take bribes, engage in malpractices for private gains, neglect his/her duties, or fail to collect, or undercollect the taxes accrued; nor may he/she abuse the power to overcollect taxes or deliberately create difficulties for taxpayers or withholding agents.	第九条 税务机关应当加强队伍建设,提高税务人员的政治业务素质。 税务机关、税务人员必须秉公执法,忠于职守,清正廉洁,礼貌待人,文明服务,尊重和保护纳税人、扣缴义务人的权利,依法接受监督。 税务人员不得索贿受贿、徇私舞弊、玩忽职守、不征或者少征应征税款;不得滥用职权多征税款或者故意刁难纳税人和扣缴义务人。

Continued

English Translation	Chinese Version
Article 10 The taxation authorities at all levels shall establish and improve the system for internal restriction and supervision. The higher level taxation authorities shall supervise over the law-enforcement activities conducted by the lower level taxation authorities by law. The taxation authorities at all levels shall supervise over and carry out inspection on compliance with the laws, administrative regulations as well as the code of conduct for honesties and self-discipline by their staff.	第十条 各级税务机关应当建立、健全内部制约和监督管理制度。 上级税务机关应当对下级税务机关的执法活动依法进行监督。 各级税务机关应当对其工作人员执行法律、行政法规和廉洁自律准则的情况进行监督检查。
Article 11 The responsibilities of the staff of the taxation authorities in charge of tax collection, administration, inspection or administrative review shall be clearly defined and separated from each other with interaction.	第十一条 税务机关负责征收、管理、稽查、行政复议的人员的职责应当明确,并相互分离、相互制约。
Article 12 In the event that a taxation official is an interested party in relation to the taxpayer, withholding agent or cases involving violation of the taxation laws in collecting taxes or investigating & dealing with cases involving violation of the taxation laws, the taxation official shall withdraw therefrom.	第十二条 税务人员征收税款和查处税收违法案件,与纳税人、扣缴义务人或者税收违法案件有利害关系的,应当回避。
Article 13 Any entity or individual may blow the whistle on the acts in violation of the laws and administrative regulations. The government agencies that receive the whistle blowing and the government agencies that are responsible for investigating and dealing with the violations shall keep confidential the whistle blower. The taxation authorities shall give the whistle blower rewards according to the regulations.	第十三条 任何单位和个人都有权检举违反税收法律、行政法规的行为。收到检举的机关和负责查处的机关应当为检举人保密。税务机关应当按照规定对检举人给予奖励。
Article 14 For the purpose of the Law, taxation authorities refers to tax bureaus at all levels, their sub-bureaus and taxation stations as well as tax offices established in accordance with the regulations of the State Council and announced to the public.	第十四条 本法所称税务机关是指各级税务局、税务分局、税务所和按照国务院规定设立的并向社会公告的税务机构。

Continued

English Translation	Chinese Version
Chapter 2 Taxation Administration **Section 1 Tax registration** **Article 15** All enterprises, the branches established thereby in non-local places to engage in production or business operations, individually-owned businesses and public institutions engaged in production or business operations (hereinafter all referred to as taxpayers engaged in production or business operations) shall, within 30 days from the date the business license is received, apply to the taxation authorities for tax registration by presenting the relevant documents. The taxation authorities shall, on the same date on which the application is received, issue the tax registration certificate. The administrative departments for industry and commerce shall keep the taxation authorities regularly informed of their handling of registration and issuing of business licenses upon examination. The scope and measures for tax registration by taxpayers other than those specified in Paragraph 1 of this Article and for registration of tax withholding by withholding agents will be formulated by the State Council.	**第二章　税务管理** **第一节　税务登记** **第十五条** 企业,企业在外地设立的分支机构和从事生产、经营的场所,个体工商户和从事生产、经营的事业单位(以下统称从事生产、经营的纳税人)自领取营业执照之日起三十日内,持有关证件,向税务机关申报办理税务登记。税务机关应当于收到申报的当日办理登记并发给税务登记证件。 工商行政管理机关应当将办理登记注册、核发营业执照的情况,定期向税务机关通报。 本条第一款规定以外的纳税人办理税务登记和扣缴义务人办理扣缴税款登记的范围和办法,由国务院规定。
Article 16 In case of changes in tax registration of a taxpayer engaged in production and/or business operations, the taxpayer shall, within 30 days from the date on which the registration change formalities are completed with the administrative department for industry & commerce or before applying to the administrative department for industry & commerce for cancellation of tax registration, apply to the taxation authorities for registration change or cancellation of tax registration by presenting the relevant documents.	**第十六条** 从事生产、经营的纳税人,税务登记内容发生变化的,自工商行政管理机关办理变更登记之日起三十日内或者在向工商行政管理机关申请办理注销登记之前,持有关证件向税务机关申报办理变更或者注销税务登记。

Continued

English Translation	Chinese Version
Article 17 Any taxpayer engaged in production and/or business operations shall, in accordance with applicable requirements of the State and by presenting the tax registration certificate, open a basic deposit account and other deposit accounts with banks or other financial entities and shall report all the account numbers to the taxation authorities. The banks and other financial entities shall record in the accounts of the taxpayers engaged in production and/ or business operations the number of their tax registration certificate, and record in the tax registration certificate the account numbers of the taxpayers engaged in production and/ or business operations. Where the taxation authorities, in accordance with law, inquire about the accounts opened by a taxpayer engaged in production and/or business operations, the banks or other financial entities concerned shall provide assistance.	**第十七条** 从事生产、经营的纳税人应当按照国家有关规定,持税务登记证件,在银行或者其他金融机构开立基本存款帐户和其他存款帐户,并将其全部帐号向税务机关报告。 银行和其他金融机构应当在从事生产、经营的纳税人的帐户中登录税务登记证件号码,并在税务登记证件中登录从事生产、经营的纳税人的帐户帐号。 税务机关依法查询从事生产、经营的纳税人开立帐户的情况时,有关银行和其他金融机构应当予以协助。
Article 18 Taxpayers shall use the tax registration certificate in accordance with applicable requirements of the competent department in charge of taxation under the State Council. No tax registration certificate may be lent, altered, damaged, traded or forged.	**第十八条** 纳税人按照国务院税务主管部门的规定使用税务登记证件。税务登记证件不得转借、涂改、损毁、买卖或者伪造。
Section 2 Administration of accounting books and vouchers **Article 19** Taxpayers and withholding agents shall, pursuant to the relevant laws, administrative regulations and regulations of the competent departments for finance and taxation under the State Council, set accounting books, keep accounts on the basis of lawful and valid vouchers and conduct accounting.	**第二节 帐簿、凭证管理** **第十九条** 纳税人、扣缴义务人按照有关法律、行政法规和国务院财政、税务主管部门的规定设置帐簿,根据合法、有效凭证记帐,进行核算。

315

Continued

English Translation	Chinese Version
Article 20 The financial and accounting systems or the financial and accounting procedures and the accounting software of taxpayers engaged in production and/or business operations shall be filed with the taxation authorities. Where the financial and accounting systems or the financial and accounting procedures of taxpayers or withholding agents contravene the relevant regulations on tax collection formulated by the State Council or the competent departments for finance and taxation under the State Council, the tax payable, the tax withheld and remitted, or collected and remitted shall be calculated in accordance with the said regulations.	**第二十条** 从事生产、经营的纳税人的财务、会计制度或者财务、会计处理办法和会计核算软件,应当报送税务机关备案。 纳税人、扣缴义务人的财务、会计制度或者财务、会计处理办法与国务院或者国务院财政、税务主管部门有关税收的规定抵触的,依照国务院或者国务院财政、税务主管部门有关税收的规定计算应纳税款、代扣代缴和代收代缴税款。
Article 21 The taxation authorities are the competent departments in charge of invoices responsible for the control and supervision over printing, purchasing, issuing, obtaining, keeping and handing in for cancellation of invoices. When purchasing or selling commodities, providing or receiving business services or engaging in other business activities, entities and individuals shall issue, use or obtain invoices as required. The measures for the administration of invoices will be formulated by the State Council.	**第二十一条** 税务机关是发票的主管机关,负责发票印制、领购、开具、取得、保管、缴销的管理和监督。 单位、个人在购销商品、提供或者接受经营服务以及从事其他经营活动中,应当按照规定开具、使用、取得发票。 发票的管理办法由国务院规定。
Article 22 The special invoices for value-added tax shall be printed by enterprises designated by the competent department for taxation under the State Council; other invoices shall, pursuant to the regulations of the competent department for taxation under the State Council, be printed by the enterprises designated respectively by the state taxation bureaus or local taxation bureaus of the provinces, autonomous regions or the centrally-administered municipalities. No enterprise other than those designated by the taxation authorities specified in the preceding paragraph may print invoices.	**第二十二条** 增值税专用发票由国务院税务主管部门指定的企业印制;其他发票,按照国务院税务主管部门的规定,分别由省、自治区、直辖市国家税务局、地方税务局指定企业印制。 未经前款规定的税务机关指定,不得印制发票。

Continued

English Translation	Chinese Version
Article 23 The State, according to the needs of the administration of tax collection, actively promotes the use of tax-control devices. Taxpayers shall, in accordance with applicable regulations, install and use tax-control devices, and shall not damage, destroy or alter such devices without authorization.	第二十三条 国家根据税收征收管理的需要，积极推广使用税控装置。纳税人应当按照规定安装、使用税控装置，不得损毁或者擅自改动税控装置。
Article 24 All taxpayers engaged in production or business operations and withholding agents shall keep their accounting books, vouchers for the accounts, tax payment receipts and other relevant documents for a period as specified by the competent departments for finance and taxation under the State Council. No accounting books, vouchers for the accounts, tax-payment receipts or other relevant documents may be forged, altered or, damaged or destroyed without authorization.	第二十四条 从事生产、经营的纳税人、扣缴义务人必须按照国务院财政、税务主管部门规定的保管期限保管帐簿、记帐凭证、完税凭证及其他有关资料。 帐簿、记帐凭证、完税凭证及其他有关资料不得伪造、变造或者擅自损毁。
Section 3 Tax declaration Article 25 Taxpayers shall, within the specified time limit and according to the contents of tax declaration as prescribed by the laws or administrative regulations, or as determined by the taxation authorities in accordance with the laws or administrative regulations, truthfully complete the formalities for tax declaration and submit tax returns, financial and accounting statements as well as other relevant documents on tax payments as required by the taxation authorities according to actual needs. Withholding agents shall, within the specified time limit and according to the contents of tax declaration as prescribed by the laws or administrative regulations, or as determined by the taxation authorities in accordance with the laws or administrative regulations, submit statements on taxes withheld and remitted, or collected and remitted as well as other relevant documents as required by the taxation authorities according to actual needs in a truthful manner.	第三节　纳税申报 第二十五条 纳税人必须依照法律、行政法规规定或者税务机关依照法律、行政法规的规定确定的申报期限、申报内容如实办理纳税申报，报送纳税申报表、财务会计报表以及税务机关根据实际需要要求纳税人报送的其他纳税资料。 扣缴义务人必须依照法律、行政法规规定或者税务机关依照法律、行政法规的规定确定的申报期限、申报内容如实报送代扣代缴、代收代缴税款报告表以及税务机关根据实际需要要求扣缴义务人报送的其他有关资料。

Continued

English Translation	Chinese Version
Article 26 Taxpayers and withholding agents may directly go to the taxation authorities to complete the formalities for tax declaration or submit statements on taxes withheld and remitted, or collected and remitted, or, in accordance with regulations, handle the declaration or submission matters mentioned above by mail, electronic data transmission or other means.	第二十六条 纳税人、扣缴义务人可以直接到税务机关办理纳税申报或者报送代扣代缴、代收代缴税款报告表，也可以按照规定采取邮寄、数据电文或者其他方式办理上述申报、报送事项。
Article 27 Where a taxpayer or a withholding agent is unable to complete the formalities for tax declaration or submit statements on the taxes withheld and remitted, or collected and remitted within the specified time limit, the declaration may be postponed upon examination and approval by the taxation authorities. In the event that a taxpayer or withholding agent is permitted to handle the above declaration or submission matters with delay, the taxpayer or withholding agent shall, within the specified time limit for tax payment, prepay the tax on the basis of the amount of the tax actually paid f or the amount determined by the taxation authorities upon examination or during the previous period, and settle the tax payment within the extended time limit.	第二十七条 纳税人、扣缴义务人不能按期办理纳税申报或者报送代扣代缴、代收代缴税款报告表的，经税务机关核准，可以延期申报。 经核准延期办理前款规定的申报、报送事项的，应当在纳税期内按照上期实际缴纳的税额或者税务机关核定的税额预缴税款，并在核准的延期内办理税款结算。
Chapter 3 Tax Collection **Article 28** The taxation authorities shall collect taxes in accordance with applicable requirements of the laws or administrative regulations and shall not, in violation of such requirements, impose, cease to collect, overcollect, undercollect, collect in advance, postpone the collection of, or apportion taxes. The amount of agricultural taxes payable shall be determined in accordance with the provisions of applicable laws and administrative regulations.	第三章 税款征收 第二十八条 税务机关依照法律、行政法规的规定征收税款，不得违反法律、行政法规的规定开征、停征、多征、少征、提前征收、延缓征收或者摊派税款。 农业税应纳税额按照法律、行政法规的规定核定。
Article 29 No entity or individual other than the taxation authorities, taxation officials as well as entities and individuals entrusted by the taxation authorities pursuant to applicable laws and administrative regulations may engage in tax collection activities.	第二十九条 除税务机关、税务人员以及经税务机关依照法律、行政法规委托的单位和人员外，任何单位和个人不得进行税款征收活动。

Continued

English Translation	Chinese Version
Article 30 Withholding agents shall perform their obligations of withholding or collecting taxes in accordance with the provisions of the laws or administrative regulations. No taxation authorities may request the entities or individuals that are not obligated to withhold or collect taxes as prescribed by laws or administrative regulations to perform such obligations. When a withholding agent performs its obligations of withholding or collecting taxes in accordance with law, no taxpayer may refuse to pay taxes thereto. Where a taxpayer refuses to do so, the withholding agent shall promptly report the matter to the taxation authorities for handling. The taxation authorities shall, in accordance with relevant regulations, pay to withholding agents service fees for withholding or collecting taxes.	**第三十条** 扣缴义务人依照法律、行政法规的规定履行代扣、代收税款的义务。对法律、行政法规没有规定负有代扣、代收税款义务的单位和个人，税务机关不得要求其履行代扣、代收税款义务。 扣缴义务人依法履行代扣、代收税款义务时，纳税人不得拒绝。纳税人拒绝的，扣缴义务人应当及时报告税务机关处理。 税务机关按照规定付给扣缴义务人代扣、代收手续费。
Article 31 A taxpayer or withholding agent shall pay or deliver tax payments in compliance within the time limit specified by laws or administrative regulations, or as determined by taxation authorities in accordance with laws or administrative regulations. Where a taxpayer is unable to pay taxes within the prescribed time limit due to special difficulties, the taxpayer may, upon approval by the State tax bureau or the local tax bureau of a province, autonomous region or centrally-administered municipality, defer the payment of taxes for a maximum period of three months.	**第三十一条** 纳税人、扣缴义务人按照法律、行政法规规定或者税务机关依照法律、行政法规的规定确定的期限，缴纳或者解缴税款。 纳税人因有特殊困难，不能按期缴纳税款的，经省、自治区、直辖市国家税务局、地方税务局批准，可以延期缴纳税款，但是最长不得超过三个月。
Article 32 Where a taxpayer fails to pay taxes or a withholding agent fails to remit tax payments within the specified time limit, the taxation authorities shall, in addition to ordering the taxpayer or withholding agent to pay or remit the tax within the specified time limit, impose a penalty for late payment on a daily basis at the rate of 0.05% of the amount of tax in arrears, from the date the tax payment is defaulted.	**第三十二条** 纳税人未按照规定期限缴纳税款的，扣缴义务人未按照规定期限解缴税款的，税务机关除责令限期缴纳外，从滞纳税款之日起，按日加收滞纳税款万分之五的滞纳金。

Continued

English Translation	Chinese Version
Article 33 A taxpayer may, in accordance with laws or administrative regulations, apply for tax reduction or exemption. All decisions on tax reduction or exemption made in violation of laws or administrative regulations by the local people's governments at all levels, the competent departments under the said people's governments, or by entities or individuals shall be null and void. No taxation authorities may implement such decisions, and they shall instead report the matter to the higher level taxation authorities.	**第三十三条** 纳税人依照法律、行政法规的规定办理减税、免税。 地方各级人民政府、各级人民政府主管部门、单位和个人违反法律、行政法规规定,擅自作出的减税、免税决定无效,税务机关不得执行,并向上级税务机关报告。
Article 34 When collecting taxes, the taxation authorities shall issue tax payment receipts to taxpayers. When withholding or collecting taxes, the withholding agents shall, upon request by taxpayers, issue to them receipts for withholding or collecting taxes.	**第三十四条** 税务机关征收税款时,必须给纳税人开具完税凭证。扣缴义务人代扣、代收税款时,纳税人要求扣缴义务人开具代扣、代收税款凭证的,扣缴义务人应当开具。
Article 35 If a taxpayer comes under one of the following circumstances, the taxation authorities have the power to assess the tax amount payable: (1) Where the setting of accounting books is not required in accordance with the provisions of laws and administrative regulations; (2) the accounting books are not set as required by theprovisions of laws and administrative regulations; (3) where the taxpayer damages or destroys accounting books without authorization or refuses to provide information on tax payments; (4) where accounting books are set, but the accounts are in a mess or information on costs, receipt vouchers and expense vouchers are incomplete, making it difficult to check the books; (5) where, when the obligation to pay taxes arises, the taxpayer fails to complete the formalities for tax declaration within the specified time limit and, after being ordered by taxation authorities to make tax declaration within the specified time limit, still fails to do so upon expiration of the specified time limit; and (6) where the basis for assessing tax declared by the taxpayer is obviously on the low side and without justified reasons. The specific procedure and measures for the taxation authorities to determine the tax amount payable will be formulated by the competent department for taxation under the State Council.	**第三十五条** 纳税人有下列情形之一的,税务机关有权核定其应纳税额: (一)依照法律、行政法规的规定可以不设置帐簿的; (二)依照法律、行政法规的规定应当设置帐簿但未设置的; (三)擅自销毁帐簿或者拒不提供纳税资料的; (四)虽设置帐簿,但帐目混乱或者成本资料、收入凭证、费用凭证残缺不全,难以查帐的; (五)发生纳税义务,未按照规定的期限办理纳税申报,经税务机关责令限期申报,逾期仍不申报的; (六)纳税人申报的计税依据明显偏低,又无正当理由的。 税务机关核定应纳税额的具体程序和方法由国务院税务主管部门规定。

Continued

English Translation	Chinese Version
Article 36 The payment or receipt of money or charges in business transactions between an enterprise, or the establishment or site engaged in production or business operations which is set up by a foreign enterprise in China, and its affiliated enterprises shall be made in the same manner as the payment or receipt of money or charges in business transactions between independent enterprises. Where the payment or receipt of money or charges is not made in the said manner and thus results in a reduction of the taxable revenue or income, the taxation authorities have the power to make reasonable adjustments.	**第三十六条** 企业或者外国企业在中国境内设立的从事生产、经营的机构、场所与其关联企业之间的业务往来，应当按照独立企业之间的业务往来收取或者支付价款、费用；不按照独立企业之间的业务往来收取或者支付价款、费用，而减少其应纳税的收入或者所得额的，税务机关有权进行合理调整。
Article 37 Where a taxpayer engaged in production or business operations or a taxpayer temporarily engaged in business operations fails to complete the formalities for tax registration in accordance with regulations, the taxation authorities shall determine the tax amount payable by the taxpayer and order the taxpayer to make payments; if the taxpayer fails to do so, the taxation authorities may attach the commodities or goods valued equivalent to the tax amount payable; if the taxpayer pays the taxes payable after the attachment, the taxation authorities shall immediately cancel the attachment and return the commodities or goods attached; if the taxpayer still fails to pay the taxes payable after the attachment, the commodities or goods attached shall, upon approval of the director of the taxation bureau (or sub-bureau) at or above the county level, be auctioned or disposed of in accordance with law and the proceeds therefrom shall be used to offset the taxes payable.	**第三十七条** 对未按照规定办理税务登记的从事生产、经营的纳税人以及临时从事经营的纳税人，由税务机关核定其应纳税额，责令缴纳；不缴纳的，税务机关可以扣押其价值相当于应纳税款的商品、货物。扣押后缴纳应纳税款的，税务机关必须立即解除扣押，并归还所扣押的商品、货物；扣押后仍不缴纳应纳税款的，经县以上税务局（分局）局长批准，依法拍卖或者变卖所扣押的商品、货物，以拍卖或者变卖所得抵缴税款。

Continued

English Translation	Chinese Version
Article 38 Where the taxation authorities have grounds to believe that a taxpayer engaged in production or business operations commits an act of tax evasion, the taxation authorities may, prior to the specified date of tax payment, order the taxpayer to pay the taxes payable within the specified time limit. If, within the specified time limit, the taxation authorities discover evident signs that the taxpayer is transferring or concealing the taxable commodities, goods or other property, or taxable income, the taxation authorities may order the taxpayer to provide a guaranty for tax payment. If the taxpayer is unable to do so, the taxation authorities may, upon approval of the director of the taxation bureau (or sub-bureau) at or above the county level, adopt the following tax preservation measures: (1) To notify in writing the bank or any other financial institution with which the taxpayer has opened an account to freeze the taxpayer's deposits valued equivalent to the taxes payable; and (2) to attach or seal up the taxpayer's commodities, goods or other property valued equivalent to the taxes payable. Where the taxpayer makes the tax payment within the time limit specified in the preceding paragraph, the taxation authorities shall immediately cancel the tax preservative measures. Where the taxpayer fails to do so upon the expiration of the specified time, the taxation authorities may, upon approval of the director of the tax bureau (or sub-bureau) at or above the county level, notify in writing the bank or any other financial institution with which the taxpayer has opened an account to withhold and remit the taxes payable from the taxpayer's frozen deposits, or, in accordance with law, auction or dispose of the commodities, goods or other property attached or sealed up and use the proceeds therefrom to offset the taxes payable. Any housing or articles for use which are necessary for the daily lives of an individual and the family members he/she supports shall not be subjected to the tax preservation measures.	**第三十八条** 税务机关有根据认为从事生产、经营的纳税人有逃避纳税义务行为的,可以在规定的纳税期之前,责令限期缴纳应纳税款;在限期内发现纳税人有明显的转移、隐匿其应纳税的商品、货物以及其他财产或者应纳税的收入的迹象的,税务机关可以责成纳税人提供纳税担保。如果纳税人不能提供纳税担保,经县以上税务局(分局)局长批准,税务机关可以采取下列税收保全措施: (一)书面通知纳税人开户银行或者其他金融机构冻结纳税人的金额相当于应纳税款的存款; (二)扣押、查封纳税人的价值相当于应纳税款的商品、货物或者其他财产。 纳税人在前款规定的限期内缴纳税款的,税务机关必须立即解除税收保全措施;限期期满仍未缴纳税款的,经县以上税务局(分局)局长批准,税务机关可以书面通知纳税人开户银行或者其他金融机构从其冻结的存款中扣缴税款,或者依法拍卖或者变卖所扣押、查封的商品、货物或者其他财产,以拍卖或者变卖所得抵缴税款。 个人及其所扶养家属维持生活必需的住房和用品,不在税收保全措施的范围之内。

Continued

English Translation	Chinese Version
Article 39 Where a taxpayer makes the tax payment within the specified time limit but the taxation authorities fail to immediately cancel the tax preservation measures, therefore causing losses to the lawful interests of the taxpayer, the taxation authorities shall be liable for compensation.	**第三十九条** 纳税人在限期内已缴纳税款,税务机关未立即解除税收保全措施,使纳税人的合法利益遭受损失的,税务机关应当承担赔偿责任。
Article 40 Where a taxpayer engaged in production or business operations or a withholding agent fails to pay or remit tax within the specified time limit, or a tax payment guarantor fails to pay the guaranteed amount of tax within the specified time limit, the taxation authorities will order it to pay the tax within a specified time limit, failing which the taxation authorities may, upon approval of the director of the taxation bureau (or sub-bureau) at or above the county level, adopt the following compulsory enforcement measures: (1)To notify in writing the bank or any other financial institution with which the taxpayer, withholding agent or tax payment guarantor has opened an account to withhold and remit the taxes from its deposits; (2)to attach, seal up or, in accordance with law, auction or dispose of the commodities, goods or other property of the taxpayer, withholding agent or tax payment guarantor, valued equivalent to the taxes payable, and to use the proceeds therefrom to offset the taxes payable. When executing the compulsory enforcement measures, the taxation authorities shall also apply the compulsory enforcement measures to the penalty for payment which is not paid by the taxpayer, withholding agent or tax payment guarantor mentioned in the preceding paragraph. Any housing or articles for use which are necessary for the daily lives of an individual and the family members he/she supports shall not be subjected to the compulsory enforcement measures.	**第四十条** 从事生产、经营的纳税人、扣缴义务人未按照规定的期限缴纳或者解缴税款,纳税担保人未按照规定的期限缴纳所担保的税款,由税务机关责令限期缴纳,逾期仍未缴纳的,经县以上税务局(分局)局长批准,税务机关可以采取下列强制执行措施: (一)书面通知其开户银行或者其他金融机构从其存款中扣缴税款; (二)扣押、查封、依法拍卖或者变卖其价值相当于应纳税款的商品、货物或者其他财产,以拍卖或者变卖所得抵缴税款。 税务机关采取强制执行措施时,对前款所列纳税人、扣缴义务人、纳税担保人未缴纳的滞纳金同时强制执行。 个人及其所扶养家属维持生活必需的住房和用品,不在强制执行措施的范围之内。

Continued

English Translation	Chinese Version
Article 41 No entity or individual other than the statutory taxation authorities may exercise the power to adopt tax preservative measures or compulsory enforcement measures provided for in Articles 37，38 and 40 of this Law.	**第四十一条** 本法第三十七条、第三十八条、第四十条规定的采取税收保全措施、强制执行措施的权力,不得由法定的税务机关以外的单位和个人行使。
Article 42 The taxation authorities shall adopt tax preservative measures or compulsory enforcement measures in compliance with the authorities and procedures prescribed by law，and shall not seal up or attach any housing and articles for use which are necessary for the daily lives of the taxpayer itself and the family members it supports.	**第四十二条** 税务机关采取税收保全措施和强制执行措施必须依照法定权限和法定程序,不得查封、扣押纳税人个人及其所扶养家属维持生活必需的住房和用品。
Article 43 Where the taxation authorities abuse their powers in violation of the laws to adopt tax preservative measures or compulsory enforcement measures，or inappropriately adopt such measures，thus causing losses to the lawful rights and interests of taxpayers，withholding agents or tax payment guarantors，the taxation authorities shall be liable for compensation in accordance with law.	**第四十三条** 税务机关滥用职权违法采取税收保全措施、强制执行措施,或者采取税收保全措施、强制执行措施不当,使纳税人、扣缴义务人或者纳税担保人的合法权益遭受损失的,应当依法承担赔偿责任。
Article 44 Any taxpayer who defaults on tax payment or its legal representative needs to leave China shall pay the taxes payable and the penalty for late payment，or provide a guaranty to，the taxation authorities before leaving China. If neither the tax amount payable and the penalties for late payment are paid nor a guaranty is provided，the taxation authorities may notify the exit administration to prevent the taxpayer or its legal representative from leaving China.	**第四十四条** 欠缴税款的纳税人或者他的法定代表人需要出境的,应当在出境前向税务机关结清应纳税款、滞纳金或者提供担保。未结清税款、滞纳金,又不提供担保的,税务机关可以通知出境管理机关阻止其出境。

Continued

English Translation	Chinese Version
Article 45 Taxes collected by the taxation authorities shall have precedence over unsecured claims, except as otherwise provided for by law; where tax is defaulted before the taxpayer mortgages or pledges its property or before the taxpayer's property is liened, the taxes shall have the precedence over the exercise of the right of mortgage, pledge or lien. In the event that a taxpayer defaults on tax payment and in the meanwhile receives administrative sanctions such as fines and confiscation of illegal earnings pursuant to decisions made by the administrative agencies, the taxes shall have precedence over the fines and confiscation of illegal earnings. The taxation authorities shall announce the tax payments defaulted by taxpayers regularly.	**第四十五条** 税务机关征收税款,税收优先于无担保债权,法律另有规定的除外;纳税人欠缴的税款发生在纳税人以其财产设定抵押、质押或者纳税人的财产被留置之前的,税收应当先于抵押权、质权、留置权执行。 纳税人欠缴税款,同时又被行政机关决定处以罚款、没收违法所得的,税收优先于罚款、没收违法所得。 税务机关应当对纳税人欠缴税款的情况定期予以公告。
Article 46 In the event that a taxpayer defaults on tax payment and mortgages or pledges its property, the taxpayer shall explain to the mortgagee or pledgee about its default on tax payment. The mortgagee or pledgee may request the taxation authorities to provide information about the default.	**第四十六条** 纳税人有欠税情形而以其财产设定抵押、质押的,应当向抵押权人、质权人说明其欠税情况。抵押权人、质权人可以请求税务机关提供有关的欠税情况。
Article 47 The taxation authorities shall issue a receipt when attaching commodities, goods or other property, and issue a detailed list when sealing up commodities, goods or other property.	**第四十七条** 税务机关扣押商品、货物或者其他财产时,必须开付收据;查封商品、货物或者其他财产时,必须开付清单。
Article 48 In case of merger or division, the taxpayer shall report to the taxation authorities and pay off the taxes payable in accordance with law. If the taxpayer fails to pay off the tax payable at the time of merger, the new taxpayer after the merger shall continue to fulfill the duty to pay taxes; if the taxpayer fails to pay off the taxes payable upon division, the new taxpayer after the division shall bear joint and several liabilities for the unfulfilled duty.	**第四十八条** 纳税人有合并、分立情形的,应当向税务机关报告,并依法缴清税款。纳税人合并时未缴清税款的,应当由合并后的纳税人继续履行未履行的纳税义务;纳税人分立时未缴清税款的,分立后的纳税人对未履行的纳税义务应当承担连带责任。
Article 49 Any taxpayer who defaults on payment of a considerable amount of tax shall, before disposing of its real estate or large sum fixed assets, report to the taxation authorities.	**第四十九条** 欠缴税款数额较大的纳税人在处分其不动产或者大额资产之前,应当向税务机关报告。

Continued

English Translation	Chinese Version
Article 50 In the event that a taxpayer who defaults on tax payment fails to exercise its natural creditor's rights, or waives such rights, or transfers its property gratuitously or at a low price obviously unreasonable, which the transferee is aware of, therefore causing losses to tax revenues of the State, the taxation authorities may, in accordance with the provisions in Articles 73 and 74 of the *Contract Law*, exercise the rights of subrogation and rescission. The exercise the rights of subrogation and rescission in accordance with the provisions in the preceding paragraph by the taxation authorities shall not release the taxpayer who defaults on tax payment from the tax payment obligations and the legal liabilities that should be borne.	**第五十条** 欠缴税款的纳税人因怠于行使到期债权,或者放弃到期债权,或者无偿转让财产,或者以明显不合理的低价转让财产而受让人知道该情形,对国家税收造成损害的,税务机关可以依照合同法第七十三条、第七十四条的规定行使代位权、撤销权。 税务机关依照前款规定行使代位权、撤销权的,不免除欠缴税款的纳税人尚未履行的纳税义务和应承担的法律责任。
Article 51 Where the taxation authorities discover that a taxpayer makes a tax payment in excess of the amount of tax payable, the taxation authorities shall immediately refund the excess payment; where a taxpayer discovers the same, the taxpayer may, within three years from the date the payment is made, claim from the taxation authorities a refund of the excess payment, plus the interests accrued according to the bank interest rates at the time, and the taxation authorities shall immediately pay back the money upon examination and verification of the case; where such refund involves the State Treasury, it shall be dealt with in accordance with the provisions on the administration of the State Treasury in relevant laws and administrative regulations.	**第五十一条** 纳税人超过应纳税额缴纳的税款,税务机关发现后应当立即退还;纳税人自结算缴纳税款之日起三年内发现的,可以向税务机关要求退还多缴的税款并加算银行同期存款利息,税务机关及时查实后应当立即退还;涉及从国库中退库的,依照法律、行政法规有关国库管理的规定退还。

Continued

English Translation	Chinese Version
Article 52 Where a taxpayer or withholding agent fails to pay or underpays taxes for reasons attributable to the taxation authorities, the latter may, within three years, require the taxpayer or withholding agent to pay the tax in arrears without, however, the imposition of any penalty for late payment. Where a taxpayer or withholding agent fails to pay or underpays taxes owing to its own miscalculation or other faults, the taxation authorities may, within three years, recover the taxes in arrears and the penalties for late payment; under special circumstances, the time limit for recovering the taxes in arrears may be extended to five years. Where a taxpayer evades, refuses to pay or practises fraud in tax payment and the taxation authorities recover the collection of the unpaid or underpaid tax, the penalties for late payment, or the tax payment defrauded on, the latter shall not be restricted by the time limit prescribed in the preceding paragraph.	**第五十二条** 因税务机关的责任,致使纳税人、扣缴义务人未缴或者少缴税款的,税务机关在三年内可以要求纳税人、扣缴义务人补缴税款,但是不得加收滞纳金。 因纳税人、扣缴义务人计算错误等失误,未缴或者少缴税款的,税务机关在三年内可以追征税款、滞纳金;有特殊情况的,追征期可以延长到五年。 对偷税、抗税、骗税的,税务机关追征其未缴或者少缴的税款、滞纳金或者所骗取的税款,不受前款规定期限的限制。
Article 53 The State and local tax bureaus shall, in conformity with their respective areas of administration for tax collection and the levels of budgeted tax for the State Treasury prescribed by the State, turn over the collected taxes to the State Treasury. Where, in accordance with law, the auditing or finance authorities identify any violation of law on tax collection, the taxation authorities shall, based on the decisions or written suggestions of the related authorities and in accordance with law, turn over the taxes and penalties for late payment collected to the State Treasury in conformity with the levels of budgeted tax for the State Treasury, and provide the related authorities with feedback on the results without delay.	**第五十三条** 国家税务局和地方税务局应当按照国家规定的税收征收管理范围和税款入库预算级次,将征收的税款缴入国库。 对审计机关、财政机关依法查出的税收违法行为,税务机关应当根据有关机关的决定、意见书,依法将应收的税款、滞纳金按照税款入库预算级次缴入国库,并将结果及时回复有关机关。

Continued

English Translation	Chinese Version
Chapter 4 Tax Inspection **Article 54** The taxation authorities have the powers to conduct the following tax inspections: (1) to inspect a taxpayer's accounting books, vouchers for the accounts, statements and relevant information; to inspect a withholding agent's accounting books, vouchers for the accounts and relevant documents in respect of the amount of tax withheld and remitted or collected and remitted; (2) to inspect a taxpayer's taxable commodities, goods or other property at the taxpayer's premises where production or business operations are conducted and places where goods are stored; to inspect a withholding agent's operational conditions relating to the withholding and remittance of tax or the collection and remittance of tax; (3) to order a taxpayer or withholding agent to furnish documents, certifying documents and materials pertaining to the payment of tax or the amount of tax withheld and remitted or collected and remitted; (4) to inquire a taxpayer or withholding agent regarding issues and particulars relevant to the payment of tax or the amount of tax withheld and remitted or collected and remitted; (5) to inspect, at railway stations, docks, airports, postal enterprises and their branches, the supporting documents, vouchers and materials pertaining to the taxable commodities, goods or other property consigned or mailed by a taxpayer; and (6) upon approval of the director of the tax bureau (or sub-bureau) at or above the county level and by presenting the permit for deposit account inspection in the national unified format, to inquire about the deposit accounts that a taxpayer engaged in production or business operations or a withholding agent has opened with a bank or any other financial institution. Upon approval of the director of the tax bureau (sub-bureau) at or above the level of the city with districts or the autonomous prefecture, inquire about the savings a suspect involved in a case. No information obtained through inquiry by the taxation authorities may be used for purposes other than tax collection.	**第四章　税务检查** **第五十四条** 税务机关有权进行下列税务检查： （一）检查纳税人的帐簿、记帐凭证、报表和有关资料，检查扣缴义务人代扣代缴、代收代缴税款帐簿、记帐凭证和有关资料； （二）到纳税人的生产、经营场所和货物存放地检查纳税人应纳税的商品、货物或者其他财产，检查扣缴义务人与代扣代缴、代收代缴税款有关的经营情况； （三）责成纳税人、扣缴义务人提供与纳税或者代扣代缴、代收代缴税款有关的文件、证明材料和有关资料； （四）询问纳税人、扣缴义务人与纳税或者代扣代缴、代收代缴税款有关的问题和情况； （五）到车站、码头、机场、邮政企业及其分支机构检查纳税人托运、邮寄应纳税商品、货物或者其他财产的有关单据、凭证和有关资料； （六）经县以上税务局（分局）局长批准，凭全国统一格式的检查存款帐户许可证明，查询从事生产、经营的纳税人、扣缴义务人在银行或者其他金融机构的存款帐户。税务机关在调查税收违法案件时，经设区的市、自治州以上税务局（分局）局长批准，可以查询案件涉嫌人员的储蓄存款。税务机关查询所获得的资料，不得用于税收以外的用途。

Continued

English Translation	Chinese Version
Article 55 When the taxation authorities, in accordance with law, conduct tax inspection of a taxpayer engaged in production or business operations in respect of the tax payment made during earlier tax periods and discover the taxpayer's evasion of the obligation to paytaxes and evident signs of transfer or concealment of taxable commodities, goods or other property or incomes, the taxation authorities may adopt tax preservative measures or compulsory enforcement measures in conformity with the powers vested by the Law.	**第五十五条** 税务机关对从事生产、经营的纳税人以前纳税期的纳税情况依法进行税务检查时,发现纳税人有逃避纳税义务行为,并有明显的转移、隐匿其应纳税的商品、货物以及其他财产或者应纳税的收入的迹象的,可以按照本法规定的批准权限采取税收保全措施或者强制执行措施。
Article 56 A taxpayer or withholding agent must accept tax inspection conducted by the taxation authorities in accordance with law, report the particulars truthfully and provide relevant documents, and may not refuse to accept such inspection or conceal any facts.	**第五十六条** 纳税人、扣缴义务人必须接受税务机关依法进行的税务检查,如实反映情况,提供有关资料,不得拒绝、隐瞒。
Article 57 When conducting tax inspection in accordance with law, the taxation authorities have the power to inquire the related entities and individuals about the particulars of taxpayers, withholding agents and other parties in respect of the payment of tax and the amount of tax withheld and remitted or collected and remitted, and the said entities and individuals shall truthfully provide the relevant materials and certifying documents to the taxation authorities.	**第五十七条** 税务机关依法进行税务检查时,有权向有关单位和个人调查纳税人、扣缴义务人和其他当事人与纳税或者代扣代缴、代收代缴税款有关的情况,有关单位和个人有义务向税务机关如实提供有关资料及证明材料。
Article 58 When investigating a case involving violation of laws or regulations on tax collection, the taxation authorities may take notes and make tape-recordings, video-recordings, photographings and duplications of the particulars and documents pertaining to the case.	**第五十八条** 税务机关调查税务违法案件时,对与案件有关的情况和资料,可以记录、录音、录像、照相和复制。
Article 59 When conducting tax inspection, the officials sent by the taxation authorities shall present tax inspection certificate and tax inspection notice, and have the duty to keep confidential the persons under inspection; where no such certificate and notice are presented, the persons subject to inspection have the right to refuse to accept the inspection.	**第五十九条** 税务机关派出的人员进行税务检查时,应当出示税务检查证和税务检查通知书,并有责任为被检查人保守秘密;未出示税务检查证和税务检查通知书的,被检查人有权拒绝检查。

Continued

English Translation	Chinese Version
Chapter 5 Legal Liability **Article 60** Where a taxpayer commits one of the following acts, the taxpayer shall be ordered by the taxation authorities to rectify within the specified time limit and may be fined not more than 2,000 yuan; if the offenses are serious, the taxpayer may be fined not less than 2,000 yuan but not more than 10,000 yuan: (1)Fails to apply for tax registration or for change or cancellation of tax registration within the prescribed time limit; (2)fails to set and/or keep the accounting books, or keep the vouchers for the accounts and the relevant documents in accordance with regulations; (3)fails to submit the financial and accounting systems or the financial and accounting procedures, the accounting software to the taxation authorities for reference in accordance with regulations; (4)fails to report all the numbers of bank accounts to the taxation authorities in accordance with regulations; and (5)fails to install or use tax-control devices in accordance with regulations, damages or destroys or alters such devices without authorization. Where a taxpayer fails to go through the formalities for tax registration, the taxation authorities shall order the taxpayer to rectify within the specified time; if the taxpayer still fails to rectify upon expiry of the specified time limit, the administrative department for industry and commerce shall, upon proposal and request of the taxation authorities, revoke the business license of the taxpayer. Where a taxpayer fails to use the tax registration certificate in accordance with regulations, or lends, alters, damages or destroys, trades or forges tax registration certificate, the taxpayer shall be fined not less than 2,000 yuan but not more than 10,000 yuan; if the offenses are serious, the taxpayer shall be fined not less than 10,000 yuan but not more than 50,000 yuan.	**第五章　法律责任** **第六十条** 纳税人有下列行为之一的,由税务机关责令限期改正,可以处二千元以下的罚款;情节严重的,处二千元以上一万元以下的罚款: (一)未按照规定的期限申报办理税务登记、变更或者注销登记的; (二)未按照规定设置、保管帐簿或者保管记帐凭证和有关资料的; (三)未按照规定将财务、会计制度或者财务、会计处理办法和会计核算软件报送税务机关备查的; (四)未按照规定将其全部银行帐号向税务机关报告的; (五)未按照规定安装、使用税控装置,或者损毁或者擅自改动税控装置的。 纳税人不办理税务登记的,由税务机关责令限期改正;逾期不改正的,经税务机关提请,由工商行政管理机关吊销其营业执照。 纳税人未按照规定使用税务登记证件,或者转借、涂改、损毁、买卖、伪造税务登记证件的,处二千元以上一万元以下的罚款;情节严重的,处一万元以上五万元以下的罚款。

Continued

English Translation	Chinese Version
Article 61 Where a withholding agent fails to create and keep the accounting books for the tax withheld and remitted, or collected and remitted, or keeps the vouchers for the accounts and the relevant documents regarding the tax withheld and remitted, or collected and remitted, in accordance with relevant regulations, the withholding agent shall be ordered by the taxation authorities to rectify within the specified time and may be fined not more than 2,000 yuan; if the offenses are serious, the withholding agent shall be fined not less than 2,000 yuan but not more than 5,000 yuan.	**第六十一条** 扣缴义务人未按照规定设置、保管代扣代缴、代收代缴税款帐簿或者保管代扣代缴、代收代缴税款记帐凭证及有关资料的,由税务机关责令限期改正,可以处二千元以下的罚款;情节严重的,处二千元以上五千元以下的罚款。
Article 62 Where, within the specified time limit, a taxpayer fails to go through the formalities for tax declaration and submit information on tax payment or a withholding agent fails to submit to the taxation authorities statements on taxes withheld and remitted, or collected and remitted and other relevant documents, the taxpayer or withholding agent shall be ordered by the taxation authorities to rectify within the specified time and may be fined not more than 2,000 yuan; if the offenses are serious, the taxpayer or withholding agent may be fined not less than 2,000 yuan but not more than 10,000 yuan.	**第六十二条** 纳税人未按照规定的期限办理纳税申报和报送纳税资料的,或者扣缴义务人未按照规定的期限向税务机关报送代扣代缴、代收代缴税款报告表和有关资料的,由税务机关责令限期改正,可以处二千元以下的罚款;情节严重的,可以处二千元以上一万元以下的罚款。

Continued

English Translation	Chinese Version
Article 63 Tax evasion means that a taxpayer forges, alters, conceals or, without authorization, destroys accounting books or vouchers for the accounts, or overstates expenses or omits or understates incomes in the accounting books, or, after being notified by the taxation authorities to make tax declaration, refuses to do so or makes false tax declaration, or fails to pay or underpays the amount of tax payable. Where a taxpayer evades tax, the taxation authorities shall recover the payment of the amount of tax the taxpayer fails to pay or underpays and the penalties for late payment, and the taxpayer shall also be fined not less than 50 percent but not more than five times the amount of tax the taxpayer fails to pay or underpays; if a crime is constituted, the taxpayer shall be investigated for criminal liability in accordance with law. Where a withholding agent fails to pay, or underpays the tax withheld or collected through means mentioned in the preceding paragraph, the taxation authorities shall recover the payment of the amount of tax the taxpayer or withholding agent fails to pay or underpays and the penalties for late payment, and the taxpayer or withholding agent shall also be fined not less than 50 percent but not more than five times the amount of tax it fails to pay or underpays; if a crime is constituted, the taxpayer or withholding agent shall be investigated for criminal liability in accordance with law.	**第六十三条** 纳税人伪造、变造、隐匿、擅自销毁帐簿、记帐凭证，或者在帐簿上多列支出或者不列、少列收入，或者经税务机关通知申报而拒不申报或者进行虚假的纳税申报，不缴或者少缴应纳税款的，是偷税。对纳税人偷税的，由税务机关追缴其不缴或者少缴的税款、滞纳金，并处不缴或者少缴的税款百分之五十以上五倍以下的罚款；构成犯罪的，依法追究刑事责任。 扣缴义务人采取前款所列手段，不缴或者少缴已扣、已收税款，由税务机关追缴其不缴或者少缴的税款、滞纳金，并处不缴或者少缴的税款百分之五十以上五倍以下的罚款；构成犯罪的，依法追究刑事责任。
Article 64 Where a taxpayer or withholding agent fabricates the basis on which tax is assessed, the taxpayer or withholding agent shall be ordered by the taxation authorities to rectify within the specified time and shall also be fined not more than 50,000 yuan. Where a taxpayer fails to make tax declaration, or fails to pay or underpays the tax payable, the taxation authorities shall recover the payment of the amount of tax the taxpayer fails to pay or underpays and the penalties for late payment, and the taxpayer shall also be fined not less than 50 percent but not more than five times the amount of tax it fails to pay or underpays.	**第六十四条** 纳税人、扣缴义务人编造虚假计税依据的，由税务机关责令限期改正，并处五万元以下的罚款。 纳税人不进行纳税申报，不缴或者少缴应纳税款的，由税务机关追缴其不缴或者少缴的税款、滞纳金，并处不缴或者少缴的税款百分之五十以上五倍以下的罚款。

Continued

English Translation	Chinese Version
Article 65 Where a taxpayer who fails to pay the tax payable, by means of transferring or concealing the property, prevents the taxation authorities from recovering the payment of the tax in arrears, the taxation authorities shall recover the payment of the tax and the penalties for late payment and shall also give the person a fine of not less than 50 percent but not more than five times the amount of tax in arrears; if a crime is constituted, the person shall be investigated for criminal liability in accordance with law.	**第六十五条** 纳税人欠缴应纳税款,采取转移或者隐匿财产的手段,妨碍税务机关追缴欠缴的税款的,由税务机关追缴欠缴的税款、滞纳金,并处欠缴税款百分之五十以上五倍以下的罚款;构成犯罪的,依法追究刑事责任。
Article 66 Where a person, by making false export declaration or through other means, receives export tax rebate from the State, the taxation authorities shall recover the export taxes refunded, and the person shall also be fined not less than the amount of the refund taxes but not more than five times that amount; if a crime is constituted, the person shall be investigated for criminal liability in accordance with law. Where a person receives export tax rebate from the State through deception, the taxation authorities may, within the specified time limit, suspend export tax rebate for the person.	**第六十六条** 以假报出口或者其他欺骗手段,骗取国家出口退税款的,由税务机关追缴其骗取的退税款,并处骗取税款一倍以上五倍以下的罚款;构成犯罪的,依法追究刑事责任。 对骗取国家出口退税款的,税务机关可以在规定期间内停止为其办理出口退税。
Article 67 Refusal to pay taxes means refusing to pay taxes by resort to violence or threats. In such a case, the taxation authorities shall, in addition to recovering the payment of the amount of tax a person refuses to pay and the penalties for late payment, conduct investigation for criminal liability in accordance with law. If the offenses are not serious and no crime is constituted, the taxation authorities shall recover the payment of the amount of tax the person refuses to pay and the penalties for late payment and shall also give the person a fine of not less than the amount of the tax the person refuses to pay but not more than five times that amount.	**第六十七条** 以暴力、威胁方法拒不缴纳税款的,是抗税,除由税务机关追缴其拒缴的税款、滞纳金外,依法追究刑事责任。情节轻微,未构成犯罪的,由税务机关追缴其拒缴的税款、滞纳金,并处拒缴税款一倍以上五倍以下的罚款。

Continued

English Translation	Chinese Version
Article 68 Where a taxpayer or a withholding agent fails to pay or underpays the amount of tax that should be paid or remitted within the specified time and, after being ordered by the taxation authorities to pay or remit within the specified time, still fails to do so on the expiration of the time limit, the taxation authorities may, in addition to recovering, by adopting compulsory enforcement measures in accordance with the provisions in Article 40 of this Law, the payment of the amount of tax the taxpayer or withholding agent fails to pay or underpays or fails to remit, impose a fine of not less than 50 percent but not more than five times the amount of tax the taxpayer or withholding agent fails to pay or underpays or fails to remit.	**第六十八条** 纳税人、扣缴义务人在规定期限内不缴或者少缴应纳或者应解缴的税款,经税务机关责令限期缴纳,逾期仍未缴纳的,税务机关除依照本法第四十条的规定采取强制执行措施追缴其不缴或者少缴的税款外,可以处不缴或者少缴的税款百分之五十以上五倍以下的罚款。
Article 69 Where a withholding agent fails to withhold or collect the amount of tax which should be withheld or collected, the taxation authorities shall recover the payment of the said amount, and give the withholding-agent a fine of not less than 50 percent but not more than three times the amount of tax that should have been withheld or collected.	**第六十九条** 扣缴义务人应扣未扣、应收而不收税款的,由税务机关向纳税人追缴税款,对扣缴义务人处应扣未扣、应收未收税款百分之五十以上三倍以下的罚款。
Article 70 Where a taxpayer or a withholding agent evades, refuses to undergo or, by other means, hinders inspection by the taxation authorities, the taxpayer or withholding agent shall be ordered by the taxation authorities to rectify and may be fined not more than 10,000 yuan; if the offenses are serious, the taxpayer or withholding agent shall be fined not less than 10,000 yuan but not more than 50,000 yuan.	**第七十条** 纳税人、扣缴义务人逃避、拒绝或者以其他方式阻挠税务机关检查的,由税务机关责令改正,可以处一万元以下的罚款;情节严重的,处一万元以上五万元以下的罚款。
Article 71 Where a person, in violation of the provisions in Article 22 of this Law, illegally prints invoices, the taxation authorities shall destroy the invoices illegally printed, confiscate the illegal gains and tools for criminal purposes and give the person a fine of not less than 10,000 yuan but not more than 50,000 yuan; if a crime is constituted, the person shall be investigated for criminal liability in accordance with law.	**第七十一条** 违反本法第二十二条规定,非法印制发票的,由税务机关销毁非法印制的发票,没收违法所得和作案工具,并处一万元以上五万元以下的罚款;构成犯罪的,依法追究刑事责任。

Continued

English Translation	Chinese Version
Article 72 Where a taxpayer engaged in production or business operations or a withholding agent commits an act in violation of the provisions in this Law on tax collection and refuses to accept the sanctions given by the taxation authorities, the taxation authorities may confiscate the invoices or discontinue selling invoices to it.	**第七十二条** 从事生产、经营的纳税人、扣缴义务人有本法规定的税收违法行为，拒不接受税务机关处理的，税务机关可以收缴其发票或者停止向其发售发票。
Article 73 Where a bank or other financial institution with which a taxpayer or a withholding agent has opened deposit accounts refuses to accept the taxation authorities' inspection of the deposit accounts of the said taxpayer or withholding agent in accordance with law, or refuses to execute the decision made by the taxation authorities on freezing the deposits or withholding the tax, or, after receiving the written notice of the taxation authorities, assists the taxpayer or withholding agent in transferring the deposits, therefore causing the loss of taxes, the bank or other financial institution shall be fined by the taxation authorities not less than 100,000 yuan but not more than 500,000 yuan and the persons that are directly in charge and the other directly liable persons shall be fined not less than 1,000 yuan but not more than 10,000 yuan.	**第七十三条** 纳税人、扣缴义务人的开户银行或者其他金融机构拒绝接受税务机关依法检查纳税人、扣缴义务人存款帐户，或者拒绝执行税务机关作出的冻结存款或者扣缴税款的决定，或者在接到税务机关的书面通知后帮助纳税人、扣缴义务人转移存款，造成税款流失的，由税务机关处十万元以上五十万元以下的罚款，对直接负责的主管人员和其他直接责任人员处一千元以上一万元以下的罚款。
Article 74 Any administrative sanction specified under the Law may be decided by the taxation stations if the amount of the fine is less than 2000 yuan.	**第七十四条** 本法规定的行政处罚，罚款额在二千元以下的，可以由税务所决定。
Article 75 The taxation and judicial authorities shall, in conformity with the levels of budgeted tax for the State Treasury, turn over all the revenues from tax-related fines and confiscations to the State Treasury.	**第七十五条** 税务机关和司法机关的涉税罚没收入，应当按照税款入库预算级次上缴国库。
Article 76 Any taxation authorities that, in violation of regulations and without authorization, alters the administrative areas for tax collection and the levels of budgeted tax for the State Treasury shall be ordered to rectify within the specified time limit, and the persons that are directly in charge and the other directly liable persons shall, in accordance with law, be given administrative sanctions such as demotion or dismissal from office.	**第七十六条** 税务机关违反规定擅自改变税收征收管理范围和税款入库预算级次的，责令限期改正，对直接负责的主管人员和其他直接责任人员依法给予降级或者撤职的行政处分。

Continued

English Translation	Chinese Version
Article 77 Where a taxpayer or withholding agent is suspected of committing an offense against the provisions in Article 63, 65, 66, 67 or 71 of this Law, the taxation authorities shall refer the case to the judicial authorities to be investigated for criminal liability in accordance with law. Where a taxation official fails to refer a case that should be referred to the judicial authorities to the judicial authorities for investigation for criminal liability by engaging in malpractice for private gains, the taxation official shall be investigated for criminal liability by law if the offense is serious.	第七十七条 纳税人、扣缴义务人有本法第六十三条、第六十五条、第六十六条、第六十七条、第七十一条规定的行为涉嫌犯罪的,税务机关应当依法移交司法机关追究刑事责任。 税务人员徇私舞弊,对依法应当移交司法机关追究刑事责任的不移交,情节严重的,依法追究刑事责任。
Article 78 Any person that collects tax without authorization by the taxation authorities by law shall be ordered to return the money and things of value collected and be given administrative sanctions or penalties by law; where losses are caused to other people's lawful rights or interests, the person shall be liable for compensation in accordance with law; if a crime is constituted, the person shall be investigated for criminal liability in accordance with law.	第七十八条 未经税务机关依法委托征收税款的,责令退还收取的财物,依法给予行政处分或者行政处罚;致使他人合法权益受到损失的,依法承担赔偿责任;构成犯罪的,依法追究刑事责任。
Article 79 Where the tax authority or tax official seals up or attaches a taxpayer's housing and articles of use which are necessary for the daily lives of the taxpayer and the family members it supports, the taxation authorities or taxation official shall be ordered to return the said housing and articles for use and be given administrative sanctions by law; if a crime is constituted, the taxation authorities or taxation official shall be investigated for criminal liability in accordance with law.	第七十九条 税务机关、税务人员查封、扣押纳税人个人及其所扶养家属维持生活必需的住房和用品的,责令退还,依法给予行政处分;构成犯罪的,依法追究刑事责任。
Article 80 Where a tax official colludes with the taxpayers or withholding agents, instigates or assists them in committing an offense against the provisions in Article 63, 65 or 66 of this Law, the tax official shall be investigated for criminal liability in accordance with law if a crime is constituted; if no crime is constituted, the taxation official shall be given administrative sanctions in accordance with law.	第八十条 税务人员与纳税人、扣缴义务人勾结,唆使或者协助纳税人、扣缴义务人有本法第六十三条、第六十五条、第六十六条规定的行为,构成犯罪的,依法追究刑事责任;尚不构成犯罪的,依法给予行政处分。

Continued

English Translation	Chinese Version
Article 81 Where a tax official, by taking advantage of the post, accepts or solicits money or things of value from taxpayers or withholding agents, or seeks other illegal interests, the taxation official shall be investigated for criminal liability in accordance with law if a crime is constituted; if no crime is constituted, the taxation official shall be given administrative sanctions in accordance with law.	第八十一条 税务人员利用职务上的便利,收受或者索取纳税人、扣缴义务人财物或者谋取其他不正当利益,构成犯罪的,依法追究刑事责任;尚不构成犯罪的,依法给予行政处分。
Article 82 Where a tax official is engaged in malpractices for privates gain, neglects the duty, fails to collect or under-collects the tax that should be collected, thus causing serious losses to State revenue, the taxation official shall be investigated for criminal liability in accordance with law if a crime is constituted; if no crime is constituted, the taxation official shall be given administrative sanctions in accordance with law. Any taxation official who abusing the power to deliberately create difficulties for taxpayers or withholding agents shall be transferred from the post for tax collection and be given administrative sanctions by law. Where a tax official retaliates against taxpayers or withholding agents who complain about or blow whistle on violations of the laws or rules of discipline on tax collection, or any other whistle blowers, the taxation official shall be given administrative sanctions in accordance with law; if a crime is constituted, the taxation official shall be investigated for criminal liability in accordance with law. Where a tax official, in violation of the provisions of laws and/or administrative regulations, deliberately over-or under-assess the agricultural yield taxable, thus resulting in over-or under-collection of tax, infringing upon the farmers' lawful rights and interests or undermining the interests of the State , the taxation official shall be investigated for criminal liability in accordance with law if a crime is constituted; if no crime is constituted, the taxation official shall be given administrative sanctions in accordance with law.	第八十二条 税务人员徇私舞弊或者玩忽职守,不征或者少征应征税款,致使国家税收遭受重大损失,构成犯罪的,依法追究刑事责任;尚不构成犯罪的,依法给予行政处分。 税务人员滥用职权,故意刁难纳税人、扣缴义务人的,调离税收工作岗位,并依法给予行政处分。 税务人员对控告、检举税收违法违纪行为的纳税人、扣缴义务人以及其他检举人进行打击报复的,依法给予行政处分;构成犯罪的,依法追究刑事责任。 税务人员违反法律、行政法规的规定,故意高估或者低估农业税计税产量,致使多征或者少征税款,侵犯农民合法权益或者损害国家利益,构成犯罪的,依法追究刑事责任;尚不构成犯罪的,依法给予行政处分。

Continued

English Translation	Chinese Version
Article 83 In case of early collection, delayed collection or apportionment of taxes by the taxation authorities in violation of the laws and/or administrative regulations, the higher level authority or administrative supervision authority shall order it to take corrective measures, and the persons that are directly in charge and other directly liable persons shall be given administrative sanctions by law.	**第八十三条** 违反法律、行政法规的规定提前征收、延缓征收或者摊派税款的，由其上级机关或者行政监察机关责令改正，对直接负责的主管人员和其他直接责任人员依法给予行政处分。
Article 84 Where decisions regarding the imposition or cessation of tax, tax reduction, tax exemption, refund of tax or payment of tax underpaid, or other decisions contravening the laws or administrative regulations on tax collection are made without authorization and in violation of the provisions of laws or administrative regulations, in addition to revocation of such decisions in accordance with the provisions of this Law, the amount of tax that should have been collected shall be collected, the amount of tax that should not have been collected shall be refunded, and the persons that are directly in charge and the other persons who are directly liable shall be prosecuted for administrative liability by the higher level authorities; if a crime is constituted, investigation for criminal liability hall be conducted by law.	**第八十四条** 违反法律、行政法规的规定，擅自作出税收的开征、停征或者减税、免税、退税、补税以及其他同税收法律、行政法规相抵触的决定的，除依照本法规定撤销其擅自作出的决定外，补征应征未征税款，退还不应征收而征收的税款，并由上级机关追究直接负责的主管人员和其他直接责任人员的行政责任；构成犯罪的，依法追究刑事责任。
Article 85 In case of failure of any taxation official to withdraw therefrom in collecting taxes, investigating or dealing with cases involving violation of taxation laws in accordance with the Law, the persons that are directly in charge and other directly liable persons shall be given administrative sanctions by law.	**第八十五条** 税务人员在征收税款或者查处税收违法案件时，未按照本法规定进行回避的，对直接负责的主管人员和其他直接责任人员，依法给予行政处分。
Article 86 In case that any violation of the tax-related laws and/or administrative regulations that should be given administrative sanctions is not identified within 5 years, no administrative sanctions shall be given.	**第八十六条** 违反税收法律、行政法规应当给予行政处罚的行为，在五年内未被发现的，不再给予行政处罚。

Continued

English Translation	Chinese Version
Article 87 In case of failure to keep the taxpayer, withholding agent or reporter in confidence in accordance with the Law, the persons that are directly in charge and the other directly liable persons shall, in accordance with Law, be given administrative sanctions by their employers or the departments concerned.	**第八十七条** 未按照本法规定为纳税人、扣缴义务人、检举人保密的,对直接负责的主管人员和其他直接责任人员,由所在单位或者有关单位依法给予行政处分。
Article 88 In case that any dispute arises over taxation between a taxpayer, withholding agent or tax guarantor with the taxation authorities, the taxpayer, withholdingagent or tax guarantor must pay or release the tax and penalty for late payment or provide corresponding guarantee in accordance with the tax payment decision made by the taxation authorities before applying for administrative review by law; if dissatisfied with the decision of administrative review, the taxpayer, withholding agent or tax guarantor may institute a litigation at the people's court. In the event that the party concerned is dissatisfied with the taxation authorities' penalty decision, mandatory enforcement measures or tax preservative measures, it may apply for administrative review or institute litigation at the people's court by law. In the event that the party concerned neither applies for administrative review of the penalty decision made by the taxation authorities in a timely manner, nor institutes a litigation at the people's court or refuses to implement the decision, the taxation authorities that makes the penalty decision may, in accordance with Article 40 of the Law, take enforcement measures or apply to the people's court for enforcement.	**第八十八条** 纳税人、扣缴义务人、纳税担保人同税务机关在纳税上发生争议时,必须先依照税务机关的纳税决定缴纳或者解缴税款及滞纳金或者提供相应的担保,然后可以依法申请行政复议;对行政复议决定不服的,可以依法向人民法院起诉。 当事人对税务机关的处罚决定、强制执行措施或者税收保全措施不服的,可以依法申请行政复议,也可以依法向人民法院起诉。 当事人对税务机关的处罚决定逾期不申请行政复议也不向人民法院起诉、又不履行的,作出处罚决定的税务机关可以采取本法第四十条规定的强制执行措施,或者申请人民法院强制执行。
Chapter 6 Supplementary Provisions **Article 89** Taxpayers and withholding agents may entrust the tax agents to deal with the tax-related matters on their behalf.	**第六章　附则** **第八十九条** 纳税人、扣缴义务人可以委托税务代理人代为办理税务事宜。

Continued

English Translation	Chinese Version
Article 90 The specific measures for the administration of collection of cultivated land use tax, deed tax, agricultural tax and animal husbandry tax shall be formulated by the State Council separately. The administration of collection of the Customs duties and the taxes collected by the Customs on behalf of the taxation authorities shall be in accordance with the provisions of relevant laws or administrative regulations.	第九十条 耕地占用税、契税、农业税、牧业税征收管理的具体办法，由国务院另行制定。 关税及海关代征税收的征收管理，依照法律、行政法规的有关规定执行。
Article 91 Where the provisions of treaties or agreements on tax concluded between the People's Republic of China and other countries contain provisions different from those of this Law, the provisions of such treaties or agreements shall prevail.	第九十一条 中华人民共和国同外国缔结的有关税收的条约、协定同本法有不同规定的，依照条约、协定的规定办理。
Article 92 Where the tax laws promulgated prior to the effectiveness of this Law contain provisions different from those of this Law, the provisions of the latter shall prevail.	第九十二条 本法施行前颁布的税收法律与本法有不同规定的，适用本法规定。
Article 93 The detailed rules for implementation of this Law shall be formulated by the State Council in accordance with this Law.	第九十三条 国务院根据本法制定实施细则。
Article 94 This Law shall enter into force on May 1 2001.	第九十四条 本法自 2001 年 5 月 1 日起施行。

Appendix Ⅱ : Exercises

1. What are the governing laws for tax administration in China?

2. What's the difference between domestic law and the tax treaties in terms of tax administration in China?

3. Which executive institutions are in charge of tax collections in China?

4. Which executive institutions are in charge of social contribution collections in China?

5. Which executive institutions are in charge of tax audits in China?

6. Which executive institutions are in charge of exchange of tax information with the Contracting States of China?

7. What's the difference in the mode of exchange of information between the provisions of the Chinese DTAs and the two multilateral conventions?

8. What are the roles of the SAT in China?

CHAPTER 9
ANTI-TAX AVOIDANCE MEASURES[①]

9.1 Introduction

Before the BEPS project was launched by the OECD/G20 in 2013, China already had its own tax avoidance regime, consisting of both specific anti-tax avoidance rules (SAARs) and a general anti-avoidance rule (GAAR), in its domestic tax laws, and also had a number of anti-treaty abuse provisions in the Chinese DTAs. However, these anti-tax avoidance measures seem not

---

① The content of this chapter is based on the publications of Dr. Li on journals, books and international conferences, for example, her papers "China's CFC Regime: Existing Rules and Improvement Suggestions", *International Tax Bulletin*, 2014, Vol.68, No. 10; "Status of the Implementation of the OECD/G20 BEPS Initiative in China and Future Developments", *International Tax Bulletin*, 2016, Vol.82, No.4; "Advance Pricing Agreements in China", *International Tax Bulletin*, 2016, Vol.70, No.5; "General Anti-Avoidance Rules (GAARs)-A Key Element of Tax Systems in the Post-BEPS Tax World: China", co-authored with Mingxing Cao, in Michael Lang et al (eds.), *General Anti-Avoidance Rules (GAARs)-A Key Element of Tax Systems in the Post-BEPS Tax World*, Amsterdam: IBFD, 2016; "The Impact of the Multilateral Instrument on China", *Asia-Pacific Tax Bulletin*, 2018, Vol.17, No.6; "The TCI Case-A Milestone Case for China Taxing Offshore Indirect Shares Transfer", *Asia-Pacific Tax Bulletin*, 2019, Vol.25, No.6; "The Adoption of BEPS in China", in Sadiq, Sawyer and McCredie (eds.), *Tax Design and Administration in a Post-BEPS Era: A Study of Key Reform Measures in* 18 *Jurisdictions*, Fiscal Publications, 2019; and "BEPS MLI-China Report", in Studies on International Fiscal Law by the International Fiscal Association 2020-Volume 105A: Restricting the treaty network, IFA, 2021.

effectively implemented in China to invalidate MNEs' base erosion and profit shifting arrangements, because China's corporate income tax revenue loss in 2011 as a result of MNEs' tax avoidance practices reached RMB 10.637 billion.[1] Therefore, active involvement in the BEPS project is one necessary approach as well as an opportunity for the Chinese government to enhance its tax avoidance regime. In implementing the BEPS actions, China has not created any new tax (such as the diverted profits tax), but has made efforts in issuing new measures to enforce its existing anti-tax avoidance regime and to improve tax transparency.

9.2   Domestic Measures

In 2008 a whole regime of tax avoidance measures was introduced as part of China's enterprise income tax, including four SAARs and one GAAR.[2] The four SAARs relate to transfer pricing rules, cost-sharing arrangement rules, controlled foreign company (CFC) rules and thin capitalization rules. The GAAR is designed as the Chinese tax authorities' last resort which tests whether transactions have a "reasonable business purpose".[3] If taxpayers fail to demonstrate such a purpose, the Chinese authorities may disregard the legal form of a transaction and tax the transaction according to its economic substance.[4]

---

[1]   The total of RMB 10.637 billion represented approximately USD 1.668 billion at the USD/RMB exchange rate of 6.3763 as on 31 December, 2011 published by the Bank of China; see Bank of China, http://srh.bankofchina.com/search/whpj/search.jsp (accessed on 20 March, 2021).

[2]   Enterprise Income Tax Law (EIT Law) 2008, promulgated by the NPC on 16 March, 2007 with effect from 1 January, 2008.

[3]   Chapter 6 of the EIT Law.

[4]   Measures for the Administration of General Anti-Tax Avoidance (for Trial) (SAT Order 32), enacted by the SAT on 25 November, 2014 with effect from 1 February, 2015.

9.2.1 Transfer Pricing

The first transfer pricing rule was introduced as part of China's enterprise income tax law applicable to the foreign companies and foreign investment companies,[①] and was also introduced into the Tax Administration Law in 1993.[②] The current applicable transfer pricing rules are provided in the Article 36 of the Tax Administration Law, Articles 41-44 of the EIT Law and Articles 109-115 of the EIT Regulation. All transactions amongst associated parties should be subject to the assessment of the transfer pricing rules.

9.2.1.1 Associated parties

The associated parties subject to the transfer pricing rules in China shall include the taxpayers satisfying any of the following situations:

(1) the total direct or indirect shareholding by one party in the other, or by a common third party in both, exceeds 25%; in an indirect shareholding, if a party holds more than 25% of the shares in an intermediary, which in turn holds shares in a subsidiary, the full percentage of shareholding of the intermediary in the subsidiary is regarded as the shareholding percentage of the first party in the subsidiary. In the case of two natural persons who are spouses, relatives or siblings or because of custodianship or family maintenance are related to each other, and hold equity interests in the same enterprise, the percentages of the shares held by them should be aggregated in computing the related-party relationship;

(2) one party owns shares in another party or a common third party owns shares in both parties of less than 25%, but a loan granted by one party to the other constitutes 50% or more of the paid-in capital or one party guarantees 10% or more of the total debts of the other (loans or guarantees granted by independent financial institutions are excluded);

(3) one party owns shares in another party or a common third party

---

① Article 13 of the Income Tax Law for Foreign-Invested Enterprises and Foreign Enterprises (Tax Law in 1991).

② Article 24 of the Tax Administration Law.

owns shares in both parties of less than 25%, but the normal production and business operations of one party are only possible if patents, know-how, trademarks, copyrights or other intellectual property are provided by the other party;

(4) one party owns shares in another party or a common third party owns shares in both parties of less than 25%, but purchases, sales, receipt or provision of services, etc. of one party are controlled by the other party. "Control" means that one party may take decisions in respect of financial and business policies of the other party and derive benefits from the other party's business operations;

(5) more than half of the board members or the senior management (including the secretary of the board of directors, managers, deputy managers, financial controllers or other personnel prescribed by Articles of association of listed companies) of one party are appointed or assigned by the other party or concurrently serve as directors or senior management of the other party, or more than half of the directors or senior management of both parties are appointed or assigned by a common third party;

(6) two natural persons who are spouses, relatives by lineal consanguinity, siblings or because of custodianship or family maintenance are related to each other have one of the relationships described above under 1-5; and

(7) two parties effectively have common interests in other ways.

9.2.1.2 Arm's length principle

The "arm's length principle" is provided in both Chinese domestic laws and all Chinese DTAs as the principal approach to assess the pricing of associated parties. It is in principle to be decided in according to the price adopted by unrelated parties conducting business transactions based on fair transactional prices and normal business practices. However, Chinese tax authorities have criticized this principle too vague and requiring a process of locating an appropriate comparable which is too difficult in practice. For example, lack of appropriate comparable, quantification and allocation of location-specific advantages, and identification and valuation of intangibles. Therefore, in the UN Transfer Pricing Manual in 2013, Chinese tax authorities for the first time proposed some innovative measure in the chapter sharing Chinese practice,① especially the concept of "location-specific advantages" (LSAs) as a response to Chinese concern on Chinese affiliates having been under-compensated in the global value chain of the MNEs② and some factors of the LSAs in fact are quite in line with the value creation concept later proposed by the BEPS Actions 8-10 and the 2017 OECD Transfer Pricing Guidelines.③

The Chinese tax authorities have been putting efforts into investigating whether MNEs have allocated "reasonable profits" to China.④ Chinese domestic law, however, only provides a general approach to the arm's length principle and does not contain any specific rule as to how to identify and calculate the comparative advantages derived from China attributable to LSA factors. Consequently, significant uncertainty remains for taxpayers as to how much profit should be allocated to China to demonstrate that they have satisfied the request of the Chinese tax authorities to allocate "reasonable profits" to China.

This may also explain why certain deviations from the OECD approach are found in China's transfer pricing rules. For example, no preference is specified in relation to the transfer pricing methods to be applied, and methods such as the comparable uncontrolled price method, resale price method, cost-plus method, transactional net margin method and profit split method are all of the same importance when analyzing transfer pricing amongst asso-

① United Nations Practical Manual on Transfer Pricing, supran. 12.

② Yuesheng Jiang, Value Creation Theory of the BEPS Report and China's Reasonable Share in Global Value Allocation, *Intl. Transfer Pricing J.* 2015, Vol.22, No.4; Jinyan Li, China and BEPS: From Norm-Taker to Norm-Shaker, *Bull. Intl.Taxn.*, June/July 2015, IBFD; Brett A. Norwood, Location Savings and Other Location-Specific Advantages, *Asia-Pac. Tax Bull.*, September/October 2013, IBFD.

③ Jinyan Li and Stephen Ji, Location-Specific Advantages: A Rising Disruptive Factor in Transfer Pricing, *Bull. Intl.Taxn*, May 2017; Rafael TriginelliMiraglia, Mimi Wang and Cheng Chi, The New China Country Practice Chapter of the UN Practical Manual on Transfer Pricing: Reflections on Post-BEPS Transfer Pricing in the Middle-Kingdom, *Asia-Pac. Tax Bull.* 2017, Vol.23, No.4.

④ SAT, Jiangsu Provincial Office, 2016-2018 Compliance Plan on International Tax Administration (Suguoshuifa 〔2016〕 No 125), published on 30 May, 2016 with effect from the same day.

ciated enterprises. In addition, other methods, such as the cost method, market method and income method and so forth are also applicable, as long as they comply with the independent transaction principle.

2.1.3 9.Reporting obligation

Resident companies and non-resident companies having an establishment in China are required to submit, along with the annual enterprise income tax return, a report on related-party transactions if such companies are not taxed on a deemed profit basis. The contemporaneous documentation includes master file, local file and special issue file. Companies are required to prepare such documentation for each year and present it to the competent tax authorities at their request if the thresholds and other conditions for each file are fulfilled.

Furthermore, an ultimate holding company is required to submit a (Country-by-Country) report if its consolidated group revenue of the preceding year exceeds CNY 5.5 billion or it is nominated as the CbC report entity. Such a CbC report is intended to disclose the business operations, global income and the amount of taxes of all the group members. The Chinese tax authorities are authorized to exchange CbC reports with other tax jurisdictions according to the tax treaties or other agreements concluded by China.

9.2.1.4 Advance pricing agreement

The APA programme was introduced into Chinese legislation by the SAT in 1998 by issuance of the tax circular [1998] No. 59.[1] The background to the introduction of the APA programme was that the SAT wished to explore all of the potential approaches to counter transferring of profits by MNEs from China by way of misuse of transfer pricing methodologies.[2] As a result, the SAT, in Guoshuifa [1998] No. 59, briefly stated that an APA could be concluded with them by taxpayers as a way of resolving potential

---

[1]   Regulation on the Taxation of Transactions between Related Parties (Trial), Guoshuifa [1998] No. 59 was issued by the SAT on 23 April, 1998 and with effect from the same date. Guoshuifa [1998] No. 59 was replaced with effect on and after 30 April, 2006 by Guoshuifa [2004] No. 143.

[2]   B. Li, X. Liu, Comparison of the APAs in China, Japan and Korea, *Intl. Taxn. in China*, 2006, Vol.6, pp. 47-51.

transfer pricing disputes in advance. However, the SAT did not provide any procedural guidance as to how to conclude an APA. Consequently, the local tax authorities applied various criteria when they started to negotiate APAs with taxpayers in 1998 and the concluded APAs varied widely. In 2002, China's State Council formally encoded the APA programme into a law as Article 53 of the Implementation Regulations of Tax Administration Law.[①] There was, however, still no nationwide procedure for concluding an APA in China. For this reason, the SAT did not include the APAs concluded before 1 January, 2005 when it published its statistics regarding APAs concluded by China. The 113 concluded APAs that were referred to in Section 1. are, therefore, a statistic published by the SAT for the period from 1 January 2005 to 12 December, 2014.

From 1 January, 2005, all Chinese tax authorities have started to apply the same criteria and follow the same procedure in negotiating APAs according to the SAT's Guoshuifa [2004] No. 118.[②] In January 2008, the SAT replaced Guoshuifa [2004] No. 118 with Guoshuifa [2009] No. 2, which was entitled "Notice on Issuing the Measures for the Implementation of Special Tax Adjustments (Trial)". Guoshuifa [2009] No. 2 contained detailed procedures for concluding, implementing and monitoring APAs in China, and it is valid as of today. The APA procedure nowadays includes the pre-filing meeting, formal application, examination and evaluation, negotiation and signing the APA. Chinese law does not provide any statutory time limit for the completion of the APA process. Consequently, the time taken to negotiate and conclude APAs varies widely with Chinese tax authorities. More than 200 APAs have been concluded by China so far. Most of these APAs were

---

① The Implementation Regulations of the Administration of Tax Collection and Administration Law of the People's Republic of China), Guowuyuanling No. 362, which was promulgated by the State Council on 7 September, 2002 with effect from 15 October, 2002.

② The Implementation Rules on Advance Pricing Arrangements for Transactions between Related Parties (Trial Version)), Guoshuifa [2004] No. 118, which was enacted by the SAT on 3 September, 2004 with effect on and after the same date. Guoshuifa [2004] No. 118 was replaced by Notice on Issuing the Measures for the implementation of Special Tax Adjustments (Trial) (Guoshuifa [2009] No. 2) on 1 January, 2008.

unilateral APAs covering tangible-assets transactions, and the most commonly used transfer pricing method in these APAs was the transactional net margin method (TNMM). These features reflect the common features of the business operations of multinational enterprises (MNEs) in China, which have been mainly engaged in manufacturing and are not proactive in negotiating taxation agreements with the Chinese tax authorities.

9.2.2 Thin Capitalization

Thin capitalization rules were also introduced in China as Article 46 of the EIT Law of 2008. The Chinese thin capitalization rules only apply to interest paid to related parties and concern only the debt-to-equity ratio, i.e., that the ratio of the loan capital received from affiliated parties to the equity capital received from affiliated parties in an enterprise is in excess of a stipulated criterion. This debt-to-equity ratio is 5 : 1 for a financial enterprise and 2 : 1 for any other type of enterprise.[①] The debt herein refers to the finance obtained from an associated party including:

(1)financing (investment) provided by the related party through a third party;

(2)financing (investment) provided by a third party but guaranteed and pledged with collateral liability by the related party; or

(3)any other financing (investment) indirectly made by the related party with the substance of debt.

If the debt-to-equity ratio of an enterprise exceeds the prescribed ratios, taxpayers are not allowed to deduct interest expenses relating to excess loan capital received from affiliated parties when computing the taxable income of that enterprise. Such non-deductible interest may not be carried over to the following years and is re-characterized as dividends and subject to income tax. If any tax paid in this regard exceeds the tax due on the deemed dividends, the overpaid tax amount is not refunded.

---

①　EIT Regulation, Art. 119.

9.2.3 CFC

The CFC rules were for the first time introduced into China in 2008 as Article 45 the EIT Law. The Chinese CFC rules provide that, where an enterprise is located in a tax jurisdiction where the actual tax burden is clearly lower than the normal 25 per cent enterprise income tax rate, and the enterprise is controlled by one or more Chinese resident enterprises or jointly by Chinese resident enterprise(s) and individual(s), the profits of the enterprise that are not distributed or are insufficiently distributed without reasonable business needs shall be included in the income of the current period of the controlling Chinese resident enterprise(s), to the extent that those profits are attributable to the Chinese controlling enterprise(s).

The key provisions in these rules include the following factors:

(1)Effective control

The meaning of "control" is defined as effective control in terms of shareholding, financing, business operations, purchases and sales. The control in terms of shareholding refers to the cases where a resident shareholder, either directly or indirectly:

①direct or indirect participation in a foreign company exceeds 10% or more of share capital or share capital with voting rights of the foreign company;

②direct or indirect participation in a foreign company is increased from less than 10% to 10% or more; and

③direct or indirect participation in a foreign company is decreased from 10% or more to less than 10%.

(2)Actual tax burden

The term that "the actual tax burden is clearly lower than normal 25 per cent enterprise income tax rate", which refers to a situation where the actual tax burden is more than 50 per cent lower than the normal 25 per cent enterprise income tax rate.[①]

---

① See EIT Regulation, Art. 118.

However, there are certain jurisdictions are treated as the white-listed jurisdictions where the SAT in 2009 announced not to apply the CFC rule if CFCs are incorporated in these jurisdictions. These jurisdictions include Australia, Canada, France, Germany, India, Italy, Japan, New Zealand, Norway, South Africa, the United Kingdom and the United States.[①]

(3) Deemed distribution

The income to be included in the taxable income of the resident shareholder shall be calculated as follows:

> Income of a Chinese resident corporation shareholder in the current period=(The deemed dividends×Number of days of the shareholding/number of days comprising a controlled company's tax year)×The proportion of the shareholding

(4) Exceptions

The Chinese CFC rules do not apply to CFCs:

① that are located in the white-listed jurisdictions;

② that are mainly engaged in active business operations; or

③ whose annual profits do not exceed CNY 5 million.

The participation and income must be calculated in accordance with the Chinese accounting rules, and the form must be filed together with the annual corporate income tax return.

9.2.4 GAAR

China introduced the general anti-avoidance rule (GAAR) as Article 47 of the EIT Law coming into force in 2008, providing that "where an enterprise makes any other arrangement not having a reasonable business purpose and leading to a decrease of its taxable income or tax liabilities, the tax authorities shall have the power to make an adjustment through a reasonable method". Then Articles 120 and 123 of the EIT Regulation defines the

---

① SAT, Notice on Simplifying Procedures for Identifying the Effective Tax Rate of the Jurisdictions Where the Foreign Controlled Company Is Incorporated, Guoshuihan [2009] No. 37 (issued on 21 January, 2009).

phrase "not having a reasonable business purpose" as "having as the main purpose to reduce, exempt, or defer the payment of taxes" and provided that statute of limitations for Chinese tax authorities applying the GAAR is ten years starting from the time the transaction takes place.

9.2.4.1 Transactions subject to GAAR

The transactions subject to the GAAR must satisfy the following two objective elements:

(1) A transaction exists and must be the entire arrangement or a part of the arrangements planned by a natural person.

Chinese tax law has no definition of what a "transaction" is; therefore, the transaction referred to in the Guidance could be the whole arrangement or a part of a series of activities or arrangements. It could be one action mutually agreed upon by all the parties involved (for instance, a share transfer transaction between the buyer and the seller); it could also be a one-sided action (for example, an enterprise distributing dividends to its investors).

(2) The taxpayer must have obtained "tax benefits" from carrying out such a transaction.

The term tax benefits herein refers to the "decrease of taxable income or tax liabilities" in Article 47 of the EIT Law, and Article 120 of the EIT Regulation further defines tax benefits also "reduce, exempt or defer the payment of taxes". The SAT did not clarify in the Guidance what the tax benefits obtained in a tax avoidance transaction are. In addition, the transaction should also satisfy one subjective element, which is to obtain tax benefits is the main purpose of the taxpayer in carrying out the transaction.

There are four specific scenarios and one general scenario under which Chinese tax authorities can initiate a GAAR investigation. The four specific scenarios are: (1) abuse of tax incentives; (2) abuse of a tax treaty; (3) abuse of the legal form of a company; and (4) avoidance of tax by using tax havens. The general scenario is "other arrangements having no reasonable business purposes".

Chinese tax authorities must apply the substance over form principle when investigating avoidance transactions, but the burden of proof is on the taxpayer. There are six reference factors that should be considered when assessing whether a tax avoidance arrangement exists: (1) the form and substance of the arrangement; (2) the conclusion time and execution period of the arrangement; (3) the implementation method of the arrangement; (4) relationship between each step or part of the arrangement; (5) the changes in the financial performance of each party involved in the arrangement; and (6) the tax consequences of the arrangement.

9.2.4.2 Adjustment measures

The burden of proof is on the taxpayer when the tax authorities challenge a transaction on tax avoidance grounds. The taxpayer must prove that its transaction has a reasonable business purpose and, most importantly, that its main purpose was not to obtain tax benefits. And it is up to the Chinese tax authorities to accept or reject such proof on a case-by-case basis. China's tax law has no "safe harbour" for transactions which could be excluded from being challenged on tax avoidance grounds.

Article 47 of the EIT Law provides that "the tax authorities have the power to make an adjustment through a reasonable method" when finding a transaction a tax avoidance arrangement. In terms of the "reasonable method" for adjustment, Method 28 provides that the tax authorities may use any of the following three methods:

(1) re-characterizing the taxpayer's business arrangements based on economic substance;

(2) disregarding the legal status of the company; and/or

(3) denying the tax benefits obtained from the tax avoidance arrangement.

It is clear that these adjustment methods should be closely related to the tax benefits obtained by the taxpayer in the tax avoidance transaction. Adjustment of the tax liability is a process of finding an alternative transaction model to replace the original one. There can be many alternative models, and these models could result in different tax benefits for the taxpayer.

Chinese law does not specify which alternative should be given priority, so the discretion to apply an alternative method lies with the tax authorities. Some Chinese academics are of the opinion that the alternative method should be the one which would bring the largest tax benefits to the taxpayer, given that the taxpayer under the EIT Law is usually an enterprise which aims to maximize its after-tax profits. They suggest the tax authorities focus on the "economic substance" and apply an alternative model by standing in the shoes of the taxpayer.

The penalty resulting from application of the GAAR in China takes the form of increased interest, which is imposed at a rate of 500 basis points above the benchmark lending interest rate published by the People's Bank of China for the year in which the tax payment is due. Chinese law does not specify whether a corresponding adjustment is possible when application of the GAAR in China would change the tax costs of the taxpayer in a cross-border transaction.

9.2.4.3 Indirect shares transfer

One notable measure is that the Chinese tax authorities have strengthened the application of GAAR in recent years, in particular on indirect share transfer arrangements.

Indirect shares transfer, in the view of Chinese tax authorities, is a type of tax avoidance arrangement where non-Chinese tax residents indirectly transfer the shares of Chinese resident enterprises through arrangements, such as an abuse of the organization form incorporated outside of China, for the purpose of avoiding to pay taxes in China. The key test that Chinese tax authorities apply to these shares transfers is the "reasonable business purpose" test provided by the Chinese general anti-avoidance rule (GAAR), to which the burden of proof is on the non-Chinese tax residents. If the "reasonable business purpose" cannot be proved, Chinese tax authorities may deny the existence of the offshore middle companies, and re-characterize the shares transfer in accordance with its economic substance. The result usually is that the non-Chinese tax resident is taxed in China for the gains derived from the shares transfer. Since 2009, the SAT has issued several circulars in an attempt to guide taxpayers as to what circumstances would be deemed to have "no reasonable business purpose": for instance, whether the transaction is an artificial scheme with a primary purpose of obtaining tax benefits, whether 75 per cent or more of the value of the shares in the foreign target company is derived, directly or indirectly, from Chinese taxable assets, whether 90 per cent or more of the income of the foreign target company is derived from investments in China at any time within one year prior to the indirect transfer, and so forth.① It is, however, not possible for the SAT to list all relevant circumstances. Consequently, as long as the sole test with regard to such offshore indirect shares transfer is subjective, i.e., the business purpose of the seller, uncertainty will remain in carrying out such transfers.

9.3   Anti-treaty Abuse Measures

All of the Chinese DTAs have a purpose of prevention of fiscal evasion. The exchange of information provisions in the Chinese DTAs is a method for the competent authorities of China and the Contracting States to obtain the foreseeable relevant information. In the meanwhile, the DTAs have provided certain additional provisions for anti-treaty abuse purpose.

9.3.1 Beneficial Ownership

All Chinese DTAs are using the term of "beneficial owner" when ensuring the treaty benefits in respect of dividends, interest and royalties shall not be abused. A "beneficial owner" is referred to as a person who is in pos-

---

① SAT, Notice on Issuing the Measures for the Implementation of Special Tax Adjustments (Trial)(Guoshuifa 〔2009〕 No. 2), issued by the SAT on 8 January, 2009 but with retrospective effect from 1 January, 2008; SAT, Circular of the State Administration of Taxation on Strengthening the Administration of Enterprise Income Tax on Incomes from Non-resident Enterprises' Equity Transfers(Guoshuihan 〔2009〕 No. 698), enacted on 10 December, 2009 but with retrospective effect from 1 January, 2008; SAT, Notice on Several Issues on Administration of Non-residents Income Taxes (Notice 24〔2011〕), enacted by the SAT on 28 March, 2011 with effect from 1 April, 2011; SAT, Announcement on Several Issues Concerning the Enterprise Income Tax on Income from the Indirect Transfer of Assets by Non-resident Enterprises (Announcement No. 7 〔2015〕), enacted by the SAT on 3 February, 2015 with effect from the same date.

session, and has the power to dispose, of the income or the rights and assets from which the income is derived. A beneficial owner is generally supposed to carry on a substantial business and may be an individual, a company or any other organization. An agent or a conduit company may not be regarded a beneficial owner.

Given that there is no definition of the term "beneficial owner", the SAT issued a number of circulars for the purpose of interpreting and implementing the DTAs.[①] In general, beneficial ownership must be determined for each transaction on the basis of factors and factual circumstances. But the following occurrences may be treated as the factors determining for a beneficial owners:

(1)The recipient has the obligation to pass on more than 50% of the received payments to a resident of a third country (or region) within 12 months. "Obligation" means contractual obligation and de facto obligation;

(2) activities conducted by the recipient do not constitute substantial business activities. Substantial business activities include substantial manufacturing, sales and management activities. Substance must be determined by reference to functions performed and risks assumed, e.g. equity holding may be regarded as a substantial business activity;

(3)the income of the recipient is not subject to tax, is exempt from tax or is taxed at a very low effective tax rate in the jurisdiction in which the recipient resides;

(4)in the case of interest income, in addition to the loan agreement from which the interest income is derived, there are other similar (in terms of amount, interest rate and time) loan or deposit agreements with a third party; and

---

① SAT, Notice on Administration Method for Non-residents to Benefit from Tax Treaties (Circular 124 〔2009〕), with effect from 1 October, 2009; SAT, Notice of the State Administration of Taxation on How to Understand and Determine the "Beneficial Owners" in Tax Treaties (Circular 601 〔2009〕), with effect from 27 October 2009; SAT, Bulletin on the Recognition of Beneficial Owners in Tax Treaties (Notice 〔2012〕), with effect from 29 June, 2012; SAT, Supplementary Rules on "Beneficial Owners" (Notice 24 〔2014〕, with effect from 1 June, 2014.

(5)in the case of royalty income, in addition to the contracts on copyright, patent and know-how in respect of which the royalties arise, there are other contracts on copyright, patents and know-how with a third party.

At the same time, there are certain safe harbors where the recipients are to be considered as a beneficial owner without any need for a test:

(1)the government of a tax treaty jurisdiction;

(2)a resident company listed in the tax treaty jurisdiction;

(3)an individual resident in the tax treaty jurisdiction; and

(4)a direct or indirect 100% owned subsidiary of the above (in the case of indirect shareholding, the intermediate company must be a resident of China or the recipient's jurisdiction).

9.3.2 Principal Purpose Test (PPT)

Some Chinese DTAs have provided with a purpose test provision in the distributive rules for dividends, interest and royalties. For example, Article 10(6) of the China-Singapore Tax Treaty (2007) provides that "the provisions of this Article shall not apply if it was the main purpose of any person concerned with the creation or assignment of the shares or other rights in respect of which the dividend is paid to take advantage of this Article by means of that creation or assignment."

Clearly, this Article is an anti-abuse clause, and the preferential provisions in the dividend clauses of tax agreements shall not apply to the transactions or arrangements of which the main purpose is to obtain favorable tax status. Where a taxpayer improperly enjoys the treatment in the DTA due to such transaction or arrangement, the competent tax authority shall have the right to make adjustment. In the implementation of this Article, the relevant provisions on special tax adjustments in the domestic laws of China shall be considered. The same anti-abuse clauses are provided in Articles 11 and 12 of the China-Singapore Tax Treaty (2007) respectively for interest and royalties.

9.3.3 Application of Domestic Anti-tax Avoidance Measures

Some Chinese DTAs have an article named the "miscellaneous rule", which generally provides that the domestic anti-tax avoidance laws and regulations of the Contracting States shall not be affected by the DTA. For example, Article 26 of the China-Singapore Tax Treaty (2007) provides that "nothing in this Agreement shall prejudice the right of each Contracting State to apply its domestic laws and measures concerning the prevention of tax avoidance, whether or not described as such, insofar as they do not give rise to taxation contrary to the Agreement." Accordingly, both Contracting States may implement their domestic anti-tax avoidance rules when application and interpretation of these Chinese DTAs. The SAARs and GAAR which are described above in this chapter shall be applicable when China implementing and interpreting these Chinese DTAs.

9.4   Implementation of the BEPS Project

China, despite not being an OECD member country, has been actively involved in the BEPS(Base Erosion and Profit Shifting) project launched. For instance, China was nominated as an "associate" with the same standing as the OECD member countries with regard to the discussions on the BEPS initiatives, and China also held the vice-chair of the Ad Hoc Group for developing multilateral instruments. The SAT, being the highest level Chinese tax authority, has played a key role in China's involvement in the BEPS project, including (but not being limited to) attendance at the various meetings and conferences on behalf of China regarding the BEPS project, enactment of new tax measures, instruction and supervision of local tax authorities in China in undertaking anti-tax avoidance measures, and addition of new anti-treaty abuse provisions to tax treaties when negotiating bilateral tax treaties and multilateral agreements. China's active role in BEPS project is due to the fact that China has over a long period suffered from tax avoidance arrangements, in particular transfer pricing, treaty abuse and offshore indirect transfers of shares. Especially since 2008, when China abolished its foreign-oriented tax incentive policies in the form of tax holidays, reduced tax rates and tax exemptions, many multinational enterprises (MNEs) have entered into tax avoidance arrangements more aggressively for the purpose of shifting their profits out of China.

9.4.1 Implementing the Four Minimum Standards

China has taken actions in compliance with all four minimum standards under the BEPS project's Inclusive Framework, namely Action 5 (Countering Harmful Tax Practices), Action 6 (Prevention of Treaty Benefits in Inappropriate Circumstances), Action 13 (Transfer Pricing Documentation and Country-by-Country Reporting) and Action 14 (More Effective Dispute Resolution Mechanisms).

9.4.1.1 Compliance with Action 5

Harmful tax practices under Action 5 were no longer concerns for China, even before the BEPS project was launched. From as early as 1 January 2008, China had already abolished all foreign-oriented tax incentive measures which may be interpreted as harmful tax practices as defined in the 1998 OECD report (OECD, 1998).[①] Nowadays all Chinese tax resident enterprises, whether foreign-invested or domestically-owned, are subject to the same income tax at a standard tax rate of 25 per cent, with a few tax incentives designed for certain industry sectors or rural areas rather than for attracting geographically-mobile activities. Industry sectors benefiting from these tax incentives are agriculture, forestry and fishery industries, public

---

① Prior to 1 January, 2008, China provided tremendous tax incentives to attract foreign investment, including but not limited to tax holidays, lower income tax rates, accelerated depreciation, and refunds of tax paid when reinvestment took place. Chinese domestic investment however barely received any tax incentive. When its new EITL Law came into force on 1 January, 2008, China abolished all these foreign-oriented incentives.

infrastructure projects, environmental protection projects, energy and water saving projects, etc. These tax incentives are also clearly provided through tax laws and the process for taxpayers to become entitled to these incentives is transparent too, as China has so far does not provided any advance rulings to taxpayers.

In 2015, the OECD Forum in fact placed China's tax incentives provided to high-tech enterprises under review, as such tax incentives in the form of lower tax rates, additional deductions and tax exemptions applied to all income of qualified high-tech enterprises, rather than solely to their intellectual property-related income. The Forum in the first three peer reviews respectively in May 2015, November 2016 and March 2017 decided that these tax incentives did not satisfy the nexus approach for intellectual property tax incentives, but it subsequently changed its decision after the SAT proved that the criteria for enterprises to qualify as high-tech enterprises eligible for these tax incentives are of a more comprehensive nature and of a higher threshold than needed under the nexus approach, and also that a finding of qualification should be reviewed and approved by the Ministry of Science and the SAT for each high-tech enterprise on a case by case basis. Thus, the Forum finally decided in May 2017 that China's tax incentives to high-tech enterprises are "not harmful".[1]

9.4.1.2 Compliance with Action 6

Countering treaty abuse under Action 6 is in line with Chinese tax authorities' practice. Given that China has a large treaty network which by the end of May 2018 already consisted of 106 bilateral tax treaties, treaty-shopping issues exist in both inbound investment into China and Chinese outbound investment.[2] In order to counter treaty abuse, the SAT has issued circulars narrowing down the scope of eligible "beneficial ownership" and

---

[1] SAT, Report on the development of rule of law by the State Administration of Taxation in 2017 (27 April, 2018), http://www. chinatax. gov. cn/n810214/n2897183/c3427202/content.html (accessed on 30 March, 2021).

[2] Dongmei Qiu, Collecting Unpaid Tax Offshore: Caribbean Tax Havens and Foreign Direct Investment in China, *Bulletin for International Taxation*, Vol.68, No.12.

has also extended the list of the documentation which taxpayers must provide for the purpose of benefiting from treaty entitlement.①

The SAT has also added anti-avoidance provisions into some newly concluded bilateral tax treaties. For instance, the Belgium-China Income Tax
Treaty (2009) clearly provides that the application of the domestic anti-tax
avoidance rules of Belgium or China should not be overridden by the tax
treaty.② In 2015, for the first time, China included both a principal purpose
test (PPT) clause and a limitation on benefits (LOB) clause into one of its
bilateral tax treaties, namely the Chile-China Income Tax Treaty.③The LOB
clause provides that the entitlement to treaty benefits should be solely to
"qualified persons" while the PPT clause requires consideration of taxpayers'
principal purpose in conducting transactions.④ In addition, the Chile-China
Income Tax Treaty (2015) in the preamble paragraph also states that the
purpose of the tax treaty includes the prevention of double non-taxation.⑤
China and Chile included such multiple anti-treaty abuse provisions into their
tax treaty in part due to the influence of Action 6 (OECD, 2015), and due to
the fact that a low withholding tax rate (only 4 per cent) is provided in this
treaty in respect of interest derived from loans granted by banks, insurance

---

① SAT, Administrative Method for Non-Tax Residents to Benefit from Tax Treaties
(Announcement No. 60 [2015]), issued on 27 August, 2015 with effect from that date.

② Article 23 of the Agreement between the Government of the Kingdom of Belgium
and the Government of the People's Republic of China for the Avoidance of Double Taxation and the Prevention of Fiscal Evasion with Respect to Taxes on Income, signed on 7
October, 2009.

③ Agreement between the Government of the People's Republic of China and the
Government of the Republic of Chile for the Elimination of Double Taxation and the Pre-
vention of Tax Evasion and Avoidance with Respect to Taxes on Income, signed on 25
May, 2015.

④ Article 26(5) of the Chile-PRC Income Tax Treaty.

⑤ The preamble to the Chile-PRC Income Tax Treaty (2015) states that the tax
treaty should not give rise to "opportunities for non-taxation or reduced taxation through
tax evasion or avoidance (including through treaty-shopping arrangements aimed at obtaining reliefs provided in this Agreement for the indirect benefit of residents of third
States)".

companies and other financial institutions, which is much lower than the tax rate suggested by the OECD Model Convention or UN Model Convention (10 per cent). Thus, the Contracting States inevitably have greater concerns in this case about treaty abuse.

9.4.1.3 Compliance with Action 13

China signed the Multilateral Competent Authority Agreement for the Automatic Exchange of Country-by-Country (CbC) Reports in May 2016; [1] and the SAT introduced the CbC reporting regime into China in July 2016 through issuing Bulletin [2016] No. 42, [2] which sets out certain requirements for taxpayers to maintain and submit contemporaneous transfer pricing documentation including a master file, local file and special issues file. This CbC reporting regime can help Chinese tax authorities to assess the data about the whole picture of MNEs' business activities around the world as well as the value chain (including the location specific advantage factors) in China, which Chinese tax authorities previously had very great difficulty assessing. Concerns on the part of MNEs include the cost for preparing and submitting the CbC reports and how the tax authorities (both of China and of other countries) will use these reports.

The definition of "associated enterprises" China adopts under the CbC reporting regime is broad, taking into account factors in shareholding control, loan control, franchise control, procurement, sales and acceptance of services control, personnel control and all other common interests. This CbC reporting regime also covers a broad range of transactions amongst associated enterprises, including financial asset transfers, intangible asset transactions, service transactions, and includes cash pooling in financing transactions, etc. MNEs in China having total consolidated revenue of more than RMB 5.5 billion must file CbC reports with Chinese tax authorities contai-

---

[1] SAT, Bulletin on the 10th Tax Administration Forum, Beijing, 13 May 2016, www.chinatax.gov.cn/n810219/n810744/n2128547/n2128559/c2140587/content.html (accessed on 20 March, 2020).

[2] SAT, Bulletin on Refining the Filing of Related Party Transactions and Administration of Contemporaneous Transfer Pricing Documentation (SAT Bulletin [2016] No. 42).

ning details of their overall operations and information regarding transaction-swith affiliates, the restructuring of business or functions, the MNEs' value chains and, in particular, the location specific advantage factors that the MNEs have taken into account in locating profits in China. For example, where an enterprise engages in a single manufacturing business such as processing-on order, processing of imported materials etc. for its overseas related parties, or engages in distribution, contracted research and development business, Chinese tax authorities request that such an enterprise in principle maintains a reasonable profit level in China. Where such an enterprise incurs losses, regardless of whether it attains the standards for preparation of contemporaneous documentation, it still needs to prepare local files for contemporaneous documentation with respect to the loss-making year. Chinese tax authorities then focus on examination of the local files of the enterprise in question, and strengthen monitoring and administration.

This CbC reporting regime also provides MNEs with a self-assessment opportunity. The SAT in Bulletin [2016] No. 42 listed nine risk indicators for tax audits, including where an MNE's business involves: (1) related-party transactions in large transaction amounts, or varied types of related-party transactions; (2) incurring of long-term losses, low profits or non-linear profits; (3) profit lower than the industry's level; (4) a profit level that does not match the functional risks borne, or earnings shared which do not match the costs shared; (5) carrying out of related-party transactions where the related parties are located in low tax countries (regions); (6) failure to declare related-party transactions or prepare contemporaneous documentation pursuant to the provisions; (7) ratios of debt investments and equity investments accepted from related parties which exceed the stipulated standards; (8) a group structure containing an enterprise controlled by a resident enterprise or by a resident enterprise and a Chinese resident which is established in a country (region) with an actual tax burden lower than 12.5 per cent which does not distribute profit or reduces profit distribution and such non-distribution or reduced distribution is not due to reasonable business needs; and finally (9) implementation of other tax planning or arrangements which do not have a reasonable business objective. These risk indicators may assist MNEs in self-assessing their risk as well as in providing simplicity and certainty to both the MNEs and Chinese tax authorities.

9.4.1.4 Compliance with Action 14

Action 14 addresses concerns which the Chinese government also holds. A great numb of tax disputes arose following the Chinese tax authorities' strengthening of enforcement of anti-tax avoidance measures and the increase in Chinese outbound investment. However, China's bilateral tax treaties all provide only for the mutual agreement procedures (MAPs), without any mediation or arbitration options. Given that the MAPs are inefficient for resolving tax disputes between Contracting States, Chinese residents are encountering a substantial risk of double taxation. China's approach is to enhance the MAP process through provision of a more detailed indication of the procedure for taxpayers when filing MAP applications involving treaty-related disputes[1] or transfer pricing related disputes.[2] The challenge however is that the SAT has very limited human resources to handle the MAPs at this point in time. Given China's refusal to adopt the arbitration option under the MLI,[3] it is likely that the SAT will have to increase its MAP team staffing levels for the purpose of increasing the efficiency of resolution of disputes.

9.4.2 Implementing Other BEPS Measures

9.4.2.1 Response to Action 1

Determining how to tax digital economy is a major challenge for the Chinese government, so by the end of May 2018, Chinese government had not enacted any new income tax measures in this area. With regard to value

---

[1] SAT, Implementation Method of the Mutual Agreement Procedure in Tax Treaties (Gong Gao [2013] No. 56), issued by the SAT on 24 September, 2013 with effect from 1 November, 2013.

[2] SAT, Bulletin on Administrative Measures for Special Tax Investigations and Adjustments and the Mutual Agreement Procedure (SAT Bulletin [2017] No. 6).

[3] OECD, People's Republic of China-Status of List of Reservations and Notifications at the Time of Signature, http://www.oecd.org/tax/treaties/beps-mli-position-china.pdf (accessed on 20 March, 2021).

added tax (VAT), China has already included electronic commerce activities within the taxable scope of VAT, but the challenge remains as to how to collect the VAT due from business-to-customer (B2C) suppliers. With regard to income tax, despite the fact that non-Chinese residents are subject to tax in China in respect of the income sourced in China, China's domestic laws do not contain a source rule with regard to the digital economy. However, China will need to reform its tax system and/or tax treaties to deal with digital economy activities, as China on the one hand is one of the largest consumption markets for digital products and services, on the other hand, many Chinese MNEs engage in electronic commerce throughout the world.

9.4.2.2 Response to Action 2

Not applicable in China, as Chinese company laws do not allow hybrid mismatch arrangements.

9.4.2.3 Response to Action 3

When compared with the suggestions in Action 3, the Chinese CFC rules may be found to have been drafted in a very limited and ambiguous way. First, the "control test" in China's CFC rules mainly addresses shareholding control, as management control is only for supplementary purposes;[①]second, although an exemption is provided with respect to the profits derived from an "active business operation", the law has not defined what constitutes such an active business operation; third, only CFCs in a form of corporations are subject to the rules, while the look-through entities and permanent establishments are not covered; fourth, in order to reduce the tax administrative burden and taxpayer compliance costs and increase certainty,

---

①   See EIT Regulation, Art. 117.The term "controlled by one or more Chinese resident enterprises or jointly by Chinese resident enterprise(s) and individual(s)" refers to two circumstances: (i) more than 10 per cent of the equity with voting rights of a foreign enterprise is directly or indirectly held by each such Chinese resident enterprise or individual and more than 50 per cent of the equity is held by all Chinese resident enterprise(s) and individual(s) jointly; (ii) with respect to equity, capital, business management, sale or purchase, a foreign enterprise is effectively controlled by one or more Chinese resident enterprises or jointly by Chinese resident enterprise(s) and individual(s), where the equity holding ratios in (i) are not reached.

the SAT issued a "white list" carve out of some high-tax jurisdictions (as determined by the SAT) from the application of the CFC rules.① However, after almost ten years so far, this list has never been updated and some jurisdictions can no longer be considered high-tax jurisdictions.② The Chinese government has not amended these defects yet, but they are becoming concerns to the Chinese government with the rapid increase in Chinese outbound investment.

9.4.2.4 Response to Action 4

No change yet as of March 2021.

9.4.2.5 Response to Action 7

China has reserved its right in the MLI not to apply the permanent establishment (PE) provisions.

9.4.2.6 Response to Actions 8-10

The BEPS project has influenced China in enacting transfer pricing rules as well as conducting tax adjustments. The SAT has issued Bulletin [2017] No.6③ which reflects the result of the BEPS report that "the place where profit and economic activities occur matches the place of value creation", and also reshapes China's transfer pricing rules on "location-specific advantages" (LSAs) and intra-group services. This is most significant with regard to assessing the value of, and payments arising from, intangibles, as follows:

(1) First, the Bulletin extends the definition of intangibles in China to include both application intangibles (e.g., local efforts to make technological improvements to the production process) and marketing intangibles (related to local marketing activities) which are treated as intangibles for tax purposes.

---

① These jurisdictions include the US, the UK, France, Germany, Japan, Italy, Canada, Australia, India, South Africa and Norway; see the Circular on Simplified Determination of Actual Tax Burden of Foreign Enterprises Controlled by Chinese Resident Shareholders (Guoshuihan [2009] No. 37).

② Li (2014).

③ SAT, Bulletin on Administrative Measures for Special Tax Investigations and Adjustments and the Mutual Agreement Procedure (Bulletin [2017] No.6), issued in March 2017.

(2)Second, it clarifies that legal ownership of intangibles alone no longer determines entitlement to a return on the intangible, and thus having legal ownership alone of intangibles is not accepted as giving rise to a right to all (or indeed any) of the return that is generated by the exploitation of the intangibles. In order to assess the value of the intangible, a full analysis must be conducted of the global operational process of the enterprise's group, that fully considers the value contribution of each party to the development, value increase, maintenance, protection, application and promotion of the intangible assets, and methods for realization of the value of the intangible assets, as well as the interaction between the intangible assets and the functions, risks and assets of other businesses within the group. For those enterprises owning only the intangible assets but not contributing to the value of the intangible assets, they are not allowed to participate in profit distribution of the intangible assets; and for those enterprises only providing funding in the process of formation and use of the intangible assets but not actually performing the relevant functions and bearing the corresponding risks, they are allowed to receive only a reasonable return on the cost of capital. In other words, royalties payments must match the economic benefits brought by the intangible assets to the payer.

(3)Third, it affirms again that LSAs in China are considered by the Chinese tax authorities as being amongst those most important elements in the value creation chain. This is in accordance with China's consistently maintained position that MNEs must allocate to China "reasonable profits" reflecting their LSAs generating benefits from China, a position which China has taken steps to ensure is expressly stated in the UN Transfer Pricing Manual of both the 2013 first edition and the 2017 second edition.[1] Tax audits in recent years have particularly paid attention to the question of whether MNEs have attributed such "reasonable profits" to China when their Chinese subsidiaries have paid their foreign affiliates in respect of interest, serv-

---

① United Nations (2013); and theUnited Nations Practical Manual on Transfer Pricing for Developing Countries (2017)

ice charges, management and technical fees, and royalties.[①]One further important but still outstanding issue is then how to determine whether the profits being allocated to China are reasonable and sufficient to reflect the LSA factors. Chinese laws have not provided any apportionment formula or safe harbor for this issue, and thus significant uncertainty remains for both Chinese tax authorities and taxpayers in practice. Thus, the challenge China is facing at this point in time is how to provide simplicity and certainty when applying the transfer pricing rules.

9.4.2.7 Response to Action 11

This is an OECD measure, not for country implementation.

9.4.2.8 Response to Action 12

A mandatory disclosure regime is still not imposed on tax advisors in China at present, although there is no constraint under Chinese constitutional laws on introducing such a regime. In May 2017, the SAT issued a circular specifying that all tax advisors, and tax planning and filing agents must register with tax authorities and also receive supervision from China's Tax Agent Association;[②] however, this circular nevertheless did not impose any disclosure obligation on tax advisors and agents.

9.4.2.9 Response to Action 15

The SAT signed the Multilateral Convention to Implement Tax Treaty Related Measures to Prevent Base Erosion and Profit Shifting (MLI) on 7 June 2017. The MLI is currently under the ratification process in China. Upon the MLI coming into force in China, the 102 bilateral DTAs will be modified by matching with the positions and reservations of the corresponding signatories. Clearly, China needs the MLI to amend its DTAs with Contracting States. It is obviously infeasible for China to negotiate individually with

---

① SAT, Notice on Conducting Anti-tax Avoidance Investigation on Excessive Payment to Abroad (Circular 146 [2014]), issued by the SAT on 29 July, 2014; SAT, Announcement on Issues concerning Enterprise Income Tax on Expenses Paid by Enterprises to Their Overseas Affiliates (Announcement No. 16 [2015]), enacted by the SAT on 18 March, 2015.

② Bulletin [2017] No.13, Supervision Method on Tax Related Professional Service (Trial), issued by the SAT on 5 May, 2017 and entering into force on 1 September, 2017.

its more than 100 contracting jurisdictions to amend each of their bilateral DTAs respectively.

The SAT included 102 of the total of 107 Chinese tax treaties, which were concluded before 7 June, 2017,[①] in the provisional list of China's Covered Tax Agreements. The five bilateral tax treaties that were not included in the list of the Covered Tax Agreements are as follows:

- China-India Tax Treaty (signed in 1994);
- China-Chile Tax Treaty (signed in 2015);[②]
- Chinese Mainland-Macao Special Administrative Region (SAR) Tax Arrangement (signed in 2003);
- Chinese Mainland-Hong Kong SAR Tax Arrangement (signed in 2006); and
- Chinese Mainland-Taiwan Tax Cooperation Agreement (signed in 2015).

China made the following positions and reservations in its Status of List of Reservations and Notifications ("the Notice") at the time of signature of the MLI. It opted into eight MLI articles, opted out of six articles and did not choose the optional articles for the exemption methods and mandatory arbitration.

Upon the MLI coming into force in China, the Covered Tax Agreements will be modified according to the matching of the positions and reservations made by China and the other Contracting States. Once they change the Covered Tax Agreements, the opt-in articles may in practice significant-

---

① The list of these 102 Covered Tax Agreements is slightly different from the tax treaties list shown on the SAT's website (see http://www.chinatax.gov.cn/n810341/n810770/index.html). The two differences are: (i) China signed two tax treaties with Romania, in 1991 and 2016, respectively, which are listed as two treaties in the list of the 102 Covered Tax Agreements, but are counted as one on the list shown on the SAT's website; and (ii) the tax treaty with Yugoslavia is listed as two treaties (one applicable to Montenegro and the other applicable to Serbia) in the list of the 102 Covered Tax Agreements, while it is counted as one on the list shown on the SAT's website.

② The Agreement between the Government of the People's Republic of China and the Government of the Republic of Chile for the Elimination of Double Taxation and the Prevention of Tax Evasion and Avoidance with Respect to Taxes on Income (25 May, 2015).

ly increase the discretionary power of the tax authorities.

China has opted into all three MLI articles that reflect the minimum standards of BEPS Actions 6 and 14. These articles consist of:

(1)Article 6 (Purpose of a Covered Tax Agreement), reflecting the Action 6 minimum standard that Contracting States should include in their tax treaties an express statement that the common intention of the parties to the treaty is to eliminate double taxation without creating opportunities for non-taxation or reduced taxation through tax evasion or avoidance, including through treaty shopping arrangements;

(2) Article 7 (Prevention of Treaty Abuse), reflecting the Action 6 minimum standard of choosing the PPT; and

(3)Article 16 (Mutual Agreement Procedure), reflecting the Action 14 requirement to improve the efficiency of its mutual agreement procedure (MAP) with other Contracting States.

These opt-in actions may demonstrate China's determination to implement the BEPS measures. At the same time, the reason could also be that China is a member of the Inclusive Framework, and is subject to the monitoring mechanism to review its compliance with the BEPS minimum standards.

China also opted into some other measures in the MLI, for example, Article 4 (Dual Resident Entities), at the same time, it chose not to adopt certain other measures, for example, Part IV-Avoidance of Permanent Establishment Status and Part VI-Arbitration. These behaviors could demonstrate China's quite positive attitude, at least at the time of signing the MLI, to the "common approach" or the "best practice" measures of the BEPS project.

Of the eight MLI clauses that China opted into, two of them were opted in with reservations, vz. Article 9—Capital Gains from Alienation of Shares or Interests of Entities Deriving Their Value Principally from Immovable Property and Article 16—Mutual Agreement Procedure. Therefore, the following three different modification results may be achieved when the reservations conflict with the provisions of the corresponding articles in the Covered Tax Agreements:

(1)the MLI clauses apply "in place of" the provisions in the Covered

Tax Agreements;

(2) the MLI clauses "apply to" or "modify" (but do not replace) the provisions in the Covered Tax Agreements; or

(3) the MLI clauses apply "in the absence of" an existing provision in the Covered Tax Agreements.

However, the signing of the MLI only indicates a provisional position for supporting the multilateral instrument approach and such a position is still subject to change before being ratified in China. The impact of the MLI in China will not only be on the modified treaty articles of the Covered Tax Agreements but also on China's negotiation of new tax treaties and amendments to its existing tax treaties in the future. We can deduce from the fact that China has opted into all of the MLI clauses reflecting the minimum standards that China might also have to insist on having these minimum standards clauses when negotiating tax treaties with jurisdictions that have not yet signed the MLI. One example is the China-Kenya tax treaty, which was signed three months after the MLI signature day, and where Kenya is a not yet an MLI signatory. All three minimum standards clauses are incorporated into that treaty, while only some of those clauses reflecting best practice or common approaches were included (for example, the corresponding adjustment), while others were not (for example, dual resident entities). While the China-Kenya Tax Treaty is the only bilateral tax treaty so far that China has signed after it signed the MLI, with one or two more new tax treaties that China will sign with non-MLI countries, we can expect to get a clearer picture of the practical impact of the MLI.

Appendix: Exercises

1. Which anti-tax avoidance measures are provided in domestic laws?
2. Which anti-treaty abuse measures are provided in Chinese tax treaties?
3. How to apply the arm's length principle in China?
4. What would be the consequence when applying the transfer pricing

rule?

5.What would be the consequence when applying the thin-capitalisation rule?

6.What would be the consequence when applying the CFC rule?

7.Which factors are determinant when applying the GAAR to a transaction?

8.What would be the consequence when applying the GAAR?

9.Who will take the burden of proof in tax investigations in China?

10. What measures China have implemented by taking into account of the deliveries of the BEPS project?

11.Research questions：

• Fact

Offshore indirect shares transfers refer to those transactions being carried out by foreign shareholders through selling the shares they hold in a company located outside China. In the view of Chinese tax authorities，offshore indirect shares transfer is a type of tax avoidance arrangement where foreign shareholders indirectly transfer the shares of Chinese resident enterprises.

• Questions

（1）Can Chinese tax authorities apply the transfer pricing rule to tax offshore indirect shares transfers? Why?

（2）Can Chinese tax authorities apply the controlled foreign corporation （CFC） rule to tax offshore indirect shares transfers? Why?

（3）Can Chinese tax authorities apply the thin capitalization rule to tax offshore indirect shares transfers? Why?

（4）Can Chinese tax authorities apply the general anti-tax avoidance rule （GAAR） to tax offshore indirect shares transfers? Why?

CHAPTER 10
TAX DISPUTE RESOLUTION^①

10.1   Introduction

Tax disputes in China are generally arising from the following three types of disputes:

(1)disputes over tax imposition activities according to tax laws and tax treaties;

(2)disputes over other tax administrative measures; and

(3)disputes over application of anti-avoidance measures.

Resolving tax disputes in China normally should be subject to two approaches for resolution purpose: the domestic legal remedy approach and the treaty approach. The domestic approach refers to the administrative review firstly and then the administrative litigation procedures, which will be de-

---

① The content of this chapter is based on the publications of Dr. Li on journals, books and international conferences, for example, her papers "General Anti-Avoidance Rules (GAARs)-A Key Element of Tax Systems in the Post-BEPS Tax World: China", co-authored with Mingxing Cao, in Michael Lang et al (eds.), *General Anti-Avoidance Rules (GAARs)-A Key Element of Tax Systems in the Post-BEPS Tax World*, Amsterdam: IBFD, 2016; "China's Employment Income Case", in Michael Lang et al (eds.), *Tax Treaty Case Around the Global 2017*, Vienna: Linde, 2018; "The TCI Case-A Milestone Case for China Taxing Offshore Indirect Shares Transfer", *Asia-Pacific Tax Bulletin*, 2019, Vol.25, No.6; and "China: A tax relief for corporate reorganizations was denied to an Italian company (Article 24 of the OECD Model)", in Michael Lang et al (eds.), *Tax Treaty Case Around the Global 2019*, Vienna: Linde, 2020.

scribed in Section 3 (Judicial Cases) herein. The taxpayers must complete an administrative review procedure at competent tax authorities, before they could bring the tax dispute to the Chinese courts. The authorities hearing such review applications normally should be the higher-ranking tax authorities of the one making the tax assessment. The appeal must be issued within 60 days after the taxpayer has received the tax assessment. Before submitting the application for review, however, the tax assessment and eventual surcharge must be paid or a corresponding guarantee for the payments must be provided. The hearing tax authorities are required to make a decision on the appeal within 60 days after the date the appeal is received. This period of handling an appeal may be extended with 30 extra days if the tax authorities decide to do so. If the review panel at such administrative review process could settle the disputes, then few taxpayers would continue to seek judicial remedies.[1]

The treaty approach refers to the mutual agreement procedure (the "MAP"), provided in all Chinese DTAs, with regard to resolving the tax disputes arising from implementation and interpretation of the Chinese DTAs by a mutual agreement mechanism between the competent authorities of China and the Contracting States. As of today, China has not accepted for any arbitration approach, therefore, tax disputes must be resolved either by the domestic approaches or in accordance with the mutual agreement procedure provided in the Chinese DTAs. It seems that these two approaches in theory could be applied in parallel, because the MAP provisions in the Chinese DTAs usually provide that "irrespective of the remedies provided by the domestic law of the Contracting States", the taxpayers may apply for the MAP under the Chinese DTAs. And even without receiving any MAP application, the competent authorities of the Contracting States shall also be obliged to endeavor to resolve by mutual agreement any difficulties or doubts arising as to the interpretation or application of the DTAs. And they may also consult together for the elimination of double taxation in cases not provided for in the DTAs.

---

[1] Wei Cui, What Is "Law" in Chinese Tax Administration, *Asia Pacific Law Review*, 2011, Vol.19, No.1.

10.2   Tax Cases

The term "tax case" in Chinese language is usually used to describe two types of tax-related disputes. One type refers to the judicial cases ruled by courts. China has no tax court yet, so all tax-related cases are heard at the administrative chamber of Chinese courts. In theory, these judicial cases should not become precedents, as China is a civil law country adopting a doctrine of textualism in its legislation; in practice, however, these cases have informal but significant influence on taxing cross-border transactions in China. The number of these tax-related judicial cases is limited, around only 400 cases filed with courts nationwide every year[1]and few of them were for cross-border related tax issues. To date, there are only a very few of reported cross-border tax cases (for example, the PanAmSat case, the Hardie case, the ILLVA case, and the TCI case).

Another type refers to the administrative investigations conducted by Chinese tax authorities on tax avoidance transactions. Strictly speaking, the results of these investigations are only administrative decisions and have not been heard at any court. But from time to time, the in-charge Chinese tax authorities published on their website or on newspapers sponsored by Chinese government with some brief information about these transactions, including the laws they applied, investigation methods they used and the amount of additional taxes they collected. And occasionally, the SAT which is the highest-level tax authority in China, also publishes such investigation results in a form of "internal rulings" which are sent to all Chinese tax author-

---

[1]   Data published by the National Bureau of China Statistics at http://data.stats.gov. cn/easyquery.htm? cn=C01 (accessed on 7 March, 2021).

ities.[①]In these internal rulings, the SAT often announces that the in-charge tax authorities applied certain anti-tax measures correctly and as a consequence succeeded in collecting additional tax revenues. Then all Chinese tax authorities in practice are likely to take the practice of these tax investigations mentioned the publications and internal rulings as references when they conduct anti-tax avoidance investigations. In this sense, analyzing the three such investigations (For example, the Xinjiang case, the Suzhou case, and the Jiamusi case) in this chapter could provide implications on where cross-border tax disputes might most possibly arise in China.

10.3   Judicial Cases

The jurisdiction of Chinese courts is limited to review of the only the validity of specific administrative conduct of Chinese tax authorities, rather than the reasonability of tax authorities' conduct. Given that Chinese tax legislations in general are written in a brief and abstract context, Chinese tax authorities then could exercise a wide discretionary power when applying these legislations in practice. Consequently a very few of tax administrative conduct maybe brought to the courts for review purpose even if they might not comply with principles of proportionality, appropriateness or necessity, as long as they are legitimate conducts.[②]

---

① For example, SAT, Notice of a Case Correctly Handled by Xinjiang Provincial Tax Authorities to Counterfeit Abuse of Tax Treaty (Guoshuihan [2008] No. 1076), issued on and effective on 30 December, 2008; and SAT, International Transport Cases Involved in the Implementation of Tax Treaties by the Office of the State Administration of Taxation in Shandong Province" (Guoshuibanfa [2011] No. 34), issued no 21 March, 2011.

② Article 12 of the Administrative Litigation Law of the People's Republic of China, promulgated by the NPC on 4 April, 1989 and effective on 1 October, 1990; and Article 3 and Article 56 of the Interpretations of Certain Issues in the Implementation of the Administrative Litigation Law (Fashi No. 8 [2000]), issued by the Supreme People's Court on 8 March, 2000 and effective on 10 March, 2000.

There is no tax court yet in China, the tax cases must be heard at the administrative courts in China. Looking into the structure of the Chinese courts, which in general are called the "People's Courts", both the Supreme Court and the local courts might hear a tax case. The Supreme Court is the highest judicial organ in China, supervising the administration of justice by the local courts at different levels and by the special courts. The local courts are divided into three levels: (1) the Higher Court; (2) the Intermediate Court; and (3) the Basic Court. The higher levels supervise the administration of justice by those at lower levels in a regime of first trial and then appeal process. The Supreme Court may hear some cases as the last review if it believes necessary.

10.3.1 PanAmSat Case

The PanAmSat case was a judicial case ruled by the Higher People's Court of Beijing in December 2002[①], where the courted supported the Beijing tax authorities. The question at issue was whether the income of PanAmSat derived from China should be taxed in China as royalties.

The fact of case was that PamAmSat was a U.S. tax resident, which entered into a "Services Agreement" with a Chinese state-owned television channel — CCTV for providing CCTV with satellite transmission services. For the fee that CCTV payable to PanAmSat under this service agreement, PanAmSat argued that it should be characterized as its business profits derived from China and it should not be taxed in China as PanAmSat did not constitute any permanent establishment in China. But the Beijing tax authorities argued that this payment should be characterized as royalties, as the it could fall into the definition of royalties under China-US tax treaty for the

---

① PanAmSat International Systems, Inc. v. Second Department in the External Substation of the Beijing State Tax Authority (court judgement at the first instance (2001) 168), ruled by the First Intermediate People's Court of Beijing on 20 December, 2001; And PanAmSat International Systems, Inc. v. Second Department in the External Substation of the Beijing State Tax Authority (court judgement at appeal (Gaoxingzhongzi [2002] 24), ruled by the Higher People's Court of Beijing on 20 December, 2002.

"payments of any kind received as consideration…for the use of, or the right to use, industrial commercial or scientific equipment…", and then such royalties should be taxed in China.

Chinese tax legislations in 2002 had no any definition about royalties yet, so the Higher People's Court of Beijing applied the China-US tax treaty directly as the legal basis for reaching its decision. The Higher People's Court of Beijing interpreted this payment as a consideration for granting the right for CCTV to use certain bandwidth of PanAmSat's satellite facilities, rather than for obtaining satellite transmission services from PanAmSat. This interpretation approach is opposite to the OECD's view since 1992, as the OECD in 1992 already deleted the provision that the payment for "use, or the right to use, any industrial, commercial or scientific equipment" from its Model Convention for definitions of royalties, and in addition, the OECD in 2000 added one paragraph into its commentary specifically states that satellite service income should be characterized as business income, rather than as royalties.[①]

Although China as a non-member observer state of the OECD has engaged in various discussions on the revision work of the commentary,[②] China has made a reservation on the OECD's change of position in 1992 through deleting the terms of "payments of any kind received as consideration... for the use of, or

---

① OECD (2012), "Commentary on Article 12: Concerning the taxation of royalties", in Model Tax Convention on Income and on Capital 2010 (Full Version), OECD Publishing. http://dx.doi.org/10.1787/9789264175181-46-en: "9.1 Satellite operators and their customers (including broadcasting and telecommunication enterprises) frequently enter into 'transponder leasing' agreements under which the satellite operator allows the customer to utilize the capacity of a satellite transponder to transmit over large geographical areas. Payments made by customers under typical "transponder leasing" agreements are made for the use of the transponder transmitting capacity and will not constitute royalties under the definition of Paragraph 2: These payments are not made in consideration for the use of, or right to use, property, or for information, that is referred to in the definition (they cannot be viewed, for instance, as payments for information or for the use of, or right to use, a secret process since the satellite technology is not transferred to the customer). As regards treaties that include the leasing of industrial, commercial or scientific (ICS) equipment in the definition of royalties, the characterization of the payment will depend to a large extent on the relevant contractual arrangements. Whilst the relevant contracts often refer to the "lease" of a transponder, in most cases the customer does not acquire the physical possession of the transponder but simply its transmission capacity: The satellite is operated by the lessor and the lessee has no access to the transponder that has been assigned to it. In such cases, the payments made by the customers would therefore be in the nature of payments for services, to which Article 7 applies, rather than payments for the use, or right to use, ICS equipment. A different, but much less frequent, transaction would be where the owner of the satellite leases it to another party so that the latter may operate it and either uses it for its own purposes or offer its data transmission capacity to third parties. In such a case, the payment made by the satellite operator to the satellite owner could well be considered as a payment for the leasing of industrial, commercial or scientific equipment. Similar considerations apply to payments made to lease or purchase the capacity of cables for the transmission of electrical power or communications (e.g. through a contract granting an indefeasible right of use of such capacity) or pipelines (e.g. for the transportation of gas or oil)."

② Li Jinyan, The Great Fiscal Wall of China: Tax Treaties and Their Role in Defining and Defending China's Tax Base, *Bulletin for International Taxation*, 2012, Vol.66, No.9, pp.452-479.

the right to use, industrial commercial or scientific equipment…" from royalties' definition.[①] Hence, in the PanAmSat case, the Higher People's Court of Beijing did not take into account of the OECD's opinion and ruled in favor of Beijing tax authorities to tax PanAmSat in China under the royalty's provision under the US-China treaty.

Then royalties remain undefined in Chinese domestic tax legislations, until the SAT issued the Circular 75 in 2010 where the SAT expressly provided that "income from the use of, or the right to use, industrial, commercial or scientific equipment, for example, rental of equipment should be characterized as royalties, unless such income is the interest for payments involved in financial leasing activities."

10.3.2 Hardie Case

The Hardie case was ruled by the Guangzhou Municipal Intermediate People's Court on 14 November 2015. The question at issue was whether Mr. Macdonald-Hardie (a US tax resident) was subject to Chinese individual income tax for income he received from his US employer, during the period he worked in China as a CEO of a Chinese company, in relation to work that he claimed was non-Chinese related. This case involves application of the employment income provisions in Article 14 of the China-United States Income Tax Treaty (1984) (the China-US Tax Treaty).[②]

The fact of case was that Mr. Macdonald-Hardie (the Appellant), a US tax resident, worked as the CEO of a Chinese company (called Aquatech Guangzhou Company) from 2005 to 2007, and as a result he stayed in China for 259.5 days, 289 days and 286 days respectively in the years 2005, 2006 and 2007. Mr. Hardie received remuneration from the Chinese company and

---

① See Paragraph 8 of the Positions on the OECD MC Article 12 (Royalties) and its Commentary. China's reservation is to keep "the right to include in the definition of royalties payments for the use of, or the right to use, industrial, commercial or scientific equipment".

② Guangzhou Municipal Intermediate People's Court, 14 November, 2015, Andrew Ronald Macdonald-Hardie vs The First Investigation Branch of Guangzhou Municipal Local Tax Bureau, (2014) Huizhongfaxingzhongzi, No.1464.

had already paid Chinese individual income tax on this Chinese income. During the same period, Mr. Hardie had an employment contract with a US company (called Aquatech International), an affiliated company of Aquatech Guangzhou Company. Under his US employment contract, Mr. Hardie was stated as the Vice-President for International Business Development of Aquatech International, and he received remuneration from this US company in the United States. Mr. Hardie did not pay Chinese individual income tax on this US income.

The First Investigation Branch of Guangzhou Municipal Local Tax Bureau (the Appellate, or the Tax Bureau) conducted a tax investigation into Mr. Hardie in 2008, and then reached a decision in 2009 that Mr. Hardie's US income for the period from 2005 to 2007 should be subject to Chinese individual income tax. Mr. Hardie, however, disagreed with this assessment. After having gone through a compulsory administrative review process undertaken by the higher level Chinese tax authority, Mr. Hardie brought the case to the Chinese courts in 2013.

In 2013, the first instance court ruled in favor of the Tax Bureau, reasoning that (1) for the year 2005, Mr. Hardie, although not a Chinese tax resident, by virtue of his position at the Chinese company as a CEO was subject to a broader scope of tax liability in China according to the tax circulars issued by the State Administration of Taxation of China (the SAT). Thus, Mr. Hardie should have been subject to individual income tax in China for the income he received from the US company in 2005; and (2) for both 2006 and 2007, China had a right to tax Mr. Hardie's US income according to Paragraph 2 of Article 14 of the China-US tax treaty (i.e. employment income provisions), as Mr. Hardie stayed in China for more than 183 days in both of those years.

Mr. Hardie disagreed with the decision of the court of first instance. He argued that the first instance court wrongly applied Chinese domestic law as well as the China-US tax treaty provisions. Consequently Mr. Hardie appealed to the intermediate court (i.e. Guangzhou Municipal Intermediate People's Court) in 2013. In his petition, Mr. Hardie argued that: (1) his income received from the US company should not be treated as income sourced from China, as his employment contracts with the Chinese company and with the US company were separate, and all his US income was paid by the US company in the United States; and (2) all his work for the US company had nothing to do with China, so all the places he performed his work under his US employment contract were outside China. The appeal court, however, seems not to have accepted Mr. Hardie's arguments, and in November 2015 it ruled in favour of the Tax Bureau, again requiring Mr. Hardie to pay Chinese individual income tax on the income he received from the US company from 2005 to 2007.

10.3.3 ILLVA Case

The ILLVA Case was the first non-discrimination case having been published in China on the basis of a tax treaty article. The case was heard at the Yantai Municipal Intermediate People's Court of China on 15 August, 2016, which involved application of the non-discrimination provisions in Article 24 of the China-Italy Income Tax Treaty (1986) (the China-Italy Tax Treaty).[①] The question at issue in this case consists of three parts: (1) whether China may have taxing power over an Italian tax resident company in relation to it merging its wholly-owned Italian subsidiary; (2) whether the merger may qualify as a corporate reorganization, which could be exempted from paying Chinese income tax under the Circular 59 of Chinese domestic tax law and (3) whether the Italian tax resident was discriminated against by the Chinese tax administration on grounds of its nationality.

The fact of the case was that ILLVA Saronno Holding SpA (the appellant, hereinafter called the "ILLVA Holding"), an Italian tax resident company, owned 100% of the shares in another Italian tax resident company-IL-

---

① Agreement between the Government of the Republic of Italy and the Government of the People's Republic of China for the Avoidance of Double Taxation and the Prevention of Tax Evasion with Respect to Taxes on Income (31 Oct. 1986), Treaties IBFD [hereinafter China-US Tax Treaty]. The China-Italy tax treaty was signed on 31 October, 1986 and came into force in China on 14 November, 1989. This tax treaty is still in force as writing this chapter.

LVA Saronno investment Co, ltd. (hereinafter called the "ILLVA Investment"). On 29 September, 2005, ILLVA Investment purchased 33% of the shares in a Chinese company-Yantai Changyu Group Co., Ltd. (the "Chinese Company") at a price of RMB 481,424,260[①] and became a shareholder of the Chinese Company. From then on ILLVA Investment did not engage in any other equity-investment, and the shares it held in the Chinese Company constituted the major part of its assets.

On 17 July, 2012, ILLVA Holding conducted a merger with ILLVA Investment according to Italian laws by a way of taking over all assets and liabilities of the latter (including the 33% shareholding which ILLVA Investment had in the Chinese Company). The result of the merger was that ILLVA Holding merged ILLVA Investment into its company (i.e. the parent company merged the subsidiary company into itself), and ILLVA Investment was then de-registered in Italy in November 2012. As a consequence of the merger, ILLVA Holding replaced ILLVA Investment, becoming a shareholder in the Chinese Company, and ILLVA Holding declared that it did not make any gains from the merger, as the consideration for the merger was made on the basis of the original cost of the assets and liabilities of ILLVA Investment.

On 9 September, 2013, the State Tax Bureau in Zhixia District (the defendant, hereinafter "the Tax Bureau"), which is the tax authority with jurisdiction in respect of the Chinese Company, informed ILLVA Holding that it was liable to pay income tax in China amounting to RMB 46,342,168.32.[②] According to the Tax Bureau, the merger was in substance a transfer of the Chinese Company's shares from ILLVA Investment to ILLVA Holding, and the transfer price was not compliant with the arm's length principle. Thus, the Tax Bureau, in accordance with Circular 698 of Chinese domestic law,[③]

---

① Equivalent to USD71,747,281, at an exchange rate of 6.71 as published by the Bank of China.

② Equivalent to USD6,906,433, at an exchange rate of 6.71.

③ SAT, Tax Issues for Equity Transfers by Non-China Tax Resident Enterprises, Guoshuihan〔2009〕No. 698, promulgated on 15 December, 2009, effective on 1 January, 2008.

decided that ILLVA Investment should pay Chinese income tax as decided by the Tax Bureau for the gains derived from this share transfer transaction. The Tax Bureau used the cost method when deciding the sale price for the shares by taking the value of the net assets of the Chinese Company as of 30 June, 2012 as the sale price (i.e. RMB 2,863,169,524.88) and then taking the investment made by ILLVA Investment into the Chinese Company in 2005 as the original cost (i.e. RMB 481,424,260.00). As a result, the Tax Bureau calculated that the "gain" derived by ILLVA Holding from the merger was RMB 463,421,683.2. China, as the source state from where the shares in the Chinese Company were transferred, derived a taxing power in respect of this capital gain and could apply its domestic tax rate of 10% on the gain, which resulted in a tax due of RMB 46,342,168.32.

ILLVA Holding paid the tax due in September 2013 and then filed a petition to the higher-level Chinese tax authority (the National Tax Authority of Yantai City) requesting a tax refund. The court's judgment did not disclose whether ILLVA Holding had ever challenged the correctness of the application of Chinese domestic anti-tax avoidance measures (as provided in Circular 698), although the Tax Bureau re-characterized the arrangement at issue as a share transfer rather than a merger on the basis of that Circular. The only thing that the court's judgment mentioned was that ILLVA Holding had raised a tax refund request in the petition based on Circular [2009] 59 (hereinafter called "Circular 59")[1] which grants Chinese tax exemption to qualifying corporate reorganizations.

However, the National Tax Authority of Yantai City did not support ILLVA Holding's request, deciding that ILLVA's merger did not fit into any of the forms of tax-free corporate reorganizations. The form of ILLVA's transaction was the parent company(ILLVA Holding) merging its subsidiary(ILLVA Investment), while the tax-free form as provided in Article 7 of Circular 59 was a subsidiary merging its parent company. ILLVA Holding disagreed with this decision on its petition, so it raised an action against the

---

[1]   MOF and SAT, Notice on Enterprise Income Tax Treatment of Enterprise Reorganizations, Caishui No. 59 [2009], promulgated on 30 April, 2009, effective on 1 January, 2008.

Tax Bureau at the administrative chambers of the Chinese courts in April 2014.[1]

The Zhixia District People's Court of Yantai City, the first instance court, ruled in favour of the Tax Bureau on 15 December 2015, issuing the following decisions with regard to the three arguments raised by ILLVA Holding, especially the last argument on the discrimination of non-Chinese nationals:

(1) ILLVA's transaction should be taxed in China as a transfer of shares in the Chinese Company and Circular 698 empowers the Chinese tax authority to make adjustments to the taxable amount in a proper method, thus the Tax Bureau's behaviour, namely taxing the "gain" through using the cost method was correct when calculating the tax due in China.

(2) The transaction did not fit into any of the tax-free corporate reorganizations as provided in Article 7 of Circular 59, so ILLVA Holding could not benefit from Chinese tax reliefs granted to corporate reorganizations.

(3) There was no discrimination against ILLVA Holding, so no violation of Article 24 of the China-Italy Tax Treaty.

On December 2015, ILLVA Holding appealed the case to the intermediate court, i.e. Yantai Municipal Intermediate People's Court, with the same claims and based on the same grounds. On 15 August 2016, the appeal court delivered a decision supporting the first instance court's judgment, ruling that the Tax Bureau was correct to tax ILLVA's transaction as a transfer of shares in the Chinese Company and to refuse to grant ILLVA Holding the tax relief applicable to corporate reorganizations under Circular 59.

10.3.4 TCI Case

The TCI Case was a judicial case ruled by the Higher Court of Zhejiang Province in December 2015. It is a milestone case for China taxing offshore indirect shares transfers, as it is the first cross-border tax case going

---

[1]   There is no tax court in China, so all litigation on or relating to tax issues is heard in the administrative chambers of Chinese courts.

through the administrative review, the first trial, the appeal and a consideration for re-trial at the Supreme Court.

10.3.4.1 Litigation process

The Children's Investment (TCI) Master Fund filed its complaint with the West Lake District Court of Hangzhou City, suing the West Lake Tax Office on 24 April, 2014, TCI. As the disputed tax amount is significant and the parties to the transaction are not Chinese tax residents, the TCI's complaint was transferred by the West Lake District Court to a higher level court-the Hangzhou Intermediate People's Court on 19 December, 2014. Subsequently, the Hangzhou Intermediate People's Court (the First Trial Court) registered the case on 23 December, 2014, held a public hearing on 5 March, 2015, and then delivered a judgment on 9 July, 2015, upholding the tax collection decision of the West Lake Tax Office.[①] TCI then lodged an appeal to the Zhejiang Province People's High Court (the Appeal Court), which registered the case on 24 September 2015, had a public hearing on 8 December, 2015, and delivered a judgment on 15 December, 2015 in favor of the West Lake Tax Office.[②] Normally, the judgment delivered by the Appeal Court should be the final decision to judicial cases, as China's trial system consists of two hearing processes: the first trial and the appeal. But TCI managed to have the Supreme People's Court of China (the Supreme Court) to give a consideration for a re-trial of its case. This is very exceptional, because the Supreme Court is quite busy, being the highest trial organ and the highest supervising organ overseeing all trial practices of local courts and special courts at various levels in China. The TCI case was the first dispute on offshore indirect shares transfer being considered by the Supreme Court for a re-trial. Unfortunately, the Supreme Court ruled on 8 September, 2016 to not re-trial the case, because the Supreme Court agreed with the Appeal

---

① First Trial Judgment for the Administrative Collection Case of The Children's Investment Master Fund v. the West Lake Office of Hangzhou State Tax Bureau (Zhehangxingchuzi〔2015〕No. 4), ruled by the Hangzhou Intermediate People's Court on 9 July, 2015.

② Second Trial Judgment for the Administrative Collection Case of The Children's Investment Master Fund v. the West Lake Office of Hangzhou State Tax Bureau (Zhexingzhongzi〔2015〕No. 441), ruled by Zhejiang Province People's High Court on 15 December, 2015.

Court and the First Trial Court that TCI's transaction was an offshore indirect shares transfer of HZGY and thus TCI should be taxed in China for its gains derived from the shares transfer.[①]

10.3.4.2 Fact of the case

TCI was established in the Cayman Islands in 2003. TCI became a shareholder of Chinese Future Corporation (CFC) by acquiring 26.32% of CFC's shares in November 2005, partly through buying shares from CFC's former shareholders and partly through subscribing new shares from CFC. CFC was a Cayman Islands company established in October 2005, holding 100% shares of Guohui Co., Ltd. (GH), a Hong Kong company; and GH held 95% shares of Hangzhou Guoyi Expressway and Bridge Management Co., Ltd. (HZGY), a Chinese company which obtained a long-term concession right to the ring road expressway of Hangzhou city in October 2005.

On 9 September, 2011, TCI sold all shares it held in CFC to Moscan Developments Limited (MDL), a British Virgin Islands company, at a price of USD 280 million with additional interest payment of approximately USD 3.8 million in respect of deferred payment of consideration. This shares transfer from TCI to MDL is the transaction of the TCI case, which was trialed at the Chinese courts later for the issue of whether China may tax TCI for its gain derived from the transfer.

On 30 September, 2011, TCI, in compliance with the reporting obligation provided in the SAT Guoshuihan [2009] No. 698 (Circular 698), informed the West Lake Office of Hangzhou State Tax Bureau (West Lake Tax Office) of its shares transfer transaction, and then TCI provided the West Lake Tax Office with materials proving its transaction was not a tax avoidance arrangement. Subsequently, the West Lake Tax Office conducted an investigation on the transaction through applying the Chinese GAAR, and then submitted its investigation results to the SAT for endorsement.

In July 2013, the SAT responded to the West Lake Tax Office with its endorsement that TCI's transaction should be taxed in China according to its

---

①　Ruling for Administrative Cases (Zuigaofaxingshen [2016] No. 1867), delivered by the Supreme People's Court of China on 8 September. 2016.

economic substance, i.e. as a non-Chinese tax resident indirectly transferring the shares of the Chinese company (i.e. HZGY). The SAT authorized the West Lake Tax Office to look through both CFC and GH and then tax TCI for its gains derived from the shares transfer. Accordingly, on 12 November, 2013 the West Lake Tax Office notified TCI to pay the Chinese corporate income tax amounting to RMB 105,310,815.32[1] (the Notification) in China.[2] This tax due was calculated on the basis of a deemed gain amount of USD 173,228,521.91, taking account of the consideration for the shares transfer and the cost of TCI for obtaining the shares of CFC (about USD 50 million); the tax rate applied was 10%, which was the corporate income tax rate applicable to non-Chinese tax residents under the EIT Law.

TCI disagreed with the above Notification, so it paid off the tax due, and then on 17 January, 2014 brought the dispute to the higher level tax bureau (i.e. the Hangzhou State Tax Bureau) for an administrative review.[3] On 10 April, 2014, the Hangzhou State Tax Bureau made a review decision which upheld the tax collection Notification of the West Lake Tax Office.[4] TCI disagreed with this review decision, so it decided to seek judicial reme-

---

[1] Approximately USD 14,667,244 at the exchange rate of USD 1＝RMB 7.18 as of 8 September. 2019.

[2] Notification Letter for Tax Matters (Hangguoshuixitong〔2013〕No.004), issued by the West Lake Tax Office on 12 November. 2013.

[3] According to art. 88 of the Tax Collection and Administration Law promulgated by the National People's Congress on 4 September. 1992, and Article. 19 of the Administrative Review Law promulgated by the National People's Congress on 29 April. 1999, for the purpose of commencing an administrative review, TCI must have paid the full amount of the tax due or have provided an appropriate guaranty. Furthermore, TCI can proceed to litigation at Chinese courts only after the Hangzhou State Tax Bureau has reached a review decision with regard to the Notification. According to Dongmei Qiu, one reason for China having a very few number of judicial tax cases is that few taxpayers would continue to seek judicial remedies if the review panel at the administrative review process could settle the disputes. See Dongmei Qiu, Legal Interpretation of Tax Law: China, in Legal Interpretation of Tax Law(R. F. van Brederode &. R. Krever eds.) Kluwer Law International BV, The Netherlands 2014.

[4] Decision of Administrative Review (Hangguoshuifujuezi〔2014〕No. 1), issued by the Hangzhou State Tax Bureau on 10 April. 2014.

dies at Chinese courts.

10.3.4.3 Applicable laws

The laws and regulations applied by the Chinese courts to the TCI case are as follows:

(1) Article 47 of the EIT Law, which is the GAAR provision introduced into China in 2008, providing that "(w)here an enterprise makes any other arrangement not having a reasonable business purpose and leading to a decrease of its taxable income or tax liabilities, the tax authorities shall have the power to make an adjustment through using reasonable methods" [emphasis added].[1] Article 47 is the fundamental legal basis for applying the GAAR in China.

(2) Article 120 of the EIT Regulation, which interprets that the term in Article 47 of the EIT Law "not having a reasonable business purpose" means "the main purpose [is] to reduce, exempt, or defer the payment of taxes" [emphasis added].[2] This interpretation literally expanded the scope of purpose test from "not having a reasonable business purpose" as provided in the EIT Law to "the main purpose [is] to reduce, exempt, or defer the payment of taxes" as provided in the Implementing Rules. Consequently, the burden of proof on taxpayers is also increased from proving the parties have certain (at least one) reasonable business purposes to a burden of proving the main purpose of the parties is not to obtain tax benefits.[3]

---

[1]   The Corporate Income Tax Law of the People's Republic of China, promulgated by the NPC on 6 March. 2007 and in effect as from 1 January. 2008.

[2]   The Implementing Rules of the Corporate Income Tax Law of the People's Republic of China, enacted by the State Council on 28 November. 2007 and in effect as from 1 January. 2008.

[3]   The Administrative Measures for General Anti-avoidance Rules (Trial) (Order 32), issued by the SAT on 2 December. 2014 and came into force on 1 February, 2015, narrowed down the "main purpose" of a "tax avoidance scheme" to be "the sole or main purpose is to obtain tax benefits", while "the tax benefits are obtained by using an arrangement where it complies with the tax law in form but is not consistent with its economic substance". However, the TCI's shares transfer transaction took place in 2001, which was before the effectiveness of Order 32, thus the narrower purposive test in Order 32 was not applicable to the TCI case.

(3)Notice on Strengthening the Management of Enterprise Income Tax Collection on Proceeds from Shares Transfers by Non-residents (Guoshuihan [2009] No. 698), issued by the SAT on 10 December 2009 but with retroactive effect from 1 January 2008. This is the famous Circular 698, a technical implementing rule on how to tax non-residents for transferring shares of Chinese companies, through defining the concept of "offshore indirect shares transfer", endorsing the application of the "reasonable business purpose" test under the Chinese GAAR, and empowering Chinese tax authorities to disregard the offshore middle companies for the purpose of taxing non-residents according to the economic substance of the transactions. With these technical instruments provided by Circular 698, Chinese tax authorities have successfully investigated many offshore indirect shares transfers in the past decade.

In the meanwhile, Circular 698 itself raised concerns and controversies. One may notice that this circular was enacted by the SAT , which has a dualfunction of being both a legislative organ and an administrative organ. The legislativepower comes from the State Council to the SAT on enacting tax circulars for implementing tax laws; while the administrative power comes from the SAT's role as the highest level tax authority supervising administration work of all Chinese tax authorities, including their implementation of the tax circulars enacted by the SAT. This dual-function of the SAT was clearly demonstrated in the TCI case. When the West Lake Tax Office completed the investigation on TCI's transaction, it submitted the investigation results to the SAT for endorsement according to Circular 698. While one may not forget that the SAT was the legislative organ who issued Circular 698 and although the SAT has played a key role, it cannot be listed as a defendant in the TCI case. This is because the SAT was not the tax authority issuing the tax collection Notification (the West Lake Tax Office issued the Notification), and the SAT enacting Circular 698 was in its legislative role for which it is not liable to be sued in court.

(4)Article 7 of the EIT Regulation, which provides a source rule for China taxing non-residents, i. e. incomes derived by non-residents from transferring shares of companies located in China shall be their income sourced from China. This Article is a legal basis for the West Lake Tax Office to impose the Chinese corporate income tax on TCI, because the shares sold by TCI were deemed as the shares of HZGY when the offshore middle companies (CFC and GH) were looked through. In other words, the source rule for non-residents remains the same as that under Article 7. However, when TCI was deemed as selling the shares of Chinese company (HZGY), the gains derived from the shares transfer became TCI's income sourced from China.

10.3.4.4 Rationale of the courts' judgments

The key issue in the TCI case was whether the parties have "reasonable business purpose" to conduct the shares transfer. According to the Chinese GAAR and Circular 698, the burden of proof is on the taxpayer (i.e. TCI). While the competent Chinese tax authority should determine the purpose of the parties according to the following three elements enacted by the SAT in the circular Guoshuifa [2009] No. 2:①(1) The transaction was carried out by using artificial scheme(s); (2) the taxpayer must have obtained tax benefits; and (3) obtaining tax benefits was the main purpose of the taxpayer in carrying out the transaction. The author herein summarizes the arguments of TCI, the arguments of the West Lake Tax Office, and the decisions of the Chinese courts with regard to these three elements:

1. An artificial scheme

This element consists of both an objective test and a subjective test, where TCI needs to prove that all offshore companies involved in the transaction are not shell companies. The West Lake Tax Office argued the transaction having used artificial schemes on the basis of the following three facts which was found by the West Lake Tax Office during its investigation:

(1) Both CFC and GH were registered in tax havens or in low-tax jurisdictions, and they did not carry out substantive business activities such as manufacturing, sales or management, etc. CFC has no substantive business

---

① SAT, Notice on Issuing the Measures for the Implementation of Special Tax Adjustments (Trial) (Guoshuifa [2009] No. 2), issued by the SAT on 8 January, 2009 but with retroactive effect from 1 January, 2008.

activities except for holding the shares of GH (and indirectly holding the shares of HZGY); as for GH, its only income was the dividends distributed from HZGY.

(2) The consideration of the shares transfer was primarily determined according to the valuation of HZGY, and the most valuable assets of HZGY were the concession rights to the ring road express way of Hangzhou city.

(3) The actual target of the transfer was the shares of HZGY, according to the announcements of MDL's shareholders on the website of HK Stock Exchange.

In response to the arguments of the West Lake Tax Office, TCI raised the following statements:

(1) GH and CFC were established in 2004 and 2005 respectively, which was before Circular 698, so the founders of these two companies should be unable to predict that the SAT would enact Circular 698 in 2009. TCI and its affiliated companies were not the founders of GH and CFC, and TCI has fully contributed to the capital of CFC in 2005 when acquiring CFC's shares. Both GH and CFC were established for business purposes, rather than for tax avoidance purposes. CFC was established to raise funds outside of China. While GH becoming the shareholder of HZGY was approved by the relevant Chinese governmental institutions in accordance with the Chinese laws in force at that time; furthermore, the Chinese governmental institutions expressly requested that the shares held by GH in HZGY should not be transferred.

(2) Both GH and CFC are not shell companies, as they have their employees, offices and facilities and they have carried out business activities. GH was engaged in real estate investment business; while CFC carried out shares investment, issued bonds, managed bonds and shares, and has signed a number of contracts outside of China. All these activities should be treated as substantive business activities, because no Chinese law or regulation provides that only manufacturing and sales activities are substantive business activities.

(3) Many factors were taken into account when determining the price for the shares transfer. CFC has issued bonds amounting to USD 225 million on

the Singapore Stock Exchange, for which it has to pay interests of USD 27 million every year, thus it is improper to determine the transfer price based on the value of CFC. So the value of the HZGY was taken into account as one of the factors, but the transfer price was eventually determined according to the shareholders' willingness. There was no cause and effect relationship in a legal sense between the transfer price and the value of the HZGY, and there was no direct relevance to tax avoidance neither.

(4) The Announcement made by MDL's shareholders on the website of the HK Stock Exchange did not expressly state that the target of the transfer was the shares of HZGY. Instead, it was clearly stated that the shares of CFC were the target of the transaction. In addition, the Announcement did not state that the price was mainly based on the value of the HZGY, while it only said that the value of the HZGY was taken as one of the considerable factors when determining the price.

Clearly, TCI intended to argue with the above statements that no artificial scheme was used in the transaction and the result of the indirect shares transfer of HZGY was only a matter of fact in consequence rather than a deliberate tax avoidance. However, it would depend on the evidence TCI could provide to support its arguments, and to what extent the Chinese courts would accept TCI's arguments and evidence. Unfortunately, the Supreme Court ruled that the evidence provided by TCI was not sufficient to support its arguments on the matter that GH and CFC both having engaged in business activities. The Supreme Court also ruled that the West Lake Tax Office has provided sufficient evidence with regard to its three fact findings through proving the location of the companies involved, the specific amount and methods of shares transferred, the actual target of the shares transfer, the actual source of the income, the determinant factors of the transfer price, and the motives and purposes of the parties to the transaction. Therefore the Supreme Court ruled that "[f]rom the perspective of the objectivity, relevance and legitimacy of the evidences for administrative litigation, the evidences provided by the tax authority in the previous trials were more powerful and had a comparative advantage." As a consequence, the Supreme Court accepted the arguments of the West Lake Tax Office that TCI's transaction was carried out through using artificial schemes.

2.Tax benefits

This element is an objective test, and it is not difficult to calculate the tax benefits that TCI may enjoy if it is not paying Chinese taxes for selling the shares. Therefore, this element is the least argued issue at the courts. TCI admitted certain tax benefits occurring if no Chinese tax needs to be paid by TCI (as a non-Chinese tax resident) for the shares transfer of CFC, which is also not a Chinese tax resident.

3.Purpose to obtaining the tax benefits

This element is a subjective test, as TCI needs to prove that the main purpose of the parties for carrying out the transaction was not for obtaining the tax benefits. This element might be the most difficult one for TCI to fulfill the burden of proof, as the evidence provided must be convincing and acceptable to the Chinese courts.

TCI argued that selling the shares of CFC was the only legally permitted and reasonable business action for TCI to receive the capital gains. Thus even without obtaining any tax benefits, TCI would still have sold the shares of the CFC for the purpose of obtaining the capital gains. The West Lake Tax Office, however, raised a stronger argument with regard to this element. It pointed out that in Article 7 of the Shares Transfer Agreement for the transaction, TCI has expressly committed to report the transaction to the Chinese tax authorities according to Circular 698, and TCI has promised to pay any possible.

10.3.4.5 Impact of the BEPS Project

When the TCI case was brought to the Chinese courts, China had already confirmed its participation in the BEPS Project.[①] Thus when the case was trialed at the Appeal Court in 2015, the defendant (the West Lake Tax Office) raised an argument based on the BEPS Project that the TCI case is directly relevant to the issue of whether China may protect its tax sovereignty. The West Lake Tax Office argued that taxing offshore indirect shares

---

① Na Li, Status of the Implementation of the OECD/G20 BEPS Initiative in China and Future Developments, *International Tax Bulletin*, 2016, Vol.82, No.4, pp.387-398.

transfer is a justified act for Chinese tax authorities to protect China's tax sovereignty through tackling tax avoidance transactions. If such an indirect transfer of shares is not taxed in China according to Circular 698, "it will seriously damage China's tax sovereignty".

According to the West Lake Tax Office, TCI paid only around USD 50 million (excluding CFC's bond financing) when acquiring the shares of CFC in 2005, but it made significant amount of gains from the shares transfer in 2011 through indirectly selling the shares of HZGY. This is because HZGY is a valuable company having a 25-year concession right to the ring road expressway of Hangzhou city. Therefore, the West Lake Tax Office argued that the place where the economic activities take place and where the value creation occurs should both be in China. According to the general principles of the BEPS Project, taxation should match the substantial business activities and profit should be taxed at the place where economic activities takes place and where the value is created. So the West Lake Tax Office argued that China should have the right to tax TCI for its gains derived from the shares transfer.

Although having heard the above quite serious arguments from the West Lake Tax Office, the Appeal Court did not make any response or comment in its judgment. It was the Supreme Court which wrote the following statements in its ruling in 2016 demonstrating an obvious attitude of supporting the above arguments of West Lake Tax Office:

The application of tax laws, regulations and policies in this case is related to how to set out a basic rule and standard for Chinese tax authorities dealing with similar issues in the future, to protect the reputation of Chinese government in managing foreign trade and economy, and also to equally protect the legitimate rights and interests of foreign companies and Chinese companies. [Emphasis added.]①

One year later, when the Supreme Court announced the Ten Classical Administrative Cases of the Supreme Court on its website on 13 June 2017,

---

①   Ruling for Administrative Cases (Zuigaofaxingshen [2016] No. 1867), delivered by the Supreme People's Court of China on 8 September, 2016.

the TCI case was listed as the seventh of the ten classical cases and the Supreme Court made the following statements:

The significance of this case is that with regard to the tax avoidance arrangements through setting up companies and transferring assets outside of China while the income actually sourced from China, the People's Courts in their trials have demonstrated Chinese tax sovereignty and the prevailing international taxation rules, and it has protected the legitimate rights and interests of China in the field of foreign trade and economy. With the increasing scale of foreign trade and economic cooperation and the increasing number of ways of communication, it is clear that the taxation criteria for the transfer of shares and financing of various market entities are closely related to the country's major economic security and economic and trade interests. It is an issue of urgent practical significance and long-term strategic significance. In this case, the West Lake Tax Office issued the tax collection notification for the relevant companies to register and transfer shares in low-tax (or tax-free) jurisdictions outside of China, after having obtained endorsement from the State Administration of Taxation and fully communication with the re-trial applicant. The courts of the first trial, the appeal and the Supreme Court have fully affirmed the legality of the taxation and have clarified the applicable rules and standards for the relevant laws. This case has a clear demonstration and warning function in curbing similar tax avoidances and tax evasions. This case has received full attention from the representatives of People's Congress and several departmental institutions.[①]

The TCI case in theory should not become a precedent, as China is a civil law country adopting a doctrine of textualism in its legislation. However, the author believes that in practice the TCI case will have significant influences on China's legislation, administration and judicial practices, because the Supreme Court in the above statements clearly sent out a signal that this case is to be used as a model standard for China taxing offshore in-

---

① The Ten Classical Administrative Cases of the Supreme Court, issued by the Supreme Court on 13 June, 2017 on its website: https://www.chinacourt.org/article/detail/2017/06/id/2893953.shtml(accessed on 14 March, 2021).

direct shares transfers in the future.

10.4   Administrative Investigations

Although strictly speaking, the results of administrative investigations conducted by Chinese tax authorities on tax avoidance transactions are only administrative decisions, which should not be binding on the other taxpayers. But the brief information of these investigations published by Chinese tax authorities (especially the SAT) have significant impacts in practice.

10.4.1 Xinjiang Case

The Xinjiang case was an investigation conducted by the tax authority in Xinjiang Province in 2008, and then the SAT published an internal ruling in December 2008 announcing that this tax authority has counterfeited a treaty abuse transaction through correctly applying the procedural request for the "resident identity certificate" and applying the "substance over form" doctrine in.[1] The fact of this case is that a Barbados company sold its shares in a Chinese company in 2007 and then applied to be subject to the China-Barbados Tax Treaty effective at that time[2] which provided that China should have no taxing right no such capital gain. As the China-Barbados Tax Treaty only provided that the term "resident" means "any person who, under the

---

[1]   SAT, Notice of a Case Correctly Handled by Xinjiang Provincial Tax Authorities to Counterfeit Abuse of Tax Treaty (Guoshuihan 〔2008〕 No. 1076), issued on and effective on 30 December, 2008.

[2]   Article 13.4 of the China-Barbados Tax Treaty applicable then provided that gains from the alienation of any property other than that referred to in Paragraphs 1, 2 and 3 (that is, immovable property, movable property forming part of the business property of a permanent establishment, ships or aircraft) are only taxable in the Contracting State of which the alienator is a resident. Thus, Barbados shall have exclusive taxing right on the capital gain.

laws of that State, is liable to tax therein by reason of his domicile, residence, place of head office, place of management or any other criterion of a similar nature", the treaty itself did not provide any specific procedural requirement for the taxpayers to prove its residency. Thus, the Chinese tax authority has recourse to Chinese domestic laws requesting the Barbados seller to provide a "resident identity certificate" issued by Barbados tax authority.

However, this Barbados seller failed to provide any "resident identity certificate" issued by Barbados tax authority; instead it provided a document issued by the Chinese embassy in Barbados stating that it is a Barbados resident. In addition, when reviewing the other materials relevant to this shares transfer, the Xinjiang Province tax authorities found the following facts which disclosed that the existence of the Barbados seller was for the purpose to abusively using the China-Barbados Tax Treaty: (1) the Barbados seller purchased the shares in the Chinese company in 2003 within only one month after its incorporation, and also paid the share purchase price through a bank account opened at Cayman Islands; (2) the price for the shares sold in 2007 was not determined based on the actual operations of the Chinese company, instead the sales price was already agreed by the parties in the Barbados seller's shares purchase agreement in 2003, and (3) all three directors of the Barbados seller were US citizens, who have the same address as the parent company of the Barbados seller in the United States.

Based on these facts, the Chinese tax authorities decided that the Barbados seller should not be recognized as a tax resident of Barbados and furthermore the legal form of this Barbados seller should be looked through based on "substance over form" doctrine,[①] so the Chinese tax authority denied the Barbados Company to benefit from the China-Barbados tax treaty and then

---

① When the shares transfer transactions took place in 2007, China had no general anti-avoidance rule yet. Thus, this case was investigated according to the "substance over form" doctrine provided in the Income Tax Law of the People's Republic of China for Enterprises with Foreign Investment and Foreign Enterprises, Promulgated by the NPC on 9 April, 1991 and void on 1 January, 2008.

taxed this capital gain in China according Chinese domestic law.

From the Xinjiang Case, one may find that when a non-Chinese tax resident claims for being entitled to benefit from the tax treaty between China and a Contracting State, this taxpayer must provide to Chinese tax authorities that he is a resident of the Contracting State. The proof this taxpayer must submit is his "resident identity certificate" issued by the competent tax authority of the Contracting State in the calendar year before him raising the claim in China. In addition to requesting for this resident certificate, the Chinese tax authorities also keep the power to request for all relevant contracts, agreements, and resolutions of the boards of directors or the shareholders' meetings, payment documents and other ownership certification materials related to the relevant income obtained, in order to review the risk of this taxpayer abuse of the tax treaty[①].

10.4.2 Suzhou Case

The Suzhou Case was an investigation that the Suzhou tax authorities conducted in 2010, and some brief information about the facts and the results of this case was published on a Chinese government sponsored newspaper named the China Taxation Newspaper[②].

The fact of the case is that a Dutch company signed a management service contract with a Chinese hotel. The Dutch company was exclusively responsible for managing this Chinese hotel, and the Chinese hotel paid the Dutch company management service fee to a bank account opened in Hong Kong on a monthly basis with an amount of 2% of business profits plus 5% of its gross operating profits. The Dutch company argued that the service fee it receives should not be taxed in China, as all its management services were

---

① SAT, Administrative Method for Non-Tax Residents to Benefit from Tax Treaties (Announcement No. 60 [2015]), issued on and effective on 27 August, 2015.

② The article was published on the 2nd page of the 20 September, 2010 volume of this newspaper. See the website of this newspaper: http://www.ctaxnews.net.cn/html/2010-09/20/nw.D340100zgswb_2010-09-20_10-05.htm (accessed on 7 March, 2021).

performed outside of China. This implied that the Dutch company had no permanent establishment in China.

The Chinese tax authorities, however, in their investigations found that the general manager, operation director and financial director of this Chinese hotel, who are all residents of Hong Kong, represented the Dutch company in the monthly management meetings of the hotel, although they were employed by the Chinese hotel and were paid salaries by the Chinese hotel in China. Also, the hotel's payment records showed that the monthly payments made by the hotel to the Dutch company exceeded the management service fee provided in the contract, as it also covered the insurance premium for these three senior management in Hong Kong. With these evidences, the Dutch company admitted the existence of the employment contract with these three senior management who were actually managing the hotel in China on behalf of the Dutch company. As the presence of these three persons in China already reached the threshold of staying-length under China-Netherland tax treaty, the Chinese tax authorities deemed the Dutch company has constituted a permanent establishment in China and then taxed its business profits in China.

The guidance that the SAT gave in the Circular 75 was for where the parent company of a Contracting States ending its employees to provide services to its subsidiary in China, four factors should be taken into account when conducting a responsibility and risk analysis to test which company has the authority to instruct the employee(s) and which company bears responsibilities or risk for the results produced by the employee's work.① This Suzhou case applied this guidance on services provide between non-parent/subsidiary companies. From the Suzhou case, one can clearly find that the SAT's interpretation on the term "services" is broad, including but not lim-

---

① According to circular No. 75 [2010], the four factors include the following: (i) overseas parent company can instruct the work of seconded employees and assume the relevant responsibilities and risks resulting from their work; (ii) number of seconded employees, as well as their qualification are determined by the overseas parent company; (iii) salary of seconded employees is borne by the overseas parent company; and (iv) overseas parent company derives profits from secondment of such employees.

ited to professional services of project, technology, management, design, training, consultancy, etc. For example, technical guidance, assistance, consultancy and other services provided for the implementation of the operating projects (not responsible for the specific construction and operation); services provided for the use and reform of production technology, improvement of business operation and management, project feasibility analysis, selection of design plans, etc.; and professional services provided in the business operation and management of enterprises, etc. The Suzhou case was an example that Chinese tax authorities recognized some hotel management services provided by "employees or other personnel engaged" in China as the permanent establishment of a Dutch company in China.

China's position of protecting source states' tax rights also reflects in its approaches used to interpret the concept of permanent establishment. For example, as a general rule provided in tax treaties, constituting a PE requests the non-Chinese tax residents must have a relatively fixed place of business in China. The approach the SAT interprets such a "relatively fixed place" is broad, which does not have any limit on scale or scope of the place. Thus machinery owned or leased, houses, offices and hotel rooms rented for long or short terms, facilities or equipment are partly used for other activities could all recognized as the fixed place of non-residents in China, as long the non-residents have certain disposal space therein.

In 2013, the SAT issued a circular to provide further guidance for conducting this responsibility and risk analysis through taking into account of the following five factors: [①] (1) the Chinese receiving company pays the non-resident dispatching company management fees or makes payments in the nature of service fees; (2) the payment to the non-resident dispatching company from the Chinese receiving company exceeds the dispatched employee's wages, salaries, social security contributions, and other expenses borne by the non-resident dispatching company; (3) the non-resident dispatching com-

---

① SAT, Announcement on Imposing Enterprise Income Tax on Non-residents Providing Services in China through their Dispatched Personnel (Announcement No. 19 [2013]), issued and effective on 19 April, 2013

pany does not pass on all the related payments made by the Chinese receiving company to the dispatched employee; instead, the non-resident dispatching company retains a portion of such payments;(4) the dispatched employee's wages and salaries born by the non-resident dispatching company are not fully subject to the individual income tax in China; (5) the non-resident dispatching company may decide number, qualification, remuneration and working locations of the dispatched employees in China.

10.4.3 Jiamusi Case

The Jiamusi Case was an investigation conducted by Chinese tax authorities in Jiamusi city in 2013. It may indicate how China taxes the enterprises incorporated outside of China. Given that Chinese laws provide a broad concept for "Chinese tax residents", both for individuals and for enterprises, Chinese tax enterprise residents shall include both (1) enterprises incorporated in China, and (2) enterprises incorporated outside of China but "effectively managed" in China.[1] As the Chinese tax residents shall be subject to Chinese taxes for their worldwide income and the applicable Chinese tax rates are not low[2], there are occasions that some Chinese tax residents tend to avoid their Chinese tax liabilities through trying to be recognized as non-Chinese tax residents. Then, Chinese tax authorities in recent years have been strengthening the application of the concept of Chinese tax residents. Given of this concept having a broad scope, it is becoming an effective instrument for Chinese tax authorities to counterfeit tax avoidance schemes.

The fact of the Jiamusi Case is that a Cayman Islands company sold the shares it held in its Cayman Island subsidiary which was public listed in Hong Kong Stock Exchange. The Chinese tax authorities in Jiamusi city argued that China should have taxing right over this Cayman Islands for its

---

[1] Article 2 of Enterprise Income Tax Law promulgated by the NPC on 6 March, 2007 and effective on January 1, 2008.

[2] The marginal tax rate for individual salary's income is 45% and the standard enterprise income tax rate in China is 25%.

capital gain derived from the shares transfer, as this Cayman Islands Company is a Chinese tax resident enterprise for it being "effectively managed in China"[①]. Then, the question comes out is how to determine whether a foreign incorporated company is "effectively managed in China".

The SAT published several circulars since 2009 to interpret this term of "effectively managed in China, and all of these circulars seemed were focusing on where is the office of actual management, for example, whether the senior management responsible for daily production, operation or management and the place where such responsibilities are carried out are mainly located in China, whether decisions about its finances (such as borrowing, lending, financing and managing financial risk) and human resources (such as staff recruitment, termination and remuneration policies) are made or approved by organizations or individuals located in China, and whether 50% or more of its voting directors or its senior executives habitually reside in China.[②]This approach is different from both the common law concept of central management and control and the OECD Model Convention' concept of place of effective management.[③] Thus, it may draw concerns on the impact of applying this concept in interpretation and application of Chinese tax treaties, as well as misinterpretation of this concept by foreign courts.[④]

---

① Shanshan Shi, Kenny Z. Lin, Taxing Indirect Equity Transfers in China, *The International Tax Journal*, 2015, Vol.41, No.2, p.51.

② SAT, Notice on Issues about the Determination of Chinese-Controlled Enterprises Registered Abroad as Resident Enterprises on the Basis of Their Body of Actual Management (Guoshuifa [2009]No.182), issued and effective on 22 April, 2009; Administrative Method for Imposing Enterprise Income tax on Registered Abroad Chinese-Controlled Resident Enterprises (Bulletin [2011] No.45), issued and effective on 27 July, 2011; and Announcement of the State Administration of Taxation on Issues concerning the Accreditation of Resident Enterprises Based on the Place of Effective Management Criteria (Bulletin [2014] No. 9), issued on 29 January, 2014 and retroactively effective on 1 January, 2013.

③ Nolan Sharkey, Enterprise Residence for Chinese Income Tax Purpose: Not What It Might Be Expected to Be? *Bulletin for International Taxation*, October 2014, pp.541-547.

④ Nolan Sharkey, The Correctness of the Chinese Position of Enterprise Residence in Chinese Law: The Institutional and Treaty Implications, *Bulletin for International Taxation*, November 2014, pp.617-26.

In the Jiamusi Case, there is no tax treaty between China and Cayman Islands. So when this Cayman Islands seller satisfied all the above criteria in the SAT circulars for being "effectively managed in China"[①], it was recognized by the Chinese tax authorities in Jiamusi city as a Chinese enterprise tax resident. It means that this Cayman Islands Company should be subject to taxes in China not only for its gain derived from its shares transfer, but also for its other income derived world widely.

Appendix: Exercises

1. Which tax disputes in general may arise in China?

2. What domestic approaches can be used in China for resolving tax disputes purpose?

3. Why the administrative investigations are called "cases" but still not the "judicial cases"?

4. What treaty approach can be used in China for resolving tax disputes purpose?

5. Is there a tax court in China?

6. Which executive institution of China will be the competent authority to conduct the MAP with the competent authority of the other Contracting States?

7. Is there any statute of limit for the competent authorities to reach agreements under the MAP?

8. Has China accepted the arbitration approach proposed by the OECD?

---

①   Shanshan Shi, Kenny Z. Lin, Taxing Indirect Equity Transfers in China, *The International Tax Journal*, 2015, Vol.41, No.2.